Social Foundations of Education
An Urban Focus

THIRD EDITION

HARRY L. MILLER

Hunter College, City University of New York

HOLT, RINEHART AND WINSTON
New York   Chicago   San Francisco   Dallas
Montreal   Toronto   London   Sydney

Library of Congress Cataloging in Publication Data

Miller. Harry L., 1920–
  Social foundations of education.

  Second ed. by H. L. Miller and R. R. Woock
published under title: Social foundations of
urban education.
  Includes index.
  1. Educational sociology. 2. Education,
Urban. I. Title.
LC191.M568   1978   370.19′3   77-25992
  ISBN 0-03-017426-0

For permission to use copyrighted materials, the author is indebted to the following:

For Table 1.2, p. 15, from Edgar K. Browning, "How Much More Equality Can We Afford?" *The Public Interest,* Spring 1976, No. 43, p. 93, copyright 1976 by National Affairs, Inc.; for Table 2.1, p. 40, from James S. Coleman, "Equality of Opportunity and Equality of Results," *Harvard Educational Review,* 1973, Reprint Series No. 8, p. 97; for Figure 3.1, p. 62, from Seymour Martin Lipset and Reinhard Bendix, *Social Mobility in Industrial Society,* copyright © 1959 by The Regents of The University of California, reprinted by permission of The University of California Press, Berkeley, p. 89; for Table 4.1, p. 82, from Samuel S. Peng, "Trends in the Entry to Higher Education, 1961–1972," *Educational Researcher,* January 1977, p. 18; for Figure 5.1, p. 113, from Birger Bakke, "Detroit Schools: Mirror of a City," *NASSP Bulletin,* Vol. 55, January 1971, p. 132; for Figures 10.1, p. 237, and 10.2, p. 238, from Howard Garber and Rick Heber, *The Milwaukee Project: Early Intervention as a Technique To Prevent Mental Retardation,* Connecticut University, Storrs National Leadership Institute, 1973, pp. 3 and 10; for Table 11.1, p. 265, from Henry R. Dyer, "School Factors and Equal Educational Opportunity," *Harvard Educational Review,* Vol. 38, No. 1, Winter 1968, p. 43; for Figure 12.1, p. 281, from Gertrude Moskowitz and John L. Hayman, "Interaction Patterns of First-Year, Typical, and Best Teachers in Inner-City Schools," *Journal of Educational Research,* Vol. 67, 1974, pp. 226–229; for Table 12.1, p. 295, from Melvin Long, "Culture Shock and the Teacher Corps: The Identification of Sources of Conflict," paper presented at the annual meeting of the American Research Association, New York, 1971, pp. 2–3; for the quotation on pp. 300–301, from William Wayson, "Expressed Motives of Teachers in Slum Schools," *Urban Education,* Vol. 1, No. 4, 1965, pp. 223–238, reprinted by permission of the Publisher, Sage Publications, Inc.; for Table 13.2, p. 340, and Table 13.3, p. 341, from Alan B. Wilson, "Social Stratification and Academic Achievement," in A. H. Passow (ed.), *Education in Depressed Areas,* New York, Teachers College, 1963, pp. 223 and 226; Figure A.2, p. 394, reproduced, by permission, from Frederick E. Croxton, Dudley J. Cowden, and Sidney Klein, *Applied General Statistics,* 3d ed., Englewood Cliffs, N.J., Prentice-Hall, Inc., 1967, data provided by Mr. Bert E. Holmes.

Preface

The field of social foundations of education is characterized by a number of different theories and values. My own preferred approach to this field and to the social foundations course for which this book is designed is empirical and is based on the discipline of social science. It is this approach that determines the consistency and coherence of the subject matter treated in *Social Foundations of Education: An Urban Focus*.

Not only does the book take research seriously but its general view assumes the following:

that it is often much more difficult to define what is socially or educationally possible than it is to define what is desirable;

that the realities of history and social structure impose limits on special and professional action;

that the enhancement of cognitive skills is the most important—though not the only—task of the public schools, and that we can meaningfully measure those skills;

that deliberate efforts to bring about desirable change almost always involve a trade-off in advantages which requires that other advantages be given up or postponed;

that in the welter of demand for social services, including education, the political process represents a more democratic allocation mechanism than the value preferences of small groups of professionals.

In acknowledging the choice of a particular framework in which to view urban schools in their social context, I freely admit that other positions in the field, particularly the humanist one, are treated less completely than they are in other works, and less sympathetically than many would consider their due.

The research focus of the book has been sustained in two forms: to make the text usable by students interested in detailed data and technical education issues and to clarify such issues for those who do not need to examine them at such a complex level. The main flow of the text discusses general findings of some of the major research attempts to illuminate the policies being considered, or, at times, describes one or two illustrative studies. Detailed data underlying technical and methodological issues have been set apart from the regular text in easily identifiable sections with a different type style.

Each chapter is introduced with a brief preview of the major subjects and issues that students will encounter. There are also a few questions of the kind that I hope students might consider as they try to relate the text material to their own experiences and concerns. These are intended to be suggestive of the kinds of connections with the issues that students might find useful, rather than as an attempt to raise questions that could be described as definitive. I hope that readers will find these questions useful.

One other point should be considered, and that is the urban focus of the book. *Social Foundations of Education* loosely uses a number of terms to designate the urban field of interest. Among these are *inner city, core city,* and the like, and some preliminary definition seems necessary. The Bureau of the Census now divides the United States into three major demographic categories: *nonmetropolitan* areas, defined as rural areas or counties with a central community of less than 50,000 people; *metropolitan* areas, containing a central city of over 50,000 people; and the *suburbs* surrounding the central cities. This book is concerned with the educational problems of the central cities while giving attention to suburban schools where they are involved in central city school concerns. Except for occasional purposes of comparison, the book is not concerned with nonmetropolitan schooling issues.

Within the central city category there is a good deal in the literature about the inner city, generally understood to comprise lower-class ghetto areas into which a number of minority groups have moved in recent decades. To some considerable degree the schools in these areas pose the most challenging problems that are considered here, but it would be far too limiting to call this book *Social Foundations of Inner-City Education*. The problems of the inner cities are involved crucially in the larger problems of the central cities as whole systems and must be considered in that broader context.

New York, New York   —H.L.M.
January 1978

Contents

PART I

Social and Economic Influences in Urban Schools

Chapter 1

The Drive to Equality: Income

This chapter begins the examination of the basic social issues in which the urban school is involved with an analysis of the current pressures toward income equality. The chapter:

Describes the structure of opportunity and the influence of social class position, ethnicity, and regional residence on it.

Points out various ways of defining poverty, and indicates who the poor are.

Outlines the arguments for a more equal distribution of income, and the counterarguments of those who see dangers in forcing a redistribution.

Provides data on the particularly unequal income status of black Americans, and describes the controversy over how swiftly or slowly they are moving toward equality.

Evaluates the policy of direct income transfers as a strategy for equalizing the shares of income going to people at different levels in the society.

Some of the questions readers might address are:

Which side of the income redistribution debate seems more persuasive, and what does that say about my own value preferences? Does it seem more likely that a constriction of income spread will have little effect on people's incentives, as those who argue for equalization claim, or a greater effect, as their critics claim? What evidence, in either case, seems most convincing?

What is my own conviction about the rate of progress of black
Americans? Too slow, just about right, too fast? Did any of the
discussion of the issue here change my previously held view?
Of the various schemes for income transfers described here, which
seems most preferable, and for what reasons?

This book is about the schools of urban America, the serious problems
they face, and their response to the challenge posed to them by a public
that believes firmly in the problem-solving powers of education. Only since
the 1950s have professional educators paid much attention to urban schools
as special phenomena. Before that time, and since the establishment of
public schools for all in the first part of the nineteenth century, the stereotype of American education has been the rural or small town school, as
the movie image of the American teacher has been the "schoolmarm" confronting rows of freckle-faced children.

The nonurban focus of educational concern stubbornly persisted despite
the steady shift of American society toward urbanism and despite the
remarkable role played by a number of large city school systems in Amer-
icanizing the flood of European immigrants between the Civil War and
World War I. Only when the schools of the large central cities appeared
to fail dramatically to perform the same role with a different wave of immigrants, those completing the last great population movement from the
farm to the city, did attention focus on urban schools. Even to an American
educational establishment, whose strength lay in small town and small city
America, it became clear that the new educational frontiers lay in the
central cities of the large metropolitan areas.

The frontiers were there because by the 1950s a number of large scale
social and economic trends that had been proceeding at an individual pace
converged at last and in their mutual interaction created a crisis not only
for urban school systems but for the whole society. Shifts in occupational
opportunities, the great migration from farm to city, and the rising anger
of black Americans at their inequitable position resulted not only in a
massive retardation among the school children of the central city slums
but made the effect impossible to ignore. The same forces resulted in civil
disorders in the 1960s that, many feel, threatened the disruption of a
whole social order.

Both the social crisis and the school crisis are rooted in a formidable
complex of forces, so complicated that the task of organizing a comprehensive approach to them poses severe problems that affect both the content
and organization of this book. It may be useful to discuss a few of them:

1. Although the general term *education* is used in the title, we will deal most of the time, and particularly in the last half of the book, with *schooling*. The distinction is an important one. The school is a formal institution committed to official purposes, and run by officially designated personnel who undertake specific educational roles. But the child's education, in a more general sense, consists of everything around him that influences his attitudes, his cognitive style, his aspirations, and his behavior. This is a truism, but one that education professionals, in our concentration on the school, often tend to minimize. Although a detailed look at the impact of schooling is postponed, the early chapters are nonetheless concerned with informal education: the socializing influences of the child's position within the economic and social status system, the urban environment that immediately surrounds him, and the "curriculum" of the home.

2. The earlier focus on the economic and psychosocial environment of the urban school, instead of on the school itself, also indicates the author's conviction that a better understanding of the tangled interrelationships between the two is obtained by first considering the more basic term in the relationship. More often than not the school *reflects* change, contradictions, and conflicts in the social order rather than initiating them. An important group of educators in this century would have it otherwise; they see the school as a key institution for reconstructing the social order in a more humane and democratic image. But, although the school as it interacts with society does affect it, at present the dominant influence is the society's on the school.

As a reflector of social values, the American school has been above all expected to serve the egalitarian norms which have always had a central place among the crucial values affirmed by the nation. This and the following chapter, examine the question of the realism of the expectation that the schools can significantly serve as equalizers of both income and social status.

OPPORTUNITY STRUCTURE

What the people in a society believe is sometimes more important than what they do; and the American nation has been shaped in many ways by a widely shared belief in the idea of equality. The religious tenets of the early settlers in the Northeast downgraded the authority of a priesthood in favor of individual and congregational responsibility. The vast land resources of a virgin continent encouraged a system of individual landholdings; where property meant status, large numbers of men had property and thus equal status. The Union was founded on ideas of political democracy that started from the assumption that "all men are created equal," ideas that were socially reinforced by the conditions of an expanding frontier far from the established institutions and hardening status lines of the well-settled East.

However the concept may have been violated in actual practice, the idea is firmly rooted in the American consciousness that one man is just as good as another, as one man's opinion and his vote has equal status with another's. The economic corollary slowly came to be accepted as well: Because most Americans defined the good life as that in which one was successful, it was thought that every man should have an equal opportunity to achieve success and the good things of life.

It is not difficult to imagine a model of a society in which everyone really does have equality of opportunity to succeed, if we define success as most Americans do: having an occupation which others respect and an income that permits one to have a reasonable share of the comforts afforded by the society at any given time. Although we are all created equal politically, each man clearly differs in his aptitudes, his intelligence, and his ambition. Equality of opportunity ideally requires a state of things in which everyone, regardless of the circumstances of his birth, has an equal chance to compete for success with those at his own level of aptitude, intelligence, and ambition.

The American myth has always been that as a country we have reasonably approximated this ideal. But, although American life may have occasionally, in some places and at some times, roughly resembled the model, it is now clear that twentieth-century America is far beyond those times and places. The myth supposes, for example, that one should be willing to bet at even odds on the chances for success of two boys born with equal genetic capability, wherever they may originate. It would be a reckless gambler indeed who would place such even odds if one of the boys were born to a black, sharecropping family on an Alabama farm and the other on the East side of Manhattan Island to the family of a corporation lawyer.

Opportunity has acquired a *structure,* a term that indicates that certain relationships or events occur more consistently than one would expect them to do by chance. The opportunity structure in the United States is not by any means as rigid as, say, that of the European medieval period; an ambitious, bright serf's son had only a small chance of climbing into the relatively fixed ranks above him; and a noble's son, no matter how stupid and passive, seldom sank below the status of gentleman. But neither is it as close as some Americans believe to the fluid, random model described above. Some of the circumstances that consistently tend to decrease opportunity are:

Geographical

To be born in the South of the United States, whether one is white or black, handicaps a person unless he happens to be fortunate in his family circumstances; the less-advanced economic level of the region and its poor educational systems depress the probabilities of success relative to other regions of the country. Also, within a given region, the chances are better for those born in urban areas than in rural places.

Social class

Children born to relatively well-to-do families, with fathers engaged in high-status occupations, consistently do better than others. A later chapter will examine this in detail.

Ethnicity

To be born a nonwhite or to a family whose recent origins are not in the United States (unless those origins are in northern Europe) tends to depress access to opportunity, an effect that fluctuates with social attitudes toward the particular ethnic group.

In the current period in the United States, there are two drives toward equalizing opportunity and status: One is to better the position of the poor, the other to redress the inequality of the blacks and other minority groups. There is a clear overlap between the two, because a larger proportion of minority group members are poor than of the general population; but the problems of poverty and ethnic inequality are somewhat different in nature, and they are dealt with separately below.

EQUALITY OF INCOME

Although opportunity structure obviously is a complex phenomenon, attention has focused in recent years on one aspect of it—the uneven distribution of family income in the United States. Perhaps this is because poverty is the most visible aspect of those families that are least favored in the opportunity structure. It is a recurring concern in American life; the great national interest in doing something about the poor can be matched in several previous eras.

One of the most difficult problems in discussing the concept of poverty is that the definition of "poor" is clearly a relative matter. Very few Americans are as poor, in absolute terms, as the mass of people living in underdeveloped areas of the world. In India, an economically developing country, there are large numbers of city dwellers who do not even have shelter, families who put up a small piece of canvas in the street at night to protect them as they sleep and who do their cooking in small wooden sheds on a beach.

Though the majority of those considered poor in the United States are very well off compared to populations such as these, it is not very helpful to make such comparisons. The American who is poor does not compare himself to Indian standards but to what is roughly the average life style in his own country, which has been growing more comfortable at a very rapid rate.

There are at least two ways of measuring poverty, and the way in which it is done has a good deal to do with the solutions one is likely to come to. One approach is to assume an absolute level of income necessary to maintain a minimum living standard, defining "minimum" in relation to prevailing ideas in the society. The Department of Labor calculates a number of living standards and the income necessary to maintain them, running from poverty, through deprivation, to comfort.

Such a yardstick is based on very detailed calculations of the cost of a specific level of food expenditure, the cost of clothing, rent, insurance, etc., and though the level will move with inflation and with social ideas about what is necessary for a reasonable life, it is a fairly absolute definition. At the beginning of the 1970s, a family of four required over $9000 a year to live in a "modest" style in a metropolitan area, a figure very close to the median national income at the time. By 1973, when the system was changed to a three-category one (lower, intermediate, and higher) metropolitan lower standards required $8305, the intermediate, $12,909, and the higher level, $18,760.[1]

But because poverty is a relative term, some social scientists prefer to define it as the lowest fifth of the income distribution, a definition that permits one to examine what kinds of people are among the poor from one period of time to another. From this point of view, the pessimistic Biblical observation that the poor will always be with us becomes a logical necessity. No matter how high the living standard may rise, there will always be that lowest fifth of the families in the nation that can be considered disadvantaged in relation to the average.

The lowest-fifth definition can be carried one step further by raising this question of equality: how much of a share of the total national income goes to the lowest fifth of the income distribution, and how much to the fifths above them? It turns out that about 5 percent of the income goes to the bottom fifth, with the top fifth getting about 40 percent (the top 5 percent of the income distribution has about 20 percent). In the past thirty years there has been a fairly significant decline in the percentage of income going to the top 5 percent of the population, but the bottom fifth has increased its share only by half a percentage point.[2]

A look below at the make-up of the families in the lowest fifth of income throws some light on the problems involved in equalizing income by raising the income of the poor. These characteristics have not varied much over the past several decades:[3]

1. By 1974, 45 percent of these families were female-headed, a rise from 37 percent only four years earlier when the 1970 Census was taken. Blacks comprised 44 percent of the group.
2. 15 percent were elderly, a decline from 19 percent in 1970, because of a rise in social security benefits.
3. 10 percent were black families headed by a male of working age.
4. 33 percent were white families with a male, nonaged head; up from 1970 by about 13 percent. Some of these are low-income farmers, many of them living in the South. About one-third of them are in white-

collar or managerial occupations, many just starting on their careers and with expectations for improvement in their economic position in a relatively short time. The poverty of others in this diverse group may be due to such different factors as low intelligence, physical handicap, or just bad luck.

A later chapter will consider a variety of social strategies proposed for improving the lot of this bottom fifth of families. At this point it is necessary to note only that for the majority of the urban poor the problem is clearly an inability to be productive by reason of age, sex, or other such characteristics, and that an educational strategy is not relevant.

SHOULD WE (AND CAN WE) REDISTRIBUTE INCOME?

Since the early 1960s the argument about the fairness of income distribution in the United States and about a variety of policies aimed at making that distribution more equal has been carried on in the mass media and scholarly journals alike, in sometimes thoughtful, often bitter debate. The War on Poverty initiated by President Johnson dramatically increased public consciousness of income differences in the country at the same time that a burgeoning civil rights movement focused national attention on inequities between black and white incomes and status. The special problems involved in racial inequities merit separate consideration at a later point; the more general question to be examined here is: How unequal are we as a country, and can anything be done about it?

Table 1.1 displays the broad picture of income distribution in the United States since 1947, a span of almost thirty years, about one generation. Even at first glance it is clear that it carries both good news and bad news: Families at every level are obviously better off in income corrected for inflation, but the share of the national income pie going to various levels

TABLE 1.1 Income at Selected Positions and Percentage Share of Aggregate Income in Selected Years, 1947–1974, Received by Each Fifth and Top 5 Percent of Families (In Current Dollars)

	Lowest	Percent Share	Middle	Percent Share	Highest	Percent Share	Top 5%	Percent Share	Mean
1974	6500	(5.4)	14,916	(17.5)	20,445	(41)	31,948	(15)	14,502
1969	5000	(5.6)	10,800	(17.7)	14,751	(40.6)	22,703	(15.6)	10,577
1964	3250	(5.1)	7500	(17.7)	10,201	(41.2)	15,788	(15.9)	7336
1959	2677	(4.9)	6061	(17.9)	8380	(41.1)	12,800	(15.9)	5976
1954	2012	(4.5)	4808	(17.6)	6632	(41.9)	10,463	(16.4)	4714
1949	1543	(4.5)	3566	(17.3)	5034	(42.8)	8091	(16.9)	3505

Source: Current Population Reports Series P 60 #101, Money Income in 1974 of Families and Persons in the U.S., January 1976

has not changed very much. The debate ranges widely beyond these figures into differences of interpretation and finer breakdowns of the categories.

A voluminous literature argues the case that this distribution is overwhelmingly unequal but in the interests of clarity and consistency we have chosen a representative book, Richard Parker's *The Myth of the Middle Class,* to state that case.[4]

Although the book was published in 1972, Parker relies mainly on income data from 1969-1970; the cut-off income figures he cites are somewhat lower than they would be after a period of sharp inflationary rise, but the basic argument is not affected. He begins by dividing the income distribution into four segments: the top 10 percent (incomes over 18,000 in 1970), he calls the *rich*; the bottom fifth (incomes below 4,000) are *poor*; the middle seventy percent are divided into a bottom half (the lower middle class) and the top half (upper middle class). His upper middles receive 46 percent of the total income, the lower middles 22 percent, the rich 27 percent, and the poorest fifth 5 percent.

> . . . this means that the richest 10 percent of Americans in 1968 received more money income than the entire bottom half of the population.[5]

Since an urban family of four should have received at that time an income of $10,700 in order to maintain a "moderate" intermediate standard of living as defined by the Department of Labor, Parker thus calculates that about one-half of all American families (the poor and the lower middles) live *below* the Department's definition of a moderate life style. Thus Parker asks, "Why is it, then, that Americans think of their country as an Affluent Society? How can we speak of America as egalitarian and democratic, when such antitheses contradict equality and endanger democracy?"[6]

At the heart of his argument is Parker's contention that the belief that improvements over the past several decades have reduced the proportion of families in poverty and increased those in the middle class is wrong.

> The existence of hungry and abused men, women, and children in the midst of what is supposed to be the most prosperous and humane country on earth," he writes, "makes a mockery of American claims to 'liberty and justice for all.' Public rhetoric has occasionally admitted the presence of these human beings in our midst, but always with the promise that they would soon disappear, swept up eventually by the well-being that enfolds the rest of middle-class America. In fact, the poor have not disappeared, but are now, and always have been, a basic feature of American society. Moreover, there are no signs that this situation is changing.[7]

In the early 1960s, he points out, the federal government defined a "poverty budget" of about $3000. This included only $.75 a day per person for food, allowing only about a pound of meat a day for the family, no frozen foods, rent for a five-room flat; it permitted an electric refrigerator and iron, but no beer or tobacco, a haircut once a month for the man and a permanent once a year for the wife, not much furniture, etc. Parker argues that the decline in the number of families below the poverty level is true only because the government standard is set so low; as the general standard of living rose, fewer people must live such a bleak existence. But, he notes, in the decade between 1959 and 1969, inflation at the end of that period made necessary an income of 4365 to match the 3000 at the beginning; the poverty budget, in the same span of years, was not revised upward sufficiently to match that difference. And, in 1969, one-fifth of the families were still below $4365. So, quoting Galbraith, he concludes that the orthodox idea that a general rise in living standards for all can substitute for redistribution of income "leaves a self-perpetuating margin of poverty at the very base of the income pyramid."[8]

As for the top 1 percent, the *"very* rich," they received in one year more income than the poorest 50 million people, and accounted for 26 percent of the private holdings of wealth. The "simple rich" (those earning $25,000–$75,000 incomes) earned 56 billion in 1968, and the very top 4000 families claimed four billion alone.

Parker argues further that attempts to transfer income have largely been ineffective. Efforts to supplement the nutrition of the poor with food stamps and school lunches often fail to reach all who need them, and when they do, they may be inadequate. The tax system, which is supposedly designed to transfer some benefits from the wealthy to the poor, does not accomplish this end. The poor pay a higher percent of state and local taxes than do the better off, and though the federal tax system *rates* are progressive, the actual rates paid are not, because a variety of loopholes permits higher income families to lower their tax bill. The overall burden of taxation is, in fact, about equal in the proportion of income paid at all levels. In sum:

> A country cannot easily continue to call itself middle-class when twenty million malnourished live in its midst, or a third of the population lives in poverty, or the majority do not have what the government's own agencies describe as a "moderately comfortable" standard of living. Somewhere myth has sharply diverged from reality.[9]

Some Counterinterpretations

This view of the degree and nature of income inequality is by no means universal among economists and other social scientists; in fact, it is probably a minority position, though advanced with such heat and frequency that it often appears dominant.

In an article called "How To Increase Poverty" Stanley Lebergott has summarized the basis of what is perhaps the most general opposing interpretation. He concludes that the continued existence of a group perceived to be poor is built in to the way in which we measure poverty, and is an inevitable consequence of a number of America's most deeply held values.[10]

Lebergott agrees with Parker that an increasing standard of living, one of the central values of the society, means that some group at the bottom will always *feel* poor. He quotes the President's Commission on Income Maintenance to that effect: "Solely as a result of growing affluence a society will elevate its notions of what constitutes poverty." The disagreement arises around the question of whether, as Parker asserts, the real living standards of those now considered poor have appreciably improved. The real wages (in constant dollars) of American workers, Lebergott points out, have tripled since 1900, for an average of a third fewer hours per week. In the past generation they have doubled. Those who suggest that even if money income has grown, real welfare has not must contend with the results of a careful study by William Nordhause and James Tobin.[11] These two economists begin with a conventional measure of annual per capita income, corrected for price level changes between 1929 and 1965. They adjusted it for capital usage, allocating yearly amounts to keep the nation's capital intact; subtracted expenditures for "regrettables" (i.e., expenditures for police protection, national defense, and others); adjusted national income downward to correct for the displeasure of living under conditions that are more crowded and polluted; and offset these subtractions by a value contributed by the growth of leisure. The result was a doubling of per capita income over the period studied.

Forty-one percent of our officially poor own an automobile; a half-million of them own more than one. In 1900 15 percent of all U.S. families had flush toilets; 86 percent of poor families have them now; 3 percent had electricity then; 99 percent of the poor have it now. To define poverty as an income that does not cover what is, for the society at the time, a subsistence minimum makes critical the question of what is "subsistence." To equate it with the government's current definition of a "modest but adequate" budget, as Parker and others do, one must insist that a family is poor if it cannot afford to buy air fresheners, replace the car at frequent intervals, or buy a variety of other items not included in the standard of living for many at higher incomes. Lebergott concludes: "If American industry speeds productivity, and pays higher wages, and if advertising helps persuade American workers to buy new, more elegant products, then American capitalism must continue to generate poverty."[12]

Ben Wattenberg has recently addressed the allied issue of middle-classness.[13] By 1969, he points out, 8 percent of American families were below the income necessary to maintain the Labor Department's "low" budget, 19 percent were between lower and intermediate budget levels, 31 percent earned incomes between the intermediate and the higher standard, and 43 percent were above the higher budget. About three-quarters, thus, were living at some level *above* "modest but adequate." Wattenberg argues that an income of roughly $7000 represents the entry-level for middle-class status because it is just at that point that families of four exhibit some discretionary income, the ability to buy things that they *want* rather than what they *need*. The proportion of families in 1970 with incomes above that figure was 72 percent, which dovetails with the similar percentage of those with better than modest-but-adequate budgets.

A second way to increase poverty, writes Lebergott, is to allow older people to live apart from their children. As more of them choose to live on their social security checks, the proportion of families in poverty inevitably increases, since no monetary value is set on the convenience and freedom which many older people gain from making the choice.

Third, we increase poverty by permitting what Lebergott calls the Men's Liberation Front, the freedom of large numbers of men to abandon their family responsibilities to the taxpayer. The percent of families in poverty rises from 8 percent of those with husbands present to 32 percent of female-headed families. Simon Kuznets has directly calculated the effects of such changes in family structure on the distribution of income.[14] Considering separately female-headed families and families with heads over 65 or under 25, he finds that their incomes fall below the national average by from 33 percent to 40 percent; moreover, the proportion of these types of family has risen and with them the formation of more households with low incomes relative to the rest of the population. If one excludes these three types of families, the share of the lowest income fifth rises to 7.3 percent of the total income, the share of the second fifth from 12.9 percent to 13.6 percent and the top 5 percent drops from 16 percent to 12.8 percent.

Fourth, Lebergott goes on, pay old people not to work. In 1939 40 percent of men over 65 were employed and earning incomes, but by 1973 only 24 percent were at work. And, fifth, raise social standards. In 1900, 18 percent of all children 10 to 15 years of age worked and contributed to family income. Very few do so today. Few families now overcrowd themselves by taking in lodgers, whereas early in the century almost half of the Polish immigrants and 39 percent of the Italians, for example, lived with three or more persons in each sleeping room, a condition that housing codes now prohibit.

Sixth and seventh, permit the poor to have more children and keep them alive longer. As the number of children per family increases from two to nine or more, the proportion of families in poverty rises from 9 percent to 40 percent. A century ago only 64 percent of all infants lived to age 25, today, 94 percent do; much of that improvement benefitted poor families.

Lebergott asks, Do we want to reduce poverty by challenging social standards we have come to approve of as a society, or by changing such moral and religious principles that allow people freedom to have as many children as they want? He concludes: "Most Americans do not want to abolish poverty because they accept certain moral values. Even if these attitudes disappeared, a rise in living standards would continue relative poverty."[15]

As for the role of taxation in the argument, Irving Kristol points to a number of flaws in the position that any income of $20–25,000 puts a family among the "rich," or that the tax system is regressive.[16] One of the favorite assertions of the distribution advocates, that families with incomes below $2000 pay 50 percent of their income in taxes, is addressed directly by Kristol, who points out that the taxes in question are neither income nor sales tax, but payments that most people do not regard as taxes at all; prominently they include, for example, the portion of rent that represents the landlord's tax bill. Most such incomes, furthermore, consist not of earnings but of income transfers of various sorts.

The only group for whom the tax system is not progressive, Kristol argues, is the middle class earning $7000 to $20,000; they receive 60 percent of the total income and pay only 54 percent of the tax burden. The over-$20,000 group receive 21 percent of the adjusted gross income, and pay 36 percent of the taxes. Our income distribution is not an inverted pyramid, from which a small slice off the top yields visible dividends for distribution, but is diamond-shaped. The top 5 percent have incomes over $30,000, the top 20 percent incomes over $20,000. Instead of "rich" they are middle class; one high government official recently resigned his post because on his salary of over $40,000 he could not afford to pay for his children's higher education. A "tax-the-rich" movement, says Kristol, would end up in a middle-class tax rebellion.

Kristol quotes another supporter of Parker's view, Michael Harrington, as saying: "The unconscionable fact is that the Internal Revenue Code is a perverse welfare system that hands out 77 billion a year, primarily to the rich."[17] This figure is derived from a study by a respected tax expert, and actually represents *all* federal tax exemptions and allowances. If all were repealed, 55 percent of the increased taxes would come from families earning under $25,000; ten million families with incomes under $10,000 would also be added to the tax rolls. Perhaps 10 to 15 billion of it would actually come from the well-to-do, but the so-called loopholes include capital gains, municipal bond interest, depletion allowances, and interest on home mortgages, much of it benefitting the middle class. The tax system as a whole, he argues, is not only directed toward the end of equalization, but is supposed to provide incentives of various kinds that help society as a whole and sustain social values such as home ownership and municipal credit needs. Of the residual 10 to 15 billion in tax exemptions, Congress would be unlikely to repeal much more than half.

Kristol's conclusion that the tax system is ultimately progressive is supported by a tax study that takes into account transfer payments already made to the poor. Parker is correct in his claim that most families pay about the same rate, 30 percent, when *all* taxes are counted in; but when government payments are included, the results are progressive. Herman Miller has calculated that families with earned incomes of less than $2000 paid 50 percent in taxes but got back 106 percent of that in payments; families with over $50,000 paid 45 percent in taxes, and got back less than 1 percent.[18]

If both taxation and government transfers to the poor are taken into account, a radically different view of the income distribution picture emerges. An HEW report in 1974 shows the growth in federal outlays benefitting the poor as 7.9 billion in 1964 to 26.2 billion in 1973.[19] Edgar Browning has recalculated the relative income distribution after deducting for taxes and adding transfers, not only of cash but in-kind benefits as well. His results are shown in Table 1.2.[20]

The degree of inequality one sees, then, is clearly related to how deprivation is defined, who is considered rich, and how realistic are one's views of expected income differences due to groups of widely varying productivity. Parker's dismay at finding that the lower middle class, as he defines it, earns half of the income going to his upper middle class would not be shared by many who would regard such a disparity with equanimity. One reasonable criterion for inequality might be assumed to be represented by the most stable, favored, and productive of all groups; adult, white, fully-employed males; Lester Thurow found that the top 14.5 percent of this group earn 28 percent of the total earnings of the group, which seems a fairly modest degree of inequality considering the wide variations in occupations that are included.[21] It nevertheless represents the same two-to-one ratio that Parker deplores in his middle-class comparison.

The Stability of Inequality

One of the greatest puzzles in this crucial problem area is the remarkable stability of the relative distribution of incomes, not only in the United States (see Table 1.1 on p. 9) but in countries that have tried much harder than ours to moderate income inequalities. In developing countries of the Third World economic development usually increases inequality.[22] Parker himself does not see socialism as an effective instrument for equalization, though many of his persuasion, such as Michael Harrington, do. Kenneth Boulding has concluded that as an equalizer, socialism has been disappointing; it has produced enormous inequalities of power and "it is doubtful as to whether the distribution of income outside the top 1/1000 of the

TABLE 1.2   Adjusted Relative Income Distribution (Expressed As Percentage Shares of Income Received by Quintile)

Year	Lowest Quintile	Second Quintile	Third Quintile	Fourth Quintile	Highest Quintile
1952	8.1	14.2	17.8	23.2	36.7
1962	8.8	14.4	18.2	23.1	35.4
1972	11.7	15.0	18.2	22.3	32.8

Source: Edgar K. Browning, "How Much More Equality Can We Afford," The Public Interest, *no. 43 (Spring 1976), p. 93.*

population is very different in socialist countries than it is in countries of comparable per capita income which are not socialist."[23]

A 1975 report by a British Royal Commission found that ten years of steep progressive taxation and income transfers has accomplished very little change in the income shares going to the top 20 percent or bottom 20 percent. The share of the top 1 percent dropped dramatically, and the share of capital assets held by the top 10 percent has declined, but the share of the bottom fifth rose only from 6 percent to 6.8 percent in the decade.[24] According to Barbara Preston's report, it is even odder to find that, in the related area of health, for a generation of Britons under a full-scale, free, national health plan there has been increased, rather than decreased, social class differences in mortality rates, even when the differences in rates are controlled for occupational hazards, income, and leisure time available.[25]

It is difficult not to conclude, with Boulding, who is himself on the liberal side of the equalization argument, that the *demand* for equality may not influence the degree of income equality one actually finds among societies. Historically, changes in *supply* appear to be much more important, by which he means that the more there is of something that income buys, the more likely it is that almost everyone will have it. Egalitarian demand depends for its satisfaction on social agreement that it must have high priority; in fact, as Milton Rokeach's research on values has found, equality does not rate very high on Americans' scale of relative values, nor does individual status appear to have very much to do with people's position on the issue.[26]

One reason, perhaps, for the relative lack of interest is that the majority of Americans do generally feel a sense of improvement in their economic position. This is in contrast with the image projected by the advocates of income redistribution of a mass of "The Poor" lying inert at the bottom of the population. Bradley Schiller has compared the relative earning position of males aged 30 to 34 in 1957 to their position in 1971, by breaking the earnings distribution into categories representing twentieths of the distribution.[27] He found that over 70 percent of these men moved up or down the income ladder, and that the average move was 20 percentiles, or a fifth of the entire distribution. Two-thirds of the lowest earners in 1957 moved up an average of 12 percentiles in earnings during the 14-year period.

EQUAL STATUS FOR MINORITIES

The issues raised by the drive for equality for minorities are considerably more complex than the problems of poverty as such, although they overlap. In the first instance, there is a wide variation among minorities not only in the whole context of their social circumstance, but also in the data available about their position. Until recently the arguments have focused on American black income disparities and we shall do so here. Even in this case there are ambiguities in data. Until the 1970 Census, data were available only on "nonwhites" or "Negro and other races." Blacks did represent about 90 percent of that category, however, so comparisons from one period to another are not very substantially in error.

In order to clarify the subsequent discussion of the controversy on the progress of equalization, one needs to address two separate questions: What is the present comparative status of blacks and whites on any significant measure, and to what extent is the gap on that measure narrowing? Panel 1.1 summarizes where matters stand in the areas of income, employment, and occupational status.

PANEL 1.1   Economic and Educational Status of the Black Population[28]

Median black income in 1947 was $7800; median white income $13,400. In the years between 1950 and 1970, nonwhite income has risen at a faster rate than white, 132 percent for nonwhites versus 88 percent for whites, but gains in absolute dollars were greater for whites because they started at a higher level. This relative advantage for blacks did not persist in the period from 1970 to 1974.

The most generally useful comparison is the *ratio* between black/white incomes which was 60 percent in 1970, declined to 58 percent in the early 1970s, then remained stable for several years as of 1976. The ratio varies considerably by region, from 57 percent in the South to 77 percent in the West. In 1960 it was 53 percent.

By the late 1960s the most economically viable families in the most favored geographical position achieved parity: in the North and West the median income of young black families with a head under 35 years of age and in which both husband and wife were working did not differ from that of similar white families. In the first part of the 1970s such families in the South moved toward parity—87 percent of white income by 1973.

Despite the public concentration on urban blacks, they are comparatively better off than their rural counterparts. Three-quarters of all black families live in metropolitan areas and only 20 percent of them are below the poverty line; 50 percent of those in nonmetropolitan areas of the South (most of the rural blacks in the country) are poor.

The economically least viable family unit, that headed by a woman, is increasing in numbers for both blacks and whites, from .9 to 1.6 million in the 1960s for blacks, and from 3.3 to 4.4 million for whites. In the first half of the decade of the 1970s, the proportion of black husband-wife families declined further, from 68 percent to 61 percent.

EDUCATION

By the end of the 1960s 56 percent of all young adult blacks (25 to 29 years old) had completed high school, up from 38 percent ten years earlier; the percentage of young whites doing so was 78 percent. By 1974 the proportion of young blacks completing high school was 72 percent, rising faster than whites but still below the current figure of 85 percent for whites.

Between 1965 and 1970 college enrollment among blacks 18 to 24 years old almost doubled, reaching 7 percent of total college enrollment. In 1970 one of every six college-age black men was enrolled in college, versus one of every three whites. In the four years following, a 56 percent increase in black college enrollments was reported, versus 15 percent increase for whites. The proportion of young blacks in college was, by 1977, within a few percentage points of whites, 21 percent versus 24 percent.

By 1970 a gap of only a half year separated the median educational level of white and nonwhite members of the labor force; in 1952 nonwhite median education was 7.6 years compared with 11.4 for whites in the labor force, and by 1970 the difference was 11.7 versus 12.4.

EMPLOYMENT

During the decade of the 1960s, nonwhite employment rose by 22 percent and employment in professional, technical, and clerical occupations doubled. Blacks continued to move into white-collar jobs in the 1970s but at a slower pace.

Black unemployment rate fell from 12.4 in 1961 to a low of 6.5 in 1969; then, with the recession, it rose to 8.2. The recession rise was smaller for nonwhites than whites, however, a rare occurrence. During the 1970s recession, the unemployment rate for blacks again rose to its historical 2:1 ratio.

During the 1960s, the unemployment rate for married nonwhite men decreased by half. The teenager rate, which had peaked in 1963, was 29 percent by 1970, and is continuing its rise toward the earlier peak in the 1970s.

The interpretation of these comparisons and changes can and does vary enormously; perhaps the only conclusion not possible is that there is no improvement in the position of American blacks at all. The issue of how much improvement there has been is widely debated, often with a good deal of emotion, and was publicly dramatized at the beginning of the decade by the publication of a confidential memorandum by Daniel Patrick Moynihan, then a presidential adviser. The memorandum on the status of the Negro, intended for the President's private consideration, reviewed the decade's progress and suggested that "The time may have come when the issue of race could benefit from a period of 'benign neglect.'" Moynihan argued that the issue had been taken over by "hysterics, paranoids and blood-letters on all sides," and advised the Administration to encourage progress while letting the racial rhetoric fade, and to pay greater attention to Indians, Mexican-Americans, and Puerto Ricans.[29]

The prolonged controversy that followed did little to clear the political air, but it did help to clarify the question of why it was possible, from several political and philosophical positions, to read the same evidence quite differently.

1. The degree to which general equality has been achieved depends to a considerable extent on the measurement one uses. The nonwhite/white income ratio uses the median income for each group, which is a fairly rough measure. Thus, Palmore and Whittington compute the degree to which the distributions overlap at all points (the incomes of whites and blacks at a number of different levels of income) and find that black incomes are about 80 percent of white incomes, instead of the 60 or so percent indicated by the comparison of medians.[30]

2. Most people would agree that equality of income and occupation depends on existing skills and training; previous restrictions on opportunity for blacks leave them at the present historical moment less well equipped than whites, which accounts for some of the differences of income and occupation. The question is: How much of the difference can be explained by discrimination itself? In a pioneering work, *The Economics of Discrimination,* Becker calculated that in the *absence* of discrimination the nonwhite/white income ratio during the fifties would have been 66 (that is, 66 percent of white income), instead of the actual ratio at the time of 57.[31] Using 1960 income data and employing somewhat different procedures, Rasmussen comes to much the same conclusion: removal of discrimination would permit a rise of 16 percent in black incomes in the North and West, and a rise of 45 percent in the South.[32]

Another way of measuring discrimination is to estimate the earnings of the black working force *if* it were equal to the white in age, education, and scholastic achievement. Gwartney's calculation is that, in that event, non-white earnings would range from 83.9–92.8 percent of white incomes in the North, and from 68 to 78 percent of white incomes in the South.[33]

From one point of view, of course, this more precise information comforts some because it explains a sizable proportion of the income gap as due to labor market mechanisms; but from another, it enrages those who concentrate on the also considerable proportion of the gap that is clearly due to discrimination, and who further argue that the differences in education and scholastic achievement are merely evidences of past discrimination.

3. Progress toward equality is inevitably uneven for different groups among the blacks. The most pessimistic picture emerges from a consideration of total population figures, all living blacks, no matter where they live. Such a measure includes a large number of older people whose position reflects the opportunity structure of the past. As Eckstein notes in the matter of education:

> It is impossible within a reasonable time span to have 15 percent of the black labor force as college graduates, and 68 percent as high school graduates. The figures apply to the entire stock of the black labor force up to age 65, not just new workers. Even if you now achieve 100 percent high school completion, you would not reach the necessary average for the entire black labor force by 1985. You might reach that average some 10 or 15 years later . . .[34]

The optimists can cite the progress in income of the younger marrieds and those of school age, the pessimists the increase in the number of families headed by women and the lack of progress in the South. In an answer to Moynihan, Cook notes that there has been no improvement in the South, where almost half of the black population still lives.[35] There is no question that geography and already attained position make very considerable differences, but this is merely another way of saying that half of a distribution will be above a given median, and half below it. Eleven percent of blacks in New York City are in professional and technical occupations, much above the national average;[36] the median income of black families headed by skilled and semiskilled wage earners is (outside of the South) 86 percent of white workers in the same occupations, considerably above the national general ratio. On the other hand, the 1.5 million black families with no father present made no gain relative to white during the sixties.[37] The continuing high unemployment rate of black teenagers is similarly subject to differential interpretation by those who point out that it can partly be explained by the frequent job changes among youth in general, supported by the fact that in 1969, for example, six out of ten jobless workers between the ages of 16 and 21 had been unemployed for less than five weeks.[38] Furthermore, it is argued, the enticements of the lower-class street culture include a number of illicit and rewarding jobs that go unreported.

The exceedingly high unemployment rates for teenage blacks can appear quite different when they are "disaggregated." In 1972 there were 2.2 million of them between the ages of 16 and 19. About two-thirds were "not in the labor force," that is, not looking for work; almost all of these were students. Of the remaining 770,000 in the labor force, two-thirds or about 510,000 are working, leaving 260,000 unemployed. But of these (the unemployed), 45 percent are in school, and 83 percent are looking for part-time work. The out-of-school, out-of-work group, approximating what most people think of as unemployed, consists of 144,000 youths, 18 percent of the black teenage work force, and 6.6 percent of the total number of black teenagers.[39]

4.   Finally, the greatest differences in interpretation probably result from whether one looks at the relative gains within the black population over time, or at the existing absolute differences between white and black. For example, although the rate of gain in income over the past twenty years has been greater for blacks, the gain in actual dollars has been greater for whites because they started at a higher level. The welcome news that black couples under the age of 35 reached income equality with their white counterparts has been interpreted as misleading because it was true only of families in which the wife also worked; further, 63 percent of black wives worked, as compared with 54 percent of white wives, and more of the black wives worked year round than white wives.

Cook makes a similar point by comparing the average earnings of whites and nonwhites with equal educational attainment.[40] In 1968, white college graduates earned an average of $13,100 versus $11,400 for blacks at the same educational level (an 87 percent ratio); black high school graduates earned only 62.5 percent as much as white high school graduates. Again one is dealing with the entire age span and including the South. And one can further explain the differences by citing variations in school quality and academic achievement, as well as the fact that black college graduates tend to select occupations, teaching rather than engineering, for example, that pay less well; but the fact remains that *absolute* comparisons support the view that we have a long way to go to equality.

Is general progress toward equality likely to accelerate in this decade? Economists such as Gwartney are dubious.[41] He notes the following reasons why "future relative income gains of nonwhite males are likely to be slow, even if there is some reduction in employment discrimination":

A considerable part of the differences in productivity result from the impact of the past, and cannot be changed very rapidly.

Migration has played a significant part in the gains of the last twenty years, but will be less important in the future. Past migration was primarily from rural areas in the South, but now the majority of Southern blacks are in metropolitan areas of the South, and migration from the urban South or urban North is less potent.

The only bright indicator is the increasing parity in years of education, but "given the anticipated negative influence of other factors, we can expect the relative income gains of nonwhite males during the 1970s will be modest, perhaps even slower than during the 1960s."[42]

The predictions of economic analysts do not always prove out, however; and in this case there is a countervailing political force that cannot be underestimated—the continued vigor of the black civil rights movement that has become increasingly involved in economic matters. We shall have occasion at several points in later chapters to cite a variety of evidence for the widening involvement of the average black citizen in the movement toward equality for his whole group. The most relevant evidence here may be found in a study by Kahl and Goering comparing the attitudes of a group of white and black stable working-class men.[43] Both groups, they found, are similar in their job aspirations, their sense of security about their jobs, their satisfaction with their rate of job advancement and their consumption levels, and in their high hopes for their children. The differences emerged in political and social beliefs:

Despite their general satisfaction with their own positions, only 27 percent of the black workers accepted the statement that "people like me have as good a life as anybody in this country," a statement that 82 percent of the white workers accepted.

Ninety-four percent of the blacks agreed that "our country is in bad shape" (versus 68 percent of the whites); 65 percent could accept violent protest, if necessary (versus 12 percent); and 80 percent thought that poor people are unlucky and need help (versus 60 percent).

The authors conclude: "Gone is the contentment of blacks about jobs, and in its place appears a deep sense of wrongs that need to be righted, even by extreme methods *if* necessary. Most blacks are in a mood of protest that is at least potentially radical."[44]

STRATEGIES FOR EQUALIZING INCOME

If the structure of poverty and opportunity access so far described indicates the soundness of any generalization, it is that there are a large variety of different problems involved. Any one solution usually fits only one or two of the categories of poor or otherwise disadvantaged people. In the following discussions, consideration of the role of formal schooling in the efforts to equalize opportunity requires some awareness of the broad spectrum of possible solutions. The serious proposals and ongoing projects that are currently on the social scene will be grouped roughly into two major approaches, those for which the *structural* nature of the problem is paramount, and those that concentrate on *functional* disabilities of the socially disadvantaged.

There is an important general distinction between these terms. C. Wright Mills put the difference most succinctly in discussing two types of social issues when he wrote:

When, in a city of 100,000, only one man is unemployed, that is his personal trouble, and for its relief we properly look to the character of the man, his skills, and his immediate opportunities. But when in a nation of 50 million employees, 15 million men are unemployed, that is an issue, and we may not hope to find its solution within the range of opportunities open to any one individual. The very structure of opportunities has collapsed . . . Consider marriage. Inside a marriage, a man and a woman may experience personal troubles, but when the divorce rate during the first four years of marriage is 250 out of 1000 attempts, this is an indication of a structural issue having to do with the institution of marriage and the family and other institutions that bear upon them.[45]

The approach to poverty and opportunity that looks fundamentally at structure assumes primarily that consistent personal patterns of behavior can best be explained not as individual problems but as responses to particular positions within the opportunity structure of the larger society, and, consequently, that they must be dealt with by changing broad social policy rather than on an individual basis. The distinction is a particularly important one for education, because the school works with individual children and their families almost entirely. In the absence of a dramatic shift in its nature as an institution, it must take a functional approach.

Allied to this distinction are several others that are important for a consideration of social policy. One is the difference between equality and efficiency, as Tobin notes.[46] The economist, Henry Simon, has argued (and the "trained instincts" of most economists, says Tobin, lead them to agree) that in their effort to achieve a more equal distribution of social goods, governments should not interfere with the efficiencies achieved by a competitive market. "While concerned laymen who observe people with shabby housing or too little to eat instinctively want to provide them with decent housing and adequate food, economists instinctively want to provide them with more cash income."[47] So, instead of setting minimum wages, which require employers of some unskilled labor to pay higher wages than they would otherwise have to pay (an action which artificially inflates the price of their product), it is in this view better to arrange a direct payment to the worker to supplement his income. Instead of encouraging the government to build low-cost housing, one should provide low-income families with the cash to enable them to buy better housing on the existing market. The increasingly socialist bent of American liberal reformers leads them in an opposite direction toward giving a very large role to government-operated services.[48]

A second distinction to be considered is that between "less administered" and "more administered" programs. Robert Levine has noted the growing disenchantment among liberals with centralized federal programs aimed at overcoming social problems, but he argues that simply decentralizing them is not the answer:

The key, then, may not be decentralization as such, but the design of a system in which people make decisions for themselves in their own best interests, but in which the sum total comes out as a net increment to the social good—something like Adam Smith's "invisible hand." 'And if incentives or rules can be designed to induce the many "prime movers" in business, the states, and the localities to move in the same socially desirable direction at the same time, the cumulative impact of this movement would surely be greater than the power of the federal government to accomplish the same ends by administrative means.[49]

A good illustration of the difference Levine is pointing to may be seen in the contrast between two existing programs, public assistance and income tax. The welfare system depends on the application of detailed rules by an army of social workers and investigators in each individual case. Administrative costs of welfare are enormous, and the human costs in degradation and "big brotherism" are even worse. The income tax system with all its abuses is, on the other hand, an efficient way of collecting revenue *by setting general rules and allowing people to apply these to themselves.* Where it has not worked well, Levine notes, it has been because of attempts to move toward a more administered system, as in the case of those with higher incomes.

INCOME STRATEGIES

Ae we have already seen, a large proportion of families are below the poverty level because of age or disability, or because they are unable to be productive and raise dependent children at the same time. These large groups currently receive the major portion of their income from the government in the form of old-age benefits or aid-to-dependent-children payments. The reason that they are in poverty is that the payments are below the currently defined poverty line; all that is required to bring them above that line is to increase the present allowances.

A broader proposal that would include all those with low incomes and that would avoid the overadministration of the welfare system involves setting an income floor for the population as a whole, and finding a mechanism that would provide supplementary payments as soon as a family's income fell below that level. The device that is most commonly suggested is a negative income tax.

Although there is little agreement among economists about where a minimum level of income should be set, most of the guaranteed income plans use the mechanism of the federal income tax as a device for carrying out the scheme. Each family will file a return showing its income, and will pay a regular tax if that income is above a designated figure. If the income falls below the set level, the family head would file a claim for a benefit in the amount of the difference between his actual income and the maintenance level. The plan proposed by a congressional subcommittee in 1973 is shown in Table 1.3 as it would apply to a female-headed family of three children.

TABLE 1.3   Benefits and Taxes for a Mother and Three Children at Varying Earnings Levels under the Subcommittee Plan

Annual earnings	Federal income tax liability[1]	Tax credits	Net Federal income tax liability[2]	Social security tax	ABLE grant	Net cash income[4]
0	0	$900	+$900	0	$2,100	$3,000
$500	0	900	+900	$29	1,914	3,285
$1,000.............	0	900	+900	58	1,729	3,571
$1,500.............	0	900	+900	88	1,644	3,956
$2,000.............	0	900	+900	117	1,358	4,141
$2,500.............	0	900	+900	146	1,173	4,427
$3,000.............	0	900	+900	176	988	4,712
$4,000.............	0	900	+900	234	617	5,283
$5,000.............	0	900	+900	292	246	5,854
$6,000.............	[3] $124	900	+776	351	0	6,425
$7,000.............	[3] 495	900	+405	410	0	6,995
$8,000.............	907	900	7	468	0	7,525
$9,000.............	1,073	900	173	526	0	8,301
$10,000............	1,260	900	360	585	0	9,055
$15,000............	2,315	900	1,415	772	0	12,813
$20,000............	3,695	900	2,795	772	0	16,433
$25,000............	5,325	900	4,425	772	0	19,803

[1] *Based on the standard deduction but with no low-income allowance. Personal exemptions are replaced by $225 per person tax credits.*
[2] *Numbers with plus signs indicate net payments to rather than from taxpayers because of tax credits.*
[3] *Tax is a reduced amount from regular schedule because of provision for smooth transition from ABLE recipient to nonrecipient status.*
[4] *Assuming no State supplementation. Social security taxes, using the current tax rate and taxable wage base, are deductible from earnings in computing ABLE grants.*

Although an income maintenance plan was proposed by President Nixon to Congress in the early seventies, the policy has been stalled since then by inability of various political forces to compromise between those who viewed proposed minimum income levels as too low, and those who refused to agree to increase them. The issue may be resolved within the decade, however, if only because of everyone's dissatisfaction with the welfare system as it now exists. Although it takes a basically structural approach of cash transfers to the individual and the family, the system requires armies of social workers and investigators to administer means tests and to make thousands of decisions about specific needs of individual families.

Welfare rolls began their alarming increase early in the decade of the sixties, and the rise has continued unabated. By the early seventies, there were 14 million people receiving some form of relief from the system, and one of every ten children in the nation was on welfare. Criticism and alarm rose proportionately with the costs. City, state, and federal bureaucrats wrangled over the number of ineligibles receiving welfare, with general agreement that *some* proportion of the total was on the rolls illegally. A popular image of the system evolved that imagined large numbers of able-bodied men too lazy to work, families that had come North and West just to get on welfare, and families whose fathers had deserted so that the wife and children might draw benefits.

In an attempt to cool the controversy with facts, the Department of Health, Education, and Welfare widely distributed a fact sheet on welfare in 1971:[50]

Payments vary from $60 per month in Mississippi to a high of $375 in Alaska for a family of four. (In some states the allowances are higher for larger families.)

Less than 1 percent of recipients are able-bodied males. (As drug addicts appear increasingly on the rolls, this may change, depending on one's definition of "able-bodied;" in New York City over 30,000 addicts are now included.)

The largest group is composed of mothers; about 14 percent are working and an additional 7 percent are in work training programs.

The average family is on the rolls for twenty-three months; only 7 percent have been on welfare for over ten years. (By 1975 that average had risen to 31 percent.)

Forty-nine percent are white, 46 percent black. (By 1975 comparable figures were 44 percent and 50.2 percent, with the remainder other minorities.)

At the militant reform end of the political spectrum, there has been a determined and organized effort to get more eligible families on welfare and to press for the rights of welfare recipients; this movement has been spearheaded by social workers Richard Cloward and Frances Piven. They argue that the rise of 225 percent in welfare during the sixties cannot be explained by migration or unemployment; what changed was the temper of the black poor.[51] The political turmoil of the sixties, they claim, aroused the "uprooted"; and by 1970, as the recession deepened, people felt they had a right to welfare. Cloward and Piven see the welfare explosion as just another part of a vicious cycle in which the political unrest of the poor is "bought off" by the giving of direct relief, and the necessary reconstruction of the economic order is ignored. Then, "once the poor no longer constitute a political threat in any respect, they are expelled from the rolls and left to fend for themselves in a labor market where there is not enough work to go around."[52]

Full employment at decent wages, the authors argue, would draw ADC mothers and street corner men into productive life—a result that seems unlikely. The rise in the welfare rolls no longer seems to be related to changes in the unemployment rate; unemployment can go down while the rolls go steadily up. In New York City in 1971, there was a decline in welfare categories that involved unemployment or supplementing low wages, but there was a steep increase in categories that had to do with family disintegration and drug addiction. Even if any large proportion of mothers on ADC, the greatest percentage of welfare recipients, were able and willing to work, the cost of some current government-operated day-care centers to relieve them of responsibility for their children is running about $3000 per year per child.

The "regulating the poor" thesis, although popular among many social work intellectuals, has stimulated a number of critical attacks from others. Eugene Durman has disaggregated Piven and Cloward's data and concluded that it fails to support the theory;[53] Ira Cutler has pointed out that although there was little social unrest among the poor during the early seventies, welfare payments increased.[54] Gordon Rose has remarked that if the Piven-Cloward thesis is true "one cannot have a government which earnestly wants to do well by its poor; and if that is a basic tenet of the welfare state, one cannot have a welfare state."[55]

Whether the adoption of a negative income tax or some other form of income floor would solve the welfare crisis is problematical. It would do away with the army of people necessary to administer welfare, and would probably result in a more humane system, generally; but it would do little to resolve the issues that increasingly divide the public into angry camps.

One important question relates to the motivational effect—both on the affluent professional and technical class and on the poor—of an income floor set at a decent level. Tobin argues that if the guaranteed income level "is a quarter to a third of mean income, and especially if the government is purchasing for substantive use any significant fraction of national output, the necessary tax rates will be so high that incentive and allocational effects cannot be ignored."[56] Even so, he concludes that a negative income tax at some reasonable level is the best way to achieve income redistribution.

At the other end of the scale, James Vadakin sees unfortunate consequences for the poor themselves:

> While undoubtedly not intended by their proponents, there is a pervasive suggestion emanating from these plans that the payments represent a sort of "social conscience money," as it is termed by Harry G. Johnson, paid by an affluent society to those of its members who do not share in a decent standard of living. Such payments of "conscience money" are easily justified on a short-term basis. But do we want them as permanent features of American society? Do we not wish to incorporate the poor into the mainstream of American life? Although there might be some small structural gains from such plans, as a result of altered habits and motivations of the poor once they come to enjoy more acceptable levels of living, the fact is that guarantee plans would do little to improve our human resources, to equip the able-bodied and nonaged poor to earn a better livelihood, and to contribute to our total social product.[57]

The issue of incentives was the focus of a three-year study in New Jersey and Pennsylvania, where eight different plans are under test, covering a broad spectrum of income guarantees and tax rates with a sample of 1300 low income families. An early report indicates no notable impact on the work habits of the families.[58] Those within the experiment borrowed less and purchased more durable goods than the control group families; but the additional stability afforded by the income grants did not appear to result in unusual responses—"extreme, unusual, or unanticipated responses are not supported by preliminary data."[59]

The cash grants in these experiments, however, by no means truly represent in size the combined impact of the many transfer programs now in operation, many of them now part of the social security system which has long since ceased to be an insurance program and is now an umbrella covering programs that issue payments that came to 15 billion per month by 1975. A modest program designed to combat serious malnutrition by providing food stamps to the very poor and funded with a few hundred million grew into a six billion dollar program within a few years, and may come to rival social security in the future.[60]

Nathan Glazer reports on a *Boston Globe* story about a family on welfare in that city, a sympathetic story whose point was to demonstrate that the Governor's resistance to an increase in benefits was unfair.[61] The mother of six children:

> is well organized. She buys food stamps twice a month, refuses to live in a housing project, is a member of a community women's group at Catholic Charities, and is studying for her high school diploma. Her bi-monthly cash grant is $466, she gets a flat grant every three months of $142, and her monthly savings from food stamps amount to $86. Her cash income may be given as $599 monthly, or $7,188 a year.[26]

Glazer calculates that if the family spends the average amount for health care in this country (care which they receive free), an additional $1750 would accrue to their income. Three children attend alternative schools and day-care centers, which cost paying pupils $3000 a year.

> Cash income and free health and educational services for this family thus amount to $16,028. The older children work summers, and I will not cost that out. The family pays no taxes, and need put nothing aside for savings, as the welfare department is committed to meetings its needs. A working head of a family would have to earn at least $20,000 to match this standard of living.[63]

Glazer goes on to argue, as do Martin Rein and others, that the solution for welfare or any other income support program is to make secondary jobs that now cannot compete with transfer payments more attractive. We could move in that direction by linking incentives to job-holding; by offering federal health insurance, for example, or child allowances, to those who are employed, to make the jobs themselves more secure and steady.

But, at the present, the barriers of incentives and costs remain insuperable. In its broadest terms the issue is brought into sharp focus by two recent works by Arthur Okun and Edgar Browning. Okun's book *Equality and Efficiency* poses the problem as he sees it in what he calls The Leaky Bucket analogy.[64] Suppose, he says, we tax an additional $4000 each from the top 5 percent of American families; since they represent one-fourth of the bottom 20 percent of families, we should be able to distribute $1000 each to the families in the bottom fifth. But, it will be like carrying water in a leaky bucket; because of a variety of inefficiencies and loss of incentives along the way, we will be able to transfer only a portion of that $1000 grant. The question he poses is: What level of inefficiency should we accept and still approve of the policy? Okun's answer is, about 60 percent (a $400.00 grant per family), before he would reject the possibility.

Browning's reply argues that the 9 percent additional tax suggested by Okun as all that is necessary to accomplish the transfer is far from the real cost of such a policy.[65] If a person earns $20,000, and the government decides to take $4000 in taxes, it may apply a flat rate of 20 percent, or it may exclude the first $15,000 and tax the remaining $5000 of income at a "marginal" tax rate of 80 percent. It is the marginal rate, says Browning, that affects incentives; Okun's proposal would actually confront most upper income taxpayers with a marginal tax rate of 70 to 75 percent. The proposal would have even more serious consequences for the incentives of the lowest 20 percent of the families to whom the grants apply because, when the amount of assistance falls as a family's income increases, the result is the equivalent of assessing a marginal tax rate on income. In this case, he estimates, the marginal tax rate on poor families would go up to almost 100 percent, that is, any attempt to increase their real income by working would be offset almost completely by withdrawal of present benefits, particularly if one includes all benefits-in-kind (such as food stamps) along with the cash transfers.

CHAPTER NOTES

[1] *Characteristics of the Population below the Poverty Level, 1974*. U.S. Bureau of the Census, Current Population Reports P60, no. 102 (January 1976).

[2] Pamela Roby, "Inequality: A Trend Analysis," *Annals of the American Academy of Political and Social Science*, 385 (September 1969) 110–117; Pamela Roby and M. S. Miller, *The Future of Equality* (New York: Basic Books, 1970).

[3] *Characteristics of the Population*, pp. 1–4.

[4] Richard Parker, *The Myth of the Middle Class* (New York: Liveright, 1972).

[5] Parker, p. 8.

[6] Parker, p. 15.

[7] Parker, p. 60.

[8] Parker, p. 119.

[9] Parker, p. 169.

[10] Stanley Lebergott, "How To Increase Poverty," *Commentary*, (October 1975), 59–63.

[11] Cited in Glen G. Cain, *Population Change and Economic Welfare*, Working Paper Number 72–29, Center for Demography and Ecology University of Wisconsin, November 1972.

12 Lebergott, p. 60.

13 Ben Wattenberg, *The Real America* (New York: Doubleday, 1974).

14 Simon Kuznets, "Demographic Aspects of the Distribution of Income among Families," *Essays in Honor of Jan Tinberger*, vol. 3 (White Plains, N.Y.: International Arts and Sciences Press, 1974), pp. 223–245.

15 Lebergott, p. 61.

16 Irving Kristol, "Taxes, Poverty, and Equality," *The Public Interest*, no. 37 (Fall 1974).

17 Kristol, p. 11.

18 "Census Study Finds Income Shift from the Rich to the Poor," *New York Times*, March 19, 1971.

19 *Federal Outlays Benefitting the Poor—Summary Tables*, U.S. Office of Health, Education, and Welfare, Office of Program Systems (March 1974).

20 Edgar K. Browning, "How Much More Equality Can We Afford?" *The Public Interest*, no. 3 (Spring 1976), 90–110.

21 Lester Thurow, "Education and Economic Equality," *The Public Interest*, no. 28 (Summer 1972).

22 Kenneth E. Boulding, "The Stability of Inequality," *Review of Social Economy*, 33 (1975), 1–14.

23 Boulding, p. 1.

24 Robert B. Semple, Jr., "Income Inequalities in Britain Found To Change Little in Decade," *New York Times*, August 2, 1975.

25 Barbara Preston, "Statistics of Inequality," *Sociological Review*, 22 (1974), 103–118.

26 Milton Rokeach, *The Nature of Human Values* (New York: Free Press, 1973).

27 Bradley Schiller, "Equality, Opportunity, and the 'Good Job'," *The Public Interest*, no. 43 (Spring 1976), 111–120.

28 "Social and Economic Conditions of Negroes in the U.S.," 1970, Washington, D.C., Bureau of Labor Statistics, 1971; *Educational Attainment of Workers*, March 1969–1970, U.S. Department of Labor, 1970; *Annual Current Population Report*, Bureau of the Census, 1975; *Current Population Report*, Bureau of the Census, March 1976.

29 Text of Moynihan Memorandum on the Status of Negroes, *New York Times*, March 1, 1970.

30 Erdman Palmore and Frank J. Whittington, "Differential Trends toward Equality between Whites and Nonwhites," *Social Forces*, 49 (1970), 108–117.

31 Gary Becker, *The Economics of Discrimination* (Chicago: University of Chicago Press, 1957).

32 David W. Rasmussen, "Discrimination and the Income of Nonwhite Males," *American Journal of Economics and Sociology*, 30 (1971), 377–382.

33 James Gwartney, "Discrimination and Income Differentials," *American Economic Review*, LX (1970), 396–408.

34 Otto Eckstein, *Education, Employment, and Negro Equality*, U.S. Department of Labor Seminar on Manpower Policy and Programs, April 18, 1968, p. 12.

35 Thomas J. Cook, "Benign Neglect: Minimum Feasible Understanding," *Social Problems*, 18, no. 2 (Fall 1970), 145–152.

36 "More Negroes Hold Better Paying Jobs," *New York Times*, September 27, 1971.

37 "Census Data Show Blacks Still Poor," *New York Times*, February 12, 1971.

38 "Unemployment Trends for School-Age Youth Highlighted in New BLS Report," Bureau of Labor Statistics, Office of Information, November 2, 1970.

39 Wattenberg, p. 130.

40 Cook, p. 150.

41 James Gwartney, "Changes in the Nonwhite/White Income Ratio—1939–67," *American Economic Review*, LX, no. 5 (December 1970), 881.

42 Gwartney, p. 882.

43 Joseph A. Kahl and John M. Goering, "Stable Workers, Black and White," *Social Problems*, 18, no. 3 (Winter 1971), 306–318.

[44] Kahl and Goering, p. 315.

[45] C. Wright Mills, *The Sociological Imagination* (New York: Oxford University Press, 1959), p. 9.

[46] James Tobin, "On Limiting the Domain of Equality," *Journal of Law and Economics,* 13, no. 2 (October 1970), 263–277.

[47] Tobin, p. 264.

[48] See, for example, Michael Harrington, "Government Should Be the Employer of *First* Resort," *New York Times Magazine,* March 26, 1972, p. 44.

[49] Robert A. Levine, "Rethinking Our Social Strategies," *The Public Interest,* no. 10 (Winter 1968), 87.

[50] *Welfare Myths and Facts.* U.S. Department of Health, Education, and Welfare, 1971; *HEW News,* April 16, 1977.

[51] Frances Fox Piven and Richard A. Cloward, "Welfare I: A Political Response," *New York Times,* November 15, 1971, and "Welfare II: Let the Polls Rise," *New York Times,* November 16, 1971.

[52] Piven and Cloward, p. 45.

[53] Eugene Durman, "Have the Poor Been Regulated?" *Social Service Review,* 47 (1973), 339–359.

[54] Ira M. Cutler, "*Regulating the Poor* Revisited: Testing the Model against the Reality of Events," *Public Welfare* (Summer 1973), 29–33.

[55] Gordon Rose, "*Regulating the Poor:* An Essay Review," *Social Service Review,* 45 (1971), 399.

[56] Rose, p. 265.

[57] James C. Vadakin, "A Critique of the Guaranteed National Income," *The Public Interest,* no. 11 (Spring 1968), 63–64.

[58] Heather Ross, "An Experimental Study of the Negative Income Tax," *Child Welfare,* XLIX (December 1970), 562–569.

[59] Rose, p. 569.

[60] Kenneth Schlossberg, "Funny Money Is Serious," *New York Times Magazine,* September 28, 1975, p. 12+.

[61] Nathan Glazer, "Reform Work, Not Welfare," *The Public Interest,* no. 40 (Summer 1975), 3–10.

[62] Glazer, p. 4.

[63] Glazer, p. 4.

[64] Arthur M. Okun, *Equality and Efficiency* (Washington, D.C.: Brookings, 1975).

[65] Browning, p. 108.

Chapter 2

Employment and Education Strategies for Equalizing Income

Directly increasing the buying power of the poor is surely the most efficient redistribution policy, but many people look to less direct and long-term policies that would not pose a danger to the structure of incentives: upgrading the skills of the unskilled, and, even longer range, increasing the years of schooling of the youth of the poor. This section:

Describes a number of manpower training strategies such as JOBS, and reviews the data on their effectiveness.

Reviews the surprising and contradictory findings of studies of how schooling influences future income, and suggests how they can be reconciled.

Examines the role of school achievement on income equality.

Some of the questions readers might address are:

Do Jencks' conclusions about the weakness of the influence of schooling on income square with my own observations? (The reader might think about some of his or her own family and compare their years of schooling with the incomes they attained.)

Does Jencks' conclusion about the power of *luck* in determining income seem plausible? Why, or why not?

On the basis of the evidence, should we continue to persuade adolescents against dropping out of high school? On what grounds, either way?

Although a change in employment patterns is unlikely to change very drastically the position of the majority of the poor, it is a key factor in equalizing the opportunities of minorities who are disproportionately represented among the unskilled and the unemployed. A number of structural proposals have been advanced for dealing with the problem.

The first of these consists of various suggestions for manipulating the forces in the total economy with the aim of creating such a high demand for labor that even the unskilled will be pulled into the labor market at relatively high wages. The argument, in very simple terms, is that the government can, if it wishes to employ appropriate fiscal policies, encourage industry and business to increase their production to the point where the productive resources of the economy are close to being fully employed. At such a point, theoretically, even the very unskilled and marginal workers can easily find jobs; and discrimination is lessened because employers, however prejudiced they may be, find it profitable to hire people.

Those economists who advocate this proposal point to the experience of Western Germany in the first half of the decade of the sixties as proof of their thesis. In that period, production pushed so hard against labor capacity that unskilled workers from Italy and parts of Central Europe were imported to Germany in large numbers. Or, for another example, they cite the American experience during World War II, where industry working around the clock created a demand for labor that brought great numbers of both black and white marginal workers from the South to Northern cities. A major problem with this policy in the U.S. in the seventies is the fear of reigniting the inflationary spiral of the early part of the decade.

Another suggestion that has been around for some time is that the government act as employer of last resort, offering a job to any person who, because of low skill level or disability, could not find a job that would bring him a reasonable income above the poverty line. Such a policy, by the middle of the decade, had become the focus of intense political conflict, in the face of a general unemployment rate that liberals considered far too high, but that conservatives preferred as a lesser evil to inflation.

A very good trial has been made of a plan that bypasses the over-administration of job training programs by subsidizing the direct employment of hard-core unemployed. The government through JOBS provides industry with funds to cover the extra costs of training and turnover associated with such hiring, and industry agrees to hire those whom it would ordinarily reject. The results of the program have been mixed. There is no question that of the many thousands of men and women hired through the program a number have achieved work stability; but one gets the general impression (hard data are meager) that a greater proportion did not. Studies of the program have highlighted a number of explanations for the difficulties:[1]

The state of the economy and the situation of a specific business affects willingness to participate; a business decline, or any reduction in profits results in program cutback. On the other hand, program personnel are reluctant to contract with low-wage companies, because the lower the wages, the higher the turnover.

The degree of employer commitment to the goals of the program is very important, given the substantial changes in recruitment, selection, training and supervision policies demanded.

It is difficult to predict performance as an aid to selection procedures; neither work attitudes nor biographical background data predict performance or job retention rates.

The requirement for supportiveness in the work climate is very high, much higher than most supervisory personnel realize. Friedlander and Greenberg asked groups of supervisors and men to rate the supportiveness of the work situation; the men's ratings were vastly lower than those of the supervisors.

The more successful programs tended to have a full-time administrator devoting all his time to the program, well-developed orientation programs for the employees, and to offer a chance for promotion.

A significant proportion of the success that has been achieved in employing the disadvantaged has been with the "soft core," those with positive attitudes toward work and on the threshold of a stable work life.[2]

The functional equivalent of these more direct approaches to employment is manpower training of a great variety. Mangum lists the following relatively new training developments:

> Outreach to seek the discouraged and undermotivated and encourage them to partake of available services. Adult basic education. Prevocational orientation to expose those with limited experience to alternative occupational choices. Training for entry-level skills for those unprepared to profit from the normally more advanced training. Training allowances to provide support and an incentive. Residential facilities for those from areas of sparse population or whose home environment precludes successful rehabilitation. Work experience for those unaccustomed to the discipline of the work place. Job development efforts to solicit job opportunities suited to the abilities of the disadvantaged job seeker . . . Supportive services, such as medical aid for those who need corrective measures . . . Relocation allowances for residents in labor-surplus areas and special inducements to employers to bring jobs to those stranded in depressed areas.[3]

The success of all this activity is unclear. Evidence is occasionally offered of its effectiveness; for example, a survey in 1971 showed that those Puerto Ricans who had undergone job training were considerably better off than those who had not. About 43,000 Puerto Ricans live in poverty areas of New York, of whom 6000 had completed a training program; their unemployment rate was 5.2 percent compared with 10.3 percent for those who had not been trained. They were earning $.40 an hour more than the untrained group, and had triple the proportion of workers in skilled trades.[4]

On the other hand, the same city spent 40 million dollars in 1971 on its job training program involving 12,000 individuals; of these, about 8,500 actually completed training, 3500 were placed in jobs, and a check 90 days later was able to account for only 2000 of these. At that point, only a little more than half of those 2000 were still on the job. To put 1000 men to work at a cost of $40,000 each seems excessive.

Bernard Anderson, whose study of 276 evaluations of manpower training programs has become a bible in the field, sums up the effort by concluding that gains of manpower training tend to be small and, in many cases, not lasting.[5]

A more promising approach to equalizing minority group job opportunity is represented by the growing programs in subprofessional training, one of the few genuinely creative ideas about the expansion of opportunity in a whole decade of attention to that problem. In one report the idea is defined by the following characteristics:[6]

Subprofessional jobs consist of subsections of work, heretofore done by professionals, for which full professional training is not necessary, or of new functions that expand the scope of professional services.

The jobs are designed at the entry level so that persons with less than the training or academic credentials that usually accompany professional status can, in relatively short periods, become sufficiently skilled to perform the work.

The jobs allow opportunity for individual development, regardless of the traditional credentials or other arbitrary symbols of status, and permit advancement to duties of greater challenge and responsibility.

Advancement is accompanied by increments of earnings and access to promotional avenues which are not dependent exclusively on full-time formal training financed by the individual.

The fields in which most of the subprofessional job development is taking place are health, welfare, and education. A later chapter will consider in detail the use of teacher aides from the urban community itself in schools of the inner city. The broad possibilities inherent in the idea may be grasped by a look at the kinds of jobs that, unlike teacher aides, do not even exist at present:

Social work aides to help with patients in communities and hospitals.

Homemakers to help patients recover in their own homes.

Halfway house aides to care for those who no longer need hospital care but have no other place to go.

Community mental health workers to work with families and individuals, and to assist teachers in diagnosing children's problems.

Counseling aides, possibly themselves ex-addicts or ex-alcoholics, to deal with problems of alcoholism and addiction.

Health education aides.

Preventive medicine aides.

Medical aides to assist physicians in such tasks as taking histories.

Middle-management aides in hospitals to perform and supervise functions in record-keeping, supplies, and so on.

The practical problems involved in carrying through this idea have turned out to be severe, though probably surmountable. But as a means of opening access to real career opportunities for the socially disadvantaged, the approach holds such enormous promise that it is worthwhile wrestling with the problems. One fundamental advantage is that the employment focus is in the area of greatest occupational expansion, the service industries. We are moving away from a manufacturing economy to the point where two-thirds of the labor force is currently engaged in the production of services.

EDUCATION STRATEGIES

The least direct strategy of all for equalizing income is to rely on equalizing the years of schooling received by the youth of the society. It is the policy with the longest tradition in this country, and one that most people believe in most firmly. Figure 2.1 shows the typical differences in lifetime income earned by those in various schooling categories and the case seems to be overwhelming for the substantial income benefits of education.

Most education professionals share the public's faith in the relationship. Several reviews of the very considerable body of investigations of it come to positive conclusions; Levin summarizes his review thus:

> The effect of schooling on earnings has been substantiated by numerous studies, some of which are described above. Better schools have fewer dropouts and higher student achievement. Both of these factors have been shown to be related

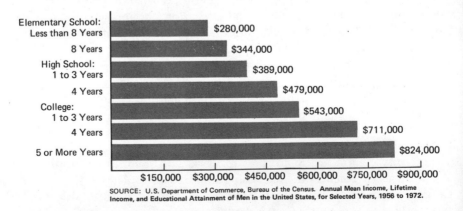

SOURCE: U.S. Department of Commerce, Bureau of the Census. **Annual Mean Income, Lifetime Income, and Educational Attainment of Men in the United States, for Selected Years, 1956 to 1972.**

FIG. 2.1 Lifetime income of men, by years of school completed: United States, 1972

to higher earnings or greater economic opportunity. Even when adjustments are made for individual ability and other intervening influences, the payoffs to better and more schooling persisted . . . While the studies differ in their findings on the relative magnitude of the schooling-earnings effect, virtually all studies on the subject show evidence of a significant effect. There are few social science hypotheses that have been tested so intensively with such consistent results.[7]

Christopher Jencks and his associates at Harvard, however, have recently reported on a number of studies of the impact of schooling that contradict the conclusions of Levin and others, and that have set off one of the great educational controversies of the decade.[8] The following chapter will examine Jenck's analysis of the influence of schooling on social status, and Chapter 11 will look at his data on the impact of schools on differences in achievement level among their students. This chapter will focus on what Jencks has to say about income.

Why the contradiction between Jencks' results and those of earlier research? One of the crucial reasons is the method he used, and some elementary understanding of that method is necessary to an appreciation of the controversy.

Figure 2.2 provides a starting point. The first set of arrows indicates the model for the way most people think about the relation between schooling and income, one that is implicit in the earlier census chart; there is a simple, direct causal connection such that additional years of school will result in higher income for an individual. But, there is also a strong correlation between the income a person attains later in life and a number of background variables, such as his father's occupation and education. It is possible that what accounts for the simple correlation between education and income is really that underlying connection, and education appears to be important only because fathers with higher levels of education see to it that their children get more years of schooling. The second set of arrows shows this particular assumption, and in the B model, years of schooling, instead of representing the basic *causal* variable, is regarded as an *intervening* variable. In the pure case, for example, if we found that children of

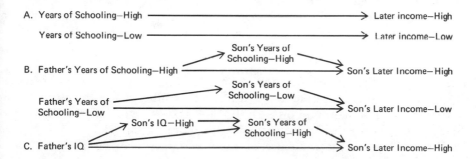

FIG. 2.2 Hypothetical relationships of educational background variables with income

fathers with the same education always achieved equal years of schooling and roughly equal incomes later, the influence of schooling itself would disappear.

The C model adds a complication. Children in the same family seldom exhibit the same interest in or talent for education, and there is a sizable correlation between IQ (as a stand-in for that variable) and years of schooling. We expect, then, that a high-IQ son of a father with poor education may well get more education, hence a higher income later, than his father; the reverse may also be the case. So IQ may be an intervening variable that modifies the direct influence of the background variables. But, we might also regard IQ as strongly linked to background, in that some part of it appears to be inherited (see Chapter 8 for a treatment of that issue). Some of the influence of IQ on the outcome variable of income may thus be seen as indirect, in its effect on how many years of schooling the child wants and is able to achieve; some is direct, in the form of the correlation between father's IQ and son's later income.

There exists, fortunately, a method of assessing the independent influence of a number of such background and intervening variables on an outcome measure such as income that permits one to ask: What difference does variation in the years of schooling make for sons whose fathers have the same level of education, and who themselves have roughly the same IQ? The method is called *path analysis*; it requires that the investigator construct a model of the relationships responsible for the outcome variable (in this case income), and it assumes that all of the variables that have any significant effect on the outcome are part of the model.

Jencks constructed such a model, and investigated the correlations among all of the variables included, using data from a number of studies that included at least some of the variables. His model includes the following:

Father's occupational status
Father's years of schooling
Father's IQ
Respondent's years of schooling
Respondent's IQ at age 11
Respondent's adult aptitude test score (the Armed Forces aptitude test)
Respondent's occupational status
Respondent's income

In addition to these actual data for a group of white males, Jencks estimated three other scores: the respondent's estimated IQ inheritance, the estimated effect of family background on early IQ, and the estimated effect of family background on the number of years of schooling he attained.

His findings on the influence of these variables may be summed up briefly as:

Very little of the differences in income is predicted by any of the variables in the system. Among individuals of the same social-class background, same level of cognitive skill, the same number of years of schooling and generally equal occupational level, income inequality is only 12 to 15 percent less than it is among a random sample of men chosen from the population.

There is a significant tendency of some to maintain the same occupational status as their fathers, which results in higher status children getting more years of schooling. But the effect of family social status and other background variables is far less than one would expect, and brothers in the same family are apt to end up with incomes almost as far apart as do two men picked from the population at random.

Men in the top fifth of aptitude scores have incomes about twice those of the bottom fifth in aptitude. But this difference is slight when compared with the six-fold difference between the best paid fifth and the worst paid fifth. That is, inequality in earned income is far greater than inequality in academic endowment.

The final number of years of schooling attained does predict income, but not very strongly. For men with the same initial ability and family background, an additional year of elementary or secondary education increases future income about 4 percent, an additional year of college 7 percent, and of graduate school, 4 percent.

If greater income equality is desired (and Jencks, himself a socialist, wants it very much), equalizing education will not bring it about; direct income transfer is the only effective means.

A summary of the debate over these conclusions is provided in Panel 2.1.

PANEL 2.1 The Controversy over Jencks' Analysis of Education and Income

Jencks' published report became an instant *cause celebre*, and within a year or so symposia on his methods and his findings had appeared in several major scholarly journals.[9] To each of them Jencks and his colleagues prepared painstaking, detailed replies, in some cases admitting error, in others defending estimates and justifying procedures. It is impossible to summarize this vast literature adequately in a short compass; little more can be done than indicate the substance of some of the more important critiques.

There was, for example, a considerable amount of disturbance about the possible negative effects of the conclusion Jencks came to, particularly from black intellectuals who accused Jencks of pulling the props from under efforts to provide adequate funding for the schooling of minorities, and taking away the last possibility of hope for dark-skinned children. A variant of this reproach is that Jencks is simply creating a straw man—that no one believes any longer in trying to reduce poverty by improving education and skills; almost 50 percent of the federal budget now goes to income maintenance or distribution programs, only 2 to 3 percent for education. But, as a policy argument, it is claimed, Jencks' report is likely to do harm; although Jencks himself has declared in favor of more educational resources for poor children, budget cutters may use his data out of context.

A second type of attack on the conclusion itself runs this way: although it may be true that the ultimate impact of schooling on income may be low, this must not be taken to mean that the immediate impact of the school on the child is not important. School life is an end in itself, and student enjoyment of learning and the expansion of individual experience through learning justify themselves. (But, as Lester Thurow remarks, if we adopt that point of view, the question is whether as a society we are willing to support an end-in-itself education in the same style.)

There is a vast amount of technical criticism that simply cannot be dealt with here, ranging from a distrust of the path analysis approach and its assumptions, to sophisticated questioning of Jencks' estimates of such measures as the average difference in brothers' incomes, and irate questioning of his estimates on IQ heredity. (It should be noted for future reference that Jencks restricts the latter estimate to the white population from which his major sample was taken.)

There are some interesting efforts to use Jencks' own data against his conclusions, and attempts by Marxist theorists to show that even when they are correct he is asking the wrong questions. An example of the former that well illustrates much of the debate is James Coleman's assertion that even if the connection between education and income does not clearly emerge from looking at individuals, Jencks' data show a relationship at the level of the entire society.[10] One of his tables (see Table 2.1), shows general inequality indices for both income and education as they have varied from 1929 to 1970. (Read it as: the degree of inequality in

TABLE 2.1   The Coefficients of Variation of Income
and Education, Relative to 1929

Year	1929	1936	1946	1960	1968	1970
Education	1.0	.89	.71	.67	.59	.61
Income	1.0	.89	.71	.67	.60	.55

Source: James S. Coleman, "Equality of Opportunity and Equality of Results," Perspectives on Inequality, Reprint Series no. 8, Harvard Educational Review, 1973, p. 97.

income in 1935–1936 was 89 percent of the inequality present in 1929, etc.)
The comparisons for each year are restricted to those of the same age
range for each period, roughly the group of men 25 to 34 years old, and
the correspondence in the decline of inequality is strikingly familiar for
education and income.

Jencks responds by pointing out that just because the two measures of
inequality vary in the same way does not mean that one is the cause of
the other; one would have to believe that more equal education "set off
system-wide sociological or technological changes that substantially al-
tered the labor market and reduced the variance in wages."[11] Such an
assumption, he argues, is implausible. Furthermore, Coleman is comparing educational inequality among young people just entering the labor
market, with income data for families of all ages, an inappropriate comparison. When the distribution of education and the distribution of income
are compared *for the same group* of individuals, the parallelism, he says,
disappears. Although the distribution of education among adult male
workers has grown steadily more equal over the past generation, the
distribution of earnings stabilized after 1950.

Education and Income: A Second Approach

The contradiction between Jencks' findings and the earlier summary of
research by Levin is not only due to methodology. As Thurow has pointed
out, Jencks uses data on individuals, and his conclusions apply to an individual's calculation of the worth, in future income, of additional schooling.[12]
Most of the other research on the question, on the other hand, has
approached the problem through data on *groups* of people, using the
methods of economics. In contrast to Jencks' procedure, economists go
through the following steps: (a) average the incomes of high school graduates and college graduates (as an example), and find the difference; (b)
average a wide variety of background factors, father's occupation, IQ, etc.,
for each of the groups and estimate the percentage of the groups' income
difference that can be attributed to these (generally about 50 percent of
the difference is left over, and is attributed to the increased education);
(c) calculate the direct and indirect costs of going to college instead of
moving directly into the labor force from high school; (d) compare the
total cost of going to college with the extra lifetime income attributable
to the additional years of education, to compute a rate of return on the
investment in college.

These estimates generally show a reasonable rate of return on the investment in additional years of schooling, but by no means is it consistent or
always very substantial:

1.   The advantage may be quite small if the investment is subtracted. Thus, for clerical workers in general, the fourth year of high school amounts to a lifetime advantage of $4300, if the costs are invested at an interest of 5 percent; at an assumption of 10 percent interest, the advantage drops to $1900.[13] Four years of college or more earn an increment of about $17,000 when corrected for an investment at 5 percent, and drop considerably at 10 percent.[14] Over a work life of forty years or so, one can see that the return, although it renders further schooling worthwhile, is not quite so urgently attractive as much of the rhetoric about schooling implies.

2.   There is much argument about whether we are measuring the effect of intelligence instead of schooling in these calculations, on the grounds that those with higher measured intelligence are more likely on the whole to continue further in school. The evidence is conflicting on the issue. Levin concludes that despite the contradictions he is satisfied that, with intelligence controlled, schooling still maintains an advantage; and he is probably generally correct. What does seem to be true is that for those lower in intelligence or scholastic achievement, the financial return for schooling is often substantially lower than for the more able. There is a gap of over $38,000 in lifetime earnings between high and low aptitude students coming from medium-quality colleges.[15]

What may account for some of the conflict in findings generally has been pointed out by Hause.[16] He discovered that IQ has a different influence on earnings depending on the level of education of the group concerned; it has a very weak effect at the lowest schooling level, increasing in influence as schooling level rises. He concludes that there is a greater incentive for those with higher IQs to attend college than others.

3.   One would suppose that the rate of return would be higher for higher levels of schooling, but strangely the opposite is true. In absolute terms, of course, the average college graduate earns more money than the average person with an elementary education. But if one asks how much better off the latter is than a person without a complete elementary school education, versus how much better off a person with a college degree is than someone with a high school degree, the return for elementary school is higher. The rate of return for the elementary school graduate is 161 percent over the nonelementary graduate; the return for the high school graduate over the nongraduate is 16 percent, and the return for the college graduate over the high school graduate, 13 percent.[17] Hines also calculated the social return on the entire investment in education made by the society, based on an estimate of how much the society could afford to pay in interest on its investment in education and still break even. In the United States, the return was 17 percent for elementary schooling, 14 percent for high school, and 9 percent for college. Thus, from the social point of view, if we could obtain as much as a 10 percent return on our investment in college education somewhere else, we would, in a sense, be losing money by running the colleges. (There are, of course, other and perhaps more significant social returns from college education.)

The greater return to elementary schooling suggests a possible answer to the question often raised about the increasing proportion of college entrants. Some have argued that as the percentage of college graduates rises, its significance will decrease and its return will be less. In the long run, of course, just the opposite should happen, as employers take a college degree for granted and demand it from everyone. Elementary school graduation is so high in value because so few lack it that to be without it represents a great disadvantage.

4.   Perhaps the greatest modification needed in the relation of schooling to earnings is to be found in the case of the blacks. Although blacks with an elementary education earn about 80 percent of the incomes of whites at that level of education, and those with a high school diploma 73 percent as much as their white counterparts, black college graduates earn only 69 percent of white college graduates' incomes.[18] In projected lifetime income terms, at the level of service and household work, the fourth year of high school is worth $4400 to whites, and $1630 to blacks; for clerical workers, it is worth $4300 for whites, $3100 for blacks.[19] With college costs discounted at 5 percent, blacks with one to three years of college, but no degree, lose money; if they had invested the cost of college, they would earn almost $2000 more over a lifetime than by going to college.[20] Black collegiates are younger, attend lower ranking colleges, and, as noted earlier, tend to select lower paying professions; all of these factors are changing to be sure, as is the discrimination at higher occupational levels that tended to keep better educated blacks in jobs that did not demand much education.

The latter thesis, however, that even well-qualified blacks will be relegated to low-skill jobs because employment discrimination is greatest at the top is challenged by Gwartney's most recent calculations. He added "average achievement" to the estimates and found the white/nonwhite income ratio is greater for black college graduates than for blacks with fewer years of schooling.[21]

What can be concluded from all this evidence? Certainly that schooling does mean something, but that it has different payoffs for different groups of people; it is a fairly rewarding, but highly risky, investment. Which suggests that school is not an independent variable that exerts very much influence by itself on the future income and occupation of people who go through it, but instead acts as a mechanism *through which* group and individual characteristics are transmuted into social status, as a number of social scientists have suggested.[22] The child begins at a given socioeconomic level and with a specific academic ability level; these interact to influence his early level of school achievement and his aspirations for both more education and future occupation; by high school, his previous academic attainment and the influence of significant others influence still further his decisions for more schooling and future occupation. Considering that something like this dynamic process must certainly go on, it is no wonder that the sometimes accidental acquisition of more years of schooling has only minor influence on what eventually happens to him. That the variable of "years of schooling" is used almost universally as a stand-in for educational achievement may well be a confounding factor in a number of contradictions. Thus, Hauser and Featherman conclude from a study of the black-white employment gap during the sixties that whites are able to turn their education into appropriate jobs to a much greater extent than blacks;[23] Robert Hall and Richard Kasten, in a 1973 Brookings Institution study, report on the contrary that a black can expect the same success in the labor market as a white with the same endowment.[24] As Gwartney and others have shown in studies cited earlier, the level of school achievement may well explain the difference in findings.

From this point of view, the reinforcing effect of academic achievement for minority group children becomes more important to the issue of ultimate equality than does the amount of schooling they have available to them. The magnitude of the effort required to equalize school performance may be estimated by examining on a very broad scale the academic retardation of minority-group children, as shown in Table 2.2.

These scores have been standardized so that the average is 50 and the standard deviation is 10. Thus, half of any normal group should fall below 50, and about 34 percent should be between 50 and 40, one standard deviation below the mean. The average for black students on general information, therefore, means that almost 85 percent of these students scored below the average of the white majority students.

It is evident that only Oriental-American youth at the twelfth-grade level come close to majority-group achievement norms. It is also interesting and important to note that black children not only lag behind the other minorities in general, but that by the end of high school their verbal scores are below those of Puerto Ricans, many of whom start school with the initial handicap of a lack of knowledge of the English language.

As is the case with access to opportunity in general, both regional and urban-rural differences strongly influence these achievement levels, particu-

TABLE 2.2 Nationwide Median Test Scores for First- and Twelfth-Grade Pupils

Test	Puerto Ricans	Indian-Americans	Mexican-Americans	Oriental-Americans	Negro	Majority
First grade:						
Nonverbal	45.8	53.0	50.1	56.6	43.4	54.1
Verbal	44.9	47.8	46.5	51.6	45.4	53.2
Twelfth grade:						
Nonverbal	43.3	47.1	45.0	51.6	40.9	52.0
Verbal	43.1	43.7	43.8	49.6	40.9	52.1
Reading	42.6	44.3	44.2	48.8	42.2	51.9
Mathematics	43.7	45.9	45.5	51.3	41.8	51.8
General information	41.7	44.7	43.3	49.0	40.6	52.2
Average of the 5 tests	43.1	45.1	44.4	50.1	41.1	52.0

Source: Equality of Educational Opportunity, Summary Report (Washington, D.C.: U.S. Department of Health, Education, and Welfare, 1966), p. 20.

larly for the black, but, as Figure 2.3 shows, even to some extent for the white majority child. James Coleman, senior author of the study from which these data are taken, argues that these curves are a rough measure of the school's failure to compensate for the differences in background that give minority-group children unequal access to opportunity in the first place. Some school professionals might view them as proof of the proposition that environment and early training are such strong forces that the school simply cannot overcome them, though it should be noted that income differences, rather than race, accounted for most of the differences. This central issue is a theme which will appear consistently throughout the second half of this book, as the role of the school in the central city is examined in depth.

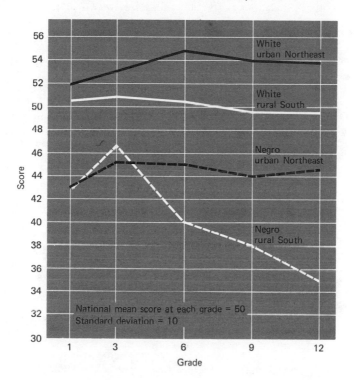

FIG. 2.3   Standardized achievement scores for Negro and white students

CHAPTER NOTES

1 Frank Friedlander and Stuart Greenberg, "Effect of Job Attitudes, Training, and Organization Climate on Performance of the Hard-Core Unemployed," *Journal of Applied Psychology*, 55 (1971), 287–295; Paul S. Goodman, Harold Paransky, and Paul Salipante, "Hiring, Training, and Retaining the Hard-Core Unemployed: A Selected Review," *Journal of Applied Psychology*, 58 (1973), 23–33.

2Elmer H. Burack, F. James Staszals, and Gopal C. Pati, "An Organizational Analysis of

Manpower Issues in Employing the Disadvantaged," *Academy of Management Journal*, 15 (1972), 255–271.

3 Garth L. Mangum, "The Why, How, and Whence of Manpower Programs," *Annals of the American Academy of Political and Social Science*, 385, 50–62 (September 1969), 58.

4 "Job Plan Helpful to Puerto Ricans," *New York Times*, June 1, 1971.

5 Bernard E. Anderson, *The Opportunities Industrialization Centers: A Decade of Community-Based Manpower Services*, (Philadelphia: The University of Pennsylvania, Wharton School, 1976).

6 Edith F. Lynton, *The Subprofessional*, (New York: National Committee on Employment of Youth, 1967).

7 Henry M. Levin, James W. Guthrie, George B. Kleindorfer, and Robert T. Stout, "School Achievement and Post-School Success: A Review," *Review of Educational Research*, 41 (1971), 321–332.

8 Christopher Jencks, et al., *Inequality: A Reassessment of the Effect of Family and Schooling in America* (New York: Basic Books, 1972).

9 *Harvard Educational Review*, 43 (1973); *School Review*, and *Sociology of Education*, 46 (1973).

10 James S. Coleman, "Equality of Opportunity and Equality of Results," *Harvard Educational Review*, 43 (1973), 129–137.

11 Christopher Jencks, "*Inequality* in Retrospect," *Harvard Educational Review*, 43 (1973) p. 124.

12 Lester C. Thurow, "Proving the Absence of Positive Associations," *Harvard Educational Review*, 43 (1973), 106–112.

13 Stuart O. Schweitzer, "Occupational Choice, High School Graduation, and Investment in Human Capital," *Journal of Human Resources*, 6, no. 3 (Summer 1971), 321–332.

14 Melvin Borland and Donald E. Yett, "The Cash Value of College for Negroes and for Whites," *Transaction* (November 1967).

15 Andre Daniere and Jerry Mechling, "Direct Marginal Productivity of College Education in Relation to College Aptitude of Students and Production Costs of Institutions," *Journal of Human Resources*, 5, no. 1 (Winter 1970), 52–69.

16 John C. Hause, "Ability and Schooling as Determinants of Lifetime Earnings or If You're So Smart Why Aren't You Rich?" *American Economic Review*, LXI (May 1971), 289–298.

17 Fred Hines, Luther Tweeten and Martin Redfern, "Social and Private Rates of Return to Investment in Schooling, By Race-Sex Groups and Regions," *Journal of Human Resources*, 5, no. 3 (Summer 1970), 318–340.

18 Ritchie H. Reed and Herman P. Miller, "Some Determinants of the Variation in Earnings for College Men," *Journal of Human Resources*, 5, no. 2 (Spring 1970) 177–190.

19 Schweitzer, p. 331.

20 Borland and Yett, p. 46.

21 James D. Gwartney, "Discrimination, Achievement, and Payoffs of a College Degree," *Journal of Human Resources*, (1972) 60–70).

22 Joe C. Spaeth, "Occupational Attainment among Male College Graduates," *American Journal of Sociology*, 75, Part 2 (1970), 632–644; William H. Sewell, Archibald O. Haller, and Alejandro Portes "The Educational and Early Occupational Attainment Process," *American Sociological Review*, 34 (1969), 82–92; Peter M. Blau and Otis D. Duncan. *The American Occupational Structure* (New York: Wiley, 1967).

23 Robert M. Hauser and David L. Featherman, "Black-white Differentials in Occupational Mobility among Men in the U.S., 1962–1970," Working Paper Number 72-32, Center for Demography and Ecology, University of Wisconsin (December 1972).

24 Robert E. Hall and Richard A. Kasten, *The Relative Occupational Success of Blacks and Whites* (Washington, D.C.: Brookings Institution Papers on Economic Activity, vol. 3, 1973).

Chapter 3

The Drive to Equality II:
Social Class and Status

A second major concern in the current movement toward social equality is for a lessening of differences in social status and prestige. Here, as we shall see, it is likely that schooling can make more of a difference than income. This section of the examination of class and social status deals with the more basic concepts and the value issues in the on-going debate. It:

Provides a definition of social-class stratification, and describes the American class system.

Reviews the argument about whether a social-class system is necessary.

Describes the value systems of the various class levels and the historical roots of "mainstream" American values in the Protestant Ethic.

Notes two major deviations from mainstream values in the attack from many upper-middle class professionals, and in the rejection by the lower-lower class.

Provides a picture of the way in which people move from one class to another in the system, and considers a number of other models for social mobility.

Reviews the debate on the question of whether the mobility of black Americans is unique to the American experience.

Some of the questions readers might address are:

Do the class categories described make sense in the framework of my own experience? To what extent do the values identified as emphases in the social class of my own family reflect the values of my family?

Are my own present values closer to what is described as the mainstream, or to one or another of the variants presented? If the latter, what life influences account for the difference?

Have I, or others I know, gone through the process of social mobility? What circumstances made it possible?

The American society has always viewed itself, and has been viewed by many in the Old World, as a land of opportunity in which anyone has the chance of getting the rewards of increased status as well as increased income from effort. If one generation did not achieve their goals, then their children well might. It was a vision that drew millions of European immigrants to a fluid social order in which their children had a real chance for success, as it still attracts a steady flow of people from Asia and the Caribbean countries.

Yet, as the preceding chapter noted at some length, a fairly substantial range of income inequalities exists in the society, which also exhibits a social-class system not much different in structure from most urbanized industrial countries of the modern world. The rhetoric of equality has continued, unabashed by the reality of social stratification, largely because most Americans, and most new Americans as well, believed that the chance for upward movement was the important element in their fate and the fate of their families. Contemporary demands for social leveling are much more impatient in tone, and this chapter will focus on the possibility of meeting these demands for a quickened pace of social mobility, and particularly on the role of the school as an instrument serving the egalitarian impulse.

SOCIAL CLASS AND SOCIAL STATUS

No one doubts the existence of fairly well-defined social strata in the American society, but one must move carefully among the shoals of terminology to get a clear picture. The Marxists, for whom class and class struggle are central features of social theory, tend to see the social order as consisting rather starkly of two classes in opposition: the working class (and in particular, the blue-collar industrial group) and the upper class, who own the means of production. Some special attention is given in this scheme to such groups as the intellectuals and the nonowner managerial group, but from a revolutionary perspective a simple break into two classes engaged in a struggle for power is sufficient.

American sociology as it developed over the past century, however, has been highly empirical in orientation, and has measured social stratification in observable categories that seem most closely to fit reality, rather than theory. In the period during which these categories were developed attempts were made to identify to which class a given person belonged, with reference to both subjective and objective criteria. In the first case, people were simply asked to indicate their own social-class membership; the overwhelming majority responded, "middle class." This kind of response is a matter of some interest to social scientists, because it contributes to an understanding of how people *perceive* themselves in relation to others, but it is not very accurate; furthermore, differing percentages of respondents answer "middle class" when the alternative category is presented as "working class" or "lower class." Not very many Americans choose to regard themselves in the latter group.

Early investigations by Hollingshead, Warner, and Lunt discovered that people are very sensitive to differences among various groups in their communities, and that the differences accurately relate to objective indicators of status, among them education, occupation, income, and life style.[1] A roughly accurate measure commonly employed in social studies simply uses occupation; more refined measures include education and life style (type of housing, furnishings, reading matter, etc.). Income, for reasons to be discussed later, is a rather chancy criterion. The most commonly employed categories now in use consist of a set of four or five strata, defined as follows:

1. *Upper class.* Many contemporary investigations simply eliminate this category altogether in data gathering, since it contains such a small number of individuals; or they lump different types of upper-class individuals or families together. The public schools, for example, contain so few genuinely upper-class children that the use of the category would be meaningless. All modern societies do contain two types of upper-class individuals: those whose status depends on the traditionally defined prestige of their family over a period of time, and those "new" members whose "upperness" is created by the recent accumulation of wealth or power. The United States has always encouraged the entrepreneurial risk-taker and lavishly rewarded the lucky or able ones, so our national upper class often features a number of *nouveau riche*; one finds in the smaller cities and towns the "old families", recognized by all citizens as "society", though their wealth may in some instances have eroded.

2. *Upper-middle class.* In this category are the professionals (doctors, lawyers, engineers, writers and journalists, politicians, etc.) and the managers. Most of these occupations increasingly demand a college education, and many of them postgraduate degrees. By virtue of their strategic position in mass industrial societies, upper middles often represent a significantly powerful force; they write the news and the journals of opinion, write and direct the movies and television drama, approve new legislation, and judge

that legislation in the courts. In a period in which ownership of business has become increasingly impersonal, salaried managers make key industrial and financial decisions.

3. *Lower-middle class.* Some of the literature of social science refers to the upper middles as "major white collar," and to the lower middles as "minor white collar." Occupations in this group require some verbal or number skills, job descriptions often assume at least a high school diploma, and the category includes a wide range of occupations from typist, bank clerk and insurance salesman, to retail store personnel and school paraprofessionals.

4. *Upper-lower class.* The significant split between the middle class generally and the lower class is, in occupational terms, roughly between working with paper and working with machinery or muscle; hence the common term "blue collar" for the latter. The upper level of the lower class consists of skilled or semiskilled workers who make up what is sometimes referred to as the stable working class. Although their jobs depend on business cycle swings to a much greater degree than do those of the middle class, union organization over the past generation has introduced greater security than before at this level, machinery has in many cases reduced the physical exertion of many of the jobs, and the more powerful unions have gained appreciable influence on working conditions. Educational level used to have little relevance for blue-collar jobs, but with the general increase in years of schooling, many of them now require a high school diploma.

5. *Lower-lower class.* Terminology becomes particularly confusing here. The objective indicators are fairly clear: low, if any, occupational skills, instability of work life, with sporadic jobs interspersed with long periods of unemployment or, like the migrant farm workers, a work life dependent on seasonal events. Some writers refer to this group as "the underclass," suggesting that they are in some fashion outside the class structure itself. (As, indeed, are those who are part of the world of celebrities containing top athletes, movie and television stars, and nationally known "personalities.") The class contains a disproportionate number of "beginners," immigrants from other countries, migrants from rural areas to the city, as well as those permanently settled in bleak rural areas with few economic resources. Because of the large migrational component, this group also contains a disproportionate number of ethnic group members, and the lengthy history of discrimination against American blacks has resulted in their greater representation in the class than one would expect from their proportion in the population.

Although these social strata differ from one another on a variety of dimensions, their primary social significance lies in the fact that the various positions along the scale represent different degrees of prestige. These differences have been validated by asking representative samples of people in a number of societies to rank order lists of occupations, from those with the greatest prestige to those with the least; Duncan lists some 20,000 occupations, each with a rank order index based on such surveys.[2] As David Featherman and Robert Hauser point out:[3]

1. The rank order of occupations provided by different individuals has no connection with their own social standing, sex, age, religion, or education.
2. Different instructions emphasizing either the social standing of the occupation, its honor, or the intelligence required for it, produce the same rank order.
3. Since 1925, when such surveys began, the rank order has been static. Scores in two different surveys separated by forty years correlated + .93 with one another.
4. The prestige rank order is stable over space as well as time; the same occupations occupy the same rank in both western and nonwestern societies.
5. Eighty-three percent of the variations in prestige are accounted for by the education and income characteristics of the detailed occupational titles, although the schooling and income of the actual incumbents of the various occupations correlate only moderately to modestly: .6 with schooling, and .4 with income.

Are Social Classes Necessary?

Despite this evidence of the ubiquity and stability of social stratification, a lively debate among sociologists has developed about whether it is not possible to realize the ideals of egalitarianism by eliminating variations in social prestige. The pure communism of early Marxism envisaged such a classless society, although Maoist China appears to be the only contemporary Marxist society making a good try at attaining it, and with a good deal of accompanying social turmoil.

A classic debate on the issue began with an article by Kingsley Davis and Wilbur Moore outlining a theory of social stratification.[4] Differences in prestige, they argued, are a functional necessity because every society must distribute its members into social positions, and induce them to perform the duties of those positions. If all duties were equally pleasant and important, and required the same talents, there would be no difficulty. But, in fact, they do differ in these regards, and consequently societies must have available a system of rewards and a way of distributing them unequally in order to motivate some individuals to take on specific positions.

The rewards are built into the position, and consist of those things that add to sustenance and comfort, those that contribute to diversion or humor, and those psychological rewards that lead to self-respect and ego-enhancement. If, in order to fill some positions, these rewards must be unequal, then society must by definition be stratified, since differences in the allocation of these rewards are what stratification is.

The rank order of positions is determined by their importance to the society or by their demand for a particular talent or training. In the first case, positions that are important need not be rewarded proportionately; the reward need only be large enough to make sure they are filled. In the second instance, although all positions require some skill or capacity, some may require such a high degree of talent that persons able to fill them are comparatively rare. In other cases, the talent may be readily available, but the training process is long, costly, and elaborate, and requires sacrifice on the part of those undergoing it.

In a critical attack on this theory, Melvin Tumin raised a number of questions.[5] First, the assertion that certain positions are functionally more important than others must be based on some idea of a difference in indispensability. But, he argued, although engineers may be more indispensable than factory workers, at some point we must face the problem of motivating factory workers as well as engineers or the factory cannot work. Indispensability also involves bargaining power, and such power is shaped by the existing system of occupational prestige rating itself.

Second, the theory assumes that only a limited number of individuals have the talent to be trained into important positions, but in fact we do not know much about the real range of talents available in a society, and the more stratified a society is the less chance we have of discovering talent. If existing differences are allowed to be inherited, then the stratification system works against the discovery of talent in the next generation. Furthermore, elites, when they can, try to restrict access to their privileged positions, as in the case of medicine.

Third, a lengthy period of training is a sacrifice either because of its cost, or because of earnings the student foregoes in order to go to school. However, families generally bear the costs of training out of earnings due to their own privileged positions. And, although earnings are sacrificed, the real value of those foregone wages are earned back in about the first ten years of the individual's work life, leaving him or her with an additional twenty years of higher than the average earnings of those in lesser positions. Nor does the person lack other rewards during the training period, such as prestige, self-development, a delay in assuming adult responsibilities, and access to freedom and leisure.

Tumin further argues that there are ways of motivating people other than by differential reward; there is joy in work, the recognition of social duty, and so on. He concludes that if an unequal distribution of power and property is necessary to perform certain roles, they should be regarded as resources rather than rewards. But no differentiation in prestige and esteem need follow; everyone, regardless of position, should be equally esteemed.

The interested reader may wish to pursue the argument as it developed in further articles; it is not appropriate here to go into the sometimes technical complications that were involved.[6] One of Davis' most important points in response, however, should be noted: that is, that Davis and

Moore had proposed their theory in order to explain why stratification is, indeed, universal, while Tumin is interested in getting rid of it and offers no explanation of its universality.

THE SOCIAL-CLASS VALUE SYSTEM

To categorize individuals and families into social-class strata does more than indicate the differences in their social prestige; because of the way social groups function, it also says something about the way in which they view life and the values they attach to different aspects of life experience. Social psychologists investigate the operation of these phenomena using two key concepts—*solidarity* and *status*.[7] The first of these represents the conditions and feelings that draw people together and lead to feelings of similarity and fellow membership in the same group; the second expresses the opposite situation, namely those conditions that lead to feelings of difference, which are often expressed in social life with overtones of higher versus lower, or superior versus inferior.

These aspects of group life are so fundamental that, whether or not the precise terms are familiar, most people would find the concepts themselves transparent and perhaps obvious. But some obvious notions turn out to be inaccurate, and others, like these, are more complicated than they appear. One of the most universal characteristics that creates powerful feelings of both similarity and difference, for instance, is sex; one has only to note how magically parties often split into subgroups of men and women to appreciate the pervasiveness of sexual identification. Yet, some people are nowadays brought together in intense feelings of solidarity because they share the idea that man and women should *not* behave differently, or be treated as different.

Sex is one important determinant of solidarity and status, but there are many others.

1. *Space.* People who live in the same neighborhood, or who spend their workdays in close proximity, tend to develop feelings of solidarity; people with common life styles tend also to select the same kind of community. Conversely, in American communities those of higher status are often found living on higher ground (Nob Hill in San Francisco, Murray Hill in New York), and the lower class is often "across the tracks."

2. *Language.* Common use of a particular slang is often a signal of belonging to some hip crowd. Those who use the pure or standard form of a language demonstrate to one another that they share a common upbringing and education; others may view this type of speech as fancy and sometimes faintly funny.

3. *Age.* An almost universal norm dictates that an older person may address a younger one familiarly, using the first name, but the younger one uses formal address (Mr. Jones) unless some other ground for solidarity

exists. On the other hand, the awkwardness felt by groups of mixed younger and older people is a common source of hilarity in television series and movies.

4. *Appearance and demeanor.* Prior to the recent relaxation of dress codes, young businessmen solidarily wore neat suits, white shirts, and carefully knotted ties (most of them still do). The scruffy blue jeans and straggly hair of the college student is just as much a uniform, and just as solidarity-producing. The musical *Hair!* profitably celebrated the solidarity of youth in revolt from convention, and their superiority over the well-trimmed squares at the same time.

5. *Common fate.* Roger Brown uses the fascinating example of the Swiss mountain guides, who address the members of climbing groups, their employers, with the formal *Sie,* until the climb reaches dangerous heights, at which time they switch to the familiar *Du.* Coal miners and other special occupational groups feel the same solidarity. One study of the effect on prejudice of personal contact found that white and black miners worked together with great friendliness, but had no social contact with one another once they left the mine.

Most of these influences combine to assure that different social-class groups, facing different fates, undergoing somewhat different educational experiences, raised in different environments, will choose to emphasize different values and life styles. In modern western industrial countries available evidence suggests the following class value emphases:[8]

1. *Lower-lowers.* The key word for the life style of this social level is instability, in both work and family life. Dominant in the male culture is a search for excitement and a rejection of routine and order. An orientation toward the present rather than the future is often referred to in the literature as a disinclination to delay gratification; it is accompanied by a belief that life is ruled by luck or chance rather than influenced by men's actions. The male culture, then, is indifferent or hostile to education, a process that requires routine and future-orientation. Women in this stratum, however, are much more likely to share the values of the stratum above them, the working class.

It is absolutely crucial to an understanding of the controversy that currently surrounds this social-class level, of which there will be more later, to recognize that poverty, in itself, does not constitute its distinguishing feature. Some sociologists rather clinically designate this group as "the disreputable poor," to make that distinction, meaning that these poor are looked at disparagingly by other groups in the society.

2. *Upper-lowers.* The values of this stable, blue-collar working class emphasize the solidarity of the groups with which its members are in intimate contact—family, church, and work group. As Herbert Gans and others have pointed out, the focus for life at this level is the "adult peer group," members of the extended family as well as the immediate family, close neighbors, and workmates (often overlapping in membership). In

contrast with the wider community and national perspective of the middle class, the working class tends to view the world through the interests of groups in which they have personal relationships and to which they owe loyalty.

Education is valued, but often in very specific, short-term, contexts; for example, to get the skills necessary for a better-paying job. Working class families with ambitions for their children are likely to emphasize mobility chances for their sons rather than their daughters.

3. *Lower-Middles.* Appropriately enough, the values of this class, which is closest to the middle of the distribution of strata, put most visible emphasis on what one might call the traditional mainstream beliefs of the society. This class is oriented to the future, particularly to the future of the children; it believes in the efficacy of education and in the rewards that educational effort will bring; it is strongly aware of status differences and seeks to better its position in the long term. Lower-middle class families are often intensely child-oriented (in contrast to the exclusion of children from the working-class adult peer group), and sacrifice of present gratification in order to give children a better chance is common (though the sacrificial act may well be used as a weapon to insure the children's effort).

4. *Upper-middles.* The value themes of the *professional* upper-middles represent the most distinctive values in this stratum; the technical and managerial groups at this level may perhaps represent a mixture of the lower- and upper-middle preferences. The major theme is individual development. Education and work, instead of being viewed as merely instrumental to other things in life such as social advancement and economic reward, are seen as goods in themselves. Education must be intrinsically interesting, and must contribute to the enhancement of the "self." Work that is interesting, or noble, or socially useful may be preferred even if it is less materially rewarding. The contemporary shape of the feminist movement was foreshadowed decades before by the growing sense of upper-middle women that their own development as individuals was being sacrificed in response to social role demands that women in other classes simply took for granted.

A second major difference in emphasis is the upper-middle belief in the importance of social abstractions, such as "the public good," "equality," and, indeed, "the self." Although this shift from the almost purely personal and group loyalties of the working class can be seen in the broader community awareness of the lower-middles, the tendency to objectify abstractions reaches full flower here. Radio and television drama, written by upper-middle professionals, has widely disseminated this attitude toward life, but one is unlikely to find outside of this class, for example, a wife saying to her husband, "John, what's happened to our relationship?" as if, in addition to the two real persons present, there is a third abstract entity that must be seriously dealt with.

Upper-middles concentrate intensely on their children, but Gans has perceptively noted the difference between lower- and upper-middle parents in this regard. The former push children *to do* what is necessary, to exert effort, to do the best they can, and to obey the rules that will get them ahead; the latter, however, have a clear image of the kind of *person* they want to develop—curious, individualistic, thinking for himself, socially aware.

Some Caveats

Differences among class value systems as described above are subject to a number of qualifications. The reality is far from being as sharp as these simplified categories; it is not as if one could put an individual into a neatly circumscribed box, with reference to occupation and education, and then expect to be able to predict his values. As Brown has probably more correctly argued, social values shift by small increments along a continuum without any noticeable major breaking points on the way. So, values of individuals in classes close to one another show considerable similarities, particularly if the individuals are near the margins; working-class adolescent "street corner" groups resemble in many ways adolescent gangs in lower-lower neighborhoods. Some social scientists also see an on-going convergence of the values of some social classes; Robert Havighurst and others call the upper-lowers and the lower-middles the Common Man class because of their closeness to each other on the class scale as well as their sharing of many values.

There exist, furthermore, within each class relatively well-defined subcultures that develop specific value variations. We have already noted the male subculture in the lower-lower stratum that differs substantially from the female. Criminologists talk about a "delinquent subculture;" in large cities there are subcultures consisting of "singles" and of "bohemians," as well as a variety of ethnic subcultures; during the 1960s a fairly well-defined "youth subculture" emerged, which some observers explained partly by pointing to the market possibilities opened up by the presence of a larger-than-usual number of young people. So, some degree of caution must be observed in discussing class value differences, although their existence is indisputable and their explanatory power often considerable.

TWO ENDS OF THE SCALE: THE "CULTURE OF POVERTY" AND THE "COUNTERCULTURE"

Two subcultures in the recent past have aroused a very considerable amount of controversy and social conflict: The lower-lower male subculture and a sizeable group of highly educated upper-middle, at the opposite ends of the social scale, allied in one way or another with a set of values that has been called countercultural. Because they represent in different ways a rejection of or an attack on the range of traditional values recognized by most of the rest of the society, the controversies over these subcultures emerge in many of the policy issues dealt with in later chapters, and are crucial to those discussed here.

One must first ask, what are they rejecting? One of the most insightful available answers to that question was suggested some time ago by Max Weber in his study of the Protestant Ethic and the rise of capitalism.[9] Struck by the coincident appearance on the historical scene of the Reformation and the development of capitalism as the predominant economic organizational form in the West, Weber sought to explain the second of these phenomena as a consequence of the first. A vastly simplified version of the argument runs this way:

The religious protest of those who broke away from Catholicism focused on a number of disputed doctrines. One was the role of the priesthood; the Church viewed the priest as the mediator between the individual and God, with no direct communication necessary. A second had to do with the nature of grace and salvation; the good Catholic could expect salvation as a matter or right. The doctrines of early Protestanism were far from comforting. The individual had to develop his own relationship with God. The role of the priest was minimized; in some sects it almost disappeared. This put the burden on the faithful to know the scriptures directly and led to the first translation of the Bible into common languages where before only the priest was required to know the Latin in which the scriptures were available. (It also resulted in a distinct emphasis on literacy and on schooling generally among the early American colonists.)

As for salvation, good works and a state of grace were no longer guarantees. One was either elected for salvation or condemned to damnation, one had to live with the uncertainty of his fate. An austere life style, however, would certainly put one on the safe side. And success in earthly endeavors might well constitute a sign that one was a member of the elect, and destined for salvation.

In sum, Protestantism forced the development of new emphases in human character. Instead of dependence on the priest, a self-reliant individualism was stressed. In place of a yearning for security and certainty, an ability to endure a very substantial degree of uncertainty, and to wait a long time for future rewards, was encouraged. Sensual gratification, as represented by the drama of the mass and the incense and music of the traditional church, was rejected, material success encouraged.

Such a character, Weber argues, was extraordinarily well-suited to the needs of mercantile capitalism, which required a disposition toward saving in order to accumulate capital in the first instance, and the strength necessary to deny oneself impulse spending, an individualistic faith in one's own interests and ability to influence events and achieve success, and a preference for risk required for investing in chancy enterprises. So, he concludes, the new religious doctrines shaped the values that made the spread of capitalism feasible. Later historians argued that the process went the other way about, that the development of capitalism was hindered by the ideas of the Church and led, therefore, to the religious schism.

The theoretical disagreement matters little. The Protestant Ethic, as Weber called it, provided the driving force for economic development and as it slowly lost its direct connection with religion remained as a basic set of beliefs in this culture's middle class. Because American schools began under the domination of the Protestant Church, at least in the northern colonies, and were later heavily influenced by the expanding business class, the *effort/reward* principle continued as the prevailing set of ideas in mainstream culture. There is some debate today over the question of whether there is much left of the ethic: There is little doubt that with the rise of a consumption-oriented society the austerity and self-denial values have almost vanished, and in doing so has posed some real difficulties in ensuring the society the capital investment necessary for its economic health. But work is still a strong theme in the culture, and success still a driving force of considerable magnitude.

THE ATTACK ON MIDDLE-CLASS VALUES

A rejection, in whole or in part, of these values has come from both the top and bottom of the social-class scale. By the sixties, a substantial number of upper-middle intellectuals in academia and in the arts had adopted a number of "countercultural" values that represent almost a mirror-image of the traditional middle-class American value system. They emphasize equality rather than a struggle to attain status; they are antimaterialist and antitechnological; they champion the causes of groups whom they see as oppressed by the dominant culture; and at times they reject the country itself, much as the nineteenth century American literary expatriates had done.

At the other end of the scale the contemporary controversy focuses on the question of whether the lower-lower value system, which rejects mainstream beliefs such as effort and reward, acceptance of routine, centrality of family life, and the value of future-orientation, is embedded in a *culture* or is a response to the immediate economic and social opportunity structure confronting the class. The question bears seriously on fundamental social policy; in the first case, such options as minimum income floors might be expected to have little effect on ultimately helping lower-lower families out of poverty; in the second case, the policy might well be effective.

The "Culture of Poverty" Thesis
On the basis of several intensive anthropological investigations of poor families in Mexico, and of similar Puerto Rican families in both San Juan and New York, Oscar Lewis developed the view that the subculture of the poor that he studied constituted a special culture.[10] The characteristics of

that culture, he suggested, moving from the broad social level to the personal, are:

1.   Separation from both the institutions and values of the larger society. There is no stable or consistent interaction with workplace, financial or commercial institutions, the school, or the political organizations. Culture members are aware of the mainstream values, and may even agree with them on paper, but do not act them out in daily life. Lewis stressed the fact that the collection of value data that relies on verbal agreement to the statement of particular preferences does not accurately reflect the real values of the culture; one must live with and observe those who live in the poverty culture for some time to obtain the real picture.

2.   A distinct absence of organization or patterned interaction at the community level. Voluntary associations, one of the most prominent features of middle-class life, are missing, as are the communal bonds of church, union, and neighborhood that provide cohesiveness in working-class communities. Attempts to stimulate organization in lower-lower communities, as in the efforts during the sixties of the Office of Economic Opportunity, have largely failed.

3.   Typically unstable families, with a high proportion of female-headed units. Child-bearing practices encourage neither the group loyalty emphasized in working-class families nor the long period of dependency aimed at future payoffs of the middle class. Lewis stresses the importance in the poverty culture family of early responsibility for children, which encourages earlier sexual experience and marriage, leading inevitably to a greater probability of family instability.

4.   Feelings of marginality, helplessness, dependency and despair. Lewis points out that these psychological states are more or less appropriate to the reality they face.

He argues, nevertheless, that despite the appropriateness of the response on the psychological level, the life style is not a reaction to the immediate social situation but a coherent set of norms that prescribe what is important or desirable, that are part of a self-maintaining system passed on from one generation to another. Many other groups of people in a variety of societies across time have undergone prolonged poverty (e.g., in India), sharp separation from the main society (e.g., Eastern European Jews), or unstable economic life (a number of primitive cultures), and yet have developed strong family structures and maintained a stable community life.

To define these values as embedded in a culture creates an inevitably pessimistic prognosis. If a way could be found to increase family income, for instance, higher educational achievement for the children would not necessarily follow; if the children belong to a peer group that rewards manliness, immediate gratification, and scorns scholastic achievement, peer-group pressure will simply cancel out the potential for change in improved income.[11] Lewis also believes that the origin of the culture of poverty lies in the existence of a market economy with success values that blame failure on personal inadequacy. The Cubans, he argues, have done away with their poverty culture by organizing and integrating the poor into the revolutionary society; Castro eliminated juvenile delinquency by giving the delinquents guns (to defend the island). Since social revolution is regarded by most people in the United States as a rather remote possibility, the pessimism inherent in the theory is even deeper than at first appearance.

The "Blocked-Opportunity" Thesis

This theory of lower-lower values views them as an adaptation to a particular environment and to the circumstances faced by the group. Why do its members reject the value of delaying immediate gratification? Because the future is too precarious. Why do they engage in muggings and running numbers? Because socially acceptable jobs are not available to them. One does not need to invoke deviant value systems, it is argued, if one views the behavior as a rational response to blocked opportunity.[12]

Theoretically, the more a group identifies with mainstream values, the more likely its members are to adopt illicit means. The lethargy and disinterest in work among lower-lower men can be seen as a result of their acceptance of dominant attitudes toward occupations. The only available jobs are dirty, hard, and uninteresting; their attitude toward them may simply reflect the same attitude toward those kinds of jobs that one finds among the middle class.

The argument about whether such an entity as a "culture of poverty" even exists, and, if it does, what its causes and cure are, has grown in recent years. Almost everyone agrees that what we are talking about is a relatively small proportion of families; the best guess is about 20 percent of the lower class, or 7 to 8 percent of the population as a whole. The majority of those among the "very poor" manage to maintain a good measure of family stability and some contact with the institutional life of the society, even though they often require assistance from an outside source. But here the consensus ends.

A second widely argued issue is why members of what Lewis calls the culture of poverty agree *verbally* with the values of the middle class even though, as Lewis noted, their behavior does not conform to the values. In fact, although some attitude studies have demonstrated verbal acceptance by lower-class respondents of some middle-class values, success orientation, one of the dominant middle-class values, has been shown to vary systematically by social-class position.[13] There is, however, some evidence of a "lower-class value-stretch," a larger range of values among lower-class members that expands to include some of the values of the middle class.

SOCIAL MOBILITY

Assuming the existence of some form of social stratification, the key question to be adressed, if one is interested in equality, is: How much chance is there of moving from one stratum to another? The American ideal has occasionally in the past fostered the belief that opportunity to move up was unlimited; recent social critics claim that such opportunity is almost a myth. However, neither of these extreme views is accurate.

Since very little is known about the social mobility of women, most conclusions noted here describe mobility rates for sons, and compare fathers' occupations with sons' occupations as a measure of movement. In the United States, in any generation about 33 percent of blue-collar workers' sons move into the white-collar class.[14] Figure 3.1, showing the changes in the preceding generation, indicates that there has been little significant change in the immediate past, and Stephen Thernstrom, the historian, has concluded that we have had about the same high rate of mobility for the past eighty years.[15] Also relatively unchanged have been the rates of downward mobility (the proportion of middle-class sons who skid down the occupational scale), which has fluctuated around 25 percent.

Mobility rates, like the occupational prestige structure, are remarkably similar across societies, at least if one restricts the view to industrial societies. In western countries the rate ranges from 17 percent for Finland to 33 percent in Britain;[16] Blau and Duncan have concluded that there is little difference among industrialized countries in blue-collar mobility into the middle class, and empirical surveys in Communist countries show similar rates as well.[17] Lipset notes the conclusions of a Czechoslovakian study in the late sixties, in which the Czech sociologist compares his findings with those in the U.S., that "the openness of both systems . . . is surprisingly great."[18] The Czech scholar uses his data to refute the thesis of some western sociologists that a "mobility blockade" exists in socialist countries. In other words, says Lipset, "Safer argues it is not true that socialism means a lower rate of social mobility, that in fact its rate is as high as that under capitalism!"[19] Such comparability supports the view of many students that mobility rates are primarily linked to economic development rather than to political or economic systems as such.

It is simple to infer that some upward mobility occurs as a result of the downward mobility noted earlier; middle-class positions are vacant, thus drawing members of the lower class up to fill them. Over the long run, other forces also operate to make mobility possible:

1. As countries industrialize the demands of technology and culture create a variety of technical and professional positions some of which either did not exist before or represent expansions of work forces that were relatively small in the past. For example, an entire field of computer technology grew from nothing in the past generation; during the same period the demand for better health care enormously accelerated the growth of professional and semiprofessional positions in that field.

2. Nineteenth century political theorists predicated that, along with industrialization, bureaucracy would bring about a rigidification of class boundaries. It has, in fact, promoted mobility in a number of ways. The

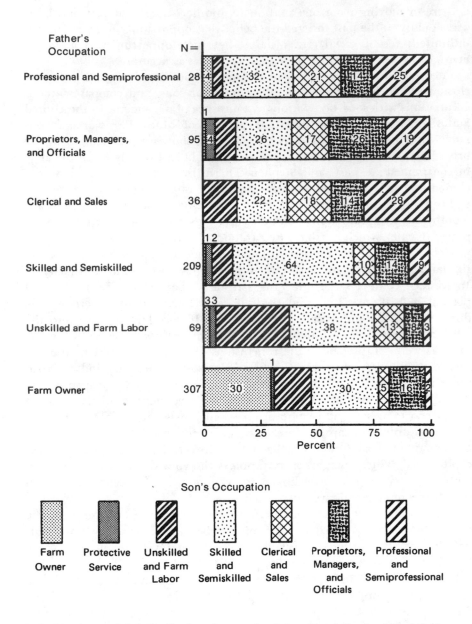

FIG. 3.1   Occupational distribution of a sample of American males by their father's occupation. Protective Service omitted from "father's occupation" because of too few cases.

Source: Seymour Martin Lipset and Reinhard Bendix, *Social Mobility in Industrial Society* (Berkeley: University of California Press, 1959), p. 89.

decline of the family business in favor of public corporations reduced the number of higher positions that passed from one generation to another within a family; the bureaucratic propensity toward recruiting from the ranks of college graduates, ranks that increasingly include members of the working class, opened new avenues of mobility; so did the bureaucratic habit of allocating higher posts through a competitive promotion process.

3.   Industrialized countries tend to exhibit a fertility differential between social classes, with lower birth rates characteristic of middle classes. There may thus be created a shortage of middle-class youth to fill available middle-class positions, offering further opportunity to working -class youth from larger families to move up.

PANEL 3.1   Four Models of Mobility

The recent and more radical version of the traditional concept of equality of opportunity demands not merely that lower-class youth have a realistic opportunity of achieving occupational success, but that the results be equal. In this view we may consider ourselves equal only if college populations and all privileged positions should be filled, in proportion to their numbers, by members from each social-class level.

Richard Merelman has analyzed this problem at considerable length and complexity, and the following consideration of alternative mobility models follows his line of reasoning.[20] He begins with the concept of "perfect mobility," in which, at any given time, each social-class group contains the same proportion of people from all social groups in proportion to the population. Thus, in a system in which the upper-middle elite is 10 percent, the lower middle 40 percent, the working class 40 percent and the lower-lower class 10 percent, only 10 percent of the elite should have originated in the elite, 40 percent should have come from the lower-middle class, and so on.

Examining the mobility data from nine western countries, Merelman concludes that even when one restricts the focus to movement between contiguous class (lower middle to upper middle or to working class, working class to lower middle or to lower lower), all countries represented do poorly in meeting the equal-mobility standard of the ideal:

"In not one case is the opportunity of manual children to move into the middle class as great as the opportunity of middle-class children to become part of the elite."[21]

In a majority of the studies, "manual workers are less well insured against falling into the lower class than are middle-class people against demotion into the manual sector."[22]

"The overall balance of class opportunities tilts markedly in favor of the middle class in each of the nine countries we have examined. Most middle-class children bask in a quite favorable mobility climate."[23]

Yet, he notes, despite much class inequality, moderate, stable mobility rates in all of these countries *do* redistribute people in the society. In industrial societies the rate of downward mobility for middle-class sons is twice the rate of their upward mobility; on the other hand, sons of manual workers are twice as likely to move upward as downward. (Figure 3.1 does not conform to these estimates because of somewhat different class categories.)

The apparent contradiction is easily resolved. These overall mobility rates do not take into account the size of the classes of origin and destination. Because there are large middle classes in industrial countries "the flow of manuals to the middle class must also be sizeable in order for the manual disadvantage to disappear. By contrast, the elite class is fairly small; therefore it need receive but a trickle of middle-class people before it yields a positive mobility ratio to the middle class."[24] The same logic applies to movements downward.

Merelman compares this model of "redistributive mobility" that predominates in all western industrial societies, with a number of other forms of mobility; the diagram in Figure 3.2 may help in understanding the comparisons.

1. *Upgrading* occurs when there is a sizeable expansion in prestigious white-collar positions and a contraction in lower-class unskilled jobs; as a result, a predominantly upward movement occurs at all levels. All mobile middle-class members move up, and almost all mobile sons of the working class do so as well. Working-class sons are at an advantage, because they do not experience the downward mobility of the redistributive model. But it does even better for middle-class sons, directing all their mobility into the elite, and relieving them of the considerable downward movement in the redistributive

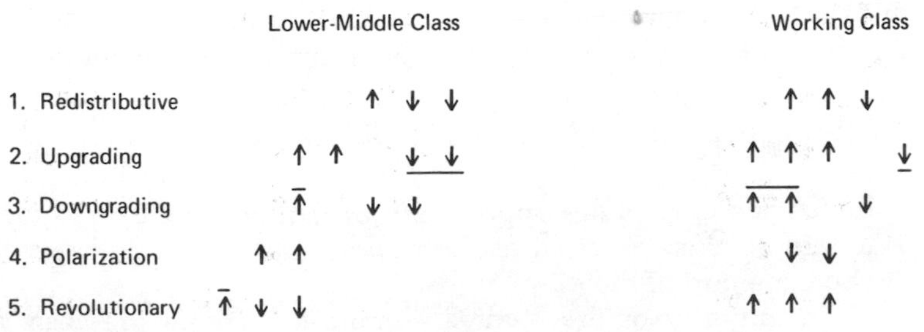

	Lower-Middle Class		Working Class	
1. Redistributive	↑ ↓ ↓		↑ ↑ ↓	
2. Upgrading	↑ ↑ ↓ ↓		↑ ↑ ↑	↓
3. Downgrading	↑ ↓ ↓		↑ ↑ ↓	
4. Polarization	↑ ↑		↓ ↓	
5. Revolutionary	↑ ↓ ↓		↑ ↑ ↑	

FIG. 3.2   Comparison of five models of social mobility

model. The actual amount of inequality between classes is not much affected.

Its impact on the society itself is mixed. In the present redistributive system, some incompetent middle-class sons are demoted, and some able working-class sons promoted. Upgrading assures working-class talent of opportunity, but it tends to promote middle-class incompetents into demanding elite positions which they do not have the talent to fill. On balance, argues Merelman, "redistribution sorts the intellectual wheat from the chaff more effectively than does upgrading."[25]

2. *Downgrading* presents the opposite situation, one in which there is a shortage of white-collar jobs and an expansion of lower-class positions. Upward mobility declines drastically, downward mobility rates increase. In such conditions, middle-class sons can no longer be protected from the full effects of downward mobility, and their mobility approaches the "perfect" ratio. But, downgrading also puts an end to upward mobility of manual sons depressing their upward movement more drastically than does the redistributive model. As in upgrading, the terms of the inequality are changed little.

For the society as a whole, downgrading has little to recommend it. Some deserving working-class sons are demoted, others are denied upward movement, which is likely to produce a wave of bitterness among the working class. The middle class is bound to feel precarious, and may "turn their incipient status panic into political reaction." The class conflict that the redistributive model prevents by providing opportunities for both classes is made highly probable by the downgrading model.

3. *Polarization* reverses the pattern of a redistributive mobility, by turning middle-class mobility primarily upward, and working-class mobility predominantly downward. It provides an even greater advantage for the middle-class son than does redistribution, and worsens the situation of the manual son. The increasing gap between the classes "increases the likelihood of class warfare, as formerly middle-class people attempt to protect their newfound elite status and newly impoverished people of manual origin recoil from their sudden degradation."[26] Furthermore, it protects incompetent middle-class members and wastes almost all working-class talent, in contrast to the fairly successful job of matching talent to reward by the redistribution model.

4. *Revolutionary mobility* demotes middle-class sons in proportion to their numbers, and fills their places with a massive upward movement of manual sons, and in the process brings the mobility ratios of the two classes close to the egalitarian "perfect mobility" rate. It also demotes all incompetent middle-class sons, and utilizes all of the talents of the manual class. So, in regard to both equality and

talent allocation, it would seem preferable to the redistribution model, were it not, says Merelman, for its effect on class conflict. Revolutionary mobility creates a belief that mobility is the accidental result of membership in a particular group, rather than a consequence of individual competition. The middle class, seeing that they are likely to fail no matter what their individual merits, will acquire a sense of collective deprivation; the manual class will create rationalizations for their inevitable rise. Organizing against one another represents a probable next step.

Redistribution, concludes Merelman, is an

"uneasy compromise between the incompatible demands enunciated by differently placed social groups, some of whom wish to equalize opportunities, and still others of whom are preoccupied with deterring class conflict. Redistribution is the only form of mobility that goes some distance toward meeting all three of these demands, although it accomplishes none completely. Indeed, the price of attempting to meet each demand is the failure to satisfy any one fully. As with so many other common practices in modern societies, redistributive mobility juggles competing and strongly held ideologies: meritocracy, the desire to utilize talent effectively; egalitarianism, the humanitarian impulse toward equal opportunity; and conservatism, the fear that class conflict will rip the social fabric asunder."[27]

THE DISADVANTAGE OF BEING BLACK

The moderate redistribution process described above appears to work acceptably for the labor force as a whole; not only is there a reasonable amount of circulation through the occupational structure, there is also evidence of a net shift over the past generation toward employment as professionals and managers, skilled blue-collar jobs, and away from self-employed management positions and farm and nonfarm labor. These movements are accounted for largely by changes in occupational status that occur between the first job that individuals get and the occupation they have at the time of the survey.[28]

As with income, however, a major lag occurs in the occupational mobility of black men. Little was known until recently about their mobility at any period, and analyses of black subsamples that are part of general random samples of the population are of uncertain reliability because of their small size. On the basis of a 1962 subsample analysis, nevertheless, Duncan concluded that:

Negro men who originated at the lower levels were likely to remain there; white men were likely to move up. Negro men who originated at the higher levels were likely to move down; white men were likely to stay there. Although Negro social origins are not as favorable as whites, this is the lesser part of the explanation of racial differences in occupational achievement. The greater part of the explanation lies in inequalities within the process of mobility itself.[29]

As a result of the programs of the sixties aimed at improving opportunities for blacks there is some evidence of a better occupational picture by the end of that decade. Reynolds Farley and Albert Hermalin found a gradual upgrading of the occupational distribution for both blacks and whites during that decade, and a large gain for blacks during the second half of the period. Such shifts are best expressed in an *index of dissimilarity,* the percentage of black men who would have had to change major occupational categories in order to produce equality between blacks and whites. That index declined from 38 percent in 1960 to 36 percent in 1966 and to 31 percent in 1970.[30]

Hauser and Featherman tested the possibility of convergence between the occupational mobility patterns of the two groups, based on the data of the sixties. They conclude that there has been some convergence from 1962 to 1970, to a rather modest degree, but "that in spite of some gains the mobility chances of blacks in 1970 are less favorable than those of white men of the same age in 1962."[31] The results of the analysis appear to bear out their remark earlier in the report that "the large remaining occupational differences between the races give little ground for complacency among those who would seek equality of achievement between the races."[32]

Such data seem to offer powerful support for one of the major positions taken during the current debate about mobility in America, the argument that as a group blacks represent a very special case, one that differs in fundamental respects from other ethnic groups in the country's past. The argument is made for American-born blacks alone, but sometimes it includes nonwhites from previously colonial countries. The issue is an important one because it represents, for some of those who believe in the "special case" argument, a basis for rejecting the possibility of assimilation into the mainstream society.

It is certainly true that during the mass migrations before and after the turn of the century a steady improvement in mobility chances for the incoming groups was visible; the census of 1890, the first time that information on the occupations of native-born children of immigrants was gathered, showed considerable difference between the two generations. The second generation more closely resembled the occupational distribution of the entire labor force than did their fathers.[33]

As a later chapter will show, however, the ability of different white groups to successfully utilize the educational opportunities offered by host cities such as New York varied widely. Chapter 1 discussed a number of features of the black income lag that are not necessarily permanent but which explain the slowness of gains; many of them relate as well to the mobility gap. Hauser and Featherman, moreover, do not differentiate between the difficulty of moving up into an adjacent class and making the two-class move into the elite upper-middle class, a much more difficult shift. They appear to be calling for what Merelman called "revolutionary mobility," which is most unlikely to result from the redistributive system that is the basis of American mobility.

A good illustration of the terms of the current debate on this issue may be found in a piece by Robert Blauner and a reply to it by Nathan Glazer. Blauner's thesis is essentially that the American black ghettos, unlike the urban ghettos of ethnic immigrant groups, must be regarded as internal colonies rather than as temporary way-stations on the road to ultimate assimilation. His reasoning, and Glazer's rebuttal, is outlined below:[34]

1.   Although whites too have lived in ghettos, says Blauner, they migrated into them voluntarily, and often chose to stay for some time because of the pull of a common culture. But the black migration into the cities, Glazer points out, was not that much different.[35] Almost 20 percent of the nonwhites in New York City are recent migrants from the West Indies; the urban migration from the South had much the same quality of the European migration earlier, a voluntary move in search of job opportunity. And, although one cannot deny the existence of economic and discriminatory limitations to blacks moving out of the ghetto, the pull of common culture just as undeniably exists.

2.   Immigrant ghettos were a one- or two-generation phenomenon, Blauner argues, temporary accommodations on the way out and up; black ghettos have a permanence reminiscent of settled populations ruled by a colonial power. Glazer notes that, though the Jewish and Italian ghettos of two or three generations ago have decreased in size, they are still to some extent in existence, and the New York Harlem population is already declining. He suggests that the significant question is which timeline is used to measure change. From a national point of view the black population is much older than other groups, but from the perspective of the urban north and west, they are newcomers. In 1900 blacks represented only 2 percent of the population of New York City, as against a German and Irish 20 percent; by 1920 Russians constituted 18 percent of the city, Italians 14 percent, but blacks only 3 percent. Only by 1940 did the blacks begin to equal the proportion of Italians in the city. As an *urban* group, then, black Americans have been on the northern and western scene for barely a generation.

3.   Blauner argues that a third indication of colonial status lies in differences in power; for only a brief period, less than a generation, did outsiders control the buildings and businesses in white ethnic ghettos. The economic life of the black ghettos, in contrast, remains under outside control. Again, replies Glazer, the period of time is important; Blauner is right if the comparison is made with the entire span of time spent by blacks

on the continent. In terms of time in the northern cities, the argument does not hold up. White ethnics, furthermore, varied widely in their success on a number of important scales of economics and power. The Irish also had little success in establishing small businesses, and part of the difficulties facing black small businessmen lies in the lack of patronage by blacks themselves. Except for the phenomenal success of the Irish, in politics blacks seem to follow much the same pattern as earlier white ethnic groups on the political scene, and if one considers blacks as one group among a number of varied others, blacks probably have more college graduates than Poles, more political influence than Mexican-Americans, and more clout with the mass media than Italians.

Glazer concludes that although blacks may be near the bottom on some scales, their disadvantage is not so uniformly, or so radically, different from the pattern that we are justified in setting up a new separatist model. But the separatist view is a strong one, particularly among black intellectuals, and we shall encounter it in the policy arguments of several later issues.

CHAPTER NOTES

[1] W. Lloyd Warner and Paul S. Lunt, *The Status System of a Modern Community* (New Haven: Yale University Press, 1942), and *The Social Life of a Modern Community* (New Haven: Yale University Press, 1942); August B. Hollingshead, *Elmtown's Youth* (New York: Wiley, 1949).

[2] Otis Dudley Duncan, "A Socioeconomic Index for All Occupations," in A. J. Reiss, Jr. (ed.), *Occupations and Social Status* (New York: Free Press, 1961).

[3] David Featherman and Robert M. Hauser, *On the Measurement of Occupation in Social Surveys* (Madison: University of Wisconsin, Institute for Research on Poverty, 1973).

[4] Kingsley Davis and Wilbur E. Moore, "Some Principles of Stratification," *American Sociological Review*, 10 (1945), 242–249.

[5] Melvin M. Tumin, "Some Principles of Stratification, A Critical Analysis," *American Sociological Review*, 18 (1953), 387–393.

[6] See Reinhard Bendix and Seymour Martin Lipset (eds.), *Class, Status and Power* (New York: Free Press, 1966) 59–72, for later articles on the controversy.

[7] Roger Brown, *Social Psychology* (New York: Free Press, 1965).

[8] Herbert Gans, *The Urban Villagers* (New York: Free Press, 1962).

[9] Max Weber, *The Protestant Ethic and the Spirit of Capitalism* (New York: Scribner's, 1958).

[10] Oscar Lewis, *La Vida* (New York: Random House, 1965), xlii–lii.

[11] Seymour Spilerman and David Elesh, "Alternative Conceptions of Poverty and Their Implications for Income Maintenance," *Social Problems*, 18 (1971), 358–373.

[12] Lee Rainwater, "The Problem of Lower Class Culture," *Journal of Social Issues*, 26 (1970), 133–148.

[13] Lola M. Irelan, Oliver C. Moles, and Robert M. O'Shea, "Ethnicity, Poverty, and Selected Attitudes: A Test of the Culture of Poverty Hypothesis," *Social Forces*, 47 (1969), 405–413.

[14] Seymour M. Lipset and Reinhard Bendix, *Social Mobility in Industrial Society* (Berkeley: University of California Press, 1959), 55–60.

[15] Stephan Thernstrom, "Migration and Social Mobility, 1880–1970: The Boston Case

and the American Pattern." Paper prepared for the Conference on Social Mobility in Past Societies, (Princeton, N.J.: Institute for Advanced Studies, June 15–17, 1972).

[16] Richard M. Merelman, "Social Mobility and Equal Opportunity," *American Journal of Political Science, XII* (1973), 213–236.

[17] Peter M. Blau and Otis D. Duncan, *The American Opportunity Structure* (New York: Wiley, 1967).

[18] Seymour M. Lipset, "Social Mobility and Equal Opportunity," *The Public Interest*, no. 29 (Fall 1972), 88–108.

[19] Lipset, "Social Mobility," p. 99.

[20] Merelman.

[21] Merelman, p. 224.

[22] Merelman, p. 225.

[23] Merelman, p. 226.

[24] Merelman, p. 227.

[25] Merelman, p. 229.

[26] Merelman, p. 230.

[27] Merelman, pp. 232–233.

[28] Robert M. Hauser and David L. Featherman, "Black-White Differentials in Occupational Mobility among Men in the U.S., 1962–1970." Working Paper 72–32, University of Wisconsin Center for Demography and Ecology, Madison, December 1972.

[29] Otis D. Duncan, "Patterns of Occupational Mobility among Negro Men," *Demography* 5 (1968), 11.

[30] Reynolds Farley and Albert Hermalin, "The 1960s: A Decade of Progress for Blacks?" *Demography*, 9 (1972), 353–370.

[31] Hauser and Featherman, p. 21.

[32] Hauser and Featherman, p. 4.

[33] E. P. Hutchinson, *Immigrants and Their Children* (New York: Wiley, 1956).

[34] Robert Blauner, "Internal Colonializing and Ghetto Revolt," *Social Problems*, 16 (1969), 393–408.

[35] Nathan Glazer, "Blacks and Ethnic Groups: The Difference and the Political Difference It Makes," *Social Problems*, 18 (1971), 444–461.

Chapter 4

Schooling and Mobility

The American public school has always been regarded as a major force in providing the opportunity for new groups to move up in the society. This chapter addresses the question: To what extent is that belief real? It:

Summarizes the research into the influence of schooling on occupational level.

Reviews a variety of suggestions for making the school a more potent force for social mobility: reducing class bias in the schools, decreasing the use of school credentials as requirements for many jobs, and eliminating the barriers to entry into higher education. Considers the problems that arise from the pressures to equalize group status very quickly, instead of generationally.

Some of the questions readers might address are:

Which of the proposals for changing the current relation of schooling to occupation seems to be the most sound and the most realistic? What evidence would I use to support that choice?

Of the people I know who moved from one social-class level to a higher one, how many did so primarily through schooling? If some did not, what accounted for their mobility?

Of the people I know who went to college but ended up in an occupation of a fairly low level, what appears to account for the downward move?

In the past decade the traditional American belief that more schooling will inevitably lead to better occupational status has undergone a series of critical examinations, aided by new and sophisticated statistical techniques described in an earlier chapter. The results raise some doubts not only about the old faith in education, but also about the new orthodoxy, the view that class and status lines are overwhelmingly determined by the status of the family.

Colin Greer, the revisionist historian of education, mounted a savage attack on the American public school in his book, *The Great School Legend,* arguing that the schools, over the past century and a half, served well only the favored few, and were successful only in maintaining economic and social deprivation on a massive scale. His indictment makes the following major points:[1]

1.   Although the picture we have been given by American historians claims that the school has enhanced opportunity, equality, and cultural harmony, it has brought no real change in the status quo in regards to the relative place of various social groups. Because the society, and in turn the school, has assumed "the perpetual immobility of a relatively static lower class base," there has really been no progress at all.

2.   Early in the nineteenth century revered early educational figures such as Horace Mann, who was a major advocate of tax-supported schools for all, may have called for universal schooling as a great equalizer of the conditions of man, but also saw it as necessary for the maintenance of public order and the protection of property. Greer says, "It was the schools as 'the balance wheel of the social machinery,' which triumphed—the balance being the imposition of controls for social stability (through schooling) in favor of the moneyed and powerful, and not the substance behind egalitarian rhetoric."[2]

3.   In relation to incoming minorities, beginning with the Irish in the 1840s and 1850s, the school has operated not as an equalizer but as an inculcator of values that would protect society from the "moral cesspool" they created in the cities. Only a few of the "best minds" were selected from these groups; large numbers simply failed throughout the school system.

4.   The growth of the high school is seen as an opportunity for mobility, as a democratizing movement, but few poor or working-class children attended it, and others were increasingly siphoned off into vocational programs or impelled to drop out and go into the world of work. The high school was primarily a service to middle-class parents, by removing the burden of paying for private secondary schooling, or at least spreading that fiscal burden.

5.   The American school replaced the church as the agent for assimilating the migrant poor into the new industrial order, reinforcing certain kinds of family patterns and punishing others. Its success in doing so aborted the kind of revolutionary movements that flourished in Europe, where such a

mechanism had not developed. The American school, thus has served to buy off the poor, to reach them more easily and deal with undesirable behavior, while offering them few gains.

This view of the American school is rather fashionable among the educational elite, and must be addressed seriously. Aside from its gross misreading of what was historically regarded as "equality of opportunity," and its inability to suggest what the American school might have done as an alternative when confronted with children from generations of peasant families and from cultures often inimical to schooling as such, the argument rests fundamentally on the thesis that social class has represented an enormously greater influence on mobility than has the school. On this question, at least, we now have some substantial evidence (see Panel 4.1 for a summary) that such is not the case, that the influence of family background on mobility is more moderate than is often supposed.

PANEL 4.1   Schooling and Occupation

All of the important studies that have examined the relation between schooling and income have also included occupational attainment as an output variable and have employed the same instrument, path analysis. The general conclusions of these intensive investigations by Sewell and Hauser,[3] the Duncans and Featherman,[4] and Jencks and his colleagues,[5] are summarized below:

Family background factors, such as the education and occupation of the father, has its greatest impact on the number of years of schooling attained by the son, least impact on later income, with an intermediate impact on occupational status. Broadly speaking, most of the influence of family background variables are felt *through* their impact on years of schooling, rather than directly on occupational status. Family background, then, "matters most for attainments that are close in time to the period of residence in the family or orientation, and has a progressively attenuated influence...."[6]

The direct influence of family background, however, though clear, is not very large in realistic terms. Jencks has estimated that the average occupational inequality among *brothers* (family background identical) is 87 percent of the degree of occupational inequality in the society as a whole.

Much the same can be said for the impact of family background on years of schooling. Although Sewell and Hauser regard this influence as "impressive," their estimates do not appear so. It takes a shift of $7000 in income, for example (from $3000 a year to $10,000) to lead to an increase in *half of a year* of postsecondary education for the son. Each year of additional education of the father or mother is related to *.08* of a year of higher education for the son.

The influence of schooling itself on occupational status is substantial, says Jencks, and it is important in itself, not merely a proxy for family background or cognitive skills. That is, even for individuals with the same background and the same cognitive abilities, extra schooling makes a difference. But, "anyone who thinks that a man's family background, test scores, and educational credentials are the only things that determine the kind of work he can do in America is fooling himself."[7] At best, taken together they explain about 50 percent of the variations in occupational status, leaving an equal amount to be accounted for.

An extra year of schooling, independent of other variables, yields an average of 6 points on Duncan's occupational status scale; four years of college roughly four times that. This difference corresponds to the difference, for example, between a doctor and an accountant, the manager of a clothing store and the manager of an auto repair shop. As men get older the correlation between schooling and status falls.

Various studies appear to agree that family background factors, in combination, explain from 15–20 percent of the variations in years of schooling.

To the specific point of social mobility, Jencks summarizes his findings this way: The difference between a person in the top fifth of the occupational hierarchy and the bottom fifth is about 60 to 65 points on Duncan's occupational status scale (that runs from 0–96). Only half of the father's status is passed on, so the sons will differ by 31 points. (The status of random individuals differs by an average of 28 points on the scale.) Of this gap, Jencks estimates that 5 to 10 percent is due to differences in inherited IQ, 10 to 20 percent to the cognitive skills developed in favorable home environments; 40 to 50 percent is due to educational attainments. The remaining 35 percent has nothing to do with social class, skills, or education. Some may be explained by the inheritance of jobs either directly or by the father's ability to pass on job skills; it may be due to individual aspiration levels unrelated to family background, or to habits and values.

In sum, although the traditional historical view that the American school played a significant role in upward mobility was probably much exaggerated, schooling does have an independent influence on status, and one that, at least in the past generation on which these data are largely based, makes a greater contribution than does family background as an independent factor. The "Movement" view, on the other hand, that the poor are overwhelmingly denied opportunity, seems to have little basis in reality.

One final anomaly: If school attainment has a significant effect on occupational status, why does it have so little effect on income? Jencks' answer is a simple one. The income variations *within* the same general occupational categories are so great that the achievement of a particular occupational status has little predictive values for the income one gets. Indeed, he claims, this variability is so great that if all occupations were made to have the same average income (all lawyers averaged the same as all plumbers, and so on), but the income disparities within each occupation remained constant, we should reduce income inequalities in general by only about 20 percent.

SCHOOLING AND THE EQUALIZATION OF STATUS

So potent is the belief in schooling as the central lever of social status that most policies intended to equalize social status involve either the school and its operations or some relationship of the school to the social order. In the final section that follows we examine three major diagnoses of the equalization problem and the policies that flow from them.

Eliminate Social-Class Bias of the School

Social scientists who study the school have, for a generation, focused on the function of the institution as a "sorting" mechanism. The image presented is of a vast funnel from kindergarten to college into which all children are dropped; as they progress through it, some are eliminated at various stages, or sorted into alternative tracks on the basis of ability, interest, behavior, and motivation.

The sorting process in most school systems involves any or all of the following practices: (a) homogeneous grouping at the elementary-school level, the procedure widely employed to group children in different classrooms within the same grade by ability; (b) high-school tracking, in which those children who are going on to college pursue one curriculum while others follow a vocational or "general" track; (c) in the larger cities, the development of separate high schools that are themselves tracks, devoted primarily to college preparatory or vocational studies; (d) the existence of private schools, again mostly in the cities, providing expensive and relatively exclusive educations for the affluent; (e) variations in participation in extracurricular activities, and in the availability of these activities from school to school.

All of these characteristic practices of schools, though usually based on objective test scores or expressed interests of students, inevitably sort by social class while they are sorting for these other variables. In studies of class-associated factors in schools, such as Havighurst and Neugarten's in Chicago,[8] any rank ordering of schools by socioeconomic status variables inevitably also ranks them roughly by achievement level.

Studies of teachers in lower-class urban schools also demonstrate the operation of class biases, as a study by Robert Herriott and Nancy Hoyt St. John shows.[9] Teachers in lower-class schools are less experienced, less satisfied with their jobs, and more eager to move to other schools than are teachers in middle-class schools. Lower-class schools tend to have more teachers whose origins are in the lower-class than middle-class schools. There is some evidence that differences in teacher performance correlate with differences in school social class:

> The prediction that the performance of teachers in schools of lowest SES would be found to be poorer than the performance of teachers in schools of highest SES is supported by the data. This conclusion is based on the evidence of two independent sets of observers—principals and teachers—and it is supported by the trend across a large number of items and by the high proportion of statistically significant differences between schools of highest and lowest SES. Although *it* would seem safe to generalize this finding of SES difference in teacher performance to the population of schools from which this sample was drawn, it should be noted that in general the observed differences are not very large.[10]

W. W. Charters has summed up a generation of research on the relation between social-class background and school success in the following often-quoted conclusion:

> It is proper to conclude that pupils of the lower classes will experience frustration and failure and pupils of the higher classes will experience gratification and success in their educational experiences. The evidence supporting this conclusion is overwhelming.
>
> To categorize youth according to the social-class position of their parents is to order them on the extent of their participation and degree of success in the American educational system. This has been so consistently confirmed by research that it now can be regarded as an empirical law. It appears to hold regardless of whether the social-class categorization is based upon the exhaustive procedures used in Elmstown (Hollingshead 1949) or upon more casual indicators of socioeconomic status such as occupation or income level. It seems to hold in any educational institution, public or private, where there is some diversity in social class, including universities, colleges, and teacher training institutions, as well as elementary and secondary schools. Social class position predicts grades, achievement, and intelligence test scores, retentions at grade level, course failure, truancy, suspensions from school, high school dropouts, plans for college attendance and total amount of formal schooling. It predicts academic honors and awards in the public school, elected school offices, extent of participation in extra-curricular activities and in social affairs sponsored by the school, to say nothing of a variety of indicators of "success" and formal structure of the student society. Where differences in prestige value exist in high school clubs and activities, in high school curricula, or in types of advanced training institutions, the social-class composition of the membership will vary accordingly.
>
> The predictions noted above are far from perfect inasmuch as the social class position rarely accounts for more than half the variance of school success, the

law holds only for differences in group averages, not for differences in individual successes.[11]

There is little doubt that the social-class biases observed do exist. The interpretations drawn from their existence, and the policies developed to counter them, are another matter, particularly in light of the more recent analyses of schooling and occupation described earlier.

1. If such biases in favor of middle-class and against working-class students were of any magnitude, it would be almost impossible to account for the demonstrated complexity of the influences on school attainment. Charters' remark in the quote above that "pupils of the lower classes will experience frustration and failure and pupils of the higher classes will experience gratification and success in their educational experience" is so flatly unequivocal, and so exaggerated that it is difficult to believe that it was made by an eminent social scientist. In fact, to turn attention to his final sentence, it is generally the case that social-class position rarely accounts for *as much as* half the variance in school measures, and in simple correlation studies, where all of the important variables are not taken into account, family background seldom explains more than about a third of the variation examined. Thus, Herriott and St. John carefully note that the differences in teacher performance observed were not very large; they are also based on comparisons between the highest and lowest categories of social-class schools, omitting the large middle range.

2. Few of the studies in the considerable literature on social-class bias in the schools control for IQ, which has a substantial effect on school performance. Jencks suggests that if we could equalize the genetic contribution to IQ, inequality in achievement test scores would probably fall by 33 to 50 percent.[12] And, although there are some differences among various estimates of the effect of IQ on how *much* schooling one gets, there is agreement that it is sizeable. Duncan puts the independent effect of IQ at 29 percent of the variations in years of schooling, and as more important than the effect of family background;[13] Jencks' estimate is somewhat lower, as about equal to family background. (The real effect is also something on the order of that of family: Two brothers with an IQ difference of 15 points are likely to vary in attainment by .6 to 1.2 years of schooling.)

It would be surprising if teachers did not treat differently students with varying IQs and academic ability, since the school is the primary institution for the development of cognitive skills. Sewell and his associates' intensive analysis of Wisconsin student data shows that, in doing so, schools are comparatively class-blind. In discussing the effects on educational attainment (in years of schooling) of perceived parental encouragement, teacher's encouragement, and friends' educational plans, they note that "we are struck by the evidence that parental encouragement and friends' plans depend heavily on the son's socioeconomic origin, while teachers' encouragement is more heavily dependent on the student's academic ability and performance. Indeed, teachers are not perceived to engage in direct socio-economic discrimination, as parents and peers apparently do, but rather depend mainly on judgments of the student's academic ability as it is validated by school performance."[14]

The policies that flow from this critique of the school as socially biased are discussed in a number of sections in the second part of this book: the greater employment of ethnically similar teachers and teacher training strategies in general (Chapter 12); making the schools accountable (Chapter 11); compensatory programs for the poor (Chapter 10).

Eliminate the Diploma Curtain

A second, and very different approach to the problem is embodied in an attack on what Peter Drucker calls "The Diploma Curtain" and M. S. Miller "The Credential Society." Both refer to the demand by private industry and government for advance evidence of ability to perform a job before hiring, in the form of degrees, diplomas, or the ability to pass a written test.[15] The crux of the matter, it is now being argued, is whether a great many jobs do not demand far higher credentials than the actual work requires.

Thus, Drucker notes that a great many forces have operated to keep people in school longer than in many cases is necessary. As people live longer, their life lengthens; he suggests that one of the ways the society has tried to cope with that fact is to shorten it at the entry end by keeping people in school. Then, faced with a population with greater years of schooling, it has been compelled to upgrade many jobs to make them attractive to a new kind of labor force. Some of the work for which we now require several years of college, or a college degree, is being done in other countries quite adequately by high school graduates or those with less education. Some observers have also suggested that part of the labor movement's interest in education has been the desire to keep young people off the labor market as long as possible.

The Diploma Curtain, says Drucker, prevents us from hiring people who can prove their ability through performance; the pressure on that curtain is likely to grow more intense during the seventies. The courts are being asked to determine whether written tests, in civil service and in the private sector, are relevant to the jobs for which they are taken.

In a review of the evidence on whether formal training is relevant to the jobs that people end up in, and whether school success is connected with job effectiveness, Ivar Berg[16] and Randall Collins[17] come to the following conclusions:

1. The educational level of the U.S. job force has increased considerably beyond the increase in the skill requirements of the jobs that must be filled. Overeducation is particularly apparent among male college graduates, and appears to be on the increase.

2. Better educated employees are not necessarily the most productive,

and may in some cases be less productive than the less well-educated; this finding appears in studies of groups ranging from factory workers to research scientists.

3.   Training for high-level professional positions, law, medicine, scholarly research, engineering, and so forth, is probably vocationally relevant. In some instances it is impossible to judge, because entry into the field is completely determined by educational credentials and no comparison group is therefore available. Outside of the traditional professions, the result of the attempt in many occupations to "professionalize" by setting increasingly higher training requirements suggests that these requirements do not genuinely embody skills useful in the occupation itself.

4.   At the level of manual skills, industry itself conducts extensive on-the-job training whether the employee brings with him training credentials or not. Graduates of vocational training programs are not more likely to be employed than high-school dropouts.

There is, nevertheless, a long-term trend toward requiring minimum educational levels for most jobs that people perceive as worth having, and a gradual rise in the minimum levels themselves, although the rise is not spectacular. Collins cites comparisons between a 1967 study in the Bay Area and a national survey conducted thirty years earlier; in the earlier period only 11 percent of employers demanded a high-school diploma for a skilled manual job versus 28 percent in the sixties study. The diploma was required for clerical workers by 63 percent of employers earlier, versus 68 percent at the later date, a not very sizeable increase and perhaps due mostly to the special nature of the San Francisco area. But, there is a very substantial increase in the demand for the college degree at higher job levels, from 12 percent to 41 percent for managers, and from 52 percent to 70 percent for professionals.

However uneven the effect may be, there is no doubt of the essential soundness of the basic credentialism argument; employers tend to hire on the basis of educational credentials that in many and perhaps most cases are not reliable predictors of the performance of the employee. The policy suggested as a response is to do away with years of education as a criterion for employment wherever possible, and substitute other more relevant criteria.

The practical pursuit of the policy is a good deal less clear than its justification. Jencks has considered the problems in implementing it at some length in his *Inequality*; some of his reflections are summariezd below:[18]

1.   Employers may not be quite so irrational as the data suggest. When two workers with unequal amounts of education end up in the same job, it is likely that the one with less schooling exhibits some compensating virtues known to the employer. If this happened very often, we would not expect to find a relation between differences in productivity by comparing workers with different education in the same job.

2.   Educational requirements act to ration the allocation of jobs because many adolescents dislike school. "The fact that high-status occupations are believed to require a lot of schooling deters many young people from trying to enter these occupations. As a result, the distribution of occupational aspirations among high school students is surprisingly congruent with the distribution of actual opportunities."[19]

3.   Educational credentials represent a reasonably objective criterion for hiring, in the same way that seniority provides an objective standard for retention. Although tests of actual skill or aptitude with sufficient reliability may be developed for some specific jobs, prediction on the basis of tests is very difficult for most positions in the upper occupational range. Should we require employers to ration access on the basis of subjective criteria, such as appearance, impression made during an interview, or supervisor's rating after a short period on the job? Such criteria, Jencks suggests, are more likely than the use of education to work to the disadvantage of minority groups.

4.   It is this problem of choosing an alternative to credentials that is an especially difficult one, particularly if we are interested in pursuing egalitarian goals of reducing the connection between social background and occupational status. Jencks presents the following set of correlations from his data between father's status and various characteristics of sons:

School grades	.194	Occupational aspiration	
Test scores	.288	in 12th grade	.366
Actual occupational		Educational aspiration	
status at age 25	.331	in 12th grade	.380
		Educational attainment	.417

The current correlation of occupation with family status, .331, would fall somewhat to .288 if we persuaded employers to hire only on the basis of test scores. It would fall further, to .194, if school grades were used as the only hiring criterion. If people were hired only on the basis of educational attainment, years of schooling, the influence of family status would increase to .417. A pure meritocracy would thus give us more social mobility than we now have.

> Yet, as we have already noted, a system which emphasizes cognitive skills would be far less satisfactory for blacks than for poor whites. For blacks, the ideal system is one which discounts test scores and emphasizes aspirations. Failing this, a system that emphasizes credentials is better for blacks than one that emphasizes test scores. The right policy thus depends on whose opportunities you want to equalize.[20]

Eliminate Bars to Higher Education

If one believes both of the preceding propositions, that the schools' social-class bias and ethnic prejudice is responsible for the lower achievement and aspiration of minority group children, *and* that educational credentials importantly determine occupational status, the logic of the current pressure for a massive increase in college enrollments of minority youth is clear.

Although careless commencement orators often give the impression that almost everyone is going to college these days, the evidence provides a more sober picture:

The Carnegie Commission on Higher Education reports that little over 50 percent of high-school graduates go on to college. Of this group, 52 percent earn bachelor degrees, 30 percent enter graduate school, 8 percent enter doctoral programs and 4 percent earn doctorates.[21] In 1975, 14 percent of the population had completed a four-year college degree program.[22]

By the mid-seventies the attendance rate in four-year colleges was decreasing, but the rate in two-year colleges was increasing. Differences in college-entry for both sex and social class have been reduced substantially over the period 1965 to 1975.[23]

The size of the black-white gap in college attendance is uncertain. In 1970 the American Council on Education reported that low-achieving whites were nearly three times as likely to be enrolled in universities than were low-achieving blacks; male high-achieving blacks were three times as likely to attend a two-year college than whites of equal ability.[24] A more recent survey by the National Center for Educational Statistics, however, paints a different picture (see Table 4.1). When controlled for ability, ethnic differences in their national probability sample disappear. Proportionately more black students than whites at each ability level attend four-year colleges.[25]

In the face of this evidence, the continuing and vigorous movement for the admission to the university of greater numbers of minority students gives the argument over equality a different cast. Those who argue for mass education at the college level do so on one or another of the following assumptions: since the degree is an entry requisite for a number of professions and subprofessional jobs, one cannot restrict its acquisition to a particular part of the population. If restrictions based on proven academic performance, or on tests designed to predict that kind of performance, eliminate an unequal proportion of minority group youth, then they are clearly unfair and a form of institutional racism. If the college curriculum demands performance of a certain type that cannot be mastered by minority group students because of their disadvantaged backgrounds, they should be judged on the basis of the kinds of things they *can* do, and the curriculum should be reformed.

Thus, the economist Mary Jean Bowman says:

Table 4.1   Percentage of High-School Graduates in Each Postsecondary
Educational Activity by Race and Ability (NLS-1972)

Race	Ability Quartile	Four-year College	Two-year College	Other	Non-Study	Sample Size
Black						
	1st (Low)	15.5	10.0	14.0	60.5	1167
	2nd	42.2	11.3	9.1	37.4	367
	3rd	54.7	10.5	5.1	29.6	145
	4th (High)	73.8	4.6	8.0	13.7	50
White						
	1st (Low)	6.4	10.7	11.8	72.1	2180
	2nd	15.0	17.4	11.8	55.8	2863
	3rd	33.7	18.9	10.2	37.2	3050
	4th (High)	61.3	13.2	5.8	19.7	3193
Hispanic						
	1st (Low)	9.6	19.4	11.3	59.7	371
	2nd	20.2	30.2	6.8	42.7	152
	3rd	33.8	26.4	5.9	33.9	72
	4th (High)	52.1	26.3	0.0	21.6	19

Source: Samuel S. Peng, "Trends in the Entry to Higher Education: 1961–1972," Educational Researcher (January 1977), p. 18. Based on the National Longitudinal Study of the
High School Class of 1972.

What, then, are the grounds for using control by qualification? I suggest that
one or more of three underlying attitudes or perceptions are entailed. One
notion, very flattering to the intellectual but dubious on moral grounds, is that
people born with brains are somehow nobler or "more deserving" of special
rewards. This is intellectual elitism in its most arrogant form. The second is a
belief that the more able will benefit more from additional schooling and that
individuals in making their choices will not allow adequately for that fact; this
is a special version of the 'superior wisdom' theme noted earlier. Third, it could
be argued that the external benefits are especially great from educating the most
able individuals. Only the third of these arguments, I submit, has even a whisper
of empirical and moral validity.[26]

Robert Staff and Gordon Tullock have similarly argued that higher
education acts to redistribute incomes from the poor to the middle class.
Because college going increases the degree of differentiation among incomes,
those with natural talent who would earn higher incomes in any event are
sent to college at the taxpayer's expense and thus given higher incomes.[27]
Herman Branson, arguing for increased black enrollments in medical
schools, discusses the differences in scores on qualifying tests in science
and offers a "modest proposal" for weighting the scores of black applicant:

Surely the score for the second group (i.e., the black students) should have been
the absolute score, multiplied by the factor of the average expenditure per pupil
in the white school, divided by the average expenditure per student in the black

school. If that were done, it would reveal that the average black student is so bright that he would have a score of roughly 80 points on the verbal test.[28]

He goes on to suggest the further need for "realistic, meaningful" programs in medical schools, and asks whether the courses taken "relate to the hard realities of general practice".[29] Speaking of a practicing physician of his acquaintance, he notes:

> I doubt that he has had any need to know anything about the alpha helix for the last six months. I doubt that he's worried about DNA, or messenger DNA, or messenger RNA, or anything of a similarly exotic nature. In short, there is a profound difference between what we are doing in the medical curriculum and what people are actually doing in the practice of medicine.[30]

In another example of the current mood, members of one of New York's local school boards have charged that the Bronx High School of Science discriminates because its entrance examination screens out most black and Puerto Rican pupils. The school is one of the best in the country for students talented in the sciences and mathematics. Although 140 blacks and Puerto Rican students enter each year on the basis of recommendations from local elementary schools, the community board is seeking to have all admissions based on recommendations rather than test.[31]

The resistance to this movement to exalt egalitarianism above competence and ability comes from a number of quarters, mainly the ranks of the academics themselves, who see in it a strong strain of the anti-intellectualism that has always been a part of American life. Indeed the arguments of those who wish to open the university to all on the basis of a general equality are almost precisely the reasons advanced in the nineteenth century for making high school available to all. As Hofstadter notes, since, in American education, the egalitarian "opening of the doors" has always been followed by making entry compulsory,

> The situation of the school administrators can hardly fail to command our sympathies. Even in the 1920s, to a very large degree, they had been entrusted by the fiat of society with the management of quasi-custodial institutions. For custodial institutions the schools were, to the extent that they had to hold pupils uninterested in study but bound to the schools by laws. Moreover, the schools were under pressure not merely to fulfill the laws, but to become attractive enough to hold the voluntary allegiance of as large a proportion of the young for as long as they could.[32]

The pressure might be mitigated by a greater use of the junior college to provide a much more varied and relevant curriculum. The most rapidly growing segment of higher education, these community-based institutions also provide the least amount of dislocation for the student, and an excellent testing ground for those who are capable of moving on to higher levels.

As for the four-year colleges, Thomas Sowell, a black professor of economics, has argued (in agreement with many white colleagues) that the proportion of black students can be greatly increased without being indiscriminate and without forcing a lowering of academic standards.[33] In absolute numbers, he notes, there are tens of thousands of black students who score above average on standardized tests. Many of those who do are forced to go to the lowest level Southern Negro colleges, "while many other black students without the necessary academic skills are being maneuvered through top-level colleges at a cost to the integrity of the educational process which is exceeded only by the psychic costs borne by the students themselves."[34] Because of an ideological commitment on the part of those who administer special aid programs, he claims, "authentic" ghetto blacks are consistently preferred over students who have the ability to make it through demanding institutions on their own.

The issue, it is clear, is more complex in this period than the simpler arguments over equality during earlier eras of the extension of educational opportunity, though many of the themes are the same. Curriculum reform in the high school came after decades of experience with a new student population had brought educators to the realization that the students could not cope with the old curriculum requirements. The opening of the colleges is taking place during a period of ferment about the aims of education generally (see Chapters 10 and 14), and in the context of a black civil rights movement with a particular ideology.

PANEL 4.2   Increasing Minority Access to College: Some Program Models

A look at several programs aimed at increasing minority group admission to college will provide a more specific idea of the promises and the problems of the movement. The first is the federal government's Upward Bound, for low-income high-school students who are doing C− work and who normally would not enter college. During the summer phase of the program, students spend eight weeks in residence on a college campus for intensive tutoring and counseling. Similar support is provided during the school year while they are juniors and seniors. About half of the participants are blacks, a third white, with Spanish-speaking, Indians, and Orientals making up the remainder:

> About 20,000 students are enrolled in Upward Bound, and in a typical year 6000 graduate high school; about two-thirds, then, stay in the program during high school.[35]
> Sixty-eight percent of the graduates enroll in some form or other

of higher education, compared to an enrollment rate of 48 percent in a matched control sample.[36]

By the end of their college sophomore year, the dropout rate is about 20 percent.

Although there are some shifts in attitudes (e.g., motivation for college, self-esteem, self-evaluated intelligence) during the two high-school years in the program, the changes are small, and in some cases the scores actually decline by the senior year. During the same period academic averages for white Upward Bound students in one group studied remained about the same, and averages of the blacks declined.[37]

Comparing a group of Upward Bound students who went on to college with a group of program participants who did not go, Egelund and his associate found the first group higher on measures of interpersonal flexibility, self-evaluated intelligence, possibility of college graduation, and importance of college graduation.[38] The college group also came from larger high schools, did not fall in the lowest income level, and tended to have mothers who remained at home.

As with most of the programs examined in this chapter, the results are at best mixed. Although Upward Bound seems to increase the probability of college entry, the fact that almost half of their controls started college without the program suggests that an equal proportion of Upward Bound students would have done so in any event. This is confirmed by a benefit-cost analysis by Garms, who compared his Upward Bound sample with their own siblings; he estimated that 43 percent of the siblings will enter college.[39] He concludes that instead of selecting students who would otherwise be very unlikely to attend college, the program has actually selected a group slightly below average in likelihood of college attendance.

Garms went on to calculate the net benefits associated with having been a participant in Upward Bound by comparing lifetime incomes (see previous section on schooling and income) of the students with their siblings. He also calculated the benefits and costs from the society's point of view by including government program costs and costs to the colleges. From the individual point of view, the program yields net economic benefits, something on the order of $2000 (over a lifetime). From the social viewpoint, if the interest rate on program costs is assumed to be 10 percent, social costs are greater than benefits.

A second, even more massive, effort has been the open admission program of the City University of New York. In 1970, that institution began to admit any student graduating from a city high school either to a community college or to one of the senior four-year colleges in the system. Although some form of open admissions has been in force for many years at some state universities, it has traditionally operated as a "revolving door" system, with vast numbers of the academically unprepared being flunked out in their freshman year. The significance of New York's program was in its promise of intensive remedial, tutoring, and counseling services, and its commitment to retain open admissions students for at least two years.

Even after a period of six years the success of the program is difficult to evaluate. The hopes of its most fervent advocates, that special admissions students, even if they do not do as well as those regularly admitted, will stay on and complete college if given a chance, proved to be unsupported. The drop out rates of New York City's open admissions students was much greater than normal, and only a handful graduated at the end of the first four-year period after the program began.[40] The large-scale remedial program that was developed to help them proved in practice to be at best marginally effective.[41] Efforts to slow the pace of normal work proved even less useful; one chemistry course was extended to cover three semesters, but only four of seventy-three students registered survived to take the third semester. Faculty and outside observers complained that academic quality deteriorated severely; Martin Mayer wrote of special ethnic studies programs as shelters for untalented students, spending much of their time on field trips and showing slides in class in a sort of "fourth-grade show and tell."[42]

What proved to be the undoing of the policy was its cost. In the course of the city's severe fiscal crisis that began in 1975 much of the tens of millions allocated to support open admissions had to be cut back as the very survival of the university itself came into question. As a national policy, the widespread and growing difficulties which higher education generally confronts may well postpone any further massive experiment with open admissions for this decade, at least.

VALUE CONFRONTATIONS AND THE PACE OF CHANGE

The line between the advocates of far more equalization of both income and status and those who tend to see more danger than benefit in such policies come to sharp focus in the debate over higher education, but the value conflicts are general ones.

Jencks has cited the equalization theories of Jeremy Bentham as justification for his call for income distribution; Bentham argued that since happiness is the ultimate good, and since the addition of resources to those who have little will make them happier than the same increment will make the wealthy, the sum of happiness can obviously be increased more effectively by redistributing income. Most egalitarians turn these days to the contemporary philosopher, John Rawls, and his theory of justice. Rawls asserts that justice demands an equal sharing of all of life's goods including income, status, and respect, unless it can be shown that some degree of inequality will be to the advantage of the deprived. His theory is based on a rather involved argument; peoples' self-interest, he says, interferes with a valid judgment of how equally life's goods should be distributed, because the poor and the well-off would give very different answers to the question. We must estimate how everyone would answer it behind a veil of ignorance, that is, without foreknowledge of what their individual life chance will be. Since no one would be likely to run the risk of spending his life poor and looked-down-upon, the philosophical judgment must be to equalize.

The critics of the current egalitarian drive, as we have indicated, tend to view the problem of providing incentives as much more serious than do the equalizers. Moreover, since men *are* different, they doubt that their conditions can be made equal and kept equal without an unacceptable amount of state interference with individual freedom and without unconstitutional reverse discrimination in the form of quotas. Although meritocracy can hardly be said to have worked perfectly, they are inclined to argue, the alternatives must appear to the realist as far worse. In the long run, we will substitute for discrimination *against* groups discrimination *for* groups, but discrimination all the same.

As in many such conflicts, we must decide between the ideally desirable and the possible, which raises a question that will arise again and again throughout this book—the payoffs on social engineering in large-scale programs aimed at solving formidable social and educational problems. We do not intend to imply that it is futile to pour vast sums of money into improving the conditions of people or into efforts to equalize status, but if one looks at the results of doing so the payoffs are not anywhere near the expectations. Perhaps it is because most of the funds in the functional programs we have described here have gone to pay already fairly affluent professionals, a fact that some poor people have noted with bitterness. Perhaps it is because of Forrester's Law, that the most obvious solution to a social problem is inevitably the wrong or counterproductive one. Perhaps it is that problems like poverty and inequality yield only to slow processes of historical change. We tend to telescope the immediate past, and forget that it took two to three generations for the nineteenth century immigrants to get where they are; and some are still, as a group, in a disadvantaged status. Although the blacks have been in this country for 300 years, they are, as Glazer has pointed out, recent immigrants to the cities and to city life.

Much of the polarization in contemporary American life is around the issue of how fast social change can be effected; almost every one of the major controversies in urban education inevitably gets involved in that issue. There is no way in which we can resolve it here, because one's position depends on individual temperament, age, state of social commitment, willingness or unwillingness to accept modest gains as significant, and tolerance of frustration. All we can do is present the available evidence on the pace of change in"the here and now," and the reader must make of it what he will.

CHAPTER NOTES

1 Colin Greer, *The Great School Legend* (New York: Viking, 1972). For a critique of Greer and his fellow revisionists, see Diane Ravitch, "The Revisionists Revised," *Proceedings of the National Academy of Education*, 4 (1977), 1–84.

2 Greer, p. 63.

3 William H. Sewell and Robert M. Hauser, "Causes and Consequences of Higher Education: Models of the Status Attainment Process," *American Journal of Agricultural Economics*, 54 (1972), 851–861.

4 Otis D. Duncan, David L. Featherman, and Beverly Duncan, *Socioeconomic Background and Achievement* (New York: Seminar Press, 1972).

5 Christopher Jencks, et al., *Inequality: A Reassessment of Family and Schooling in America* (New York: Basic Books, 1972).

6 Duncan, et al., p. 43.

7 Jencks, p. 192.

8 Robert J. Havighurst and Bernice Neugarten, *Society and Education*, 3d ed. (Boston: Allyn & Bacon, 1967), p. 84.

9 Robert E. Herriott and Nancy Hoyt St. John, *Social Class and the Urban School* (New York: Wiley, 1966).

10 Herriott and St. John, p. 115.

11 W. W. Charters, Jr., "The Social Background of Teaching," in N. L. Gage (ed.), *Handbook of Research in Teaching* (Skokie, Ill.: Rand McNally, 1963), 739–740.

12 Jencks, p. 109.

13 Duncan, et al., p. 100.

14 Sewell and Hauser, p. 857.

15 Peter F. Drucker, "Worker and Work in the Metropolis," *National Elementary Principal* XLVII (1969), 32–43.

16 Ivar Berg, *Education and Jobs: The Great Training Robbery* (New York: Praeger, 1970).

17 Randall Collins, "Functional and Conflict Theories of Educational Stratification," *American Sociological Review*, 36 (1971), 1002–1019.

18 Jencks, pp. 192–199.

19 Jencks, p. 183.

20 Jencks, p. 194.

21 "Degrees: A Plan To Alter the Role They Play," *The New York Times*, September 29, 1970.

22 *Current Population Reports*, no. 292, p. 20.

23 Samuel S. Peng, "Trends in the Entry to Higher Education: 1961–1972," *Educational Researcher* (January 1977), 15–19.

24 *National Norms of Entering College Freshmen*, American Council on Education (Fall 1970).

25 Peng, p. 18.

26 Mary Jean Bowman, "Mass Elites on the Threshold of the 1970's," *Comparative Education*, 6, no. 3 (November 1970), 158.

27 Robert J. Staaf and Gordon Tullock, "Education and Equality," *Annals of the American Academy of Political and Social Science*, 409 (1973), 125–134.

28 Herman R. Branson, *Producing More Black Doctors: Psychometric Barriers*, Occasional Paper No. 5 of the Education Research Center, Massachusetts Institute of Technology, 1969, p. 3.

29 Branson, p. 4.

30 Branson, p. 5.

31 "Bronx High School of Science Accused of Bias in Admissions," *New York Times*, January 22, 1971.

[32] Richard Hofstadter, *Anti Intellectualism in American Life* (New York: Knopf, 1969), 327.

[33] Thomas Sowell, "A Black Professor Says Colleges are Skipping Over Competent Blacks to Admit 'Authentic' Ghetto Types," *New York Times Magazine*, December 13, 1970.

[34] Sowell, p. 13.

[35] T. A. Billings, "Upward Bound Accomplishments," *Phi Delta Kappan*, LXXX (October 1968), 96–98.

[36] Byron Egeland and David E. Hunt, "College Enrollment of Upward Bound Students as a Foundation of Attitude and Motivation," *Journal of Educational Psychology*, 61, no. 5 (1970), 375–379.

[37] D. E. Hunt and Robert Hardt, "The Effect of Upward Bound Program on Attitudes, Motivations and Academic Achievement of Negro Students," *Journal of Social Issues*, 25 (1969), 118–127.

[38] Egeland and Hunt, p. 377.

[39] Walter I. Garms, "A Benefit-Cost Analysis of the Upward Bound Program," *Journal of Human Resources*, 6, no. 2 (Spring 1971).

[40] City University of New York, news release, March 17, 1974.

[41] Daniel Berger, *Effectiveness of College Skills and Basic Writing Courses*, City College of New York Office of Research and Testing, Report no. 13, October, 1972.

[42] Martin Meyer, "Open Admissions for All," *Commentary* (February 1973), 33–47. For an opposite view, see Alexander W. Astin, "Folklore of Selectivity," *Saturday Review*, December 20, 1969.

Chapter 5

The Urban Setting

The urban school that is the focus of this book operates in the context of a variety of problems that have afflicted particularly the larger central cities for some period of time. This chapter:

Describes the major differences in life and life style that sets urban experiences somewhat apart from nonurban ones.

Examines the idea that urban life creates pathologies, or illnesses among city dwellers.

Reviews the population trends over the past several decades, with particular attention to the effects of the large-scale rural-to-urban migration of black rural Americans to the cities of the north and west.

Describes the debate over the nature and magnitude of the "urban crisis," and assesses the proposals for solving the problems that are part of that crisis.

Describes the state of schools in the larger central cities, and their major academic and disciplinary problems.

Reports on efforts underway to equalize school funding within metropolitan areas, and between metropolitan and nonmetropolitan districts.

Some of the questions readers might address are:

Which side of the "urban crisis" debate seems more persuasive to me? On which particular grounds?

How far should equalization of school district expenditures be pressed? Is it reasonable to restrict the expenditures of districts that can afford a higher level of spending, or should the states merely set a minimum level for all?

The crisis in urban education that has featured turbulent school-community relations, desperate efforts by educators to make inner city schools more effective, and battles over integration and decentralization is only one aspect of a broader urban crisis. A catalogue of the ills that afflict large cities can be composed from the pages of almost any day's edition of a metropolitan newspaper: rising incidence of crime and inadequate police forces; civil disorders and not enough money to solve the problems that cause them; nor enough money to modernize outdated schools, or clear the polluted air or water, or finance rapid transit systems that might help to unclog the traffic jams.

The mayors of large American cities make periodic pilgrimages to Washington to testify before Congress on the desperate needs of the cities, pleas to which Congress has only recently begun to respond. The most powerful forces in the federal legislature are rural, small town, and suburban; together these constitute a sizable majority of the population, no segment of which has traditionally been friendly to the cities.

However, the legislatures are not alone in their distrust and fear of the cities, nor can one attribute the attitude merely to an uneducated and provincial know-nothingism. For, as Morton and Lucia White have pointed out, the American intellectual, too, has been traditionally anti-city:

Yet enthusiasm for the American city has not been typical or predominant in our intellectual history. Fear has been the more common reaction. For a variety of reasons our most celebrated thinkers have expressed different degrees of ambivalence and animosity toward the city . . . We have no persistent or pervasive tradition of romantic attachment to the city in our literature or our philosophy, nothing like the Greek attachment to the *polis* or the French writer's affection for Paris . . . While our society became more and more urban throughout the nineteenth century, the literary tendency to denigrate the city hardly declined; if anything, its intensity increased. One of the most typical elements in our national life, the growing city, became the bete noire of our most distinguished intellectuals rather than their favorite.[1]

Many of the problems the cities face arise from the same sources that feed the distrust and animosity of rural legislators and intellectuals alike. They are also the sources of the urban school's dilemmas and challenges. This chapter will describe the large-scale trends that have created the urban structure of this decade, show what has happened to the urban school as a result of these forces, and examine some of the broad proposals for the future of metropolitan life and school systems.

CONCEPT: URBANISM

Sociologists have approached the urban condition from several different conceptual starting points, which are useful in developing an understanding of the city. The earliest of these conceptions—in the work of Tonnies, Simmel, and later Redfield—see the city as a distinct type of human community and proceed by developing an image of an ideal urban community as compared to an ideal rural one.

This view emphasizes the differences primarily in human interaction between the homogeneous village or rural community and the large industrial city. The most fundamental contrast is between the *intimacy* of the small community and the remoteness of urban relationships, which are largely *contractual*. Compare, for example, what happens to a person who becomes ill in each of these communities.

The villager calls upon a doctor whom he has known for a long time and whom he trusts. Everyone in the community knows he is ill; there is likely to be a network of mutual aid in which he himself has participated in the past. Neighbors offer to take the children off his wife's hands for a period, or to help with the cooking. Friends can be called on to perform the necessary work on the farm or at the store. There is a web of expectation and obligation based on personal relationship and a feeling of community.

The big-city dweller may not even know those living around him, and certainly is not likely to know them well enough to call on them for help. The doctor he sees probably has a professional rather than a personal relationship to him; it is far easier to go to a hospital where other unknown professionals and employees tend to his needs as part of their duties—if he can get in. If, during convalescence, his wife needs someone to care for the children, she will probably have to hire a person to do so or, if they are poor, to call upon a welfare agency.

The details of these contrasting situations conform to the differences one would expect from ideal types; but, like all abstract models, they tend to be too extreme. Although true in general, there are many relationships in urban society that are not merely contractual. Working-class neighborhoods in big cities come closer in many respects to the village community model than to the urban industrial one. Middle-class people living in large apartments may not know their neighbors, but they do have intimate friends in other parts of the city. Though differences in the two milieus are, in general, significant, as anyone who has lived in both can attest, the ideal-type approach tends to exaggerate them.

Moreover, even sociologists can be prone to minimize the very real disadvantages of *gemeinschaft,* the term that stands for intimate relations of the small community. To know, and to be known, entails a lack of privacy that many find onerous; intimacy often demands a considerable amount of agreement on basic values that can restrict personal growth and individuality. One pays a price for the advantages of a sense of community.

Most urban sociologists in the United States analyze urbanism not by reference to ideal-type differences, but by categorizing the life of American communities at some point along the *rural-urban continuum*. Thus, Wirth has defined the city in terms of three major variables which are responsible for its special way of life: absolute numbers of population, density, and heterogeneity of population. As these three characteristics increase, it is postulated that various aspects of the community react as follows:[2]

1. Both occupational structure and social stratification increase in complexity. It is not so much that jobs are simpler in the rural community, but that they are fewer in kind and less specialized. The greater occupational specialization in urban areas develops much finer social distinctions among people, which is further encouraged by the fact that people do not know one another personally. Thus, in the city, we tend to judge strangers on the basis of occupation, life style, education, and other surface characteristics.

2. Mobility of many kinds sharply increases. Rural populations are kept relatively stable by ownership of land and by the strength of kinship ties; urban populations are on the move, not only geographically but socially. The greater variety of occupations, with small but significant variations in prestige, permits a far greater degree of social mobility in the cities.

3. The nature of social interaction not only becomes less intimate as urbanism increases, but the forms of interaction themselves shift. Neighborhood institutions, such as the church and the informal pattern of "dropping in" on neighbors, give way to voluntary associations focused on special interests and needs of individuals, transcending their purely geographical location in the city.

4. Instead of the relatively simple distribution of population in the rural area—with a few boundary lines separating farms from trading centers, rich land from poor—the city tends to segregate not only functions of many kinds, but people as well. The larger the city, the more complicated zoning regulations are likely to become, separating residential from commercial areas and commercial from industrial. Recreational land becomes not only segregated but scarce, and the competitive struggle for it is often fierce. Neighborhood lines sharpen. A black ghetto, a Puerto Rican barrio, a Chinatown, the Mexican section, an Italian working-class district, a Jewish middle-class area, the upper-class district—all can be drawn on a large city map and are easily recognized by visible differences in life style, as well as by the presence of special food shops, restaurants, movie marquees, and special behavior patterns among children in the local schools.

5. All persons play many social roles: worker, pupil, teacher, friend, church member, neighbor. Urbanism increases the separation of one role from another, because the roles are not played out in the small and intimate context of a homogeneous community. Consequently, city people have greater difficulty in integrating the many roles they play; and because some of their roles involve impersonal relations at best, it is easy to develop diver-

gent styles for different roles. The city teacher may be a sympathetic and loving mother, a supportive wife, and a member of associations interested in liberal and humane causes; but because her teaching is so separated from all of these, she can play a punishing and prejudiced role on the staff of a city slum school.

Because of these differences, most Americans generally assume that the greater the degree of urbanization the greater the pathology of life in the community. The recent increase in such social indices as crime, however, seems to have occurred in small towns and rural areas as well as in urban areas; and Hagedorn and his associates have shown that any generalization about pathology must be made very cautiously and may, in fact, be a myth.[3] They categorized the various states by the proportion of each state's population residing in urban areas—that is, in or near cities with 50,000 or more inhabitants. They then correlated that measure with a number of measures of community pathology: crime of various kinds and rates of behavior generally thought of as symptoms of "disorganization" or "alienation," such as alcoholism, suicide, narcotics arrests, and divorce. The degree of urbanization did not predict those behaviors at all in many cases. The correlation with narcotics arrests was .42, and with deaths from alcoholism .37, which show a moderate measure of relationship. The other correlations were too small to be meaningful or were, indeed, negative.

Evidence from another line of research confirms these findings. A number of sociologists have recently become interested in how Americans define the "quality of life" and have developed standard survey techniques for measuring it. Mark Schneider recently compared the subjective feelings of city residents, black and white, about the quality of life in a variety of social areas, with the objective social conditions of their cities (crime rates, crowding, etc.) and found no stable correlation between the two measures.[4]

Two different theories are often advanced to account for the supposed special pathology of city life. One of these, essentially a Marxist view, puts the stress on *alienation,* a term that has been used to describe the individual's "estrangement" from work brought about by the division of labor, feelings of powerlessness, social isolation, and low levels of political participation.[5] But, as Seeman has shown in his review of the survey literature related to this thesis, the evidence simply does not support either the view that most urban Americans feel particularly alienated or the general assertion that workers in mass industry (presumably the most important of alienating forces) feel more powerless or isolated than others.[6]

The second approach, a more recent topic of interest for social scientists, emphasizes *crowding*. The case has been summarized by George Carey:[7] Crowding creates high rates of interindividual contacts, producing endocrine system stress, and leading to pathological symptoms of many kinds. In the sixties attention was drawn to this phenomenon by several laboratory studies in which populations of rats were maintained under conditions of severe crowding, which produced equally severe disturbances in social behavior and disruption of mating and maternal patterns.

The inference to human populations is easy to make, but very difficult to substantiate. To find a correlation between population density (persons per square mile) and social pathology in urban populations, for example, proves little; correlation between two conditions does not establish that one causes the other. The correlations found in contemporary studies are, in any event, modest, showing at best 1 to 5 percent of pathology measures accounted for by density.[8] Historically, in a study of immigrant districts in the late nineteenth century, Ward has shown that their density is not associated with such variables as mortality rates.[9] For example, Italian districts were low density areas with high rates of mortality in contrast with Jewish districts which were high density with low mortality rates.

Carnahan has found that, despite the general increase over the past generation in such social pathology measures as crime, divorce, alcoholism, and mental hospital admission rates, population density during the same period has decreased for central cities almost by half.[10] If a more intimate measure is used, such as the number of persons per room in a household, density has decreased from .69 to .54 during the last thirty years; in central cities the decrease was .64 to .51. The density drop in black households was greater: .97 to .65, although a minority of black households seem to be falling increasingly behind the gains made by both whites and blacks.

A number of recent studies have shown, also, that it is a mistake to consider all cities, and thus urban life generally, as having the same impact on people. Schuman and Gruenberg, for example, found that both black and white attitudes vary according to the specific city of residence.[11] The dissatisfaction that blacks express tends to decrease as the percentage of blacks in the city goes up. In explanation of this effect, it is possible that as the number of black residents increases, the city government grows more responsive. The study also discovered that liberal racial attitudes are closely associated with the educational level of the city.

If the degree of urbanization is not a good predictor of pathology or the quality of life in cities, what *is* a good one? Some years ago a number of urban sociologists who were fascinated by that question devoted a great deal of effort to defining the characteristics of a "good" city, and to investigating what made it good. One of the most significant of the studies was Robert Angell's.[12] He defined a "good" city as one with a low rate of major crime and a high degree of civic responsibility, as expressed in peoples' willingness to contribute to community fund drives. Having assigned "goodness" scores to a number of cities, he correlated the scores with a variety of community characteristics. Being a good city, by his definition, apparently had little to do with such factors as population size, the degree of absentee ownership of business, the proportion of church members, or the proportion of middle-class citizens. What *did* make the difference were the heterogeneity of the population and the rate of movement in and out of the city. The greater the ethnic and racial mix in the city and the higher the mobility rate, the lower was the index of "goodness." Together, these two factors accounted for almost two-thirds of the variation in "goodness" score.

It is not surprising, then, that the contemporary urban crisis arose during a period in which urban trends are dramatically dominated by the movements of large numbers of people and by their subsequent mixture in the combustion chamber of the cities.

URBAN TRENDS

Two great movements of people have dominated the American scene since the 1940s: a flow of largely white families to the suburban rings of metropolitan areas, and a great migration from the Southern rural areas to the Northern and Western central cities. In the discussion that follows, the term "central city" will be used to refer to those zones inside the circle of suburban development, usually within defined city limits. "Inner city" will designate those zones of older and usually deteriorated housing in which the latest arrivals to the city tend to settle, and in which one finds the greatest densities and the highest rates of such pathologies as crime, delinquency, disease, poverty, and alienation.

Both the movement to the cities and from city to suburb are part of a longer range trend toward urbanism; it is a generally accepted proposition that in this century the United States has become "a nation of cities." This is a notion, says Daniel Elazar, "which conjures up a vision of nearly 200 million Americans living shoulder to shoulder along crowded streets, seeking their pleasures in theaters and poolrooms and suffering the pains of living under conditions of heavy congestion."[13] In fact, although a majority of Americans live in metropolitan areas, by 1970 only 15 percent of them lived in central cities with populations over one million. In order to evaluate the "nation of cities" belief, it is necessary to look closely at what is happening demographically to the country (see Panel 5.1).

We are becoming, in fact, a nation of suburbs and small cities. It might be argued that as long as population growth occurs in what the Census Bureau calls Standard Metropolitan Statistical Areas (SMSA), the distinction makes no difference. But there are several considerations that must be kept in mind in regard to those SMSA's. One is their nonurban density. Urban density is defined as at least 1000 persons per square mile; suburban density as 500 persons per square mile. Even before the current shift toward nonmetropolitan growth and decline in large city population, less than half the states had even one county with an urban density, and three-quarters of all SMSA's contained fewer than 500,000 people even when the central city and suburbs were combined.[14]

PANEL 5.1   Where People Live, and Where They Are Moving

The Bureau of the Census reports its continuing population surveys in two major categories: metropolitan areas (those with a city population of at least 50,000 and surrounding suburbs), and nonmetropolitan areas (counties with a center of less than 50,000 population); the metropolitan areas are further broken down into central cities and suburbs. In 1960 the population was evenly divided among central cities, metropolitan suburbs, and nonmetropolitan counties. As of 1970, in addition to the 15 percent in the largest cities over a million, another 14 percent lived in central cities of less than a million. Although a third of the population still lived in rural and nonmetropolitan counties, suburban metropolitan dwellers had outstripped the central cities, constituting about half of the metropolitan area population in 1960; by 1974 they were 57 percent of their areas and 36 percent of the population generally.[15]

The decade of the sixties saw very sizable growth of metropolitan area population, particularly suburban population. In the early seventies, growth rates reversed, and for the first time in American history nonmetropolitan growth exceeded metropolitan area growth.[16] Most of that shift was due to the decline in very large city populations, because the suburbs, although their *rate* of growth slowed considerably after 1970, continued to grow. The eight largest metropolitan areas have shown sharp declines in in-migration; three (San Francisco, Boston, and Washington) still maintained small net population balances, but the other five (New York, Los Angeles, Chicago, Philadelphia, and Detroit) actually lost population.[17]

Not only are people moving in greater numbers than before to rural and small city areas, they are moving south and southwest into the "sunbelt" states stretching across the country from California to Virginia. The cities of this region are the only metropolitan areas that gained substantially in population since 1970, and much of the growth in nonmetropolitan population is also taking place there. The sunbelt population increased by 60 percent between 1950 and 1975, in contrast to an increase of 32 percent in the rest of the country over the same period.[18]

A second important consideration has to do with the existence of any real cohesiveness within metropolitan areas. Although city planners have advocated cooperative metropolitan planning, and even the development of metropolitan governments since the thirties, they have made little headway against the resistance of the separate communities that make up SMSA's. The cities in the suburban rings value their autonomy and their identity, and in a number of the larger areas one can even begin to see a breakdown of the traditional dependence of the suburbs on the central city. Although the daily flow of people from the outer regions of the area into the city persists, in New York, for example, centers of industry and commerce are developing in the outer rings; and there is a very substantial movement from one part of the ring to another.

This overwhelming preference for the suburbs may well be a response in part to the massive migration of minority groups into the central city, a second key trend, to be discussed below. But it is probably a mistake to interpret it only as flight. People moving to the suburbs give many likely reasons for their shift: "better for the children," "less congested," "cleaner," "larger lot," "lower taxes," and other specific advantages; and indeed, Americans have been moving from city to suburb from the early days of the nineteenth century, and for the same reasons.

In general, Americans appear to have maintained their anti-city bias and preference for rural values through the decades of their migration to the city; they continue, as Elazar puts it, to try to transform urban life into one that conforms more closely to that of the rural past. They want space, grass, storage space, play freedom, and small schools for their children. And, despite the derision of the intellectuals for the suburban life style and the complaints of metropolitan planners about urban sprawl, Americans in increasing numbers choose the low-density suburban ring in preference to the central city. One of the most interesting single indicators of American values can be seen in the fact that the percentage of families living in owner-occupied houses has increased from 43 percent in 1940 to 62 percent in 1960, and is thus approaching the percentage of owner-occupied *farm* housing in 1900, which was 64 percent.[19] Only the escalating costs of single-family homes, as a result of the demand created by the now-grown members of the earlier baby boom, slowed the process in the late seventies.

It is also a mistake to regard the suburbs as homogeneously upper or upper-middle class. The stable working class are moving out of the central cities, as are the lower levels of the white collar population. The general public image of the prosperous suburbs, in contrast to the poverty-stricken central city, requires very considerable modification. In smaller SMSA's central cities are *more* prosperous than their suburbs. In the most recent period, about seven-and-a-half million whites left central cities for the suburbs (40 percent bound for the suburbs of central cities *other* than their own), but three-and-a-half million made a reverse move, into a central city, for a net loss of four million. The average income of the outward bounds was higher than those moving into the city, but the gap was not as much as one might expect: The average income of those moving out was $14,200, versus $12,900 for those moving in, resulting in a net loss of personal income for all cities of 11 percent. The occupational make-up of the central cities has not changed much; their proportion of college graduates and professionals, for example, has not changed. Ten percent of all city families, to be sure, are on public assistance rolls, in contrast to 4 percent of suburban families, but one-third of all such families in metropolitan areas generally are included in that 4 percent.[20] Even the affluent suburban counties around the major cities are beginning to feel the pressure of rising costs of social services for the poor.

The Black Migration

The complementary population movement that has done much to shape the current urban scene has been a migration to the cities of rural Southern blacks. During the earlier years of the century, the movement was a relatively modest one, averaging about 50,000 a year. During the forties, it leapt to 150,000 a year as unskilled blacks were drawn into the industrial activity created by World War II; the flow continued roughly at the same pace during the fifties and only slightly diminished during the sixties, when 1,380,000 blacks left the South.[21] Nearly half of this number moved into the Northeast, the remainder, in a fairly even split, into the far West and the Middle West (see Panel 5.2).[22]

PANEL 5.2   Recent Black Demographic Trends

The number of blacks living in suburbs has increased by about 550,000 since 1970 (a 18 percent increase), and there is evidence to suggest that the proportion of the metropolitan black population living in suburban areas has increased slightly, from about 21 percent to 23 percent. However, blacks represented only about 5 percent of the total suburban population at the National level in 1974, as in both 1960 and 1970.

The black population in cities increased by about 6 percent between 1970 and 1974, from 12.9 million to 13.7 million. With this increase and the concurrent decrease in white population, blacks represented about 22 percent of the population living in central cities in 1974, up from 20 percent in 1970. This proportion was higher in cities of the large SMSA's (about 27 percent) than in cities of smaller SMSA's (about 17 percent) in 1974.

(It should be noted that 81 percent of the population that is of Spanish origin now live in metropolitan areas, but are much less concentrated in the central cities—40 percent of those living in metropolitan areas are in the suburbs.)

The net growth of the Nation's white population in metropolitan areas has been confined to suburban areas; the white population of cities

declined by 5 percent between 1970 and 1974, while the suburban population increased by about 8 percent. In 1974, 62 percent of the white
metropolitan population lived outside central cities. The decrease in white
central city population and increase in suburban population occurred in
both SMSA's of 1 million or more and in those below 1 million population.

MIGRATION AND OPPORTUNITY

Despite the flood of books and articles in recent years deploring the environmental and social condition of the black ghettos in the urban North and
West, there is considerable evidence that migrants from the rural South have
as a group improved their condition and their opportunity by moving.

There is little question that the primary motivation for those large-scale
movements of people is economic. Bowles and other specialists in the field
argue that the value of expected future income in the location to which
people are moving provides the best measure of the benefits that draw them
to move in the first place.

> Although the vision of the Southern worker thumbing through his present value
> tables is the stock-in-trade of those skeptical of this approach to migration, the
> theory does not require such precise calculation on the part of individuals. In
> many race-age-schooling subgroups, those who move may expect to reap gains in
> lifetime income which constitute a sizeable fraction of what their total lifetime
> income would have been had they remained in the South. In the presence of
> these large potential gains, it is plausible to expect that rough information con-
> cerning the relevant benefits and costs would be widely available and under-
> stood by a significant portion of Southern workers.[23]

Bowles has shown that the effect of these expectations on the migration
rate depends on the level of schooling of those who are faced with the choice
to move North, and also that the greatest benefits accrue to younger workers
and to whites. Kaun's analysis of the patterns of Negro migration during
1955–1960 confirms Bowles' and others' findings; even if the "migration
process has improved the absolute levels of Negro incomes, other forces have
been at work which have worsened the relative incomes of Negro males" over
the period studied.[24]

One reason for this differential effect is that migration is not restricted to
a black South-to-North movement, but is typical of the society as a whole.[25]
About three-fifths of all adult men live in communities outside those in
which they were raised. Generally speaking, the more urban the community
of origin, the greater the chance for occupational success in the larger community; though rural migrants to large cities are better off than they would

have been if they had not moved, they are not as well off as the natives or those who come to the city from urban places.[26] Nor do recent migrants fare as well as those who are longer settled in the new city.

In an intensive study of a small group of Spanish-American rural migrants to Denver, Hansen and Simmons provide some understanding of the different experiences that migrating individuals may undergo.[27] The group had been in Denver for an average of five years when the study began. They found four subgroups within their sample:

Thrivers: those who were above the mean of the group in social and economic status at the time of arrival, and who maintained themselves without recourse to welfare help.
Stumblers: above the mean SES of the group, who had to avail themselves of welfare at some point in twelve months of the study.
Strugglers: those in the bottom half of the status range, who managed to stay off the welfare rolls during the twelve months of the study.
Losers: below the mean of the group in SES, who ended up receiving welfare help during the period of the study.

Hansen and Simmons found two variables that influence these different outcomes for groups that arrive with the same socioeconomic position. The most powerful of these is employment stability. Stable employment leads to a gradually rising standard of living, whatever the original status of the individual; unstable employment leads to an erratic income pattern, possibly to property repossessions and legal problems, and to a failure to achieve stable social relationships in the city.

Other influences are health and the migrant's family situation. Healthy single men, or heads of families in the early stage of family development—that is, with few children—are likely to thrive; those with poor health and large families are likely to need welfare assistance earlier and more extensively. It is logical that the former are likely to be the younger men. The worst outcomes can thus be predicted for older men of lowest socioeconomic status, in poor health and with large families.

THE LIBERAL CONSENSUS

It is difficult to read the popular press, and even some of the more serious journals, without a sense that there is nothing right with American cities, and that a dramatic urban crisis has for the past decade been bringing urban life to the brink of absolute disaster. Sharply rising crime rates, traffic congestion, deteriorated housing, failing schools, offensive architecture, pestilential pollution, undrinkable water, intolerable police oppression, violence amid public indifference, political corruption . . . The litany is so long and so piercing that one wonders how people can bear to live in such monstrosities.

The chorus of complaint makes it difficult for the historically minded to point out that in many respects American cities are better now than they were at the beginning of the century. Census reports over the century indicate a *decrease* in dilapidated and deteriorated housing; by 1980, most of it will be gone. Although some crime rates are up, not only is our crime record-keeping system better, but there also is a far greater proportion of young people, with whom higher crime rates are classically associated. The current outrage at the pollution of the automobile was probably equalled by the complaints about streets full of horse manure in New York in the early days of the century. Children are learning to read so much better than fifteen years ago that the Metropolitan Reading Test has to be restandardized every five years. Corruption on the part of police and politicians is an old story in this society, and few would assert that city government at least is not freer of corruption than it was in the late nineteenth century or the first half of the twentieth. Not only have central cities stopped growing, but they are growing less dense as neighborhoods change and expand, thinning out the most crowded areas of the poor. New York City's densest neighborhood has dropped from over 400,000 people per square mile in the 1880s to about 250,000 people per square mile today.

The sense of disaster arises partly because those who write about an urban crisis live and work in the largest cities, which have experienced the greatest amount of migration and where many of the pathologies listed are most visible. These cities also have the largest number of highly educated, upper-middle-class professionals who are "public regarding", and who set the tone of public discussions about what is socially desirable. The general tendency among this class to respond with intensity to a wide variety of causes and phenomena as if they were of equal importance often obscures what is going on. A general improvement in reading ability among children, for example, that leads to a redefinition of norms also results in a decline in reading scores among urban slum children, because the standards are higher (as happened in New York City in 1971). The cry inevitably goes up that the schools are getting worse, when what has actually occurred is an increase in the proportion of children who come from rural and impoverished backgrounds, and a change in the standards of measurement.

The genuine urban crisis has little to do with pollution, congestion, political corruption, or bad architecture, however offensive they may be to particular individuals; rather, it has to do with the powerful impact of the three-decade movement of millions of persons from one life context to another, bringing into collision a number of different life styles. When the mixture involves not only different backgrounds, but also racial differences that have troubled the society from its beginnings, the crisis becomes a super-crisis.

James Wilson has suggested that in a fundamental sense this mixture results in a lack of "sense of community."[28] The deepest concern of the ordinary urban citizen, as it emerges in poll after poll, is not with conventional urban problems—housing, transportation, pollution, and the like; a recent survey conducted by Wilson in Boston showed these to be significant problems for only 18 percent of those responding, a group that was disproportionately affluent and better educated. Only 9 percent mentioned jobs and employment. "The issue which concerned more respondents than any other was variously stated—crime, violence, rebellious youth, racial tension, public immorality, delinquency. However stated, the common theme seemed to be a concern for improper behavior in public places."[29]

This perhaps was an expression among some white respondents of covert antiblack feelings; but the same feelings were expressed by blacks as well as whites, and by those who, in answer to another question, expressed the most willingness for the government to do more to help blacks. In Wilson's view, what these concerns have in common is a sense of *failure of community*. By this, he does not mean a longing to return to the intimacies of the small community or a need for identification with a supraindividual entity, but "a desire for the observance of standards of right and seemly conduct in the public places in which one lives and moves, those standards to be consistent with—and supportive of—the values and life styles of the particular individual."[30]

The rational concern for community, as Wilson defines it, is often attacked as conformity or an expression of prejudice or an overconcern for the trivialties of appearance. But, argues Wilson, the purpose of social sanctions on public conduct, from the most informal frown of disapproval to the official complaint to the police, is to handle what economists call "third party effect," the external and public consequences of private behavior:

> I may wish to let my lawns go to pot, but one ugly lawn affects the appearance of the whole neighborhood, just as one sooty incinerator smudges clothes that others have hung out to dry. Rowdy children raise the noise level and tramp down the flowers for everyone, not just for their parents.[31]

This is why people prefer to live in homogeneous neighborhoods; they can expect less deviation from common standards of conduct. An unfortunate result of this desire for community is that people are likely to assume different standards of conduct on the basis of purely external differences of skin color or accent. However undesirable, such assumptions change only very slowly, and the feelings behind them cannot be wished away. Antidiscrimination laws in housing are necessary and desirable, but they are unlikely to control feelings.

The preference for community, Wilson points out, is at odds with the idea of cosmopolitanism that requires the existence of diversity within the city. But only a minority really wants that in a city—intellectuals, the young unmarrieds who have come to the city for excitement, and dropouts from society. It is a grave error, Wilson warns, to mistake the preference of the few for the needs of the many. Nor does this emphasis on the sense of community necessarily imply a defense of "middle-class values." The process is the same, whatever the neighborhood, to enforce any set of values.

> To be sure, we most often observe it enforcing the injunctions against noisy children and lawns infested with crabgrass, but I suppose it could also be used to enforce injunctions against turning children into "sissies" and being enslaved by lawn-maintenance chores. In fact, if we turn our attention to the city . . . we will find many kinds of neighborhoods with a great variety of substantive values being enforced.[32]

"Increasingly," says Wilson, "the central city is becoming made up of persons who face special disabilities in creating and maintaining a sense of community."[33] These are affluent whites without children who can at least isolate themselves in high-rise apartments; poor whites, economically unable or unwilling to leave their old neighborhood when it undergoes a change; blacks, whose segregation by color in enclaves of the central city means that various class levels among them have no spatial separation.

It is particularly in these segregated areas that the unease is greatest, because it is most difficult there to maintain different communal life styles. In such areas, the breakdown of community controls leads inevitably to a demand for more direct external controls. Thus, one even finds ghetto schools under police control at times. But the police remain largely ineffective; it is simply not feasible for them to control all conduct in public places; and disorder often arises out of disputes *among* neighborhood residents over what ought to be standards of proper conduct. Until what hour of the night, for example, should one be permitted to sit on the steps playing a guitar and singing?

As Wilson points out, the problem is likely to grow rather than recede. Efforts to eliminate poverty in the city may only increase the flow of rural migrants to the city as the advantages of migration are increased, and make it more difficult to maintain a sense of community. From this point of view, the black-and-white confrontation in the city is only one aspect of a greater problem that has to do with class more than color, and that will continue to afflict the schools of the central city after the present crisis passes.

EXPLANATIONS AND SOLUTIONS

The most radical approach to the urban crisis as defined here has been developed by the black nationalist movement. In this view, the major explanation of the plight of the inner city black, and of the consequent problems of the metropolitan areas, is the black's lack of power and control over his own life. The solution proposed is to turn over the management of inner city ghettos to the blacks themselves, and to build the economics of those areas to the point where they are self-sustaining and can offer adequate employment opportunity to their own citizens. We will deal with the proposal for community control in Chapter 14 at some length; here it is necessary to note only that although there is some sympathy for it in the federal bureaucracy, the financial basis for any massive testing of the proposal has yet to emerge.

The Liberal Consensus

The dominant view on the urban crisis, and one that has almost achieved consensus among the liberal intellectuals of the universities and in government, can be found in detail in almost any of the federal commission reports that have examined urban problems over the past decade.[34] Its apocalyptic vision of the future of American cities was spelled out most clearly by the National Commission on the Causes and Prevention of Violence in the late sixties:[35]

Central business districts, partially protected during daylight by the presence of large numbers of people, will be deserted at night save for police patrols.

High rise apartment buildings and residential compounds will be protected by private guards and "will be fortified cells for upper-middle and high income populations living at prime locations in the city."

Suburban neighborhoods will be protected by distance and by the economic homogeneity of their populations; ownership of guns will become universal, as will window grills and surveillance devices; in neighborhoods closer to the central city armed citizens in cars will patrol the area, with extreme left and right wing groups accumulating arsenals of weapons.

Armed guards will "ride shotgun" on all forms of public transportation and taxicabs as well as private vehicles will be equipped with light armor and other security devices.

Streets in residential areas will be unsafe to different degrees and ghetto neighborhoods will be "places of terror with widespread crime, perhaps entirely out of police control during nighttime hours."

Between the unsafe, deteriorating central city on the one hand, and the network of safe, prosperous areas and sanitized corridors on the other, there will be, not unnaturally, "intensifying hatred and deepening division."

In this view of increasing polarization between black cities and white suburbs, a number of major problem areas may be isolated:

1. *Job separation.* In many of the largest cities, the dynamics of growth results in a situation in which a large proportion of newly created jobs are in suburban areas, separated by many miles and bad transportation from those who need them and who live in the inner city. In part, this results from a shift in industrial technology toward horizontal designs

that require a great deal of land, and which are consequently too expensive to use in central cities; in part, it stems from the desire to follow the stream of the more sophisticated labor supply—the technicians and the professionals—to the suburbs. The question of whether to invest economically in the ghettos, to create jobs for people where they are, or to put social energy into moving people out to live where the jobs exist is one of the more furious current debates.

There are encouraging movements, particularly in the black ghettos of some of the larger cities, toward self-help programs of many kinds; Jesse Jackson's Operation PUSH in the midwest and Leon Sullivan's Opportunities Industrialization Centers are examples. Such admirable efforts deserve more support than they often get, but their impact is likely to be felt in the long run rather than the short.

2. *Housing.*   Involved in the debate is the general crisis in housing in the inner cities. Despite an apparent shortage of housing for the poor in the large cities, both private and federally financed housing is disappearing. The private housing loss seems to proceed in a standard way. The owner of an apartment building in the slums finds it more expensive to maintain the property in the face of rising vandalism and costs. Often, at the instigation of the tenants, he is sued by the city for failure to maintain the building; and to get out of the financial squeeze, he abandons the building. The tenants also slowly abandon it, and often a mysterious fire breaks out that destroys it. The bitter debates over this process involve largely unanswerable questions: whether lower class tenants are that destructive, whether the landlord has taken some form of super profit from the building before the process begins, and whether the fires are set by landlords for insurance or vandals for fun.

Much the same process has, in fact, occurred with public housing; this suggests that in addition to the war between landlords and tenants, there is another one going on between the working poor and the troubled families of the lower-lower class. Some federally supported projects have actually been abandoned, and stand as empty shells. Because of the tax shelter offered to investors in subsidized housing, until recently there was considerable capital available for it. Now, investors have become cautious; and the indications are that most such capital is going to construct housing outside the central cities, where it tends to benefit the blue-collar families rather than the very poor of the inner city.[36] If the trend continues, the inner city ghettos are likely to move further toward blight and abandonment.

3. *The Fiscal Crisis.*   In March of 1975 the Ford administration had concluded that the "urban crisis" was over, to a chorus of anguished howls of protest from city officials around the country.[37] Later that year New York City awoke to the fact that it was so deeply in debt that it could no longer sell its municipal bonds on the open market; its cliff-hanging effort to stave off bankruptcy dramatized the claim of the liberal consensus that the urban malaise ran deep.

New York's insolvency, it was argued, resulted from its humanitarian concern for the poor and for struggling ethnic groups. No other large city had to contribute as much to welfare payments, none supported a municipal hospital system of such size, a free-tuition university with open admissions, a widespread day-care center program, and other services. Moreover, as in the case of central cities generally, the movement of affluent whites to the suburbs has decreased the tax potential, and the larger proportion of needy families in the city has forced the hiring of greater numbers of civil servants during a period when municipal salaries are dramatically increasing.

The costs associated with this "politics of compassion," it is further argued, should be borne by the federal and state governments because the low income population requiring such services are in the city as part of large-scale national movements not under the city's control.

In the short-term, then, the Consensus solution is for the federal assumption of central city burdens. In the long range, since the diagnosis lays the blame for the urban crisis on white racism that has blocked access to opportunity for blacks and penned them into inner city ghettos, the suggested solution is to desegregate the suburbs, thereby breaking up the handicapping ghetto culture and finding a place for black workers to live where they will be close to jobs.

The argument is typically made in these terms by Davidoff and others:[38] The major device the suburbs use to exclude blacks is the zoning ordinance. So long as local ordinances decree that houses cannot be built on less than a certain amount of land (often one acre) "almost all blacks will be excluded from such zones."[39] So long as these zoning practices continue, the pressure of educational costs tends to maintain them, since real property taxes support suburban schools. If housing is built within the reach of low or modest income families, the taxes from that property will not be enough to meet the additional costs to the community for educating the children of those families. Furthermore, because working-class families now find it difficult to buy houses in the suburbs, the traditional "trickle down" process by which the city housing they leave becomes available to poorer families no longer operates.

Opening up the suburbs by eliminating zoning codes, the argument runs, would:

create a housing boom that would benefit the economy generally.
bring ghetto workers together with available jobs.
reduce race and class tensions by bringing people together.

Davidoff suggests not only that legislative and court action is necessary to declare zoning codes illegal, but also that no business or industry be permitted to move to suburbs where the housing market is closed to families earning what the workers in that company earn. He also calls for a restructuring of tax laws to make school costs a responsibility of the state, in order to relieve local communities of a burden that maintains high housing costs.

Critiques of the "Urban Crisis"

Responses to the liberal consensus have varied from a conservative rejection of the entire thesis to the inability of some liberals to believe in the glowing promise of some of the solutions. In the absence of any general opposing view, we can only discuss piecemeal some of the critical responses.

In Banfield's view, one that is shared by a minority of social scientists, the roots of the urban crisis lie not in white racism or oppression, but in the sharp rise in expectations among large groups of people to new levels that are unlikely to be met in reality.[40] Thus, so long as poverty is defined relatively—the lower fifth, or third, or whatever percentage one wishes to use—some people will feel poor, no matter how much better off everyone is. If police brutality is defined as hitting people with nightsticks, it has almost vanished; but if we give it the more recent definition of speaking slightingly or condescendingly to citizens, it is a matter of changed standards rather than worse behavior. At the turn of the century, when a majority of pupils failed to finish high school, there was no dropout problem. It was not until the sixties, when the majority of young people were graduating from high school, that it became an acute problem; at the same time, the dropout rate was continuing to decline.

> To a large extent, then, our urban problems are like the mechanical rabbit at the racetrack, which is set to keep just ahead of the dogs no matter how fast they may run. Our performance is better and better, but because we set our standards and expectations to keep ahead of performance, the problems are never any nearer to solution. Indeed, if standards and expectations rise *faster* than performance, the problems may get (relatively) worse as they get (absolutely) better.[41]

Kristol has noted that the end result of this process is to make people deeply unsatisfied with modest, realizable social gains.[42] We can thus, the argument runs, actually create a crisis, where no real crisis may exist, by the pressure of unrealizable expectations.

Why are the cities in such desperate financial straits? Partly, Banfield answers, because there are two kinds of urban problems—a normal-class and a lower-class form (*see* Chapter 3 for his definition of lower class). In its normal form, the unemployment problem usually consists of the presence of younger workers on the labor market who make a number of tries before finding a suitable job. In its lower-class form, it consists of people who prefer the "action" of the street to any stable job. So it is with poverty, housing, schools, crime, and the other urban problems. The costs associated with the small population Banfield calls lower class take an inordinate proportion of the whole: a Minneapolis survey showed that 5 to 10 percent of the population gets well over 50 percent of such services as social work, police, welfare, etc. A Philadelphia study found that in a sample of 10,000 boys, 6 percent accounted for 53 percent of the police contacts for personal attacks and 71 percent of the contacts for robberies.[43]

But, New York, which has suffered the most dramatic fiscal crisis, is hardly unique in its possession of a large proportion of lower class among its citizens. According to a Brookings Institution study, nine other cities are worse off than New York when large central cities are compared with their suburbs on unemployment, dependency rates, low degree of education, income level, crowded housing, and poverty.[44] It has been plausibly suggested that the problem of that particular great city lies not only in its readiness to indulge in questionable fiscal manipulation rather than face up to deficits but to its inability to resist the demands of its unions; the difficulty is not a lower-class "giveaway" but a middle-class one.[45]

The more general issue for urban policy continues to be debated: Is New York simply the tip of the iceberg, the dramatic example of a widespread urban malaise requiring far-reaching and radical change in central city–suburban relationships? A conference of mayors in 1976 contended that it was:

> The financial plight of city government is national in scope. It includes small and large cities as well as central, suburban, and Sunbelt region cities . . . For the first time, cities across the nation of every size and representing every geographical area, including the Sunbelt, are being forced to review budgets and financial positions to determine if they have sufficient revenues to avoid financial crisis.[46]

Such an urgent sense of financial stringency may simply have been the result of a deep national recession from which the country was emerging as the mayors met. A different and somewhat contradictory view of the situation is provided by some experts, such as Richard Nathan of Brookings, who points out that some central cities are better off than their suburbs, that some are on an economic upswing as the recession lightens, and that a majority of urban people live in small communities that are very different from New York.[47] A policy that will help one city, he points out, may do little for another one, and concludes:

> It may belabor the obvious, but it must be stated that there can be no single solution for what above all is no single problem. If something we should label the "urban crisis" exists today, it is highly differentiated.[48]

The Liberal Consensus solution of "opening up the suburbs" is thus regarded with some sense of dubiousness by moderates and conservatives, though it continues to be the favored policy of many urban planners and ethnic leaders. The arguments against strongly pursuing such a policy may be summarized as follows:

1.   Black suburban population is increasingly naturally and at a greater rate than is ordinarily perceived. Although, as earlier noted, the proportion of blacks in suburban rings held steady from 1960 to 1970, that was during the period of the largest increase in white suburbanization; from 1970 to 1974, black suburbanites increased at a greater rate than white.[49] In nine of the twelve metropolitan areas with the largest black population, the rate of black growth was greater in the suburbs than in the central cities. Nor were these new black suburban dwellers merely an extension of the city ghettos; they have higher incomes and better occupations.[50]

2.   In the central cities themselves, increasing proportions of black populations do not necessarily indicate increasing poverty—they are not becoming more lower class at the same rate as they are becoming more black.[51] As Wilfred Marston has shown, there is very considerable social class differentiation in black areas in American cities,[52] and Robert Jiobu and Harvey Marshall's calculations indicate that "ghettoization" is not an important variable in explaining income differences of metropolitan blacks and whites.[53] Indexes of residential segregation in American cities, furthermore, after rising for a decade between 1940 and 1950 are finally showing a decline: from 83.6 to 74.3 in Northeast cities from 1950–1970, from 83.0 to 67.9 in the West, for example.[54] (An index of segregation may be interpreted as the percentage of either of two populations that would have to change residence in order to achieve zero segregation.) Somewhat less, but significant, drops have occurred in the North Central and Southern cities.

3.   Glazer suggests that the positive benefits to be derived from the policy are uncertain. Higher levels of educational achievement may result, but there is very little hard data supporting the view (see Chapter 9 for the evidence). The effect on black political power would surely be negative, since it has so far depended on population concentration in the inner cities. An improvement in social relations is likely, but opening up the suburbs entails meeting very great resistance, and the management of integration to achieve positive results while avoiding negative ones would be very difficult. Even some urban planners are now beginning to see that social costs are involved in mixing social classes as well as races.

4.   The job-separation thesis, arguing that the increase of jobs in suburban areas leads to cutting off opportunity for blacks in the central cities, has been seriously weakened. Bennett Harrison concludes from a Brookings study that there is no evidence of a job mismatch between cities and suburbs in recent years;[55] Glazer points out that the increase in suburban jobs and shrinkage in central jobs was based on pre-1963 data which does not seem to be supported after that year. Nor does it take into account the massive growth in government employment in recent years.

5.   Attacks on suburban zoning laws must be made in the name of the poor since the establishment of racial categories has generally been found unconstitutional. The black middle class itself is often found on the side

of the whites in battles to restrict the development of subsidized housing for low-income groups in the suburbs.

Voluntary action, Glazer concludes in his review of the issue, is slowly bringing us to a more integrated society and better integrated suburbs.

> The black middle class and the black worker do not need any special help from government, aside from the strict enforcement of the laws against discrimination; these groups have made substantial progress and are steadily making more. There should be no problem for other Americans in fully accepting them as neighbors and accepting their children in schools, and if there is, the full force of the law must be brought into play to replace prejudice and silliness with reason.[56]

It is the large, depressed section of the black city population that constitutes the problem, Glazer argues.

> As long as this other problem exists, as long as it holds the key place in public consciousness that it does, as long as it continues to make the central city dangerous and unpleasant, and to many, immoral to boot, I do not see how we can expect anything but resistance—from blacks and whites—to the overruling of local governmental powers in order to open up the suburbs.[59]

THE URBAN SCHOOLS

The combined forces of in-migration, diffusion of whites toward the metropolitan periphery, and the inclination of white middle and working class to send their children to private schools have resulted in an increasing proportion of black and minority group children in the public schools. Washington, D.C., schools now have better than 90 percent black children; black and Puerto Rican children make up about 60 percent of New York schools; blacks constitute a majority in the schools of over twenty of the larger cities, including Newark, New Orleans, Philadelphia, Chicago, and Oakland.

It is generally supposed that schools in low-income areas of the cities are much inferior in facilities to schools in better neighborhoods; indeed, this is one of the complaints of the national civil rights movement. As Chapter 13 will show, minority group status *does* make a difference in the quality of school facilities available to children, though not consistently so. For economic status, independent of race or nationality, the conclusion is by no means so clear, and is, indeed, contradictory, as an analysis of Project Talent data indicates.[58]

Thus, the urban northeast is the only urbanized area in the country in which per-pupil expenditures are less for low-income students than for others; excluding the largest cities, there was a $100 per year difference.

In the other regions of the country the difference was no larger than $33 at the time the study was done. Even in the northeast, in cities over 250,000 population, the difference in per-pupil expenditures between income groups is a matter of only a few dollars.

There is a difference in the very largest cities of the country in the age of school buildings; low-income schools in New York, Los Angeles, Chicago, Philadelphia, and Detroit are distinctly older than schools in higher income areas; in fact, they are almost twice as old. But, aside from these large cities, in the urban northeast, urban southeast, and urban west, lower income school buildings are newer; and in moderate-sized cities throughout (from one-fourth to one-half million population), the average age of buildings is identical. Furthermore, in all areas, low-income students are *less* likely to be on double schedules than are higher income students; and average class sizes are approximately the same.

The assumption that low-income city children have less experienced teachers, however, seems to be true. Although average teacher experience is about the same for all income groups in small and medium-sized cities, the larger the city, the greater the disparity. In medium-large cities, higher-income pupils have teachers with an average of thirteen years experience, against ten years for lower income students. In the largest cities, the figures are thirteen and six years respectively. The urban teacher career patterns that account for these differences will be explored in Chapter 12.

There is no question, moreover, of the contrast in achievement in basic skills between middle- and lower class children, *both* black and white. Figure 5.1 shows a map of Detroit that dramatizes the usual case as one compares academic test scores in the socioeconomic pattern of the city's population. Similar differences by race in Chicago schools are somewhat larger: Sixth grade achievement scores in schools that are 100 percent black are about 5.5, as against an average of 7.2 for schools entirely white.[59] In New York City, the gap between schools in Central Harlem and the rest of the city by the sixth grade is about the same—two full grades.

National Assessment for Educational Progress data not only provides a broader national picture of these differences, but one from a different perspective since it is based on criterion-referenced tests of knowledge and skill. Table 5.1 summarizes testing from 1969–1973 for different types of communities. Medium and large central city scores, as it shows, are quite close to national medians and not very different from the urban fringe generally. The very sizable differences are for inner city pupils and those in the most affluent suburbs.

One feature of the inner city school has to do with a kind of mobility not yet mentioned; unlike in-migrant movements into the city and the movement from the central city to the suburbs, very little is known about the large amount of moving that goes on within the city itself. But school administrators and teachers are sharply aware of its effects; teachers in some schools end the year with very few of the pupils with whom they began

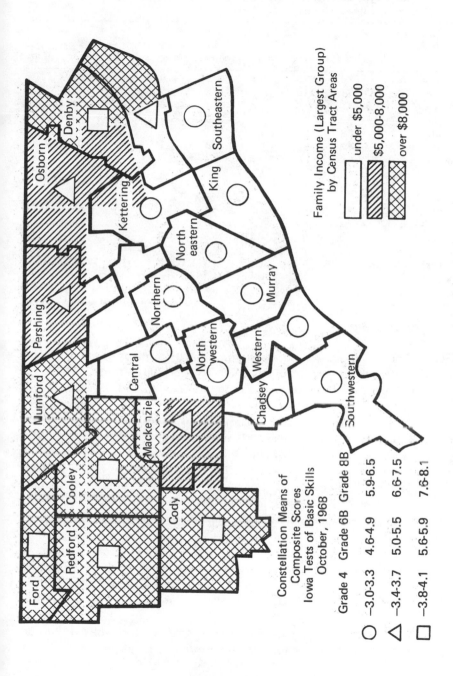

Fig. 5.1 Academic Achievement and Family Income in Detroit

Table 5.1   National Assessment of Educational Progress for Ages 9 and 13, and by Type of Community, 1969–1973 (expressed as differences from the national median)

	Science	Writing	Citizen-ship	Reading	Litera-ture	Mus.	Soc. St.	Math
				Age 9				
National Median	63.2	28.3	64.1	70.4	43.9	58.8	72.2	36.7
Inner City	− 15.1	− 14.2	− 5.7	− 14.3	− 9.4	− 8.8	− 11.1	− 10.8
Extreme Rural	− 6.3	− 4.6	− 3.3	− 4.4	− 3.6	− 2.7	− 2.8	− 3.6
Small place	0.9	− 0.6	0.0	− 0.6	0.3	0.1	0.5	− 0.5
Medium City	0.8	2.1	1.4	0.1	− 1.2	0.5	0.2	0.8
Main Big City	− 2.7	− 2.9	− 0.3	1.4	− 0.5	0.0	− 0.2	− 0.9
Urban fringe	2.6	2.4	0.4	2.1	2.4	0.3	0.6	2.4
Affluent suburbs	7.2	5.8	3.4	8.4	7.5	5.5	6.7	8.1
				Age 13				
Inner City	− 13.7	− 10.5	− 6.0	− 8.1	− 5.4	− 4.5	− 8.7	− 14.9
Extreme Rural	− 6.2	− 6.3	− 4.3	− 3.9	− 3.1	− 1.4	− 2.6	− 2.1
Small place	0.5	− 0.7	− 0.3	− 0.5	− 0.6	0.1	− 0.5	− 0.1
Medium City	1.9	1.8	1.0	0.4	0.0	0.3	0.5	0.5
Main Big City	− 3.9	− 0.4	0.0	− 1.3	− 0.8	− 1.0	− 0.2	− 1.0
Urban fringe	2.8	1.8	0.8	2.2	1.3	0.0	0.7	1.5
Affluent suburbs	6.2	7.5	4.3	5.6	5.5	3.4	7.3	10.2

Source: Digest of Educational Statistics, *U.S. Department of Health, Education, and Welfare, 1975, pp. 188 and 189.*

in September. In the largest cities, the amount of pupil transiency can be shockingly high, mounting in some schools to over 100 percent.

Moving frequently from one school to another should logically affect children's school achievement negatively; but it seems, oddly, to do so only for lower income children. Numerous studies of transiency in populations that are middle class, or where class was not isolated as a variable for study, show that there seem to be no ill effects from a greater number of moves.[60] But within the city, a high level of transiency obviously has a quite different meaning than it has normally, as is noted by the results of Justman's examination of reading test scores of pupils in New York who had been admitted to more than one school in the city during their elementary-school career:[61]

at the third grade there is a gap in word knowledge scores between pupils who had attended only one school and those who attended four schools of one grade, an average of 3.7 for the first group, 2.7 for the second group.

by the sixth grade the gap had reached two grades, scores of 6.4 for the one-admission children, 4.6 for the four-admission children.

The effects of in-migration itself from both the rural South and from Puerto Rico are evident from another New York study.[62] Not only do in-migrant children achieve at lower levels than New York-born children in the same schools (a reasonable prediction considering the quality of the schooling which they or their parents experienced earlier), but New York-born children tend to do less well in schools that are heavily saturated with in-migrants. Several probable explanations may be suggested for this finding. First, the most heavily in-migrant schools are in the worst part of the ghetto, what one urban study called "The Crisis Ghetto"; and the New York-born children in these neighborhoods are thus among the most deeply disadvantaged of their group. Second, it is equally plausible that schools with high proportions of in-migrant children are so loaded with problems and pressures that the school itself is disorganized and unable to cope with them.

The probability of the latter explanation is heightened by the descriptive materials available about these schools in the inner city. For the statistics of achievement level and saturation do nothing to convey the real crisis in human relationships one sometimes finds there: an atmosphere made up of despair, hostility, exhaustion, counteraccusation, misunderstanding, and mutual aggression. In the high schools particularly, there has been an eruption in recent years of a considerable amount of disruption and violence (see Panel 5.3).

PANEL 5.3   Violence in the Urban Schools

The first period of disruptiveness, during the late sixties and early seventies, appears to have been associated with the national wave of student activism in the universities and involved strong elements of politics and civil rights protest. Stephen Bailey's study[63] of that period surveyed twenty-seven high schools in nineteen cities, focusing on the 1968–69 school year. In that year, 10 percent of the principals reported disturbances, which is probably a good estimate of the total rate nationwide. At about the same time, a subcommittee of the House of Representatives surveyed 29,000 high schools; and among its 50 percent reply, it found 18 percent reporting serious protests. Since the principals experiencing disturbances had the greatest motivation to respond, an overall 10–15 percent rate among high schools generally is probably close to accurate.

Major issues occasioning protest were disciplinary rules, dress codes, school services and facilities, and curriculum policy.
In the larger schools (over 1000 students) race was a factor in more than half of the disturbances, in only a third of them in the smaller schools.

There was a somewhat higher probability for disturbances to occur in
schools experiencing a significant increase in minority group enrollment during the preceding five years, but that factor was clearly not
the only or major cause.

The size of the student body is a more important factor in disturbance
rate than the size of the city.

Integration is positively correlated with disturbance—all-black or all-
white schools are less likely to be disrupted.

A higher proportion of black staff in integrated schools with many black
students is associated with a *lower* rate of disturbance; integrated
schools with predominantly white staffs are more likely to be disrupted.

Disruption and daily attendance are related; where average daily attendance is lower, disruption is higher.

Bailey points to a bewildering variety of causes for this upsurge
in disruption and violence, which in some instances has forced schools
to close their doors for varying periods of time. He cites a general climate
of violence in the society, reinforced by the ready availability of its
images on television; the success of civil rights protests, as well as the
high visibility and apparent success of the college protests of the period
from 1968–1970; an emphasis on racial pride and the formulation of militant groups as expressions of it; the rhetoric of "participatory democracy" used in many government programs for the poor and minorities
and now common in low-income communities; white and black racism,
compounded by motives of black revenge and slum life styles; and "situation ethics," the doctrine that you might as well live it up today because
"you might get your head busted by the pigs tomorrow," or "you might
get drafted the minute you walk out the door." To these social influences,
Bailey adds a number of in-school causes: social codes and other types
of restrictions that in a permissive age frustrate and irritate the young.

By the middle of the seventies the high school troubles appeared to
have shifted into a second phase, one emphasizing vandalism and crime.
It is difficult to tell whether the actual events shifted in character, or
whether peoples' interpretations changed. A Congressional study indicated that school crime in various categories had increased from 200 to
7000 percent from 1964–1968, a period just preceding Bailey's study in
which he cited only poverty and historical injustice as the root of the
problem. In any event, school violence, including violence against teachers and administrators, continued to grow. New York schools reported
333 incidents of school violence in 1970, 580 in 1971, involving robberies,
muggings, attacks on teachers, and gang fights. It is estimated that only
30 to 60 percent of actual incidents are reported.[64]

Jeremiah McKenna reports that in that city during the three years
from 1970 to 1972 the number of felony arrests each year of school-age
population represents about 5 percent of junior and senior high-school

students.[65] Since almost all these juvenile rapists, robbers, burglars and drug offenders have been released back to the school, he calculates that in some schools as many as 15 percent of the student body may already have been arrested for serious crime.

There is little agreement on the solutions for this growing problem. The immediate answer is an increase in school security forces, which the strained budgets of urban school systems can ill afford. The policy of expelling the most disruptive and violent of the students involved is severely constrained by the courts, who now require strict due process standards even for suspensions. A vigorous, national child advocacy movement maintains a constant pressure on both family courts and the schools that, however well-intentioned its efforts, keeps most disruptive children in the schools and a constant stream of others moving back into them from the family courts.

In the midst of all the turmoil and in the face of the impression one gets from the popular media that all high schools are in varying states of disruption and most youths are antiestablishment, it must be noted that only a small minority of youth are involved in either criminal activity or activist disaffection. A Louis Harris study of a cross-section of youth between 15 and 21 in 1970 at the height of youth unrest reported:[66]

Eighty-one percent felt their upbringing had been just right, 73 percent agreed with their parents' values, 66 percent reported no trouble in communicating with their parents and most of those who did thought the trouble at least partially their own fault.

Ninety percent reported that their life has been happy so far, and 93 percent expect their future to be as happy or happier.

Eighty-four percent expressed satisfaction with their education so far; only 17 percent had fathers who graduated from college in contrast with 66 percent of those under 18 who expressed an intention to go to college.

Only 22 percent had great confidence in the government to solve the problems of the 70s, but an additional 54 percent had some confidence and only 22 percent expressed "hardly any confidence."

Religion is important to 77 percent of the sample. Ninety-six percent thought that sexual fidelity is important to marriage and a plurality voted against "sex for its own sake," though the sample split more or less evenly on the issues of abortion and pre-marital virginity.

Ninety percent favored penalizing polluters, and 70 percent declared they would not work for a company that did pollute; 58 percent favored

requiring the hiring of minorities, but a majority opposed an annual guaranteed income and school busing.
Fifty-nine percent identified themselves as conservative or middle-of-the-road, only 5 percent as radical.

College students on almost every issue are more skeptical and progressive than those in high school, but even that elite group is hardly revolutionary.

EQUALIZATION OF METROPOLITAN SCHOOL FINANCING

There are two general approaches to the school problems of the central city. One is to generate an enormous range of proposals and programs to improve their performance directly. These will be considered in detail in the second part of this book. The second approach can be dealt with appropriately here in the context of our examination of metropolitan areas and their problems.

Concern for metropolitan growth and its effect on the uneven development of school systems began at least as early as the forties among educators. The concern has focused on two major issues: the disparity in local financial resources available for schooling as affluent members of the area moved to the suburbs, taking with them a major source of tax revenue for schools; and the uneven distribution of educational needs, with growing numbers of educationally disadvantaged children concentrated in the central city, requiring greater than average educational efforts—efforts that central city governments do not have the tax resources to finance. What revenues they do command, furthermore, are increasingly subject to competition from other sectors of city service, such as welfare and the police.

The present crisis in school financing consists of a number of interlocking elements. Over half of school revenues are derived from the states, about 40 percent from the local communities, and an increasing, but still small, 7 percent from the federal government. The local share is most commonly generated from property taxes which, since real property does not expand (though its value slowly rises), provide a relatively inflexible base. Meanwhile, school costs are sharply increasing, keeping pace with rising construction costs and teachers' salaries; as a result, a number of cities as well as suburban communities have been the scene of taxpayer revolts. Since votes on school budgets are in most places conducted as a separate referendum (the only governmental cost so treated), citizens can vote down increases in school budgets, and have regularly been doing so. More than one city in the past few years has been forced to close its schools for a time while the board rewrote its rejected budget and submitted it anew to the voters.

One way out of the difficulty is to turn to the federal government. Though it is probable that federal contributions to the cost of education will continue to increase, it is not very likely that Congress will soon agree to the demands of some that it take over the entire burden of school costs. In the meantime, there has been a great deal of pressure exerted to distribute the federal share more equitably between the central city, the suburbs, and the rural areas.

The problem is a far larger one than the disparities between the central cities versus the suburbs. Although districts with the highest level of expenditure per pupil tend to be found in the wealthy suburbs, central cities are generally above statewide average in expenditures, generally exceeding by a slight amount the average district in their suburbs.[67] Thus, in 1970 to 1971 the per-pupil expenditure of central cities averaged $851 versus $836 for the suburbs and $702 for the nonmetropolitan areas.[68] It is nevertheless argued that the cities have far more sizable problems and should be spending more.

The most recent emphasis has been to attack the problem at the *state* level. The average per-pupil expenditure for the nation in 1974 to 1975 (including all public costs) was $1431, but the states varied widely around that mean, from $921 for Mississippi to $2241 for New York.[69] If each state's expenditure is stated as a percent of its personal income, however, the variations are substantially reduced, from about 5.4 percent to 6.3 percent. There is little support for the gigantic task of equalizing such differences nationally, but the seventies has witnessed a widespread effort to reduce the disparities between school districts within each state.

The movement began with an influential state court decision, California's Supreme Court ruling in *Serrano versus Priest*.[70] In a class action complaint the plaintiffs argued that their schools provided less money per pupil than wealthier districts that were able to raise higher taxes because of the value of their property. The court responded by ruling that education was a fundamental right under both the state and federal constitutions and must be distributed equally. The quality of education must not be a function of wealth, said the justices, but they permitted the state legislature to take any road it chose toward equalization. They did not rule out the property tax, nor the imposition of uniform spending by the legislature on the various districts, though they did not require it. (In a later decision the court finally did forbid the use of the property tax as the basis for school funding.)

What the court proposed was that each district decide on a level of spending for its schools, thus indicating its level of educational ambitions. The budget would then trigger a tax on local wealth, the same tax for each district that chose a particular level. Thus, if a central city district and a wealthy suburb each decided on $1500 per pupil, they would each impose a property tax of the same rate. If, in the case of the poorer district, the tax failed to raise the necessary amount, the state would make up the difference.

If the tax brought in a surplus above the budget, it would be redistributed to the poorer districts. All districts choosing the same tax rate would spend at the same level. So the higher property values of the more affluent suburbs would not permit them to raise more money for schools than was available for those districts whose property values did not permit setting a similar budget.

The *Serrano* decision led to a spate of such actions in many other states, and one of these, *Rodriguez versus San Antonio School District* finally reached the Supreme Court in 1973.[71] That court declared that education was not a fundamental right under the U.S. Constitution and consequently there were no constitutional grounds for equality of expenditure. It observed, however, that there were inequities within the states and these should be eliminated by state governments and courts.

Although *Rodriguez* slowed the pace of school equalization action, it by no means stopped it. Shortly after the *Serrano* decision almost a hundred separate commissions were set up in the various states to study school financing, and by 1975 a considerable amount of state legislation had been enacted. The trends, as reported by Robert Wynkoop, are:[72]

1.   A major principle adopted from *Serrano* is that of "fiscal neutrality," that is, equal availability of taxable resources per pupil. In twelve states an assumption of a greater portion of school expenditure by the state has led to more equal allocation; for example, Colorado, under its new law, assumed 51 percent of school costs, over a previous 31 percent. Some of the states have passed provisions allowing districts to choose their own level of expenditure, then make up the shortfall from the tax levy with state funds (District Power Equalization).

2.   A second common emphasis is to permit variations in expenditure per pupil due to concentrations of children with special needs. Most states taking this approach accomplish the aim by setting up weighted per-pupil formulas; Florida includes a provision for cost-of-living differences among school districts.

3.   All the states that have enacted reform place a ceiling on either the tax rates or the revenue which districts are permitted to impose or collect. This is presumably aimed at limiting the power of wealthy districts to get too far out of line, but since most such clauses permit the local voters to override the limitation, Wynkoop doubts their effectiveness.

4.   The general trend is ultimately toward full state funding of education, but the first round of reform has taken only a small step in that direction by increasing the contribution of some of the states. At the moment there is only a relatively low level of support for this goal, but Wynkoop observes, "it may be only the tip of the iceberg which may later surface."[73]

Betsy Levin, in another survey of school finance reports suggests that holding too rigorously to the principle of fiscal neutrality may, indeed, represent a disadvantage. It is encouraging, she finds, that with a lessening of reliance on property taxes, the states are now showing more sophistication by looking at a number of local district characteristics that might determine special needs. The larger cities, faced with many special problems, may thus emerge sooner or later with expanded resources on which to draw.

The development of a mechanism for equalizing dollars spent still leaves a crucial question unanswered. Though many economists seem to assume that we know how many extra dollars are needed to bring the school achievement of disadvantaged children to normal levels, we do not in fact have that knowledge, as we shall show in Chapter 10. There is a growing split among educators between those who think that the problems of the urban schools can be solved only by an infusion of vast sums and those who conclude, after a decade of sharply rising school costs, that even much of the funds currently expended are showing no payoff. We shall return to the issue of costs and benefits when we examine the in-school programs later.

CHAPTER NOTES

[1] Morton and Lucia White, *The Intellectual versus the City* (New York: New American Library 1962), 13–14.

[2] Paul K. Hatt and Albert J. Reiss, Jr. (eds.), *Cities and Society* (New York: Free Press, 1957), 18–19.

[3] Robert J. Hagedorn, John P. Miller, and Sanford Labavitz, "Industrialization, Urbanization, and Deviant Behavior," *Pacific Sociological Review*, 14 (1971), 177–195.

[4] Mark Schneider, "The Quality of Life in Large American Cities: Objective and Subjective Social Indicators," *Social Indicators Research*, 1 (1975), 495–509.

[5] R. Blauner, *Alienation and Freedom: The Factory Worker and His Industry* (Chicago: University of Chicago Press, 1964); W. Kornhauser, *The Politics of Mass Society* (New York: Free Press, 1959); Herbert Marcuse, *One-Dimensional Man* (Boston: Beacon Press, 1964).

[6] Melvin Seeman, "The Urban Alienations: Some Dubious Theses from Marx to Marcuse," *Journal of Personality and Social Psychology* 19 (1971), 135–143.

[7] George W. Carey, "Density, Crowding, Stress, and the Ghetto," *American Behavioral Scientist*, 15 (1973), 495–508.

[8] Douglas L. Carnahan, Avery M. Guest and O. R. Galle, "Congestion, Concentration and Behavior Research in the Study of Urban Population Density," *Sociological Quarterly*, 15 (1974), 488–506.

[9] D. Ward, "The Internal Spatial Structuring of Immigrant Residential Districts in the Late Nineteenth Century," *Geographical Analysis* (1969), 337–353.

[10] Douglas Carnahan, Walter Gove and O. R. Galle, "Urbanization, Population Density and Overcrowding: Trends in the Quality of Life in Urban America," *Social Forces*, 53 (1974), 62–72.

[11] Howard Schuman and Barry Gruenberg, "The Impact of City on Racial Attitudes," *American Journal of Sociology*, 76, no. 2 (September 1970), 213–261.

[12] Robert C. Angell, "The Moral Integration of American Cities," Paul K. Hatt and Albert J. Reiss Jr. (eds.), *Cities and Society* (New York: Free Press, 1957), 617–630.

[13] Daniel J. Elazar, "Are We a Nation of Cities?" *The Public Interest*, no. 4 (Summer 1966), p. 42.

[14] Elazar, p. 44.

[15] *Social and Economic Characteristics of Metropolitan and Nonmetropolitan Populations 1970–1974*, Bureau of the Census, 1975.

[16] *Social and Economic Characteristics*, p. 2.

[17] *Current Populations Reports*, Series P25-618, U.S. Bureau of the Census, 1976.

[18] *Social and Economic Characteristics*, p. 8.

[19] Elazar, p. 43.

[20] *Social and Economic Characteristics*, p. 17.

[21] "Negro Migration to North Found Steady Since 1940s," *New York Times*, March 3, 1971.

[22] *Social and Economic Characteristics*, p. 4.

[23] Samuel Bowles, "Migration as Investment," *Review of Economics and Statistics*, LII, no. 4 (November 1970) 357.

[24] David E. Kaun, "Negro Migration and Employment," *Journal of Human Resources*, 5, no. 2 (Spring 1970), 207.

[25] Peter M. Blau and Otis D. Duncan, *The American Occupational Structure* (New York: Wiley, 1967).

[26] Stanley H. Masters, "Are Black Migrants from the South to the Northern Cities Worse Off Than Blacks Already There?" *Journal of Human Resources*, VII (1972), 411–423.

[27] Robert C. Hansen and Ozzie G. Simmons, "Differential Experience Paths of Rural Migrants to the City," *American Behavioral Scientist*, 13, no. 1 (October 1969), 14–35.

[28] James Q. Wilson, "The Urban Unease," *The Public Interest*, no. 12 (Summer 1968), 25–39.

[29] Wilson, p. 26.

[30] Wilson, p. 27.

[31] Wilson, p. 20.

[32] Wilson, p. 21.

[33] Wilson, p. 30.

[34] See, for example, *Report of the National Advisory Commission on Civil Disorders* (New York: Bantam Books, 1968); *Urban School Crisis. The Problem and Solutions Proposed by the HEW Urban Education Trade Force*, National School Public Relations Association, Washington, D.C., 1970.

[35] "Excerpts from Report by the Commission on Causes and Prevention of Violence," *New York Times*, November 24, 1969.

[36] "Subsidized Housing Increase in Suburbs," *New York Times*, January 24, 1972.

[37] Ernest Holsendolph, "Urban Crisis of the 1960s Is Over, Ford Aides Say," *New York Times*, March 23, 1975, p. 1.

[38] Linda and Paul Davidoff and Neil N. Gold, "The Suburbs Have To Open Their Gates," *New York Times Magazine*, November 7, 1971, 40+.

[39] Davidoff and Gold, p. 42.

[40] Edward Banfield, *The Unheavenly City* (Boston: Little, Brown, 1970).

[41] Banfield, p. 240.

[42] Irving Kristol, "A Foolish American Ism—Utopianism," *New York Times Magazine*, November 14, 1971, 31 ff.

[43] *New York Times*, November 24, 1969.

[44] Richard P. Nathan, "For Cities, No Single Problem a Solution," *New York Times*, August 23, 1975, p. 21.

[45] James Ring Adams, "Why New York Went Broke," *Commentary*, 61 (1976), 31–37.

[46] Paul Delaney, "Mayors Say Fiscal Crisis Has Spread to Small Cities," *New York Times*, June 27, 1975, p. 1.

[47] Nathan, p. 21.

[48] Nathan, p. 21.

[49] *Social and Economic Characteristics*, p. 4.

[50] Nathan Glazer, "On 'Opening Up' The Suburbs," *The Public Interest*, no. 37 (Fall 1974).

[51] Glazer, p. 96.

[52] Wilfred G. Marston, "Socioeconomic Differentiation within Negro Areas of American Cities," *Social Forces* 48 (1969), 165–176.

[53] Robert Jiobu and Harvey H. Marshall, Jr., "Urban Structure and the Differentiation between Blacks and Whites," *American Sociological Review*, 36 (1971), 638–649.

[54] Annemette Sørenson, Karl E. Taeuber, and Leslie J. Hollingsworth, Jr., "Indexes of Racial Residential Segregation in the U.S., 1940 to 1970," *Sociological Focus* (April 1975).

[55] Bennett Harrison, *Urban Economic Development: Suburbanization, Minority Opportunity and the Condition of the Central City* (Washington, D.C.: The Urban Institute, 1974).

[56] Glazer, p. 111.

[57] Glazer, p. 111.

[58] Bernard Goldstein, *Low Income Youth in Urban Areas* (New York: Holt, Rinehart and Winston, 1967), 43–44.

[59] Robert J. Havighurst, *The Public Schools of Chicago* (Chicago: The Board of Education of the City of Chicago, 1964).

[60] John W. Evans, Jr., "The Effect of Pupil Mobility upon Academic Achievement," *National Elementary School Principal* (April 1966), 18–22.

[61] Joseph Justman, "Academic Aptitude and Reading Test Scores of Disadvantaged Children Showing Varying Degrees of Mobility," *Journal of Educational Measurement* (December 1965), p. 154.

[62] L. Moribur, "School Functioning of Pupils Born in Other Areas and in New York City," *New York City Board of Education*, 1962.

[63] Stephen K. Bailey, *Disruption in Urban Public Secondary Schools*, National Association of Secondary School Principals, 1971.

[64] "Assaults on Teachers," *Today's Education* 61 (1972), 30–32; Leonard Buder, "Crime and Violence Rise in City Schools," *New York Times*, March 19, 1972, p. 1.

[65] Ralph J. Marino and Jeremiah McKenna, "The New and Dangerous Juvenile Delinquent," *New York Affairs* (Winter 1973), 3–11.

[66] "New Youth Poll: Louis Harris Poll," *Life*, January 8, 1971, 22–27.

[67] Robert D. Reischauer and Robert W. Hartman, *Reforming School Finance*, (Washington, D.C., Brookings, 1973).

[68] *Digest of Educational Statistics*, Department of Health, Education, and Welfare, 1975.

[69] *Digest of Educational Statistics*, p. 71.

[70] *Serrano versus Priest*, S. Cal. 3d 584, 487 (p. 2d 1241, 96 Cal. Reporter, 601 1971).

[71] *Rodriguez versus San Antonio Independent School District*, 337 F. Supp. 28 (W.D. Texas 1971); 411 U.S. 1 (1973).

[72] Robert J. Wynkoop, "Trends in School Finance Reform," *Phi Delta Kappan* (April 1975), 542–546.

[73] Wynkoop, p. 545.

Chapter 6

Culture: Value and Language Differences

The general framework of economic opportunity provides the background incentives for groups of people; the central cities present a specific arena for the lives of new minority groups who migrate into them. But the daily lives of children are most importantly shaped by the intimate values and incentives given by their families, and the cultures that the families transmit. This chapter looks at some of the basics of culture and its impact. It:

Briefly reviews a variety of theories that attempt to explain why groups that are culturally different are often subjected to stereotyping and prejudice.

Considers the extent of racism in America, and estimates its future scope.

Describes the value systems of two different minority groups, and how these differences relate to success in school.

Explores the argument over "cultural deprivation" as an explanation of black/white school achievement differences, and the crucial role that theories of language play in the dispute.

Some of the questions readers might address are:

Is there some group of people I view in a less favorable light than others? Which of the various theories described is most likely to account for my feelings?

Does the theory that intergroup contact will ultimately reduce prejudice square with my own experience?

Which of the explanations for black cultural differences seem most likely—"difference," "deficit," or "bi-culture?" On what particular evidence is the judgment based?

Economic and social status and the conditions of urban life are, in a sense, statistical artifacts and do not themselves directly influence the behavior of urban school children. The factors that mediate between these large abstractions and the individual are the culture of the ethnic groups that compose our diverse society and the family relationships that characterize those cultures.

Culture, as the anthropologists view it, consists of all the enduring patterns of behavior and values of a definable social group or subgroup; what gives those patterns their durability is the family, the mechanism for passing them on to each new generation and thus maintaining their vitality. It is within the intimate relationships of the family that the child learns his most basic lessons: what to value, what to fear, what to expect from others, and what sort of life to anticipate for himself. It is also within the family that he takes the very early crucial steps of cognitive and emotional development which either prepare him for later growth or handicap him when he is provided with opportunity for growth.

Following chapters will look at the direct influence of family environment and socialization patterns on the characteristics of children that appear to correlate with their careers in school. At this point we shall be more interested in the influence of general cultural factors and the differences in them among groups. Some artificiality is inevitable in considering culture and family as separate entities, but the reader should try to keep in mind the reality, i.e., that they are indeed not separable.

CULTURAL DIFFERENCE AND INTERGROUP RELATIONS

For much of its history the United States has been what is probably the most incredibly diverse society in modern times, containing ethnic groups representing most European countries and many from Asia, the Pacific, South America and, of course, Africa, not to mention the aborigines of the continent settled by the original colonists. American history has been profoundly influenced by the troubled relationship between the white settlers and Indian Americans, and even more profoundly by black slavery and its terrible consequences for the society as a whole. White mainstream relations with other cultures that came to America during the high flood of immigration between the Civil War and World War I, though by comparison much better, were consistently marked by prejudice, discrimination, and varying degrees of exclusion.

A major explanation offered for the marked retardation in school performance of many minority group children puts the blame on the attitude of the school, reflecting deeply ingrained prejudices of the society at large. Ensuing sections will examine the basis for this view and a variety of issues that have arisen in response to, or in sympathy with, it. It may be helpful, first, to summarize briefly some of the major theories of intergroup prejudice as an aid to later clarity.

Cultural Stereotyping and Prejudice

Prejudice is, first of all, a *group* phenomenon. Though we often enough take an unreasoning dislike for an individual who has caused us no harm, we usually shrug it off as a "personality conflict." Gordon Allport has defined prejudice as "an aversive or hostile attitude toward a person who belongs to a group simply because he belongs to that group and is therefore presumed to have the objectionable qualities ascribed to the group."[1]

It is thus a special and unhappy variation of a broader psychological phenomenon that social psychologists study as "stereotyping," the human tendency to identify a new stimulus on the basis of past experience and respond to it with behavior that the experience makes appropriate. Having been burned by a stove we approach all stoves with some caution, and as Dorothy Parker observed, we don't make passes at girls who wear glasses. The difference between the two examples is that the connection between stoves and danger is usually based on one's own experience, but the stereotype about studious girls is generally based on hearsay (and has largely vanished since Parker's time).

All stereotyping saves time and energy; it is parsimonious. Cultural stereotypes, for all the damage they do, seem partly, at least, to be based on information. R. C. Gardner and his associates report that stereotypes about the same groups in different countries are more similar than one would expect by chance;[2] this does not mean, they add, that there is a "kernel of truth" to them, but rather a "shell of information." The actual characteristics imputed to groups do vary somewhat over time, however. A number of investigators have replicated a study of college students' cultural stereotypes over a three-generation span and found some fading of earlier prejudices.[3] Blacks are seen more favorably by the recent generation, and more favorable traits are also assigned to Japanese, Germans, Jews, and the English than to Americans themselves. But, some earlier stereotypes have been replaced by new ones that are rather like the old; previously "hot-tempered" Italians are now, for example, "passionate" and "impulsive."

A variety of theories have been advanced to account for cultural group prejudice, beyond its appeal as a kind of conceptual parsimony:

1. *Economic theories.* It has been suggested, particularly as an explanation for prejudice against blacks in American society, that prejudice is

primarily a device for maintaining structured patterns of dominance and subordination in order to continue an "exploitative" relationship that benefits the dominant group. Thus, O. C. Cox explains: "Race prejudice is a social attitude propagated among the public by an exploiting class for the purpose of stigmatizing some group as inferior so that the exploitation of either the group itself or its resources may both be justified."[4] Although there is no doubt that some instances of cultural prejudice appear to involve a strong element of economic exploitation, there are too many more cases of prejudice that do not, for the theory to have very widespread applicability. Cox's definition also requires us to believe that prejudices are somehow maintained by the action of an "exploiting class" presumably through the use of the mass media, which seems sharply at odds with the current situation in the U.S., where the mass media and the upper class as well seem considerably less prejudiced than the population at large.

2. *Psychological theories.* The most general psychological theory derives from what came to be known as the Yale Hypothesis, an approach based on the assumption that human aggression is closely linked to frustration. Since frustration is a common element of life, and we learn early that the resulting aggression cannot be discharged on members of our own group for fear of retaliation, it is most readily displayed toward members of any "out-group" that happens to be available. A somewhat related theory derived from Freudian psychology suggests that, unable to face up to our own "bad" motives and fantasies, we commonly project them onto others.

These and other such mechanisms have been made part of a general psychological theory of prejudice based on the concept of an *authoritarian personality.*[5] The explanation assumes that early disturbances in parent-child relationships result, for some people, in an inability to tolerate ambiguity. The child who cannot accept his own sometimes hostile feelings toward his parents and become comfortable with the knowledge that they are not all-wise, powerful, and good, cannot learn to accept ambiguity in the world at large. Everything and everyone must be either good or bad, black or white. Since the self must also be immune from criticism, all who are different from the self in appearance or behavior must be bad, hence the authoritarian personality is hostile to all minorities and to groups whose culture is different from his own.

There is a good deal of experimental and clinical evidence for the widespread existence of these types of psychological mechanisms, but they fall short of offering a complete or very convincing explanation for the pervasive existence of prejudice in human societies. Frustration does not, for example, inevitably lead to aggression against others; some people learn to deal adequately with frustration, and those who do not are likely to be regarded as "immature." Others sometimes turn their aggression inward rather than vent it on others. The concept of an "authoritarian personality" has recently been subjected to a number of criticisms. As originally conceived, it was an attempt to explain the extremes of German Nazism, and inevitably the measure took on a political dimension; many behavioral scientists prefer to talk of *dogmatism,* which is politically neutral (one can be a "left" dogmatist as well as a "right" dogmatist). The very high correlation between authoritarianism scores and both education and social class (the higher the educational level the lower the authoritarianism) also suggests that the scale is measuring variations in social norms rather than a dimension of individual personality.[6]

3. *Social conformity theories.* These approaches offer a considerably broader explanation for the phenomenon of intergroup attitudes, relying on the universal patterning of solidarity and status dealt with earlier in Chapter 3. Attitudes toward other groups than one's own are assumed to be part of the system of social norms, beliefs that we acquire in the process of growing up in the same way that we accept our society's ideas about what is good to eat or how to behave toward members of the opposite sex.

One of the most persuasive bodies of evidence supporting such a view is the work that has been done on *social distance* over the past several generations.[7] The social distance scale measures the degree of closeness people feel toward a variety of other ethnic and national groups by asking whether they would admit the group to their country, to their town, to their neighborhood, or by marriage to their family. Each group can be given an average distance score and ultimately rank-ordered by their acceptability. Although the American rank order of a number of groups has changed somewhat over time (in the same way that our stereotypes shift modestly), it has remained remarkably stable in the past half century (as has the rank ordering by people of other countries of the West).

Moreover, our suspiciousness of other peoples appears to have little to do with our knowledge of them; the Turks, for example, are consistently ranked low on the American scale, although most Americans have never met one. When the list of peoples is presented for response, a few invented nationalities are usually included, and they are commonly ranked low also.

It is fairly clear that no one theory can account for the wide range of negative intergroup attitudes one finds in the world, from the real estate practices excluding blacks from a particular neighborhood to the murder of five million Jews by the Nazis in World War II. Caution, and a hard look at specific circumstances, would appear to be the most appropriate approach to many of the issues in this chapter.

How Racist Is America?

The answer to this question, according to many upper-middle intellectuals who hold Movement ideas, is *overwhelmingly.* Black nationalists and the writers for such journals as the *New York Review of Books* now assume almost without arguing the point that "America" and "racism" are practically synonymous terms. Because such rhetoric inevitably suffuses many of the issues dealt with here and later in the book, the point requires some examination.

A convincing case can certainly be made for the proposition out of the historical record already alluded to. Those inclined to take a more balanced view of the matter, however, tend to ask: As a society, have we done any better or worse than other similar societies? Andrew Greeley, among others, argues:

> It must be said that, on the whole, American social and cultural pluralism has worked rather well. Such a statement is a dangerous one to make, for in the present climate of scholarly opinion even the most modest compliment to American society is taken as a sign of immorality and racism. Everything about the United States must be bad, and the lightest suggestion that American society may be successful at anything must be rejected out of hand. It ought to be possible, however, to steer a middle course. We ought to be able to say that there have been serious injustices done in the American society and that they are still being done; and, on the other hand, to also assert that the United States has probably coped more effectively with ethnic, religious, racial, and geographic diversity better than any large and complex society in the world. Indeed, when one considers the size, geographical diversity, heterogeneity of the population, and the sheer newness of the society, the astonishing thing is that the nation has survived at all.[8]

The evidence for Greeley's assertion is now slowly accumulating, as previously homogeneous societies have recently begun to show signs of cultural strain as their populations become more diverse. Western European countries, whose intellectuals freely criticize the United States for its ethnic difficulties, now face mounting difficulties of their own in coping with large groups of workers imported from other, less developed societies. Canada has also begun a divisive controversy over immigration restriction proposals, amid cries of "racism" from those who see the restrictions as aimed at Oriental and Pacific peoples.

The point is made with particular sharpness in a study by Ernest Chaples and his associates of attitudes among Danish university students, who often express great abhorrence for racial prejudice in the U.S.[9] Chaples obtained responses on the Situational Attitude Scale, which measures attitudes toward a variety of behavior in specific situations, to behaviors imputed to an American black, a Mediterranean, and to someone not identified by ethnic background. The Danish students were very tolerant of blacks and, indeed, preferred them to individuals who were not identified by race. But their attitudes toward persons identified as Mediterranean (who are now working in Denmark in considerable numbers) were negative, close to scores obtained in the U.S. toward blacks.

The assessment of cultural attitudes in this country is further complicated by recent ambiguities in the definition of the term "racism" itself.

It once referred to negative or hostile expressions about another racial group, or deliberate discrimination or exclusionary practices directed against it. It is now so freely used that there is some question about whether it has not been totally emptied of any meaning. There has recently been a good deal of pressure on the airlines, for example, to open for everyone the VIP lounges that they had set up for travellers who used a particular airline for some considerable number of miles a year. An article in *The New York Times* travel section on the ensuing controversy contained the following remarkable observation: "Moreover, argued American Airlines, the discrimination here has clearly never been tainted with any kind of racism or creedism. And that's perfectly true unless you consider that favoring those with money and power is a sort of racism."[10]

A new term, "institutional racism," has come into use, which further confuses the issue and makes roughly 90 percent of all American institutional behavior "racist." An organization of black psychiatrists has recently persuaded the National Institute of Mental Health of HEW to adopt such a definition of racism, which provides that *any* procedure on the part of any organization is automatically racist if it results in differential treatment for any blacks whatsoever.[11] By this definition, clearly, if the proportion of black students who drop out of a college is greater than the proportion of white dropouts, the college must be indicted for racism, and one can multiply such examples endlessly.

PANEL 6.1   The Future of Prejudice

The American faith in the school has often been extended to the hope that social patterns of prejudice, in contrast with discrimination, can be eliminated through education. It is now generally perceived that discriminatory behavior can be somewhat controlled by legislative and court action, and there is little doubt that over the past several decades such efforts have had considerable success; but feelings and beliefs are another matter, and if they are to be changed information and persuasion are necessary.

Most big city school systems make efforts in that direction; recent trends have encouraged the use of textbook materials aimed at improving intercultural understanding, and teacher training programs have increasingly involved methods and materials in that field. Though there is little evidence of any direct change of attitude as a result, it is surely better for the public schools to do as much as they can rather than to do nothing and be perceived by children as indifferent to, or worse, supportive of, social stereotypes. Social attitudes change slowly, but they do change. There is perceptibly less prejudice against Jews than there was a half-century ago; on the other hand, anti-Semitism has not fallen off to the point where the Anti-Defamation League would consider going out of business.

Similar hopes that contact between groups, in school, neighborhoods, and associations would heighten understanding and markedly decrease prejudice have likewise led to disappointment. The extensive research on the effects of racial contact provides little evidence that simple cross-cultural contact directly affects negative attitudes,[12] and doubt has recently been cast on some of the earlier classic studies of racial contact in housing developments that suggested it was effective to some extent.[13] Even those social scientists who advocated contact as a social strategy for reducing prejudice reasoned from the available research that it would be effective only under certain circumstances: Those involved must be of equal status, and their mutual interaction must be in support of movement toward common goals. In a period of escalating divisiveness in ideology, and given the slow pace of status equalization, racial contact is likely to be only marginally effective.

CULTURAL VALUES AND CULTURAL IDENTITY

In the middle of the 1960s the growing forces of the civil rights movement and black nationalism exploded into a full-scale demand for a reconsideration of the place of minority cultures in the American society. The challenge to the traditional concept of assimilation for minorities because national unity demands a unitary culture, was joined first by American-Indian spokesmen, then by the Hispanic minorities from Puerto Rico and Mexico, and finally, to some extent, by the Chinese and the "white ethnics" who had immigrated at an earlier period.

The discussion that follows will echo earlier themes encountered in the consideration of social class values; indeed, one of the most confusing problems that must be dealt with in talking about cultural values is the degree to which some of the cultural values being advocated so passionately and widely may be merely lower class values in disguise. We will return to that problem at the end of the section.

As a first cut at the issue we examine the value structure of two significant minorities. The children of one of them, the Mexican-Americans, do very poorly in American schools; those of the other, the Japanese, do well. Mexican Americans have been selected for our illustration because, for some reason, they have been studied more intensively than the Puerto Ricans.

The Mexican-American Culture

In commenting on the Spanish-American culture almost a generation ago, Talcott Parsons, the social theorist, described its most general difference from the American culture as its stress on the *particularistic-ascriptive* orientation rather than the Anglo's *universalistic-achievement* orientation.[14] These differences are, to a very considerable degree, the differences between a folk culture and an industrial one, *gemeinschaft versus gesellschaft*. Particularism means that the individual gives most importance to those people, places, and things that are part of his immediate surroundings—his family, his farm, his village—which are concrete and visible. A peasant will fight for a bit of his own land, not for grand, universalistic abstractions like justice and freedom.

Personal relations are composed of involvements with people who are "ends in themselves," as against the Anglo pattern of relating to people as the occupants of social roles. This difference is very much the same as the role separation of the urban dweller noted in Chapter 5. The individual's status is firmly anchored in his background and his family; ascriptive status is possible only in fairly small, self-contained living units, where everyone knows everyone else. The Anglo's grant of status on the basis of achievement is more fluid and appropriate to large and complex situations in which people do not know much about each other. Finally, the Mexican culture stresses feeling and emotion, and hence, immediate gratification. As Florence Kluckhohn and Fred Strodtbeck have observed, it is, in general, a mirror image of the Anglo culture in all important respects.[15]

More specifically, Norma Hernandez lists the following salient aspects of Mexican culture: central importance of the family, an authoritative father figure, present-time orientation, limited stress on material gain, simple patterns of work organization generally in the form of group cooperation, little stress on education, adjustment to problems rather than an attempt to seek solutions for them, fatalism, and an emphasis on *being* rather than *doing*.[16]

In the southwest United States there are close to two million Mexican-American students in school. The median years of schooling for the Mexican-American population as a whole ranges between 6.7 and 9.2 years, in contrast to the 12.1 years nationally.[17] Studies of the relation between the cultural factors described and the children's educational retardation present a picture that is by no means clear:

Some scholars claim that Mexican-American acculturation has moved more slowly than in European groups,[18] but others have found that, at least in some respects, it is more advanced than suspected. Audrey Schwartz presents data that show 80 percent of Mexican-American pupils in one sample attesting to the high importance of school as a means of attaining Anglo goals, to which they also subscribed.[19]

A number of studies have reported that as acculturation into Anglo values increases, school achievement increases. But Hernandez found just the opposite, and attributed the lower achievement in this case to a conflict between achievement and the family, that is, as the child moves away from family values, the resultant disturbance affects his school performance negatively.[20]

Although one would expect culture to have an independent effect on educational aspirations, when IQ, school performance, and social class are controlled, there are no differences between Mexican-American and Anglo aspirations or expectations about how much school they will get.[21]

It is possible to make a case for the following: the closer a family is to the folk culture, the more difficult it is for the child to move away from its values and toward Anglo ones; those children who do make the break may respond in one of two ways, either with an inability to handle the conflict with consequent disruption of school performance, or with enough confidence to manage the conflict and school as well.

The Japanese-American Culture

Japanese-American children in the Los Angeles area perform considerably better in school than other minority groups, and to some extent they outperform Anglo children. In some respects the cultural values of the group are not unlike the Mexican-Americans: a thorough orientation to the family, subordination of the individual to the group, reliance on hierarchy and ascriptive order, and respect for authority. Several prominent values differentiate the Japanese culture, however: a sense of duty, a belief in the effectiveness of rational effort toward long-term goals, and a high regard for the instrumental value of education.[22] In contrast with the majority of Mexican-American families in the U.S., Japanese immigrants have been relatively well-educated; before World War II Japanese parochial schools were established to socialize children into the culture, although that function has now been absorbed by other associations. Sixty percent of Japanese pupils in the Los Angeles schools report that their parents have a high school education, and 30 percent of the fathers went to college. Eighty-five percent of the pupils themselves aspire to schooling beyond high school, and an astonishing 80 percent aspire to upper-level white collar occupations.

Is it merely the case that, as the local saying has it, "Scratch a Japanese-American and find a white Anglo-Saxon Protestant"? Schwartz argues against that explanation, on the basis of her study of Japanese-American and Anglo student values.

The only values strongly held in common by the two student groups are: (a) a belief that school attendance and performance will lead to future benefits; and (b) a concern for peer group opinion. The Japanese students like school better and are more positively oriented to authority in general and to formal school compliance. They tend to reject the Anglo's stress on individual autonomy and their sense of personal mastery over the future, and they see social mobility in group, rather than individual, terms (one moves up as the family moves up). Their self-esteem is lower, perhaps, says Schwartz, because of a reluctance to view themselves in competition with others, for such competitiveness interferes with their strong orientation to the collectivity. She sums it up:

> Japanese-American pupils have certain advantages for success in the American public school that appear to be rooted in the Japanese culture: first, the traditional family, with its rigid system of obligations subordinating individual interests to those of the group, provides an environment within which children internalize family-defined achievement goals that emphasize educational success and subsequent occupational mobility and are socialized to legitimate means for attaining them; second, the structure of interpersonal relations within the family, which subordinates all members to the authority of the father, anticipates the lineal authority structure of the public school and facilitates the child's adaptation to its bureaucratic organization; and third, the "collectivity" rather than the "self" orientation of the family is congruent with the strong peer group affiliation characteristic of contemporary "teen-age" culture which, for Japanese-Americans, is supportive of achievement.[23]

It appears, then, that it is not so much the *form* of culture so much as its *content* that makes the difference. The particularism of seeing the family as the main focus in life is true of both Mexican and Japanese cultures, but in one case the family does not see education and social mobility as important, whereas in the other it does. The effects of strong peer-group attachment depend on what one's peers are interested in and supportive of. The absence of individual achievement drive and the Western striving for mastery may not be crucial if there is a culturally based sense of future orientation and desire for collective achievement.

CULTURAL DEPRIVATION: THE ISSUE
OF BLACK CULTURE AND LANGUAGE

In the early sixties, when concern surfaced over the achievement gap between low-income minority children in urban schools and their middle-class white counterparts, educators began to develop a new vocabulary to talk about the reasons for the low achievement levels. Perhaps the most common term in vogue was *cultural deprivation*. Anthropologists were among the first to point out that everyone had a culture, and that to suggest that lower-class minority children were deprived of one was nonsense. Criticism of the concept spread to others, though the current argument is still conducted mainly by anthropologists and their close colleagues, the linguistics experts. The following summary of the issues is organized in the form of a number of models—definable positions which a number of educators and behavorial scientists have taken on the relation of culture to school success.

THE DEFICIT MODEL

The earlier notion of cultural deprivation originated in part from studies by Martin Deutsch of lower class child development, in which he used the term "stimulus deprivation" to describe some common elements of lower class environment and child-rearing practices.[24]

It is not that the lower-class child is exposed to less stimulation in his environment but that the stimuli have less variety and range and are not directly related to the cognitive skills that the school later requires him to develop. Thus, even the number and variety of objects surrounding the child is limited in the lower-class home to a few pieces of furniture, a minimum of cooking and eating utensils, and a limited number of toys. Not only is the average middle-class child exposed to a greater variety of shapes and colors in the objects about him, but his parents have sufficient income to buy toys that are in many cases designed to provide cognitive growth. Deutsch points out that lacking early experience with the process of form discrimination provided by constant manipulation of objects of a variety of shapes, the child may be handicapped when he is later confronted with the need to discriminate abstract letter forms. The difference between a "C" and a "G" is a fairly subtle one, for example; and being able to tell them apart depends on a well-developed sense of form discrimination.

The ability to remember, so important a part of school skills, does not necessarily develop as the child matures, but, Deutsch argues, requires training. From his earliest years, the middle class child is gently prodded to recall previous events and experiences; and when he does remember, he is rewarded by parental approval. The often minimal level of interaction between lower-class children and adults seldom includes these persistent attempts to develop the habit of memory, and children do not themselves spontaneously stimulate one another to recall experiences.

The amount and character of parental interaction with the child accounts for many of the important elements of stimulation in other ways. A sense of time is not transmitted as a significant part of the child's life. Ordering one's life by the clock is a relatively recent development historically, and it is significant that the modern timepiece did not come into use until the rise of the European middle classes with their business activities. The middle-class family organizes its varied activities into an ordered schedule, and the child is early impressed with the need to fit into that schedule. Though a sense of time may have no direct relationship to cognitive learning, the school organizes itself in many essential ways by the clock, which makes it comfortable for the middle-class child and rather strange for many lower class children.

In a more general sense, the characteristic pattern of interaction between lower class children and adults inhibits the development of one of the most important underlying relationships in the classroom—the need for the child to see the teacher as a resource, not only for information but also for feedback to tell him if he is doing something correctly. The consistent interaction that characterizes middle-class children and parents serves to tell the child when an explanation he has offered is correct or incorrect, to answer his questions about why certain things are so, and to supply new words and concepts. As most parents will attest, this is a wearying process which demands time, stamina, and inexhaustible patience—resources seldom available to the low-income mother of a large family. The middle-class child gets accustomed, too, to obtaining adult approval and reward for successfully accomplishing fairly complicated cognitive tasks. The lower class child does many tasks also, but they tend to be concrete, physical ones, and the assurance of adult reward is less often present.

Though all of these forms of early stimulation bear an obvious relationship to school experiences, the most important class difference in family stimulation is probably linguistic. The earliest cognitive training of the family consists of teaching the child to speak the language, and much of the future hinges on what precisely that language is. Many years ago, Bernard Shaw wrote an enchanting play called *Pygmalion*, in which an expert phonetician bet that he could pass off as high society a lower class girl who sold flowers in the street simply by training her to speak the language correctly. One does not have to be a social scientist to recognize the extent to which we judge the social status of others by their pronunciation and syntax; people intuitively recognize these as more reliable indicators than dress or social context, which is why many upper-class people do not hesitate to potter about in ancient, frayed clothes or drive old jalopies.

The problem does not merely consist of the fact that the child brings lower class language habits to a school which is dedicated to their eradication—often with disastrous results for the child's self-esteem—but that lower class language is not an efficient tool for handling many of the tasks set by the curriculum. Basil Bernstein, the British linguistics expert who has studied the language of various class strata intensively, distinguishes between two forms of language: the *restricted*, which is the language of many lower class families; and the *elaborated*, which is found most often in better educated middle-class families.[25] A restricted language is characterized by:

1. Short, grammatically simple, often unfinished sentences.
2. A repetitive use of conjunctions (so, then, because).
3. Little use of subordinate clauses to modify the dominant subject.
4. An inability to hold a formal subject through a speech sequence, resulting in poor informational communication.
5. Rigid and limited use of adjectives and adverbs.

6. Frequent use of the personal pronoun, and little use of the self-reference pronoun.
7. Frequent statements that confound the reason for an action and the conclusion, to produce a categorical statement.
8. Considerable use of phrases that signal a requirement for the previous speech sequence to be reinforced: "Wouldn't it? You see? You know?"
9. Above all, it is a language of *implicit* rather than *explicit* meaning.

Because it is difficult, if not impossible, to understand complex and abstract relationships without being able to put them into clear language forms, the school difficulties of children with a restricted language are easy to understand. As Bernstein puts it:

> . . . when a child speaks he voluntarily produces changes in his field of stimuli and his subsequent behavior is modified by the nature of these changes . . . Forms of spoken language in the process of their learning initiate, generalize, and reinforce special types of relationship with the environment and thus create for the individual particular dimensions of significance.[26]

A restricted language code is particularly unable to handle abstractions adequately, and educational psychologists such as David Ausubel argue that it is primarily the lower class child's difficulty in shifting from concrete to abstract modes of thought that leaves him further behind as he progresses through the school grades.[27] Bernstein, too, has noted that the widening of the achievement gap begins at about the fourth grade, when the child encounters the concept of ratio in arithmetic—the first point at which an understanding of mathematical process depends on an ability to grasp an abstract concept rather than a relationship that can be concretely demonstrated.[28]

THE DIFFERENCE MODEL

In response to the view outlined above, which seemed to many to suggest that lower class black culture in particular was a deficient version of American white culture, William Stewart, Stephen and Joan Baratz, and others developed a theory that has been gaining support among an increasing number of anthropologists. Their assertion that black Americans are culturally different from other Americans is based primarily on demonstrated differences in linguistic structure (to such an extent that they argue for the existence of a "Black English"), as well as differences in folklore and music.[29]

Basing their point of view on the assumption of a highly distinctive black culture, the proponents of this position go on to argue that the current position of the black in American society is due to a culture conflict; and, further, that the black, brought up in a different culture, is unable to understand or practice American mainstream behavior. Some interesting consequences of the argument are the claim that trying to teach black children standard English is a form of genocide, and that the simple way to overcome the educational retardation of urban black children is to teach them in black English.

The central issue of language differences, which is crucial to the cultural difference argument, is complex, often technical; and at this point, it is unresolved. Bernstein's original studies of social class language differences, cited earlier, have been replicated in this country a number of times, with substantially the same results. Whether the subjects have been black mothers and children[30] or white mothers and children,[31] mothers of lower social class seem to talk to their children in much the same way, whether white or black. The argument for a distinctive black language thus rests on more subtle and technical linguistic grounds than ordinary observation and comparison can support.

Vernon Hall and Ralph Turner, in a thorough review and assessment of the relevant research, conclude that "no acceptable, replicated research has found that the dialect spoken by black children presents them with unique problems in comprehending standard English. If there are problems, they occur in relatively rare cases."[32] Black liberals have attacked the theory for political reasons; Bayard Rustin talks of "black cultists" who are willing to sacrifice economic advancement in the name of separate peoplehood by romanticizing black poverty.[33]

THE BICULTURATION MODEL

An alternative position to the difference model is to assume that black children, as well as Indian, Puerto Rican, Chinese, and others, grow up being socialized or enculturated in two different ways of life, that of their specific background culture and the mainstream culture as well. Charles Valentine, a major proponent of this position, notes that those who argue for a *difference* theory must overlook an enormous range of culture variation within what they assume is a distinct cultural system.[34] In a single urban community, he found fourteen different Afro-American subgroups, as well as nine other non-Afro-American subgroups. "These cultures present distinctive group identities and behavior patterns, including languages and dialects, aesthetic styles, bodies of folklore, religious beliefs and practices, political allegiances, family structures, food and clothing preferences, and other contrasts derived from specific national or regional origins and unique ethno-histories".[35]

He further suggests that much of the mainstream culture that ghetto blacks do learn remains latent and not expressed in everyday social behavior, because the opportunity to practice it is restricted by social conditions of poverty, discrimination, and segregation. "Culture competence" in the mainstream sense can be present, even though not acted out.

The linguistic experts who advocate this model also reject both the deficit and difference approaches. Of the deficit model William Labov remarks: "The most extreme view which proceeds from this orientation—and one that is now being widely accepted—is that lower class Negro children have no language at all. The notion is first drawn from Basil Bernsein's writings that 'much of lower class language consists of a kind of incidental emotional accompaniment to action here and now.' Bernstein's views are filtered through a strong bias against all forms of working-class behavior, so that middle-class language is seen as superior in every respect . . ."[36]

As for the "difference" thesis, he argues that the structural differences between the black dialect and standard English are not great enough to account for more than minor difficulties for the black child. There is, furthermore, evidence that black lower class children are familiar with both languages; in experiments in which students were read sentences in standard English, most black subjects repeated them correctly, though in their own dialect, and other studies have demonstrated that most speakers of Black English use standard forms some of the time.[37]

Labov attributes the reading failure of black children to cultural and political conflict in the classroom, a thesis that rests on several assumptions, namely that: (a) teachers have very negative feelings about Black English, and communicate their criticism to pupils and thus turn them off; (b) black children who are generally alienated from the mainstream culture turn their backs on the school and deliberately refuse to meet its requirements (to support this point Labov provides evidence demonstrating that lowest reading levels in ghetto schools are found among those who are deeply involved in street gangs; (c) in *their own milieu* black children demonstrate great verbal fluency and expressiveness, abilities which they do not display in situations that, like the classroom, are alien to them (see Panel 6.2).[38]

PANEL 6.2   Situation and Language

A strong line of research evidence is developing on the influence of situation on language. Houston, Cazden, and others[39] argue that children possess a number of language registers, styles that they use in a particular situation; they claim that the deficiencies noted in disadvantaged children, both black and white, have been observed in the "school register," which gives an impression of nonfluency and strange language use. "But it must be borne in mind that this is neither the whole of the children's linguistic performance nor in any way representative of their linguistic competence."[40]

Cazden describes a number of recent experiments that support the view that the *situation* is an important determinant of language use among children. Children talk a great deal more, and in more complex fashion, for example, when they are personally involved in what they are talking about. In one experiment, four- and five-year-olds were provided with cameras and taught to take pictures. Here is one five-year-old's stories, first about an assigned picture and then about one of his choices:

> That's a horse. You can ride it. I don't know any more about it. It's brown, black and red. I don't know any story about the horse.
> There's a picture of my tree that I climb in. There's—there's where it grows at and there's where I climb up—and sit up there—down there and that's where I look out at. First I get on this one and then I get on that other one. And then I put my foot under that big branch that are strong. And then I pull my face up and then I get ahold of a branch up at that place—and then I look around.[41]

Cazden suggests that a number of other elements of the situation have an effect on language use:

Novel, surprising, or incongruous elements.
The presence of an interviewer who is strange or different.
The demands of the topic or the task.
The formality of the situation.
The length of the dialogue.

His general conclusion, and Houston's, is that language *competence* cannot be deduced from language *performance*, a generalization that has a direct application to the classroom. But, although the relationship is clear, what one does about it is not. The result of a decade of experimentation described in Chapter 10 is testimony to the difficulty of translating scientific generalizations to the formal classroom situation and making them work there.

The Action Problem

So far as consequences are concerned, Valentine sees little difference between the *deficit* and *difference* models. Educators, he notes, subscribe to both of them, and explain the school failure of lower class black children by their cultural difference, which they link with deficit. They are unlikely, he argues, to accept with any more than lip service the assumption of the difference model that one should respect all subcultural systems as legitimate and worthy. The difference model, then, must lead to a separation strategy in which blacks avoid mainstream institutions and build black nationalism. The alternative is a radical alteration of mainstream institutions, which he does not see as probable.

But neither are the solutions that result from the bicultural view. Valentine, too, calls for educators and health specialists "not only to recognize the legitimacy and creativity of ethnic cultures, but also appreciate that Afro-Americans are already more conversant with, and competent in, mainstream culture than most nonblack Americans believe or admit".[42] He uses as an example of his thesis the story of a young black boy whose father murdered his mother. The school was later unable to handle his aberrant behavior, and he was passed on to a number of mental institutions. Valentine's interpretation of the story is that the health professionals' insistence that the boy was mentally ill was incorrect, that his aggressive and bizarre behavior was nothing but a reflection of his biculturation. He offers as proof only that the boy's behavior, at several stages of development, was relatively well accepted by the family he lived with and his peers on the street. Even if this interpretation is correct, it implies that schools and other mainstream institutions somehow must adapt themselves to behavior that constantly disrupts their operations, and that they must provide an environment as loose and aimless as the adolescent's city street life. This surely requires a radical alteration of existing institutions, which is precisely the accusation Valentine levels at the proponents of the difference model.

MOTIVATION THEORY AND CULTURAL VALUES

One fairly consistent theme in much of this discussion of cultural values has to do with fatalism, the attitude of the culture toward the possibility of control over one's individual destiny. It is around this question that considerations of culture intersect with an influential approach to individual motivation, *attribution* theory.[43] Since it offers a coherent explanation of at least some of the phenomena of interest here, it is worth taking an extended look at its assumptions and its supporting research.

When a person takes on an achievement-related task, the theory asks, to what does he attribute either his success or his failure? The attributions made by most people can be described by one, or a combination of, the following: *ability, effort, task difficulty,* or *luck.* Of the first two, a considerable amount of research indicates that Western cultures tend to emphasize effort in many situations: teachers, for example, reward the hard-working, less able child more than the lazy bright one, even if the performance is the same in each case. In general, persons who attribute their success or failure to either ability or effort, particularly the latter, tend to approach tasks confidently, to choose tasks of moderate difficulty rather than ones that are too easy or too difficult, and to try again when they fail.

Much of the work on these ideas has focused on the concepts of *internal control* (attribution to ability or effort), and *external control* (attribution to the nature of the task or luck). The concepts are defined this way: "internal control represents a person's belief that rewards follow from, or are contingent upon, his own behavior. Conversely, external control represents the belief that rewards are controlled by forces outside himself and thus may occur independently of his own actions."[44] Much of the interest in applying the concepts to minority group behavior was stimulated by Coleman's finding that, of all the variables he tested in his national study of minority pupil school performance, the child's answer to several "fate control" items did the best job of predicting his level of achievement.[45]

Obviously, "fate control" is not necessary for high achievement, as Schwartz's study of Japanese-American values demonstrated; perhaps in that case, the low value placed on individual mastery of the future by the children is compensated for by a belief in group mastery. Much of the work in the field has concentrated on the explanatory power of the concept for the academic achievement of blacks. Ronald Friend and John Neal have found experimentally that, although there is no difference between the attributions of white and black children when they were told they had succeeded at a task, differences were very sizable when informed that they had failed, or were given no feedback.[46] In these latter cases, most of the white children thought that ability or effort was the most important explanation for their performance; only a minority of the black children did.

As with language, however, the importance of the *situation* is increasingly being pointed to as an important factor in these differential responses.[47] Gurin and his associates have most thoroughly explored the possibility that the meanings of the terms "internal" and "external" control are not as simple when applied to minority groups as they are often assumed to be. Thus, the Rotter Internal-External Control Scale, the most commonly used measure of this variable, does not distinguish between a person's belief that a particular kind of control operates for *people generally,* and a belief that it operates for *me personally.* The scale contains both of these types of items: "Becoming a success is a matter of hard work, luck has little or nothing to do with it," and "There is a direct connection between how hard I study and the grades I get."

Particularly in dealing with minority group populations, the Gurins argue, such a distinction should be made; and one should further distinguish between responsibility for *success* and responsibility for *failure.*[48] A middle-class child is taught not only that it is only his own effort that can lead to achievement, but that if he fails, it is his fault. But for minority children, who in many instances face social constraints on their ability to achieve certain ends, "an internal orientation based on responsibility for their failures may be more reflective of intrapunitiveness than of efficacy."[49]

In the event of failure, a related distinction should also be made between *blaming oneself* and *blaming the system.* The Gurins point out that most of the research on internal-external control has assumed that it is a matter of belief in skill versus chance. But low-income and minority group individuals do face obstacles that have nothing to do with chance—the operation of the labor market, the location of low-income neighborhoods in relation to available jobs, and the like. The psychological literature suggests that an internal orientation, when it results in excessive self-blame on the part of minority group members, can be damaging. "Merton notes that when people subordinated in a social system react with invidious self-deprecation rather than against the system, they accept a rationale for the existing system that serves to perpetuate their subordinate position."[50]

Several studies conducted by the Gurins conclude that an external control orientation can result in more effective behavior on the part of black students. Their academically successful college student subjects were oriented toward internal controls; but a group of high school subjects who sympathized with the urban rioters of the era made high external control scores. The Gurin's interpretation thus rests on the assumption that collective, forceful action is always better coping behavior than individual effort that will more slowly equalize income and occupational disparities between blacks and whites without creating further polarization. Such a conclusion is at least debatable.

CHAPTER NOTES

[1] Gordon W. Allport, *The Nature of Prejudice* (New York: Anchor Books, 1958), p. 8.

[2] R. C. Gardner, D. M. Kirby, and J. C. Finley, "Ethnic Stereotypes: The Influence of Consensus," *Canadian Journal of Behavioral Science*, 5 (1973), 4–12.

[3] Marvin Karlins, Thomas Coffman, and Gary Walters, "On The Fading of Social Stereotypes: Studies in Three Generations of College Students," *Journal of Personality and Social Psychology*, 13 (1969), 1–16; G. M. Gilbert, "Stereotypes of Persistence and Change among College Students," *Journal of Abnormal and Social Psychology*, 46 (1951), 245–254.

[4] D. C. Cox *Caste, Class and Race* (Garden City, N.Y.: Doubleday, 1948), p. 393.

[5] T. W. Adorno, Elsie Frenkel-Brunswick, Daniel J. Levinson and R. Nevitt Sanford, *The Authoritarian Personality* (New York: Harper & Row, 1950).

[6] Roger Brown, *Social Psychology* (New York: Free Press, 1965), p. 10.

[7] Emory S. Bogardus, "Stereotypes versus Sociotypes," *Sociology and Social Research*, 34 (1950), p. 287.

[8] Andrew M. Greeley, "The Rediscovery of Diversity," *The Antioch Review*, XXXI (1971), 343–365.

[9] Ernest A. Chaples, William E. Sedlacek, and Glenwood C. Brooks, Jr., "Measuring Prejudicial Attitudes in a Situational Context: A Report on a Danish Experiment," *Scandinavian Political Studies*, 7 (1972), 235–247.

[10] *New York Times*, March 1974, Travel Section, p. 8.

[11] Charles A. Willie, Bernard M. Kramer, and Bertram S. Brown, *Racism and Mental Health* (Pittsburgh: University of Pittsburgh Press, 1973).

[12] Russell Eisenman, "Does Contact between Negroes and Whites Decrease Prejudice?" *Journal of Social Issues*, XXV (1969), 199–205; Thomas F. Pettigrew, "Racially Separate or Together?" *Journal of Social Issues*, XXV (1969), 43–69.

13 Lawrence T. Cagle, "Interracial Housing: A Reassessment of the Equal Status Contact Hypothesis," *Sociology and Social Research*, 57 (1973), 342–355.

14 Talcott Parsons, *The Social System* (New York: Free Press, 1951).

15 Florence R. Kluckhohn and Fred L. Strodtbeck, *Variations in Value Orientations* (New York: Harper & Row, 1961).

16 Norma G. Hernandez, "Variables Affecting Achievement in Middle School Mexican-American Students," *Review of Educational Research*, 43 (1973), 1–39.

17 Hernandez, 13–14.

18 Charles F. Marden and Gladys Meyer, *Minorities in American Society* (New York: American Book, 1962).

19 Audrey James Schwartz, "A Comparative Study of Values and Achievement: Mexican-American and Anglo Youth," *Sociology of Education*, 44 (1971), 438–462.

20 Hernandez, p. 9.

21 Hernandez, p. 8.

22 Audrey J. Schwartz, "The Culturally Advantaged: A Study of Japanese-American Pupils," *Sociology and Social Research*, 55 (1971), 341–353.

23 Schwartz, "The Culturally Advantaged," 350–351.

24 Martin P. Deutsch, "The Disadvantaged Child and the Learning Process," in A. Harry Passow (ed.), *Education in Depressed Areas* (New York: Teachers College, 1963), 168–178.

25 Basil Bernstein, "Linguistic Codes, Hesitation, Phenomena and Intelligence," *Language and Speech*, 5, Part I (October–December 1962), p. 31.

26 Bernstein, p. 31.

27 David P. Ausubel, "A Teaching Strategy for Culturally Deprived Pupils," *The School Review*, LXXI (Winter 1963), 454–463.

28 Bernstein, 44–45.

29 Stephen S. Baratz and J. C. Baratz, "Early Childhood Intervention: The Social Science Bases of Institutional Racism," *Harvard Educational Review*, 40 (Fall 1970), 29–50.

30 Robert D. Hess and Virginia D. Shipman, "Early Experience and the Socialization of Cognitive Modes in Children," *Child Development*, 36, no. 4 (December 1965), 869–886.

31 Helen Bee *et al.*, "Social Class Differences in Material Teaching Strategies and Speech Patterns," Developmental Psychology, 1 (1969), 726–734, for example.

32 Vernon C. Hall and Ralph Turner, "The Validity of the 'Different Language Explanation' for Poor Scholastic Performance by Black Students," *Review of Educational Research*, 44 (1974), p. 79.

33 Bayard Rustin, "Won't They Ever Learn?" *New York Times*, August 1, 1971, Section E, p. 7.

34 Charles A. Valentine, "Deficit, Difference, and Bicultural Models of Afro-American Behavior," *Harvard Educational Review*, 41 (1971), 137–157.

35 Valentine, p. 140.

36 William Labov, "The Logic of Nonstandard English," in Nell Keddie (ed.), *The Myth of Cultural Deprivation* (Baltimore: Penguin, 1973), pp. 24–25.

37 Joan C. Baratz, "Teaching Reading in an Urban Negro School System," in Frederick Williams (ed.), *Language and Poverty* (Chicago: Markham, 1970).

38 Labov, 28–32.

39 Susan H. Houston, "A Reexamination of Some Assumptions about the Language of the Disadvantaged Child," *Child Development*, 41, no. 4 (December 1970), 947–963.

40 Courtney B. Cazden, "The Situation: A Neglected Source of Social Class Differences in Language Use," *Journal of Social Issues*, 26, no. 2 (1970), 35–59.

41 Cazden, p. 45.

42 Valentine, p. 156.

43 For a general review, see Bernard Weiner, *et al.*, *Perceiving the Causes of Success and Failure* (New York: General Learning Press, 1971).

[44] Patricia Gurin, Gerald Gurin, Rosina C. Lao, and Muriel Beattie, "Internal-External Control in the Motivational Dynamics of Negro Youth," *Journal of Social Issues*, XXV, no. 3 (Summer 1969), 29–53.

[45] *Equality of Educational Opportunity* (Washington, D.C.: U.S. Government Printing Office, 1966).

[46] Ronald M. Friend and John M. Neale, "Children's Perception of Success and Failure," *Developmental Psychology*, 7 (1972), 124–128.

[47] Martin Maehr, "Culture and Achievement Motivation," *American Psychologist*, 29 (1974), 887–896.

[48] Gurin, et al., p. 32.

[49] Gurin, et al., p. 30.

[50] Gurin, et al., p. 34.

Chapter 7

Cultural Diversity: Its Impact on Socialization and Schooling

The major contemporary cultural issue that affects the school is the debate over "cultural pluralism" as an alternative to American "assimilation." This chapter brings the themes of Chapter 6 into sharper focus. It:

Describes the current movements that emphasize cultural identity and a pluralist society.

Examines those explanations of the school-achievement gap that depend on cultural differences in patterns of mental ability, with particular attention to the present status of the argument over the inheritability of IQ.

Describes the earlier experience of immigrant ethnic groups in the urban schools of America.

Assesses the potential effectiveness of the policy of bilingual schooling as an attack on the school achievement gap of minority children.

Some of the questions readers might address are:

Granted the advantages of maintaining some degree of cultural identity, how far do I believe the pluralism movement should go? All the way to separatism, as in French Quebec? The active encouragement of separate economic and social institutions? Some more modest point?

Do I agree with those who would forbid any effort to study the relation between genetics and IQ? With the author's objections to that position? What value preferences are involved in making the judgment?

What are the advantages and disadvantages of the bilingual/bicultural school movement? Should teachers, and those preparing to teach, support it or be fearful of it?

The American tradition of assimilation took its familiar name from a play by Israel Zangwill, entitled *The Melting Pot*, which was popular around the turn of the century. The work celebrated "God's Crucible," an amalgam of the best of the old world represented by the immigrants to America, and a rejection of the worst. It was far from advocacy of coercive conformity to an Anglo-Saxon tradition which the term itself has come to connote for the passionate defenders of multiculturalism and cultural identity over the past decade. Their rhetoric is often overpowering, full of injustice-collecting and lofty moral tone, as in this typical example from Manuel Guerra, a professor of education at Washington State:

> . . . Chicano defeatism is the result and aftermath of the Mexican-American War. It is caused by American institutional racism, which is in conflict with American ideals of democracy and Christian morality. American expansionism in the Southwest, the concept of Manifest Destiny, the Monroe Doctrine, and the invasion of Mexican territories created a rationale for the military acquisition of Mexican territories and the subjugation of its conquered peoples in violation of America's own commitments stated in the Treaty of Guadalupe Hidalgo . . . "Mexican towns" and "Mexican schools" quickly rose as proof that the Anglo-Saxon conqueror was not genuinely concerned with the welfare of the conquered. Segregation and prejudice were institutionalized, while the role of the Mexican American was limited from the first day of school to the menial jobs that were opened to them . . . It must be remembered that the climate of the conqueror versus the conquered has never been lifted from the *barrios* of the West; that people cling to their identity as a matter of self-preservation; that the contradictions between the American dream as it is preached and taught and the poverty, unemployment, and prejudice experienced in the *barrio* prove beyond any doubt to the Chicano youngster that common words of democracy and Christian ethos are only the rhetoric which the Anglo-Saxon community uses to expiate its guilt, rationalize its conquests, and justify its oppression . . . If the Anglo-Saxon Establishment is sincere in seeking better education for Chicanos, it should . . . realize that Chicanos are different Americans. They have a different history, different family bonds, different cultural values, and different feelings about life. Chicanos are both bilingual and bicultural. What is even more important, Chicanos do not want to become carbon copies of their Anglo-Saxon friends. They do not wish to change many of their cultural values. Chicanos want to be accepted and respected for what they are . . .[1]

A more moderate and considered case can be made against assimilation as a policy, as Andrew Greeley has shown in a prolific output of articles, mostly in support of the cultural identity movement among white ethnics.[2] Greeley argues that cultural ties are special, and potent far beyond the feelings of solidarity that other types of group loyalties engender.[3] He quotes Clifford Geertz on his concept of "primordial attachments":

> By a primordial attachment is meant one that stems from the "givens"—or more precisely, as culture is inevitably involved in such matters, the "assumed givens" —of social existence: immediate contiguity and kin connection, mainly, but beyond them, the givenness that stems from being born into a particular religious community speaking a particular language, or even a dialect of language, and following particular social patterns. These congruities of blood, speech, custom and so on, are seen to have an ineffable, and at times overpowering, coerciveness in and of themselves. One is bound to one's own kinsmen, one's neighbor, one's fellow believer, *ipso facto*, as a result not merely of one's personal affection, practical necessity, common interest, or incurred obligation, but at least in great part by the virtue of some unaccountable absolute import attributed to the very tie itself. The general strength of such primordial bonds, and the types of them that are important, differ from person to person, from society to society, and from time to time. But for virtually every person in every society at almost all times, some attachments seem to flow more from a sense of natural—some would say spiritual—affinity than from social interaction.[4]

Greeley argues that cultural diversity is real and important, and that assimilation is not the only solution to the problem of intergroup relations. He freely grants the evils that accompany ethnic diversity and the costs of disunity and conflict, but rejects as naive the optimistic liberal faith that "peace and harmony will come to the world through rational, liberal, scientific, democratic homogenization . . . that man will not need the tribal ties, and all the paraphernalia of his prerational, superstitious, unscientific past. . . ."[5]

But, man cannot live by reason alone, says Greeley, and without the power "to locate himself somewhere in the midst of the diversity man may not be able to cope with the world at all."[6] Hence, although Americans from a great variety of ethnic backgrounds have dealt uneasily and guiltily with the ambiguity and conflicts of cultural identity in a heterogeneous society, the fact is that identities persist, and that we are currently involved in a rediscovery of pluralism. It is also true that despite the injustices and conflicts, as a society we have developed an effective style of dealing with cultural diversity. "Celts and Saxons are killing each other once again in Ulster as they have for centuries. In the United States, however, Scotch-Irish Presbyterians and Celtic-Irish Catholics get along with each other moderately well. They do not feel constrained to shoot at each other from behind the hedges or out of the windows of slums. Given the history of the two groups, that is not inconsiderable progress."[7]

Greeley has "grave reservations" about some of the current emphases in the pluralist revival, notably the insistence on "organizing the ethnics" and following the example of the blacks in "getting it together" in displays of ethnic militancy. What he does suggest is the desirability of intensive study of ethnic diversity in American society in an attempt to find out what works and what did not work not only in providing for, but in encouraging the preservation of cultural diversity within a national framework.

But, the rationalist and secular liberal tradition that Greeley rejects as a support for an assimilationist position is not the only objection that can be made to a celebration of cultural pluralism. Speaking primarily, again, of the white ethnics, Arnold Stein argues that in an attempt to resolve the uncertainty and ambiguity of having both an ethnic identity and an American identity, demanding "the right to be different" results in both social and individual rigidity: polarization between "we" and "they" sharply increases, and the boundaries of the individual ego become rigid and inflexible as the "self" is restricted by the narrow demands of the cultural group.

In their efforts to resolve the paradox of identity in contemporary America, the new ethnics have created their own system of paradox. While the "new ethnicity" purports to be a system of free choice and voluntary affiliation, it is in fact a system of coercion and ascribed membership and status. While it professes an ideology of cultural relativism, tolerance, and equality, its relativism is selective, its intolerance of difference apart from its ordering of differences is complete, and its egalitarianism is ranked. While its historiography claims authenticity and truth in its efforts to correct the myths of the past, its ordering, selection, and interpretation of the "facts" of the past create a new myth that is as spurious and as much a violation of historical fact as was the myth it replaced. Finally, while a new identity is acclaimed with a newly released sense of liberation, the freedom is illusory and self-deceptive, being contained in the safety and constriction of identity foreclosure.[8]

How much of this, one might ask, may be true of the identity-consciousness and ethnic-power themes of the blacks and Hispanic groups? Many of the values of the Mexican-American culture described earlier are the values of all folk-cultures, not distinctively Spanish ones. Which of them are to be preserved in the service of cultural identity? Is it helpful to socialize Mexican-American girls into the ideal of the woman of the Mexican folk culture, cloistered in the home? Or to encourage Mexican-American boys to adopt the fatalism of a folk society? How much of the fiercely defended black culture is part of lower class norms in all societies undergoing the process of modernization?

This is, indeed, the crux of the problem for the whole contemporary movement toward accenting the subcultural. There is no gainsaying the usefulness of group cohesiveness; membership in ethnic and religious groups has been and will remain important—at least, says Marcia Guttentag, below the upper-middle class.[9] She points out that in every case where groups survived poverty and discrimination for long periods, they had a powerful group ideology to depend on. But the advantages of building such an ideology—a process visible among many groups on the current scene, from the blacks to the American Indians—accrues primarily to members of the group when they cannot overcome barriers through individual action. But if ethnic group cohesiveness persists after individuals have risen from the lower class, it becomes a handicap in further mobility.

The issue is currently being posed in absolute terms: If we reject the "melting pot," then we must either turn inward and become a set of different cultures, or, while recognizing our multiculturation, nevertheless insist that mainstream institutions adapt to all possible different cultures. In an era of rapid social change, the first solution is a fantasy, the second more possible. But to adapt such institutions as the school to what is essentially a lower class culture is likely to serve only to cut cultural groups off from the possibility of mobility, a solution for which future generations are unlikely to be grateful.

Cultural assimilation is a painful process, and one can understand the desire to have one's cake and eat it, too—to achieve affluence and yet retain what is essentially a lower class life style. But it is an unrealistic hope. All modern industrial societies are based on middle-class skills: a time sense, complex language, mathematical aptitude, reliance on written communication, planning, and the exercise of deferred gratification. Part of the demand for cultural identity consists of a desire to retain such ethnic or national elements as religion, dance, food, music, and the like. But much of it opts for acceptance of behavior patterns that are not culture-based but class-based. No system of schooling can possibly cope with a pressure to help children acquire the skills of a complex society while satisfying the simultaneous demand that those children's attitudes be left unchanged.

CULTURE AND MENTAL ABILITY

An alternative explanation, or possibly an overlapping one, for the variations in school success of different cultural groups, looks not at motivations but at the way in which culture shapes mental ability. Although we commonly speak of mental ability as "intelligence," a long and elaborate argument would be required in order to assert that IQ tests really measure intelligence, and that issue will be dealt with later. In Chapter 4 we reviewed the evidence on the effect of IQ on occupational life chances, and it is generally agreed that abilities measured by such a test as the Stanford-Binet match those demanded for successful performance in today's schools—skills of reading, writing, and mathematics. Beyond that, one steps into a quagmire of conflict.

The Culture Tradition Hypothesis

A major issue for several decades has been the question of whether the standard measures of mental ability are "culture fair." The critics claim that their stress on verbal ability, the language of administration, unfamiliarity with the context of some of the items in the test, or the alien situation, militates against success for lower class minority group children. So fashionable is it to reject IQ testing altogether that the editors of a recent full issue devoted to the question by a reputable, presumably scholarly, journal, did not bother to include even one article defending the use of the test.[10]

The complaints are not equally valid, and need some sorting out. A great deal of work, for example, has been devoted to the problem of familiarity of item content, but attempts to construct a "culture fair" test in this sense have failed; and, indeed, on some specially constructed tests minority group children do *less* well than on the Binet. If the strangeness of the test situation itself is a determining factor, why in some reported cases do lower class minority children produce superior scores on performance scales of the Binet, but not on verbal scales?[11] A recent careful attempt to administer the test using black administrators speaking Black English, moreover, failed to demonstrate any differences in scores.[12]

On the other hand, there is little doubt that the test emphasizes a narrow range of abilities and fails to measure the strengths of some cultural groups. J. S. Kleinfeld has shown, for example, that Alaskan Eskimos do very well on cognitive abilities that for them are adaptive.[13] The employment, income, and educational level of this group is lower than those of ghetto blacks, and so is their performance on Western IQ tests. But the hunting culture of which they are a part requires extreme sensitivity to visual detail and spatial patterning, and their language contains complex use of prefixes and suffixes specifying shape and location. Using a multiple IQ test, Kleinfeld found that Eskimo children achieve scores on figural and spatial tasks that are superior to mainland whites.

In another ingeniously conceived study, the investigator compared two groups of boys from a Brooklyn Jewish neighborhood. Though the groups live close to one another and are of the same middle-class composition, their ethnic backgrounds differ historically. One is Ashkenazi, the European Jew whose tradition emphasizes the importance of scholarship and learning; the other is Sephardic, whose tradition puts stress on commercial and financial success. When the average IQ's of the groups on entering school are compared, one finds a substantial and significant difference. The families representing the Ashkenazi tradition apparently provide the kind of environment in which verbal performance is rewarded and in which the child is urged to achieve in that area, enabling him to do much better on the IQ test.[14]

A number of broader studies, both in the U.S. and Canada, are summarized in Panel 7.1. They present very convincing evidence that, with

PANEL 7.1   Cross-Cultural Patterning of Mental Abilities

The current line of research into the influence of ethnic background on patterns of cognitive abilities began with an investigation by Lesser, Fifer, and Clark, who selected four groups of first-grade children: Chinese, black, Jewish, and Puerto Rican—each composed of equal numbers of girls and boys.[15] To insure that any test differences reflected real differences in ability rather than differences in the familiarity of test materials, special tests were constructed that presupposed only experiences that are common and familiar within all the various social classes and ethnic groups in New York City.

The abilities tested were verbal, reasoning, numerical, and spatial. To free the situation as much as possible from bias, the children were tested by trained psychologists of their own ethnic background; this made it possible to administer the test in the child's primary language, in English, or in the most effective combination of the languages for any particular child. The major results of the study are shown in Figure 7.1.

To a surprisingly consistent degree, each of the ethnic groups demonstrate a *pattern* of abilities that is very much the same regardless of social class position. Social class does make a difference in the level at which the ability is manifested, but not in the pattern. Ethnicity not only influences the pattern but also the level of the abilities.

The interactions between the two factors of class and ethnicity are summarized by the investigators in this way:

> a. On each mental ability scale, social class position produces more of a difference in the mental abilities of the Negro children than for the other groups. That is, middle-class Negro children are more different in the level of mental abilities from the lower class Negroes than, for example, the middle-class Chinese are from the lower-class Chinese.
>
> b. On each mental ability scale, the scores of the middle-class children from the various ethnic groups resemble each other to a greater extent than do the scores of the lower-class children from the various ethnic groups. That is, the middle-class Chinese, Jewish, Negro and Puerto Rican children are more alike in their mental ability scores than are the lower-class Chinese, Jewish, Negro and Puerto Rican children.[16]

Kevin Marjoribanks replicated this study in Canada, on a number of ethnic groups including the Canadian Eskimo and French Canadians. His results, in regard to consistent difference in the mental ability patterns of the cultures and the effects of social class, are essentially the same as

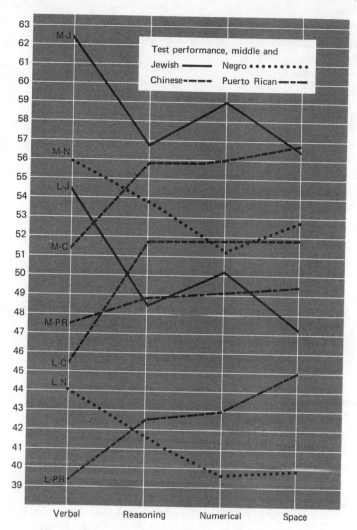

FIG. 7.1   Performance on tests of four mental abilities by children of different cultural and social class backgrounds.

Source: Gerald Lesser, *et. al., Mental Abilities of Children in Different Social and Cultural Groups,* U.S. Office of Education, Cooperative Research Project No. 1635 (1964).

those of the American study.[17] Marjoribanks carried the research one major step forward, however, by obtaining the following measures of home environment:

1. press for achievement
2. press for activeness
3. press for intellectuality
4. press for independence

5.   press for English
6.   press for ethlanguage (any language other than English)
7.   mother dominance
8.   father dominance

He found that about half of the differences among the groups in verbal and number scores can be explained by group differences in environmental measures; 16 percent of the variations in reasoning score, and only 7 percent of the variations in spatial scores, were accounted for by the environmental differences. This fits neatly with independent evidence that spatial abilities are largely genetic. And, his analysis revealed, even when environmental forces are held constant, ethnic differences still exert an independent influence on the patterns of mental ability.

social class effects controlled, culture operates through environment and perhaps something beyond it, to influence the patterning of mental ability in the child.

The Genetics Hypothesis

The discussion thus far suggests that culture and the family influence variations in IQ by determining those elements of family environment related to the development of specific abilities. But another interpretation is possible—*i.e.*, that these abilities are genetically determined by cultural inheritance, and are passed on to family members in the same way that such characteristics as height and other physical qualities are. Arthur Jensen has argued that the gap between both lower and middle class, and black and white, IQ levels is unlikely to be closed by current educational efforts because these differences are to a great extent due to genetics.[18] His case, much more persuasively argued and far better buttressed with evidence than previous attempts to argue for genetic differences between blacks and whites, developed a storm of controversy that reawakened the old argument between environment and inheritance. It is summarized below:

1.   Whatever intelligence really is, it is for all practical purposes whatever the IQ test measures. What most IQ tests measure in common is a factor that Spearman called g: the ability to see relationships, to sense similarities among different stimuli and differences among similar stimuli. "Fluid" intelligence is closest to g, less dependent on experience and education; "crystallized" intelligence depends considerably on organized knowledge and intellectual skills.

2.   Since psychologists looked for measures of social competence or superiority in devising the IQ, they inevitably arrived at qualities that correlate with high status and recognized occupational prestige. If we were a hunting culture, the IQ might have embodied measures of speed and visual acuity. It is not surprising then that estimates of the intelligence required for a given occupational level correlate very highly with the prestige that the general public accords to that occupation. Nor is it surprising that some studies find correlations as high as .71 between IQ and later occupational status.*

3.   IQ, though not fixed, argues Jensen, is due more to inheritance than to environment. He defines the issue this way:

> The legitimate question is not whether the characteristic is due to heredity or environment, but what proportion of population variation in the characteristic is attributable to genotypic variation . . . and what proportion is attributable to non-genetic or environmental variation in the population.[19]

After an extensive review of available genetic studies of IQ—studies involving parents and offspring, foster parents and adopted children, other kinship correlations, identical twins reared together and apart, and the effects of inbreeding on IQ—Jensen concludes that about 80 percent of variations in IQ are explained by inheritance, 20 percent by environmental factors.

4.   Furthermore, he argues, the evidence on environmental influence suggests that much of it is restricted to prenatal variables such as the mother's nutrition or to the very early period of life itself. How then explain the cases of sudden spurts in IQ when a child is switched from conditions of great deprivation to a normal environment, or the increases in IQ in intensive early childhood programs such as Head Start? His answers: (a) "Below a certain threshold of environmental adequacy, deprivation can have a markedly depressing effect on intelligence. But above this threshold environmental variations cause relatively small differences in intelligence."[20] Only a small proportion of the urban population we think of as disadvantaged are below that threshold, but we can expect IQ spurts only for the *severely* deprived; (b) Most of the preschool improvement in IQ (seldom greater than 10 points) he attributes to a greater familiarity with the tasks of the test or to a statistical phenomenon, "regression to the mean." When a group close to one of the extremes of a distribution is tested, then is retested at a later time, the mean of the group will tend to move toward the natural mean of the entire population (the IQ population mean is 100). Jensen reviews the literature on compensatory

---

* In contrast with the very moderate relation between years of schooling and occupational status cited earlier. IQ and years of schooling obviously themselves overlap, and the issue of whether IQ operates directly or indirectly through education is too technical to handle here.

education (*see* Chapter 10 in this book) and finds little evidence of any program that succeeded in raising group IQ's more than one could expect as a result of these phenomena.

5. Jensen's most controversial conclusion is that not only is there a sizable inheritance factor in social class variations in IQ but also in black-white differences; theoretically, this should be so because high rates of intermarriage create a "genetic pool." The evidence he cites is varied: black-white differences in IQ at all social class levels, when social amenities are presumably relatively equal; the higher group IQ's of American Indians living in worse environments than blacks; the strikingly different physiological patterns of black and white infants; the sheer magnitude of group IQ differences between blacks and whites, which he argues is unlikely to result from purely environmental influences.

6. Since the relation between both class and race and academic *achievement* is much less than that between class, race, and IQ, Jensen concludes that we are mistaken in trying to improve the ability of disadvantaged groups (individuals are another matter) to master tasks in ways that require *g* functioning. Many of these tasks and the competencies relevant to them can be learned associatively, by rote and practice, without a thorough grasp of the relationships involved. The trouble, he argues, is that we insist that all children learn *why* 1 plus 1 equals 2 before we let them go on to learn that 2 plus 2 equals 4. In this general conclusion, at least, he echoes some educational sociologists who also suggest that the aims, curricula, and methods of schools in lower socioeconomic areas be completely revamped to fit the characteristics and needs of lower-class youth more closely.

The Critical Response to Jensen

In a later issue of the same journal that carried Jensen's essay, a number of psychologists and educators responded to an invitation to comment on Jensen's thesis.[21] A literature that one could only call savage began very rapidly to accumulate as Jensen and Shockley and others, defended the genetics position against increasingly acrimonious attacks. Efforts were made to dismiss Jensen from his professorship at Berkeley for having dared to raise the question, and black student groups on a number of campuses turned the issue into political campaigns. It is difficult to summarize the diverse and often complex body of criticism; the attempt below to do so owes much to Daniel Kohl's recent excellent article pulling together the major lines of argument against the genetics thesis.[22]

1. *Quality of the data.* Kohl and most of the critics argue, in the first instance, that the validity of the IQ is too weak to represent a substantial basis for claiming heritability of intelligence. His arguments are much the same as those noted earlier in this chapter—the limitation on the mental traits it measures, the cultural bias of the items, and so on. He omits any consideration of the long history of failure to construct culture

fair tests, and dismisses the significant relationships between IQ scores and school performance; indeed, he argues that a rejection of a policy of assimilation makes such a relationship meaningless. This part of the attack might well strike a realist as the weakest element in the argument.

A much stronger case is made against the data on identical twins gathered originally by Burt, and relied on heavily by Jensen. Jensen himself admits to doubt about the trustworthiness of the data;[23] Kamin's critical review of Burt's work reveals considerable inadequacy and carelessness and concludes that it is "not worthy of serious attention."[24] Hunt and Cronbach, as well as Kohl and others, have complained that Jensen neglects to cite a variety of studies with contrary findings, and suggest that he has generally ignored a wide area of evidence outside the field of genetics, from animal laboratories and from social psychology, that argues for the existence of considerable plasticity of the organism as it interacts with the environment.[25]

2. *The meaning of heritability.*   Kohl argues that simply changing the calculation base may result in quite different estimates of the heritability of IQ. Thus, Jencks used Jensen's model for estimating heritability using data on unrelated children raised together, siblings raised together, and Burt's reports of monozygotic twins raised together. The correlations ranged from .40 in the first up to .98 in the last of these groups.[26] Bodmer and Cavalli-Sforza, using the same data, obtained a heritability estimate of 80 percent in an analysis assuming a "broad" concept of heritability, but one of 45 to 60 percent in a second analysis assuming a "narrow" concept of heritability.[27] In his own path analysis studies (see Chapters 2 and 4) Jencks finally assigned a value of about 50 percent to the heritability of IQ.

But, even if the heritability figure is a high one, argues Kohl, the fact is not necessarily meaningful when comparing two populations:

> In population genetics [heritability] has only a specific, technical meaning. The heritability of a trait within a population may have a value between 1 and 0. But a high heritability of a trait in each of two populations does not necessarily mean that the difference in the mean value of the trait is due to genetic causes. Even where the heritability is equal to its maximum value, 1, the difference between the two populations may be entirely due to environmental causes. Likewise, the heritability may have its minimum value in both populations while the observed differences in the trait between the two populations may be entirely due to genetic causes.[28]

Nor, as Crow points out, does a high heritability preclude environmental effects:

> E^2 [Jensen's symbol for the effect of environment in his general equation] tells us how much the variance would be reduced if the environment were held constant. It does not directly tell us how much improvement in IQ to expect from a given change in the environment. In particular, it offers no guidance as to the

consequences of a new environmental influence. For example, conventional heritability measures for height show a value of nearly 1. Yet, because of unidentified environmental influences, the mean height in the United States and Japan has risen by a spectacular amount. Another kind of illustration is provided by the discovery of a cure for a hereditary disease. In such cases, any information on prior heritability may become irrelevant.[29]

Kohl cites a variety of evidence tending to show that raw score differences in IQ under varying environmental conditions are often substantial, and that mental ability as measured by the IQ test may consequently be considered highly plastic. For example, he cites the famous Skodak and Skeels study of children separated from their parents shortly after birth and reared in adoptive homes. Jensen showed that the correlation of their IQs with those of their biological parents was about the same as the correlation normally observed in children reared by their natural parents. But, Kohl points out, the mean IQ of the children in the Skodak and Skeels study was almost 20 points higher than the mean of their natural mothers. Though Jensen finds that such an improvement may be consistent with an IQ heritability of 80 percent, Kohl insists that the real point is that they *did* improve, and thus demonstrated that IQ can be "boosted," to use the word in Jensen's title.

3. *The black-white comparison.* If the high heritability of a trait does not *necessarily* mean that a difference between two groups on the trait is due to genetics, on what grounds, Kohl asks, does Jensen make such a claim? Jensen has himself denied making any assertion to the effect that because there is a high heritability of intelligence within groups it can be *proven* that difference between groups is genetically based; he has said, "The relationship is one of probability or likelihood, that is, the higher the heritability of a trait *within* each of two groups, the greater is the likelihood that the group difference is attributable solely to environmental variation."[30] The argument here revolves around Jensen's reliance on a particular formula in population genetics presented by DeFries, who, Kohl says, has himself been careful to point out that no causal inference can be properly made from it.

Although Kohl thus makes a very strong case against the existence of proof of Jensen's thesis, his final conclusion, however, is considerably more controversial, for he demands that the very study of the genetic basis of IQ be forbidden. He quotes Karier approvingly:

As to social importance, a correlation between race and mean IQ (were this shown to exist) entails no social consequences except in a racist society in which each individual is assigned to a racial category and dealt with not as an individual in his own right, but as a representative of this category . . . The mean IQ of individuals of a certain racial background is irrelevant to the situation of a particular individual, who is what he is. Recognizing this perfectly obvious fact, we are left with little, if any, plausible justification for an interest between mean IQ and race, apart from the "justification" provided by the existence of racial discrimination.[31]

Suppose, Kohl argues, that population geneticists should conclude from further study that a racial or ethnic difference in intelligence is based on a genetic difference, and suppose further that they happen to be wrong. "What is the social cost of being wrong? In this case, what harm would it do a racial or ethnic group to be mistakenly labeled as intellectually inferior? The intuitive answer is clear. It would do immense harm."[32]

We are so far from understanding the neurobiological basis for "intelligence" that if we must await understanding on that level before we can do a better job of educating our children, then we may as well lay down our burdens and await the Messiah. If I am wrong and neurobiology should be on the verge of enriching our understanding of the development of the effective factors in intelligence, have no fear. Neurobiologists will inform us of their new insights. In the meantime, there is no result of population genetics which should discourage the school community in its quest to better educate all our children.[33]

One might well ask what "immense harm" to social science itself may occur as the result of taking Kohl's suggested line, as a number of scientific associations have done in the past few years by warning its members against doing research in the area. Despite Karier's concentration on the individual rather than the group, it is also true that the policy problems involved in the issue are not presented as individual ones but as claims on the school for *group* levels of performance.

Lord Snow has pointed to the dangers of the other side of the coin, the dangers of "romantic optimism" at the root of extreme environmentalism:

People like to believe that everything is open to them. Walter Mitty speaks for all of us. We should like to believe that given the right luck with our education, given the right parents, the right training, the right schools, we could do literally anything. We could produce massive theories like Einstein's. We could play the piano as well as Richter. We could pitch as well as Tom Seaver. We could be as cool-headed an astronaut as Neil Armstrong. It is just a matter of chance and environment, we feel, that we are not any or all of those things. In our saner moments, we have certain lucid intimations when we dimly realize that that is not completely true . . . In some fields—whatever the environment—we shouldn't begin to cope. It is extraordinarily hard for many of us to accept that bleak but simple truth.[34]

Snow points out that circumstances might make either heredity or environment decisive in extreme situations—*e.g.,* a person born with Einstein's equipment who is shot with a pistol at the age of two; or, on the other hand, a person born with an extra Y chromosome, or one born a mongol, in which case genotype is decisive. With evidence on both sides, Snow is disposed to throw his weight on the side of heredity as the greater influence. Nevertheless:

> God gives us a hand of cards, that's what we're born with. Education teaches us how to play that hand of cards. We all know people given hands full of aces, kings, and queens that they have not been able to use at all. It may be something intrinsic, it may be that their education was wrong. We've all known people who have had no cards higher than a ten and who have done pretty well. It is one of education's jobs—but not its only job—to see that they too get every possible opportunity to play that hand well.[35]

MINORITY CULTURES AND THE SCHOOL

The current period has witnessed a steady escalation of accusations that the schools have failed minority group children, and demands that something be done about that failure as the "new pluralism" itself grew. It is often claimed that earlier white minorities had a better experience, a view that was given brief attention in Chapter 4. It is worth taking a more specific look at it in this context.

The Nineteenth Century Immigrant Experience

Berrol has pointed out that the physical conditions then were much the same as now.[36] Poverty was the central condition of life in New York's lower East Side, and housing was considerably worse than now. Nutrition was poor, and tuberculosis was an ever-present threat. School authorities of the time noted large numbers of children with orthopedic, visual, and auditory defects. Both Jewish and Italian populations (the major groups at the turn of the century) were segregated, and their schools were overcrowded. In 1905, Berrol notes, 63 percent of the schools south of Fourteenth Street in Manhattan were using parttime schedules in order to accommodate double classes. The physical condition of the schools was deplorable: they had poorly ventilated, dark classrooms, were heated with gas burners, had inadequate and unsanitary toilet facilities, and were rat-infested and noisy. General conditions in other large cities with sizable numbers of immigrants were much the same as in New York.

Despite these conditions, there was some resistance to moving children out of their neighborhood schools. Parents, on the whole, were passive about the conditions of the schools which their children attended, and the period saw few parent demonstrations of any kind. But parents did prevent a shift of 1500 Jewish children to an underutilized school on the West Side, "because they feared that their children would be injured by the anti-Semitism they would meet".[37] The protest was unique in the time.

Smith argues that the schools did succeed with those generations of immigrant children, and that many of the innovations of the time—kindergarten classes, vacation schools, evening recreation and study centers—helped.[38] He ascribes the major reason for the schools' apparent success, however, to the great interest in education of most of the migrant families. "A direct relationship appears to have existed between the degree to which individuals had taken advantage of their educational opportunities at home and the decision to migrate."[39] For example, in 1900, only 30–50 percent of the adults in the Croatian provinces and in coastal Dalmatia and Istria could read, depending on the area surveyed; yet 63 percent of the people from these regions who landed at New York ports could read, a figure not too far off from the 72 percent of Jewish immigrants who could read.

Another important element in the picture were the numerous ethnic associations that sprang up after 1890 and displayed a remarkable commit-

---

PANEL 7.2   School Achievement among Early Immigrant Groups

Data from the public schools at least for the first generation of immigrant children show that they did not have an easy time of it. In a review of the early surveys, David Cohen shows that:[40]

> In 1908 the percentage of children retarded at least one grade varied from 16 percent for Germans to 36 percent for Italians; the American rate was 10 percent, and the Russian (mostly Jewish) was 23 percent.
> A more extensive study a year later, found that retardation was almost twice as great for the children of non-English speaking immigrants than for native urban whites.
> High school retention rates (the percentage of students entering high school who graduated) ranged one-tenth of a percent for the Irish and Italians, 10 percent for native whites, 11 percent for British, 15 percent for German, and 16 percent for Russian.
> Exposure to the culture and language of this country had an effect on retardation rates, but the effect differed from one group to another. For Russian Jews and Irish born here, the rate was half that of their ethnic brothers who had been born abroad; the rate for Italians fell by less than one-third. For Italian children born abroad, the retardation was 77 percent, the highest of all groups.
> IQ differences showed much the same differences between native whites and immigrants as they do now; in New York, for example, native white median IQ was 108.5, against 84.3 for Italian children.
> The debate over the differences was precisely the same as the contemporary one—whether the tests were culturally biasd, and whether the effect was due to environment or genetics.

ment to education. They exhorted their members to learn English, ran classes, formed night schools. Learning became not only a means to acquire money and respectability, but an integral part of the desire to preserve a new order of family and communal life. The Jews, says Smith, were not the only group in which family and religion reinforced educational values. Finally, because many of these groups managed to maintain a sense of double national identity, which fostered competition with other ethnic groups, there was a significant development of ethnic schools.

Cohen concludes that many immigrant children went through very much the same difficulties as current migrants in school—at least the non-Jewish Central and Southern European groups, and to a lesser extent, the Irish. The same explanations for group differences that appeared in the descriptions of contemporary cultures earlier in this chapter were apparent then; Smith suggests that a great deal depends on the degree of interest in education among the cultures, and Cohen stresses the extent of urbanization in the group's background experience. ". . . There is evidence which suggests that the rank order of intelligence among immigrant groups would correspond roughly to their rank order on an index of urbanization."[41] If a culture has both these strikes against it, as was the case with the Southern Italians, it was likely to lag far behind in adapting to the American school and the society as well. The Italian culture perceived children as an aid in the support of the family; they were raised to understand the nobility of labor and develop respect for elders. As with the Mexican folk culture, life revolved around the family, the church, and the province. Cavello quotes a traditional Italian saying: "Stupid and contemptible is he who makes his children better than himself," and indeed, education in Southern Italy was aimed entirely at attaining early social competence and transmitting cultural and moral values.[42]

The Bilingual, Bicultural School Policy

The mood of the current period is sharply different. A great deal of pressure has been building up in the seventies, particularly on the part of Spanish-speaking groups, for bicultural and bilingual schools. The arguments for such a policy usually involve the following reasoning:

> The dropout rates of other-language speaking groups are the highest in the country; Chicanos, for example, have the highest of all, as many as 70 percent drop out of some southwestern schools. Puerto Rican dropout rates are almost as great in eastern cities. Barriers of language and cultural conflict with Anglo-run schools must be the root cause of this phenomenon.[43]
>
> Low levels of academic performance and high rates of suspension and expulsion similarly go hand-in-hand with culture and language differences. The American school "assimilated" (and in consequence very often destroyed) the cultural identity of the child; it forces him to leave his ancestral language at the schoolhouse door; it developed in the child a haunting ambivalence of language, culture, or ethnicity, and of self-affirmation."[44]

Middle-class teachers and school administrators reject children who come to school speaking another language and refuse to recognize their needs. "Acculturation to these individuals, who have good intentions, means that the Mexican-American should change and conform to the white middle-class life-style. The fact that most teachers who teach Chicanos are not able to speak Spanish and are unfamiliar with Chicano culture illuminates a serious problem to the teaching profession.[45]

The best that can be said for the supporting evidence for these assertions, on which the bilingual school policy is based, is that it is exceedingly confusing. Even the dimensions of the problem are in doubt. The Office of Civil Rights of the Department of HEW has published estimates of the number of Spanish-speaking pupils in the schools as ranging around five million.[46] According to the Census there are three-and-a-half million children between 5 and 19 years of age with Spanish surnames, of whom only two million speak Spanish at home. Van Geel reports an estimate of between 1.8 to 2.5 million children of school age whose mother tongue was other than English and who need special instructions in English; the largest group of these is Spanish-speaking, but the number also includes American Indians, Chinese, Japanese, and about thirty other languaes.[47] Van Geel also reports an estimate of only 2 percent of pupils needing assistance with English who actually receive it in school. Critics of the bilingual school policy might suggest that even if this were accurate, the encouragement of instructional programs in English would be a less complex and less expensive remedy.

Does language difference constitute a sufficient explanation for high dropout rates and low school performance? The reader of the ample research literature can pay his money and take his choice. Some studies report sizable improvement of performance in reading when children are taught to read in their own language, then led to transfer the reading skill to the dominant tongue; others suggest that having children deal with two languages concurrently induces confusion.[48] An often-quoted French-Canadian study can be interpreted either way: English-speaking children were followed through a French school in Quebec and found to suffer no learning disability by the end of the elementary grades.[49] One can conclude either that having to live with two languages will cause no harm, and thus support bilingual schooling, or that having to learn in a foreign language is not disabling, suggesting that bilingual schooling is not necessary.

Evidence for school discrimination against minority children is clouded by often-suspect data and greatly complicated by the presence of alternative social-class explanation. HEW's Office of Civil Rights, for example, testified before Congress that of the 19,518 pupils suspended during the 1972–1973 school year in New York City, 86 percent were from minority groups, offering the figures as evidence that the schools were "pushing out" minority pupils. It turned out that the data had been forwarded by city school officials at the request of OCR, and had been gathered hastily on the basis of small sample surveys to which only a few principals had responded. The OCR had projected its reported figures from a few invalid responses gathered "helter-skelter," according to a school official, who added, "You can't say the results are inaccurate. Under such circumstances you can only say the results are worthless."[50]

Considerably better evidence is available, however. Gregg Jackson and Cecilia Cosca studied teacher behavior in a number of classrooms in a southwest district containing both Mexican-American and Anglo students.[51] They found significant differences in six out of twelve specific categories of behavior in their interactions with two groups, generally supporting the view that teachers have less verbal contact with the Mexican-American children, and give them less praise and encouragement. The difference favoring the Anglos on praise and encouragement, however, is greater for Mexican-American teachers than for Anglo teachers; the assumption of the bilingual school policy, that providing teachers of the same culture will be helpful, seems less than certain.

The school does now seem to be in a double bind on this issue of encouragement. Assailed from one side for giving minority pupils insufficient praise, a recent study by Sanford Dornbusch and associates in San Francisco accuses that system of institutional racism for giving them too much praise.[52] Dornbusch found that minority students were praised and given satisfactory grades without regard to actual performance—a system with carrots and no sticks. As a consequence, the children are unaware that their work is poor; without realistic feedback they simply proceed through the system satisfied with their poor attainments.

The Federal Presence

Although the available evidence (see Panel 7.3) suggests that the schools are not likely to change the academic achievement odds for minority group children, such evidence is just as unlikely to affect the progress of the

---

Panel 7.3 The Influence of the School Experience on Children of Different Ethnic Backgrounds— The California Study

A large-sample, very careful study by Jensen in a multicultural California school district throws some light on the more general issue of whether schools negatively influence the performance of bicultural, bilingual children.[53] Almost 7000 children were included in the study, which gathered an uncommonly wide variety of measures: (a) a series of nonverbal ability tests, including the nonverbal part of the Lorge-Thorndyke mental ability test, Figure Copying, Raven's Matrices, Listening Attention, and Memory for Numbers; (b) a number of motivation and personality measures, including a speed and persistence test, the Eysenck Personality Inventory, and a student self-report covering self-concept and attraction to school; (c) a home environment index that yielded an accurate measure of socioeconomic status; and (d) the Stanford Achievement Test for the appropriate grade.

With this range of data, and the use of very sophisticated analytical techniques, Jensen could examine variations in SAT-measured achievement holding a number of often uncontrolled variables constant.

1. The gap in achievement between Anglos and both blacks and Mexican-Americans increased in absolute scores through the grades, as Coleman and others had found; at sixth grade the minority children were one-and-a-half years behind, at ninth grade two-and-a-quarter years behind, and at twelfth grade three-and-a-quarter years. But, if measured in differences from the mean scores at each grade, there was no progression in the gap after the third grade, that is, the distribution of scores remained much the same.

2. Nonverbal ability scores exhibited a slight upward trend for both blacks and Mexican-Americans. The difference in these measures between blacks and whites is larger than the corresponding difference in school achievement measures; compared with the Mexican-Americans, Jensen notes, the blacks are overachievers and for them the school operates as an equalizer.

3. Although the Mexican-American children in that district come from homes in which English is not spoken and that are twice as deprived on the Home Index scores, they occupy an intermediate position between blacks and Anglos on both SAT scores and non-verbal mental ability scores. When achievement measures are adjusted for differences in nonverbal IQ scores (comparing school performance for children of equal ability) the differences among the three groups are substantially reduced. And, when they are further adjusted by differences in personality and motivation, the ethnic differences are almost entirely wiped out. The school's contribution to ethnic achievement differences, Jensen concludes, "must be regarded as nil."

---

bilingual school movement; the forces behind it include not only a number of politically potent minority groups but the very sizable apparatus represented by the education and civil rights bureaucracies of the federal government (HEW's Office of Civil Rights, already noted, as well as the U.S. Civil Rights Commission), and a number of influential members of Congress.

A bilingual school policy was approved by the addition of Title VII to the Elementary and Secondary Education Act in 1968, providing for the teaching of English as a second language *and* the teaching of some of the school curriculum in the native language of pupils, for the development of programs aimed at increasing knowledge and pride in ancestral cultures, and efforts to attract and retain teachers of Mexican or Puerto Rican descent (or other appropriate groups).

In 1970 the OCR of the Department of HEW issued a memorandum in accord with its powers to enforce the Civil Rights Act of 1964, which declared: "Where the inability to speak and understand the English language excludes national minority group children from effective participation in educational programs offered by a school district, the district must take affirmative steps to rectify the language deficiency in order to open its instructional program to these students."[54] As a result in part of this memorandum, a class action suit (*Lau v. Nichols*) was brought against the San Francisco schools on behalf of the city's Chinese students, demanding that the city provide special instruction in English.[55] The federal appeals court agreed with the city that its schools had no constitutionally defined duty to provide such special attention to a separate group, but the U.S. Supreme Court reversed the lower court.

ASPIRA, a New York City Puerto Rican association interested in the education of Spanish-speaking pupils, promptly brought suit demanding a bilingual school program in that city's schools, a suit that was settled by a consent decree and a commitment by the New York Board of Education to provide bilingual schooling immediately. The linking of these cases created confusion for some time; many educators believed that *Lau* required a bilingual remedy for the Chinese children involved. In fact, a simple English-as-a-Second-Language program (ESL) would clearly satisfy the Supreme Court decision, and there is as yet no existing court decision compelling the establishment of bilingual schools.

There is, however, no doubt that OCR-HEW, while not able to require a bilingual-bicultural approach, urges the use of bilingual programs on educational grounds. As Van Geel has pointed out, its similar support for bicultural programs and materials may well lead to some internal conflicts; some culturally "relevant" materials for Spanish-speaking children are very likely to include sex stereotyping, and OCR is also committed to enforcing a no-sex-discrimination policy on the nation's schools. Van Geel describes other conflicts in the federal role:

> As for the establishment of the federal policy itself, there is a division of opinion within HEW over whether and how much proof OCR is required to show that non-English-speaking students not receiving special instruction are actually being injured by the schools' policy; whether and how far to insist upon the use of bilingual cultural approaches as opposed to freely permitting the use of ESL; whether Anglo pupils should become part of the bilingual-bicultural programs,

familiar with an alternative culture, and whether speakers of Black English should also be covered by the policies of HEW-OCR.[56]

The Program and Its Critics

There is a conflict, too, in the schools. The original appropriation for Title VII was 400 million to be spent over a period of six years. By 1973 only 117 million had been spent on actual programs, and in that year only 35 million for a little over 213 projects involving 19 different languages, with about 100,000 children involved.[57]

Early enthusiasm had been generated around an ideal of a completely bilingual-bicultural school, with both English and the native language as the language of instruction, each classroom containing both English-speaking children and foreign-speakers, with both groups studying each other's language and culture. There are a few examples of this ideal (the Coral Gables school district in Florida, for one, claims to represent the ideal) but the norm appears to be a program in which non-English speaking children (if there are enough of them in the district) are taught part of the curriculum in their language in segregated classes, along with some instruction in ESL, and are gradually moved into regular classes as they become proficient in English. Some programs that call themselves bilingual consist simply of ESL instruction and some marginal cultural materials. It is difficult to tell from the literature what the situation really is like, and there has been no large-scale survey as yet.

The problems with the full-scale bilingual-bicultural school are obvious. It is possible that in a given district a respectable number of English-speaking parents would approve even enthusiastically of their children learning Spanish, but how many would be interested in having them acquire a working knowledge of Tagalog? The scarcity of bilingual teachers, even in Spanish, constitutes another very significant impediment to the development of this model. As Lawrence Wright has pointed out, the major philosophical issues have yet to be confronted, and controversy over the movement is likely both to broaden and deepen in the future.[58]

Not that it has been immune from criticism. The United Federation of Teachers, generally supportive of the movement, has severely criticized the New York City policy of establishing a separate license for bilingual teachers. Its president, Albert Shanker, suggests that it is likely to become a second-class license in which competency in another language will substitute for subject matter competence, and will lead to ethnic segregation for both teacher and pupils.[59] New York's first Puerto Rican community district superintendent, Alfredo Matthew, also warns against the danger of racial isolation:

Our devotion to bilingual education must not be merely emotional and sentimental. We cannot support it only out of the guilt that we feel for not being in our own homeland nor to overcome the shame we feel, as justified as it may be, that our homeland is not independent . . . Puerto Ricans particularly must be wary of using the bilingual program to compensate for the colonial status of the island and its people. Those campaigns and battles have to be fought and they shall, but unless we want to prostitute what is developing as a most promising program, we must not assess the bilingual program in terms of its political value, or in terms of personal gain. Let's not kid ourselves, a youngster who is the product of bilingual education will still have to compete in a culture that is English dominant.[60]

Is the program "promising" in terms of its effectiveness in attaining the concrete goals for which it was set up? It is far too early to say, particularly since the individual programs themselves differ so widely that it is difficult to identify what the policy really is. Most of the published evaluations of bilingual schools, moreover, are so methodologically weak that they are not even worth reviewing. Those that have at least employed comparison groups typically show some differences, but they are neither strong nor consistent.[61] Perhaps by the end of the decade we may be in a better position to determine in what ways the bilingual-bicultural movement is effective, or whether it is just another in a long line of educational fads in which urban minority education has indulged itself.

CHAPTER NOTES

[1] Manuel H. Guerra, "Educating Chicano Children and Youths," *Phi Delta Kappan* (January 1972), 313–314.

[2] For example, Andrew Greeley, "Ethnicity and Racial Attitudes: The Case of the Jews and the Poles," *American Journal of Sociology*, 80 (1975), 909–933; "A Model For Ethnic Political Socialization," *American Journal of Political Science*, 19 (1975), 187–206.

[3] Andrew Greeley, "The Rediscovery of Diversity," *Antioch Review*, 31 (1971), 343–365.

[4] Clifford Geertz, "The Integrative Revolution," quoted in Greeley, p. 345.

[5] Greeley, p. 349.

[6] Greeley, p. 350.

[7] Greeley, p. 365.

[8] Howard F. Stein, "Ethnicity, Identity and Ideology," *School Review*, 83 (1975), 297.

[9] Marcia Guttentag, "Group Cohesiveness, Ethnic Organization, and Poverty," *Journal of Social Issues*, 26 (1970), 105–132.

[10] *The National Elementary Principal*, 54 (1975), 4–78.

[11] Sheldon and Eleanor Glueck, *Unraveling Juvenile Delinquency* (New York: Commonwealth Fund, 1950).

[12] Lorene C. Quay, "Language Dialect, Reinforcement, and the Intelligence Test Performance of Negro Children," *Child Development*, 42 (1971), 5–15.

[13] J. S. Kleinfeld, "Intellectual Strengths in Culturally Different Groups: An Eskimo Illustration," *Review of Education Research*, 43 (1973), 341–359.

[14] Morris Gross, *Learning Readiness in Two Jewish Groups* (New York: Center For Urban Education, 1968).

[15] Gerald Lesser, Gordon Fifer, and Donald H. Clark, "Mental Abilities of Children in

Different Social and Cultural Groups," Washington, D.C.: U.S. Office of Education, Cooperative Research Project No. 1635, 1964.

[16] Lesser et al., 132–133.

[17] Kevin Marjoribanks, "Ethnicity and Learning Patterns: A Replication and an Explanation," *Sociology*, 6 (1972), 417–431.

[18] Arthur R. Jensen, "How Much Can We Boost I.Q. and Scholastic Achievement?" *Harvard Educational Review*, 39 (1969), 1–123.

[19] Jensen, p. 42.

[20] Jensen, p. 60.

[21] See *Harvard Educational Review*, vol. 39 (Spring 1969).

[22] Daniel H. Kohl, "The I.Q. Game: Bait and Switch, A Review Essay," *School Review*, 84 (1976), 572–604.

[23] Arthur R. Jensen, "Kinship Correlations Reported by Sir Cyril Burt," *Behavioral Genetics*, 4 (1974), 1–28.

[24] Leon J. Kamin, *The Science and Politics of IQ* (New York: Wiley, 1974).

[25] Lee J. Cronbach, "Heredity, Environment, and Educational Policy," *Harvard Educational Review*, 39 (1969), 343–344; J. McV. Hunt, "Has Compensatory Education Failed? Has It Been Attempted?" in Cronbach, pp. 278–300.

[26] Jencks, 69–72.

[27] W. F. Bodmer and L. S. Cavalli-Sforza, "Intelligence and Race," *Scientific American*, 223 (1970), 19–29.

[28] Kohl, p. 582.

[29] James F. Crow, "Genetic Theories and Influences: Comments on the Value of Diversity," *Harvard Educational Review*, 39 (1969), 306–307.

[30] Arthur R. Jensen, *Genetics and Education* (New York: Harper & Row, 1972), p. 30.

[31] Clarence J. Karier, *Shaping the American State* (New York: Free Press, 1975), p. 406.

[32] Kohl, p. 600.

[33] Kohl, p. 601.

[34] C. P. Snow, "Heredity, Environment, Education," *New York University Quarterly* (Spring 1970), p. 11.

[35] Snow, p. 14.

[36] Selma Berrol, "Immigrants at School, New York City, 1900–1910," *Urban Education*, 1 (October 1969), 220–230.

[37] Berrol, p. 225.

[38] Timothy L. Smith, "Immigrant Social Aspirations and American Education, 1880–1930," *American Quarterly*, 21 (1969), 523–543.

[39] Smith, p. 529.

[40] David K. Cohen, "Immigrants and the Schools," *Review of Educational Research*, 40 (February 1970), 13–18.

[41] Cohen, p. 25.

[42] Leonard Cavallo, *The Social Background of the Italo-American School-Child* (Totowa, N.J.: Rowman and Littlefield, 1972).

[43] Guerra, p. 313.

[44] Francesco Cordasco, "Educational Enlightenment Out of Texas: Toward Bilingualism," *The Record*, 71 (1970), p. 608.

[45] Guerra, p. 313.

[46] Lawrence Wright, "The Bilingual Education Movement at the Crossroads," *Phi Delta Kappan* (November 1973), 183–186.

[47] Tyll Van Geel, "Law, Politics, and the Right To Be Taught English," *School Review*, 83 (1975), 245–272.

[48] See, for example, John MacNamara, "The Effects of Instruction in a Weaker Language," *Journal of Social Issues*, 23 (1967), 121–135.

[49] Wallace E. Lambert, G. Richard Tucker, and Alison d'Anglejau, "Cognitive and

Attitudinal Consequences of Bilingual Schooling: The St. Lambert Project through Grade Five," *Journal of Educational Psychology*, 65 (1973), 141–159.

50 Will Lissner, "Data on Ouster of Pupils Here Are Scored by a School Aide," *New York Times*, March 29, 1974, p. 34.

51 Gregg Jackson and Cecilia Costa, "The Inequality of Educational Opportunity in the Southwest: An Observational Study of Ethnically Mixed Classrooms," *American Education Research Journal*, 11 (1974), 219–229.

52 Sanford M. Dornbusch, Grace C. Massey, and Mona V. Scott, *Racism without Racists: Institutional Racism in Urban Schools* (Stanford, Calif.: Stanford University, Center for Research and Development in Teaching, 1975).

53 Arthur R. Jensen, "Do Schools Cheat Minority Children?" *Educational Research*, 14 (1971), 3–28.

54 Van Geel, p. 245.

55 *Lau v. Nichols*, 39 L.Ed. 2d 1 (1974).

57 Wright, p. 183.

58 Wright, p. 185.

59 Albert Shanker, "Where We Stand," *New York Times*, March 16, 1972, Section E, p. 9.

60 Quoted in Shanker, p. 9.

61 See, for example, H. C. Barik and M. Swain, "Three Year Evaluation of a Large-Scale Early Grade French Immersion Program," *Language Learning*, 25 (1975), 1–30; R. M. Offenberg, "Evaluation of a Bilingual Evaluation," *Reading Improvement*, 10 (1974), 271–278; M. Harris and S. Stockton, "A Comparison of Bilingual and Monolingual Physical Education Instruction," *Journal of Educational Research*, 6 (1973), 53; A. D. Cohen, "The Culver City Spanish Immersion Project," *Modern Language Journal*, 58 (1974), 95–103; Warren Balinsky and Samuel Peng, "An Evaluation of Bilingual Education for Spanish-Speaking Children," *Urban Education*, 9 (1974), 271–278.

Chapter 8

The Family and the Socialization of Children

The early development of children into social beings is the task of
the family. That process has been more intensively studied and
argued about than perhaps any other subject focus of this book.
This chapter introduces readers to some of the basic concepts used
in that study, and to a major debate about the black family. It:

Describes some basic types of family structure.
Discusses the relation between family social class and the environment provided for children.
Examines the debate over the effects of the instability of the black
family and looks critically at such questions as the existence of a
"black matriarchy," the effect of father absence, and the role of
slavery.

Some of the questions readers might address are:

The described differences between lower-lower class and working
class socialization suggest that children from the former families
may pose many problems for the schools. Which behaviors are
likely to be most difficult to deal with?
What conclusions can be drawn from the debate over the black
family? What are the consequences that may flow from accepting
one viewpoint rather than another?

Because the family as an institution is the closest of all to the transmission of culture, it is not surprising that of all the controversies in this book the arguments about family structure and its effect on schooling are the most bitter and emotional. It is with the hope of providing a more objective framework for the later examination of the issues that we begin below with a general treatment of kinship from an anthropological point of view.

THE FAMILY AS AN INSTITUTION

Theoretically, it is possible for a human society to provide any form for relationship between men and women, ranging from complete promiscuity to strict monogamy. In fact, promiscuity, a state in which every male would be eligible to mate with every female or the reverse, appears to be incompatible with any known form of human organization; and of all other theoretical forms of marriage, only two are found with any great frequency: polygamy, the marriage of one man with several women, and monogamy, the marriage of one man to one woman.

Cross-cultural studies demonstrate that the only form of marriage accepted by all societies is monogamy, though some may permit and even encourage other forms at the same time. Kephart suggests that this is so because it is a system that has more to recommend it than any other:[1]

> Under a monogamous system: (a) group members at the normal marrying age have maximal opportunity to procure a mate; (b) relatively few members are "left out" of marriage, compared to the matrimonial residue inherent in polygynous and polyandrous forms; (c) an effective method of sexual gratification is provided for both men and women; (d) intra-sex jealousy and quarrels, often a problem in polygynous forms of marriage are held to a minimum; (e) socio-legal factors involved in inheritance, property rights, and lineage are relatively easy to handle; (f) emotional needs of spouses—needs associated with primary group responses—are more effectively fulfilled than under any other marital form; and (g) child-rearing practices can be effectively aimed on establishing close emotional ties between parents and children.[2]

Within the system of monogamy itself, however, there are wide cultural variations in emphasis on how the family regards children and relatives and in how much stability is sought. The American stereotype of marriage views it as a sequence of events beginning with courtship, proceeding to marriage, and then to the raising of a family within a relatively self-contained *conjugal* or *nuclear* unit. Although this is the established pattern of most Western societies, a frequently found alternative is the *consanguine* system, in which marriage and family are distinct from one another. Though a couple marry, their loyalty is primarily retained by their original family; and they may live with or near either the husband's or wife's family, depending on their culture's particular rule about how family descent runs. Their children are integrated into the larger kinship group, sometimes called the "extended family."

Each of these forms has both its strengths and weaknesses, and a society must pay the price in the disadvantages if it is to have the advantages of any system to which it is committed. The conjugal type gives freer rein to the individual choices of its members and permits each generation to adapt to social change much more quickly, since it is considerably more independent of the older generation. It is probable, too, that emotional satisfactions of a number of kinds are more available to children in the smaller, more cohesive nuclear family than in the extended one. But the nuclear family is also more structurally fragile, because death, illness, or desertion can have immediate and important consequences for all family members, particularly for the children. It also has far greater difficulty taking care of the aged, who often find themselves isolated and rejected.

Within the large, urban, fast-changing societies of the West, where the conjugal family has an obvious appropriateness, its fragility has become increasingly apparent. The current divorce rate nationally is almost at 50 percent, one divorce for every two marriages. The social causes for this contemporary instability of American marriage are well-known: Many of the older functions of the family have been taken over by other agencies; the entrance of large numbers of married women into the job market make them less dependent on their husbands; and moral and religious sanctions against divorce have declined. All of these forces make dissolution of marriage easier and thus permit the divorce rate to rise. More fundamentally, it is probably the structure of the conjugal family, so susceptible to inner and outer stresses, that lies at the root of the problem.

If this is so, one would expect those families subject to the most social and economic stress to be the most unstable, and indeed they are. Working with a random sample of divorces, Goode calculated the following "Index of Proneness to Divorce":[3]

Occupational Status	Index
Professional, proprietary	67.7
Clerical, Sales	83.2
Skilled and foremen	74.1
Semiskilled, operatives	126.1
Unskilled	197.7

Though it has been suggested that the rising divorce rate may reflect a movement away from strict monogamy to some form of "serial monogamy," in which everyone is permitted to have more than one wife or husband so long as he does not have them all at the same time, the data in the index would argue that the problem is rather one of alleviating strains associated with one's position in the social class structure.

A further reasonable supposition is that as conjugal marriage proves too fragile to take the strain of lower class life, the family tends to reform itself closer to the model of the extended family type, which is stronger in the face of outside pressures. Thus, some observers emphasize the positive aspects of lower class culture, which Frank Riessman describes as:

> The cooperativeness and mutual aid that mark the extended family, the avoidance of strain accompanying competitiveness and individualism; the equalitarianism, informality and humor; the freedom from self-blame and parental protection, the children's enjoyment of each other's company and lessened sibling rivalry.[4]

Riessman's view, however, is by no means generally accepted. Robert Havighurst replies:

> . . . there is substantial doubt that the socially disadvantaged children in our big cities have any positive qualities of potential value in urban society in which they are systematically better than the children of families who participate fully in the mass culture. The writer does not know of any comparative study which shows American lower-lower class children to be superior in any positive respect to American upper working class or middle class children.[5]

This conflict in view is one that will reverberate throughout the chapter as it examines the controversies over family environment and education.

SOCIAL STATUS AND FAMILY ENVIRONMENT

Can one predict from the cues of social class position the existence of family patterns that often relate to particular kinds of cognitive or behavioral problems in the classroom? Teachers and administrators in the urban school, in fact, do operate on the assumption that it is possible to make such predictions with some confidence. There is a good deal of evidence that family environment influences both the child's growth of conceptual abilities, through the type of stimulation provided, and his emotional development. What is not clear is the extent to which specific family practices can be related to social class position.

Berelson and Steiner, without reporting on the magnitude of the differences, summarize the state of our knowledge of behavior variations between social classes as:

> . . . lower class infants and children are subject to less parental supervision but more parental authority, to more physical punishment and less use of reasoning as a disciplinary measure, to less control of sexual and other impulses, to more freedom to express aggression (except against the parent) and to engage in violence, to earlier sex typing of behavior (i.e., to what males and females are supposed to be and do), to less development of conscience, to less stress toward

achievement, to less equalitarian treatment via à vis the parents, and to less permissive upbringing than are their middle class contemporaries.[6]

Nevertheless, the linkage between social class and family child-rearing patterns should be accepted only with a good deal of cautious reservation. In the first place, the primary evidence for sharp differences in early social class child-rearing patterns is subject to some dispute. Two separate extensive investigations in the fifties emerged with findings that were different enough from each other to give rise to years of conjecture and attempts to explain the discrepancies. There is good evidence, moreover, that middle-class child-rearing practices tend to shift fairly quickly on the basis of changes in expert opinion.

Secondly, many of the studies on which the correlation between social class and personality outcomes is based have used worrisomely small samples. Nor are the findings of these studies uniformly in the same direction; a number of them do not establish any relationship between class and child behavior. Richard Wolf, for example, in a study to be examined in a later section of this chapter, found a high correlation between aspects of family environment and IQ's of his fifth-grade subjects, but almost no correlation between the social class position of the families and IQ. McKinley found tendencies in lower-class parents to use more severe discipline with their children and for fathers to evidence more hostility toward their sons. But both of these seem to correlate just as well with the father's satisfaction with his work as with the social class.[7] To generalize, there is good evidence to show that family environment produces consistently different kinds of behavior in children; but there is not very good evidence to show that social class status consistently predicts particular family environments.

Interpretation is made even more difficult by the evidence that shows a wide variety of family styles within what is customarily considered a single social class, as in Eleanor Pavenstedt's study of two groups of lower-class families living in the same neighborhood in an Eastern city.[8] One group of multiproblem families provided an almost chaotic environment for their children, in which neglect was a predominant feature; the other more stable working class group gave their children a well-ordered setting and a great deal of attention to their needs. School professionals would do well to note Pavenstedt's conclusion that superficially "It is not easy to distinguish between these two groups of children. They come from the same neighborhood and are equally well-dressed. Yet they must be separated, for they require a totally different approach."[9]

THE BLACK FAMILY CONTROVERSY

The issue of how much one can predict family patterns from social class status is debated—when there is any disagreement about it at all—in scholarly circles. The similar question of whether the black American family at low-income levels can be described as possessing singular characteristics that set it apart—not only from middle-class family patterns, but also from the white lower class—developed, during the sixties, into great controversy that spilled over into the mass media and became a public and political issue. The storm focused on a report entitled *The Negro Family: The Case for National Action,* written by Daniel Moynihan, then (1965) Assistant Secretary of Labor in the administration of Lyndon Johnson. Because the black lower-class family is so directly a concern of the urban schools, the report, and the resultant concern over the existence or nonexistence of a black matriarchy, is of considerable significance to the field of urban education.

Accepting Frazier's classic thesis, Moynihan found the roots of the problem for blacks in slavery and the Reconstruction Era.[10] The American institution of slavery was a particularly repressive one compared to other forms that developed in the same hemisphere, and its effect on the black family was especially atrocious. The slave's children could be sold; his marriage was not recognized; his wife could be violated or sold. He was allowed no religion without his master's permission; he was kept in ignorance and given no recognition as a human being. The slave household, as a result, tended to develop as a fatherless family, with its strength and focus in the mother.

The post-Civil War period of reconstrutcion, with its development of social forms of repression to replace the legal ones of slavery, reinforced that family pattern. Jim Crow and other forms of humiliation and repression worked against the emergence of a strong father figure; "keeping the Negro in his place can be translated as keeping the Negro male in his place: The female was not a threat to anyone".[11]

In the more recent migration to Northern cities, the black male has been further penalized in the job market; work is more readily available to the woman, and again the humiliations arising out of Northern prejudice and discrimination weigh most heavily on the male ego. The central thesis of Moynihan's report was that something must be done to stabilize the nuclear black family structure:

> The fundamental problem, in which (the widening gap) is most clearly the case, is that of family structure. The evidence—not final, but powerfully persuasive— is that the Negro family in the urban ghettos is crumbling. A middle class group has managed to save itself, but for vast numbers of the unskilled, poorly educated city working class the fabric of conventional social relationships has all but disintegrated. There are indications that the situation may have been arrested in the past few years, but the general post-war trend is unmistakable. So long as this situation persists, the cycle of poverty and disadvantage will continue to repeat itself.[12]

The case for family deterioration was based on a number of measures drawn from 1960 Census data and sample studies made during the sixties:

marital instability among black families is almost three times that of white families; among urban families, the father was absent in 23 percent of nonwhite families versus 8 percent of white families.

the nonwhite illegitimacy rate was eight times that of the white, and increasing; nationally, almost one-quarter of black births were illegitimate.

a combination of these factors has led to a startling increase in welfare dependency among nonwhites. At one point or another in their childhood the majority of black children receive aid from the AFDC program, and Moynihan found particularly alarming the fact that in 1964 the number of AFDC cases sharply increased at the same time that the nonwhite unemployment rate declined, though in previous years the direction of these indices had paralleled one another.

The influence on the boy of the absence of fathers is viewed as the explanation for a variety of pathologies: poorer school performance and lower rates of persistence in school; higher rates of juvenile delinquency, crime, and narcotics addiction:

> There is, presumably, no special reason why a society in which males are dominant in family relationships is to be preferred to a matriarchal arrangement. However, it is clearly a disadvantage for a minority group to be operating on one principle, while the great majority of the population, and the one with the most advantages, to begin with, is operating on another. This is the present situation of the Negro. Ours is a society which presumes male leadership in private and public affairs. The arrangements of society facilitate such leadership and reward it. In a word, a national effort towards the problem of Negro Americans must be directed towards the question of family structure. The object should be to strengthen the Negro family so as to enable it to raise and support its members as do other families. After that, how this group of Americans chooses to run its affairs, take advantage of its opportunities, or fail to do so, is none of the nation's business.[13]

The controversy touched off by the report blazed briefly in the mass media, then persisted in the academic journals, as behavorial scientists sought to reinterpret Moynihan's data and to argue his conclusions. The 1970 Census added fresh fuel to the speculation:

> * the general rate of illegitimacy is rising sharply and nearly doubled during the decade of the sixties.[14] The increase is attributable to the teenage population now 70 percent of all unmarrieds, who are more sexually active and less knowledgeable of contraception.
>
> * At the beginning of the decade, the illegitimacy rate among black women was 10 times that of whites, by the end of the period it had dropped to a factor of 7. But the absolute difference was still large: 5 percent of all white births were illegitimate, versus 31 percent of black births; 10 percent of all first births of whites, versus 48 percent of all black first births.[15]

Family economic status is even more closely tied than before to the sex of the family head. In 1959, 28 of every 100 poor families with children were headed by a woman, ten years later the proportion of female-headed poor families was up to 47 percent. A third of black families are headed by a woman (versus 10 percent of white families); a 1972 Census Bureau study reported that 64 percent of all *poor* black families were female-headed, up 8 percent from the previous year (versus 33 percent of poor white families, up 3 percent).[16] "Although the proportion of black families without husbands and fathers is higher than for whites at every income level, it moves down sharply and continuously . . . to about 1 in 20 among higher income families."[17]

Subsequent studies of the relation between economic instability and marital breakup among blacks and whites, however, do not confirm the existence of a simple and direct connection between the position of the black male economically, and family instability (see Panel 8.1). In any event, most of the reaction to Moynihan's thesis has focused on a number of more general issues, which are examined below.

PANEL 8.1   The Economics of Marital Instability

Some of the factual basis for Moynihan's conclusions must certainly by now be revised. For example, Greta Miao has reviewed the correlation between unemployment rates and marital instability for both blacks and whites over the period of the fifties as well as the sixties and found that it dropped not only for blacks in the sixties but also for whites.[18] The same general trends appear to hold for both groups: During periods of high or fluctuating unemployment rates, marital instability does correlate with unemployment; during periods of prosperity the correlation disappears.

The assumption that both Moynihan and the black nationalists make, that black women have been more kindly treated in the labor market than black men has also been challenged. Edwin Harwood and Clair Hodge present historical data showing that sex differences are strikingly similar for both groups.[19] As late as the decade of the 30s, Harwood and Hodge report, 85 percent of black women in nonagricultural jobs were servants, in contrast to less than 25 percent of the men; three times as many men were in clerical positions as women. Although there is today a higher proportion of black women in white-collar positions than men, the same is also true of whites. Nor is it a fact that female black white-collar workers outearn male blue-collar blacks; excluding the category of "private household," black males earn more. Even black women professionals, who are mainly teachers and represent about 10 percent of employed black women, earn only $17 more per year than black male craftsmen and foremen. Harwood and Hodge go on to suggest that family instability may not be due primarily to economic variables; historically, black women were much more likely than other servant groups to stay in domestic service after marriage, and some of their historic instability may have resulted from the competition of serving a second household.

Indeed, separate studies by Reynolds Farley and by James Sweet and Larry Bumpass[20] indicate that economic background variables such as income and employment account for very little of the difference between black and white marital instability rates. Sweet and Bumpass find that only about a quarter of the difference in the disruption rate of first marriages (34 percent for blacks and 15 percent for whites) can be explained by differences in variables such as age at marriage, education, legitimacy of the first born child, region, or social status. Farley concludes from a similar analysis that "even if there were no racial differences in employment, income, or education, there would remain substantial racial differences with regard to family headship."[21]

The absence of any very significant relationships between marital instability and demographic variables is puzzling, particularly because the shift from rural to urban circumstance, at least, has been shown to have clear effects on marital stability. Peter Uhlenberg, for example, has compared the multiple-marriage rate of Mexican-Americans in rural Texas with those in California urban areas and found a very considerable difference: 3.4 to 9.3 in the rural sample, versus 6.2 to 23.9 in the urban sample.[22] The highest of these, 23.9, is about the same as the non-white rate in general. Uhlenberg, indeed, argues that Mexican-Americans, as they urbanize in the U.S., are following the patterns of the blacks: marrying young, bearing children early, exhibiting high rates of reproduction and marital instability.

IS THERE A BLACK MATRIARCHY?

Moynihan's suggestion that black family structure took on a qualitatively different form, matriarchy, has been much disputed. *Matriarchy*, technically, is a family structure in which women are considered the family head and in which the line of descent for children is their mother's family. It is used more loosely in the current literature cited here to denote a family structure characterized by female dominance, one in which a man may be only peripherally on the scene, if he is there at all. Hyman and Reed had the interesting idea of reexamining already existing data from national surveys over the past twenty years in which questions about family influence had been included.[23] In a 1951 Gallup survey, 73 percent of black respondents reported that their mother was the most important influence on them when growing up; but so did 69 percent of whites. In a 1960 NORC study, 28 percent of blacks reported that decisions about child discipline were made by the mother; so did 25 percent of whites (the majority in both cases said that such decisions were made by both parents jointly). The greatest disparity between the two groups in that survey was in the response of married couples to the question of who made the child discipline decisions in their present family: 37 percent of blacks versus 28 percent of the whites said the wife. One might be inclined to argue that in such national probability samples the black subgroup is fairly small, and certainly not large enough to allow separate examination of the black poverty family, which is what Moynihan focused on; but as Hyman and Reed point out, the samples do tend to overrepresent the black lower class, with whites being drawn from predominantly higher strata.

Other, more recent data tend to bear out these earlier surveys. Kandel collected data on a sizable group of high school students in the Northeast, 20 percent of whom were black.[24] Their families appeared to be typical of urban black families in the United States, showing about the same percentages on indices of family breakdown. On the question of the mother's authority, Kandel found that the most striking difference between black and white families in the sample was the greater authoritarianism of black mothers of girls in *intact* families. Herzog and Lewis argue that, in general, cross-cultural studies of family life show that women are dominant in some areas of family life, men in others. "Cohen and Hodges have made the same point with regard to American working-class families, pointing out that to describe the working-class family as both male-authoritarian (or patriarchal) and as mother-centered is not paradoxical. They are, indeed, both, depending upon the functional area to which one is attending."[25]

WHAT EFFECT DOES FATHER ABSENCE HAVE?

This issue is clearly more important than that of the mother's authority as such; whether black lower class families are, or are not, matriarchies, a large proportion of them are without fathers. A very considerable argument is under way about whether father absence, as an individual variable, affects the personality of the male child, his delinquency and crime rates, his intellectual development, and his school success.

The argument that it does indeed affect all of these is based both on theory and on a massive body of research. The theory goes this way: The male child without a father (particularly before the age of five or six) identifies with the most important adult figure, his mother, and thus tends to develop a feminine identification. But he soon learns that he is destined to become a man, not a woman; and, in reaction against his own feminine identification, he becomes compulsively masculine, overly masculine, as a defense. Since the definition of "good" behavior is symbolically tied to his mother, the boy is likely to identify goodness with femininity; and the opposite pole, that of being a "bad boy," becomes for him a positive goal. Most of the reviews of the research on delinquency appear to support such a formulation of the problem, as, for example, Biller's analysis of the findings specific to father absence.[26]

The general psychological literature that asserts an important causal connection between father absence and a variety of pathologies among children has been sharply questioned (see Panel 8.2), and in his specific studies of comparative black and white family data, Farley more or less concurs with the critics.[33]

PANEL 8.2   How Good Is the Research on the Effects of Father Absence?

The critics of the position that father absence is an important contributor to later difficulties among children tend to concentrate on the research base rather than on the theory itself. Herzog and Lewis[27] have raised the following objections:

1. They call the research evidence on the relation between father absence and juvenile delinquency, poor school achievement, and confused sex identity "slight and ambiguous." Although the traditional assumptions are supported by many uncontrolled studies, if one restricts the analysis to studies using a control group and a reasonably sound design, the results are contradictory. "Among 60 studies (that meet the criteria) included in one review, 24 reported a significant association between father absence and the problem under investigation, 20 reported no such association, and 16 arrived at conclusions too mixed or qualified to be counted clearly on either side. This kind of referendum can hardly be accepted as proving a proposition."[28] They note further that many positive results are highly qualified by the frequent conclusions that family conflict and discord appear to contribute as much as father absence itself, or that delinquency is more frequent in unbroken, but unhappy, families than in harmonious one-parent homes.

2. Measures of femininity and masculinity, on which much of the research is based, have been repeatedly criticized as class- and culture-bound. Girls are rated down on femininity on the California

Personality Inventory, for example, if they confess they are not afraid of thunderstorms, or of the dark, if they fail to feel they would "go to pieces," or do not want to be a librarian. "The masculinity of high-F boys was impaired by failure to feel like starting a fist fight, to want to drive a racing car, or to enjoy reading Popular Mechanics."[29]

3. A further problem is the tendency of masculinity studies to make large generalizations from small studies in one culture. One often-cited study of fatherless boys in Norway is applied to Harlem, "though the Norwegian subjects were sons of sailor officers, in the managerial class, and experiencing recurrent absence and returns for socially approved reasons. This kind of generalization is dubious in itself. It appears all the more questionable in light of a careful replication in Italy that produced findings in flat contradiction to those obtained in Norway."[30]

Herzog and Lewis might well have noted an additional problem even with the well-controlled research—that is, its frequent use of crude statistical measures to determine a relationshsip, rather than a concern with the importance or strength of the association. Thus, in a recent study, Rosen investigated the consequences of father absence among a group of Philadelphia black boys, going to great lengths to obtain an excellent sample of all adolescents in a designated slum area.[31] He found a greater likelihood of delinquency for youths from female-centered households: 35 percent of his group of delinquents were from families in which the main wage earner was *male*, versus 65 percent of his nondelinquent control group; 46 percent of the delinquents, versus 54 percent of the non-delinquents, came from female-headed families. The association was better than chance, and thus significant; but when he tested further with a measure that indicates with some precision how much better a prediction of delinquency one can make given these results, he found that the relationship was a very small one.

Herzog and Lewis conclude that the available findings do not establish clearly or conclusively the association between father absence and any social or psychological measure; nor is there conclusive evidence of no associaion. "Nevertheless, two propositions stand strong and solid. The first is that father absence is only one among an interacting complex of factors which mediate and condition its impact on a growing child. The second solid proposition is that, even if eventually a significant association can be demonstrated between father absence and one of the adverse effects attributed to it, that impact is dwarfed by other factors in the interacting complex. Among these others are: the coping ability and individual makeup of the mother, especially her ability to give adequate mothering and supervision; the economic situation of the family; and community influences."[32]

Family instability, he shows, is associated with somewhat lower levels of schooling, occupational attainment, etc., but in nearly all cases the differences are modest and less important in their impact than other factors. Beverly and Otis Duncan have calculated, for example, that an intact family for blacks is associated with about two-thirds of a year of additional schooling, and about 4 to 5 points on the occupational scale.[34] It is worth noting a by-product of this research, which is that persons from unstable families are no more likely than others to have an unstable family themselves.

It is probable that a good deal of the inconsistency of findings on this general issue results from differences in cultural norms. Glaser and Ross compared a group of successful blacks and Mexican-Americans who came from seriously disadvantaged backgrounds with their peers who had not "made it."[35] Many of their measures differentiated *both* black and Mexican-American "successfuls" from the "unsuccessfuls"; for example: warm home atmosphere, relative school success, consistent parental discipline, parental encouragement to speak good English, etc. But successful blacks tended to come from homes in which the mother was the main disciplinarian and decision-maker, the successful Mexican-American from homes in which the father performed those tasks.

WHAT ARE THE ROOTS OF THE PROBLEM?

A good deal of the early criticism of Moynihan focused on the question of his historical explanation of the current state of the black family. In adopting the view of black historians that black family instability can be traced to its situation under slavery, Moynihan unwittingly aroused the ire of many civil rights militants who had recently come to see this view as, in their words, a "copout" for the present white society, a way of saying that current discrimination is not doing the damage.

The report did, in fact, make much of job discrimination as a source for family instability; however, in *Black Rage*, a book by two black psychiatrists, this point is dismissed as "simplistic" because it assumes that overcoming employment discrimination will solve the problem. On the basis of their clinical experience, the authors argue that the psychological damage resulting from the persisting institutionalization of attitudes toward the black man is the crucial element:

> The problem is a latter-day version of the problem faced by the slave family. How does one build a family, make it strong, and breed from it strong men and women when the institutional structures of the nation make it impossible for the family to serve its primary purpose—the protection of its members? The Negro family is weak and relatively ineffective because the United States sets its hand against black people and by the strength of wealth, size, and number prevents black families from protecting their members.[36]

The role that slavery played is now, in fact, a matter of considerable controversy among historians. In a review of the situation, Stanley Elkins has pointed out that the long tradition among historians put the emphasis on the brutality of the institution and the damage it did to the family structure and personalities of the slaves; this tradition crested in the early sixties. The view that now dominates the field emphasizes the resistance of the blacks and the growth of a black culture under slavery.[37]

The earlier tradition supported the civil rights movement and gave force to political demands for equality and for overcompensation; the current position of the blacks was due to past injustices, the result of a "blanket of history and circumstance," as President Johnson put it. Moynihan's report used that tradition with the intention of shocking people into doing something, but, says Elkins, it shocked the wrong people.

The reaction to the report led to the new "resistance" view: The black slaves did not merely react to or reflect the white oppressing culture—they rejected it; the black family under slavery developed its own strengths, and with them, a rich, diverse community life that used religion, music, and folklore as mechanisms of resistance; there existed the same range of personality types among the slaves as among the masters. The strong community life of the slaves, George Rawick claims, undergirded the abolitionist movement, which was dominated by Afro-Americans with whites only playing a role in it.[38] Herbert Gutman has extensively documented the cohesiveness of the black family through slavery to the 1920s.[39]

Elkins, himself a major contributor to the historical literature on slavery, is impressed by much of the new work, but suggests that any group dispossessed of liberty and subject to the assaults that blacks endured under slavery must show evidence of having paid *some* price in the development of their culture. But, as the section below indicates, much the same viewpoint is now gaining dominance among the social scientists as well.

IS BLACK FAMILY INSTABILITY A PATHOLOGY?

Those who argue that it is *not* approach the issue from two major assumptions. From one point of view, the symptoms of family instability are not so much pathological as they are realistic social adaptations to the special situation confronting the black family in this society. As Herbert Gans puts it:

> However much the picture of family life painted in that report may grate on middle-class moral sensibilities, it may well be that instability, illegitimacy and matriarchy are the most positive adaptations possible to the economic conditions which Negroes must endure, and will only change with the removal of those conditions.[40]

He proceeds to point out that family breakdown occurs for many different reasons, and does not necessarily produce pathological reactions among children. Further, variations in family styles have different meanings for different groups. Illegitimacy is not punished among the lower class as it is in the middle class; illegitimate children are as welcome as legitimate ones, and consequently are unlikely to suffer pathological consequences.

> Illegitimacy and the bearing of children generally have a different meaning in this population than in the middle class one. Adolescent Negro girls often invite pregnancy because having children is their way of becoming adults, and of making sure that they will have a family in which they can play the dominant role for which they have been trained by their culture. If having children offers them a reason for living in the same way that sexual prowess does for Negro men, then alternate rewards and sources of hope must be available before illegitimacy can either be judged by middle class standards, or programs developed to do away with it.[41]

The authors of *Black Rage* make the same general point in discussing the black pattern of mothering:

> The mother interprets the society to the children and takes as her task the shaping of their character to meet the world as she knows it. This is every mother's task. But the black mother has a more ominous message for her child and feels more urgently the need to get the message across. The child must know that the white world is dangerous and that if he does not understand its rules it may kill him . . . She must produce and shape and mold a unique type of man. She must intuitively cut off and blunt his masculine assertiveness and aggression lest these put the boy's life in jeopardy . As a result, black men develop considerable hostility toward black women as the inhibiting instruments of an oppressive system.[42]

In another point of view Staples agrees that the basic fault lies in applying white middle-class standards to a family structure to which they are inapplicable, but goes further to state that the black family is culturally a different entity, and is in many respects superior.

> If we were to look at black family life styles objectively, we would find that its culture is not a poor imitation of its white counterpart but a fully-developed life style of its own. Whether its distinctive cultural patterns are due to its African past, alienation from the white society, or economic deprivation is not important. What matters is how it is integrated into black family life and whether it is related to the black condition in American society. This writer submits that black family culture and social achievement are largely independent of one another.[43]

Staples goes on to point to several examples of the superiority of that family culture. On the question of sexual attitudes, sexual behavior, and out-of-wedlock children, he suggests that differences between blacks and whites are due not to higher moral standards among whites, but to the existence of a double standard among whites which is absent among blacks. That is, black men and white men are equally promiscuous; but black women enjoy the same sexual freedom as their men, while white women do not. "Among blacks, the lack of a double standard means that members of this group can engage in a meaningful sexual relationship rather than participating in sex role conflicts, or developing neurotic feelings of guilt over the question of premarital sex."[44]

This position does little to meet the problem originally posed by Moynihan, the economic nonviability of black family structure in this particular society; one wonders, too, exactly how "meaningful" casual and promiscuous sexuality can be. But the greatest drawback to the viewpoint is that it seems to stereotype the black family as much as, if not more than, the stereotypes that white social scientists are accused of elaborating. It is possible that, as LaRue argues, we are replacing white myths with black myths.[45]

CHAPTER NOTES

[1] William M. Kephart, *The Family, Society, and the Individual* (Boston: Houghton Mifflin, 1966).

[2] Kephart, p. 56.

[3] William Goode, *After Divorce* (New York: Free Press, 1956), p. 47.

[4] Frank Riessman, "Low Income Culture: The Strengths of the Poor," *Journal of Marriage and the Family* (November 1964), p. 419.

[5] Robert J. Havighurst, "Who Are the Socially Disadvantaged?" in Everett T. Keach, Jr., et al. (eds.), *Education and the Social Crisis* (New York: Wiley, 1967), p. 27.

[6] Bernard Berelson and Gary A. Steiner, *Human Behavior* (New York: Harcourt, 1964), 479–480.

[7] Bernard Goldstein, *Low Income Youth in Urban Areas* (New York: Holt, Rinehart and Winston, 1967).

[8] Eleanor Pavenstadt, "A Comparison of the Child-Rearing Environment of Upper-lower and Very Low-lower Class Families," *American Journal of Orthopsychiatry*, 35 (January 1965), 92–96.

[9] Pavenstadt, 97–98.

[10] *The Negro Family, The Case for National Action*, Washington, D.C., U.S. Department of Labor, U.S. Government Printing Office, 1965.

[11] Lee Rainwater and William L. Yancey, *The Moynihan Report and the Politics of Controversy* (Cambridge, Mass.: MIT Press, 1967), p. 62.

[12] Moynihan, no page number.

[13] Moynihan, 47–48.

[14] "Marriage on Relief: A Statistical Study," *New York Times*, March 14, 1971.

[15] "Negro Illigitimacy Rate Drops as Whites' Rises," *New York Times*, April 20, 1971.

[16] *The Social and Economic Status of the Black Population in the U.S., 1973*, Bureau of the Census, Specal Studies, Series P23, No. 48.

[17] Robert L. Stein, "Economic Status of Families Headed by Women," *Monthly Labor Review* (December 19, 1970), p. 5.

[18] Greta Miao, "Marital Instability and Unemployment among Whites and Nonwhites

—the Moynihan Report Revisited, Again," *Journal of Marriage and the Family* (February 1974), 77–86.

[19] Edwin Harwood and Clair C. Hodge, "Jobs and the Negro Family, A Reappraisal," *The Public Interest*, no. 23 (Spring 1971), 125–131.

[20] James A. Sweet and Larry L. Bumpass, "Differentials in Marital Instability in the Black Population, 1970." Working Paper # 73-8, Center for Demography and Ecology, University of Wisconsin at Madison (April 1973).

[21] Reynolds Farley, "Family Types and Family Headship: A Comparison of Trends among Blacks and Whites," *Journal of Human Resources*, 6 (1971), 75–96.

[22] Peter Uhlenberg, "Marital Instability among Mexican-Americans—Following the Patterns of Blacks?" *Social Problems*, 20 (1972), 49–56.

[23] Herbert H. Hyman and John S. Reed, "Black Matriarchy Reconsidered: Evidence from Secondary Analysis of Sample Surveys," *Public Opinion Quarterly*, 33 (Fall 1969), 346–354.

[24] Denise B. Kandel, "Race, Maternal Authority, and Adolescent Aspiration," *American Journal of Sociology*, 76, no. 6 (May 1971), 99–1020.

[25] Elizabeth Herzog and Hylan Lewis, "Children in Poor Families: Myths and Realities," *American Journal of Orthopsychiatry*, 40, no. 3 (April 1970), p. 378.

[26] Henry B. Biller, "Father Absence and the Personality Development of the Male Child," *Developmntal Psychology*, 2, no. 2 (1970) 181–201.

[27] Herzog and Lewis, *op. cit.*

[28] Biller, p. 380.

[29] Biller, p. 381.

[30] Biller, p. 381.

[31] Lawrence Rosen, "Matriarchy and Lower Class Negro Male Delinquency," *Social Problems*, 17 (Fall 1969), 175–189.

[32] Herzog and Lewis, p. 382.

[33] Reynolds Farley and Albert I. Hermalin, "Family Stability: A Comparison of Trends between Blacks and Whites," *American Sociological Review*, 36 (1971), 1–17.

[34] Beverly Duncan and Otis D. Duncan, "Family Instability and Occupational Success," *Social Problems*, 16 (1969), 286–301.

[35] Edward M. Glaser and Harvey L. Ross, *A Study of Successful Persons from Seriously Disadvantaged Backgrounds* (Washington, D.C.: Department of Labor, 1970).

[36] William H. Grier and Price M. Cobbs, *Black Rage* (New York: Basic Books, 1968), p. 84.

[37] Stanley Elkins, "The Slavery Debate," *Commentary* (December 1975), 40–54.

[38] George P. Rawick, *From Sundown to Sunup: The Making of the Black Community* (Westport, Conn.: Greenwood, 1972).

[39] Herbert Gutman, *The Invisible Fact: Afro-Americans and Their Families, 1750–1950* (New York: Pantheon, 1976).

[40] Herbert J. Gans, "The Negro Family: Reflections on the Moynihan Report," *Commonweal*, October 15, 1965, p. 48.

[41] Gans, p. 50.

[42] Grier and Cobbs, p. 61.

[43] Robert Staples, "Toward a Sociology of the Black Family: A Theoretical and Methodological Assessment," *Journal of Marriage and the Family* (February 1971), p. 134.

[44] Staples, p. 134.

[45] Quoted in Leonard Liberman, "The Emerging Model of the Black Family," *International Journal of Sociology and the Family*, 3 (1973), p. 21.

Chapter 9

The Family:
Its Impact on Motivation
and Self-Concept

What accounts for children's achievement levels in school? A number of theories suggest a direct connection between family environment and achievement, and it is to these theories that this chapter turns its attention. It:

Examines the evidence for a relation between such factors as family size and parental independence training and IQ or school achievement.

Describes some explanations offered for the aspiration levels of black children.

Looks at the contradictions in various ideas about the self-concept of children, and its relation to school achievement.

Assesses some of the suggestions for how school programs might directly influence the motivations and aspirations of lower class minority children.

Some of the questions readers might address are:

How high is my own drive to achieve? Do any of the theories of achievement motivation make sense of my own developmental pattern? Do motivations differ among the children of my own family, and what might account for these differences?

Which of the findings cited on the self-concept of black children seem closer to my own experience or that of my friends? What seems to be the most likely explanation of the contradictions in the research?

We have noted the complex ways in which cultural values appear to influence the achievement motivations of members of specific cultures; family structure and environment have also been hypothesized as independently contributing to both aspiration and mastery drives.

PARENTAL INFLUENCE ON ACHIEVEMENT DRIVE

One major explanation in social psychology for family influence on achievement is that of *independence training*, a hypothesis that holds that mothers who train their sons to be independent early in life tend to produce children with higher levels of striving for achievement. In an early study Winterbottom, comparing a group of children who exhibited high achievement drive with a comparable group with low drive, found that mothers of high achievers reported expecting mastery of a number of developmental tasks (cutting one's own food, etc.) at markedly earlier ages than did mothers of low-achievers.

But though some subsequent confirming work led a number of psychologists to assume that independence training was the important variable, Zigler and Child have shown that it is far too simple to suppose that achievement need is merely a correlate of the child's ability to withdraw from the dependency of his childhood.[1] For one thing, much independent behavior is not all oriented toward striving, or toward achieving any sort of standard; in our society, dependence itself may become the object of achievement striving, as when siblings compete for parental attention; to the extent that the payoff for achievement striving comes from recognition by others, even in adulthood, it is possible to see some achievement need as a dependency upon others.

PANEL 9.1   Family Size and IQ: Is There a Connection?

Considerable scientific attention has been devoted to an indirect factor: the possibility that *family size* may affect IQ. A longitudinal study in Scotland by Nisbet and Entwhistle found sizable differences in IQ for children from families with various numbers of children—differences favoring the small families.[2] The effect is greater for those IQ tests in which verbal skill is most important, though it shows up for nonverbal tests as well. And, although upper-class families produce higher scoring children, and also are smaller, the relation holds for them, also; it is not just another aspect of the differences between social classes.

These findings are in accord with most of the studies of social mobility in the West, all of which indicate that upwardly mobile and better educated children from lower status groups are likely to come from small families. Reflecting on these studies, Lipset and Bendix remark:

> It can be argued that "small family" is simply a spurious variable which "intervenes" between the motivation and education of the parents and the motivation and education of the offspring; that it is the better educated and mobility-motivated parents from the lower strata who tend to restrict the number of their children, that these are also the parents who motivate their children to advance and would do so whatever the size of their family. Although there is an element of truth in this, research data indicate that the size of the family itself has a number of dynamic consequences which affect social mobility and should therefore be considered as an "independent variable."[3]

These effects of family size can be summarized as follows:

1. If family income is limited, the family with fewer children can obviously better afford to feed clothe, and educate them; limited resources can be more effectively channeled. This is particularly so in the provision of education, even where there are free public high schools, since the cost of keeping the child off the labor market can be prohibitive for families with many children to support.
2. The small family increases the involvement of children with adults. Lipset and Bendix summarize an extensive body of research that supports the view that stimulation for achievement in children may result from early and long-continued association with adults and their values, rather than with other children. Studies of highly successful persons tend to show, for example, that they are likely to be only children, oldest children, or children with longer than average distance between themselves and the next oldest child. Gifted children are likely to come from families that kept them isolated from other children. Available evidence also indicates that the degree of adult contact may be the most important single factor in linguistic development.

Despite the logical persuasiveness of the connection between family size and mental ability, however, some caution is in order. John McCall and Orval Johnson report very low correlations between the two variables in a sample they studied, and suggest that the higher correlations in the literature may be due to lack of control over factors such as age or social status.[4]

This last point is particularly relevant to school success. The child who achieves in school is likely to be the one who is willing to conform to the expectations of both teachers and parents, rather than the one who marches to his own drum.

In a subsequent test of the early independence training hypothesis Rosen and D'Andrade constructed a situation in which the behavior of parents could be directly observed while their son performed a difficult task.[5] Zigler and Child comment on their results:

A quite different picture emerges in Rosen and D'Andrade's comparisons of the mothers of boys with high and low achievement motivation. Here the emphasis is clearly on direct achievement training rather than on developing the child's independence or general autonomy. The mothers of high- as compared to low-achievement boys were found to be more dominant and to expect less self-reliance in their children. However, their aspirations for their sons were higher and their concern over their success greater. The mothers of the high achievement boys became very involved with their children's performance and, as compared to the mothers of low-achievement boys, were more likely to reward success with approval and to punish failure with hostility. The mothers of high achievement boys appear to Rosen and D'Andrade to be competent strivers who give their children relatively little option about doing something and doing it well.[6]

Zigler and Child conclude from their total analysis that neither independence training, nor, indeed, the often cited parental warmth-permissiveness dimension, consistently relate to achievement need, but that it does tend to follow from parents who themselves value achievement and who actively train their children toward an achievement orientation. "Such training appears to be most effective in those instances where the parent is simultaneously neither overindulgent nor overly coercive and dominating".[7]

The pressure exerted by parental expectations has also been suggested as an important mechanism behind achievement motivation (see Panel 9.2).

PANEL 9.2   Some Research on Parental Expectations

Several lines of investigation suggest that parental expectation might operate as a simpler explanation for children's aspirations than attributing them to complex parent-child interactions. One can be found in several recent studies of the relation between the mother's expectations and the child's aspiration for schooling. In a study of over five hundred tenth graders in a variety of communities in New Jersey, Eva Sandis found that a child's aspiration for schooling beyond high school had little relation to his mother's participation in school activities, nor to whether she provided him with a variety of cultural experiences.[8] But her *expectations*—i.e., whether she *planned* for him to go to college—correlated very highly with his own plans.

Kandel and Lesser came to a similar conclusion in a study that compared the college plans of over a thousand high school students with the plans of their best friends and the plans of their mothers.[9] There is a somewhat higher agreement between mothers and daughters than between mothers and sons; but overall, the influence of the mothers' plans was twice as great as the apparent influence of the best friends. Agreement with the mother remains strikingly high across social lines: "When mothers have college aspirations for their children, 80 percent of the middle class and 67 percent of lower class adolescents plan to go on to college; when mothers have no college aspirations for their children, the proportion of adolescents with college plans drops to 20 percent and 16 percent, respectively, in the middle and lower class."[10]

A second line of evidence confirms the importance of parental pressure and expectations. Using a random sample of fifth graders in a school system representing urban, rural, and suburban children, Wolf compared intelligence test scores with an elaborate series of ratings of home environment made on the basis of interviews with mothers.[11] The scales measured the amount of parental urging toward achievement, parental stress on language development, and the parents' provisions for learning in the home. The multiple correlation between IQ and the thirteen scales that made up these clusters of factors is very high, .69.

Among all of the scales, those that best predicted IQ were measures of the parents' expectations of the child's intellectual growth, the mother's information about his intellectual development, the opportunity provided for enlarging his vocabulary, and the extent to which the parents gave the child assistance in learning. When the scale measures are regrouped into an Index of Educational Environment, the correlation between that index and school grades turns out to be .80. In this sample, at least, almost two-thirds of the variations in academic achievement are explained by family environment. The relationship between home educational environment scores and social class is very small (though it should be noted that Wolf's sample underrepresented lower class children).

One fair conclusion from all this would seem to be, however, that no one coherent set of parental behaviors can broadly explain all aspects of the complicated elements that make up children's achievement. Simple parental expectations seem to play a major role in school plans and aspirations, but in order to account for academic achievement in addition, Wolf's Home Environment measure included many other aspects of parent–child interactions. Several attacks are currently developing on the underlying bases for the theories we have so far considered.

One of these argues that the assumption of a global achievement need may itself be at fault. Doris Entwistle takes sharp issue with the measurement of achievement need, particularly with the fantasy-based measures.[12] Their reliability is low, which may account for the apparent paradoxes (e.g., the findings that show relationships for men but not for women), and their use is seldom controlled for IQ or for the length of the stories produced. As sample size increases, she points out, the number of positive findings diminish. Although the more objective measures of achievement need are reasonably stable, there remain serious questions about whether children are able to report on their own state of feelings about themselves, and the measures are highly susceptible to faking. Entwisle suggests that it may be necessary to substitute for a global conception of achievement a number of relatively independent motives specific to a variety of achievement areas. Daniel Solomon's classroom studies of children's behaviors in a number of different activity contexts suggest that she may be correct.[13]

From another direction, Trevor Williams has raised some serious questions about the validity of *environmental press* theories in general.[14] The EP model, he notes, concentrates on a particular end-result skill, such as verbal achievement, and assumes that a variety of parental behaviors will strongly influence it: Parents will *stimulate* verbal development, will *reward* child behavior related to verbal and reasoning accomplishment, and *encourage* the learning of new verbal skills and verbal exploration of the environment.

Families may not focus *all* of these types of pressures on a particular developmental area, Williams argues; they may provide one type of pressure consistently across all areas, which would be consistent with a *social learning* model. They might provide stimulation, for example, for a wide range of school-related activities, but remain relatively low on the rewards they provide or encouragement to pursue them. Or, they may consistently reward a great variety of such activities, but provide little in the way of stimulus or encouragement.

The Case of Black Family Aspirations

Williams' formulation of the problem provides some insight into an important contradiction between the real world and environmental press theory. It has been long assumed that lower class black aspirations for their children are low; in fact, the opposite seems to be the case. A number of recent investigations have shown that a majority of black parents, at least those above the very lowest poverty level, have higher academic ambitions for their sons than do even middle-class parents; they report wanting their sons to have a college education, and many wish to see them enter the professions. That these aspirations communicate themselves to the children is confirmed by other surveys of comparative aspirations among children.

Irwin Katz suggests that these aspirations are the source for much anxiety in school for the lower class black child.[15] They are so high in relation to the real amount of effort that lower class parents devote to their children's educational needs, and so unrealistic in view of the existing academic retardation, that it is difficult to see them as other than wishful fantasies. In Katz's view, however, the aspirations do get communicated as parental expectations that the child is supposed to fulfill. As such, they tend to make the child overcritical of his own efforts and, since the ability to meet significant expectations creates anxiety, overanxious in the academic situation.

Values and goals have been internalized, but not:

> . . . the behavioral mechanism requisite for attaining them. The disjunction of cognitions and behaviors is not difficult to understand, for verbal attitudes are relatively easy to acquire through mere imitation of verbalizations observed in adult or peer models. If the attitudes expressed are the "correct" ones, i.e., held by socializing agents . . . they will tend to get reinforced either directly or vicariously. But performing the behaviors that are instrumental for attaining the goals is a more difficult feat than the acquisition of verbal attitudes about the goal, especially when there are no models of competency to imitate, and when achievement strivings are not socially recognized and reinforced.[16]

Thus, the reason that one finds black high-school students expressing *higher* aspirations than whites, Katz speculates, is that they are substituting verbal expressions of achievement for the achievement behavior they are unable to act out. But since the high verbal aspiration highlights the gap between what is expected and what is achieved, "as the Negro student falls increasingly behind in his school work, the expression of high verbal standards contributes to a growing demoralization."[17]

It is perhaps significant that the high achievers among black children appear to feel more distant from their parents than do the low achievers. Rubin tested a group of each type of child by asking them to paste felt figures representing their parents on a page, then to add a felt figure representing themselves.[18] The high achievers placed themselves further from both mother and father figures than did the low achievers. Perhaps this partially explains how the real achievers extricate themselves from the dilemma described by Katz above. They may feel separate enough from their parents to maintain realistic levels of aspiration, and to follow through on them.

THE FAMILY AND THE CHILD'S SELF-CONCEPT

Another measure relating parental behavior to child achievement on which an enormous amount of work has been done is *self-concept*. The construct itself is defined variously by different schools of psychology, but in one way or another the idea of "self" has played a central and crucial role in most contemporary theories of personality. The conception of self that the individual develops is generally considered to be a very potent determinant of his behavior, and the literature of education over the past several decades has become increasingly concerned with it as the interest of educators has mounted in the affective, rather than the cognitive, outcomes of schooling.

PANEL 9.3 Can We Measure Self-Concept Adequately?

Acceptance of the utility of the concept is far from universal, either among psychologists or educators; it is a very diffuse and ambiguous term. A late 1960s review of self-evaluation concepts and studies by J. C. Diggory concluded that the literature on self-concept was utterly bankrupt,[19] and some theorists of a behaviorist bent in psychology would not even consider the literature worth looking at. The investigation of self-concept in education has encountered its own problems; assessing the self-conception in the prolonged contact of therapy is likely to be considerably more reliable than the paper-and-pencil tests which educational researchers find convenient. The measure is typically administered in the form of a check list of adjectives (sad, happy, shy, etc.) on which the child checks "those that are like me." Or sometimes, in the form of a semantic differential:

sad____:____:____:____:____:____:____happy
fast____:____:____:____:____:____:____slow

and so on through a list of opposite qualities which the child checks in reference to "Myself." The validity of such measures is difficult to establish, and many studies do not even try to prove an acceptable level of reliability.

Most psychological theories of self-concept assume that it derives from cues provided to the individual by "significant others" and, since the first and most significant others are the parents during early socialization, the family is usually seen as the primary source for the evaluation of self. It has become popular, however, particularly in educational circles, to extend this assumption to include peers, teachers, and the culture at large. Gordon Allport, for example, asks:

What would happen to your own personality if you heard over and over again that you were lazy, a simple child of nature, expected to steal, and had inferior blood? Suppose this opinion were forced on you by the majority of your fellow citizens. And suppose nothing you could do would change this opinion, because you happen to have black skin?[20]

In a book that became the forerunner for an enormous literature that criticized the urban schools (see Chapter 11), Jonathan Kozol, who spent a year teaching in a Boston ghetto school, provides a widely accepted view of the impact of the school on the self-concept of black youngsters. Kozol's class was one of many that, due to overcrowding in the school, met in the assembly hall:

It was not their fault. They had done nothing to deserve substitute teachers. And it was not their fault now if they could not hear my words clearly since it also was true that I could barely hear theirs. Yet the way that they dealt with this dilemma, at least on the level at which I could observe it, was to blame not the school but themselves. Not one of these children would say to me, "Mr. Kozel, it's too noisy." Not one of them would say, "Mr. Kozol, what's going on here?" "This is a crazy place to learn." This instead is what I heard.
"Mr. Kozol, I'm trying as hard as I can but I just can't hear a word that you say." "Mr. Kozol, please don't be angry. It's so hard. I couldn't hear you." "Mr. Kozol, please would you read it to me one more time." You could not escape the absolute assumption that this mess was not only their own fault, but something to be ashamed of. It was a triumph of pedagogic brain washing. The place was ugly, noisy, rotten. Yet the children before me found it natural and automatic to accept as normal, the school's structural inadequacies and to incorporate them as it were right into themselves. As if perhaps the rotting timbers might not be objective calamities but self condemning configurations of their own making. As if the frenzied noise and overcrowding were a condition and an indictment not of the school building itself but rather of their own inadequate mentalities or of their own incapacitated souls.[21]

The general assumption clearly illustrated by this quotation in much recent educational writing is that lower class and minority children have a lower self-concept than their white middle-class counterparts. A number of recent studies challenge this assumption and have created a debate that grows increasingly acrimonious. One of the first suggestions of a contradiction between the assumption and reality was a study by Anthony and Louise Soares which compared the self-perception of over five hundred urban elementary school children—half from a disadvantaged school, half from an advantaged one—in Bridgeport. They found that the disadvantaged children not only had positive self-images, but that they scored higher than the advantaged group.[22] A later study with a sample of 2400 children supported these findings.[23]

Critics of the Soares' study base their attack primarily on the existence of other evidence that appears to contradict the Soares' findings of superior self-image among disadvantaged black children;[24] but as the Soares noted in reply, even some of the studies often used to support the assumption of a lower self-concept among blacks actually find no relationship between ethnic affiliation and self-esteem, and only a weak one between self and social class.[25]

In a recent review of the research available, Zirkel and Moses cited fourteen studies that found *lower* self-concepts among samples of black children, seven that showed *no differences*, and five that found *higher* self-concepts for black children.[26] The result is a draw. It is possible that we simply cannot measure the phenomenon very reliably, that different instruments trying to measure the same thing are actually measuring different aspects of the concept. Zirkel counted fifteen different definitions of self-concept in his general review of the literature on ethnic identity, and noted that many of the measurements used lack any evidence of validity or reliability.[27] Or, it has been suggested, the self-concept of black children who are segregated may be quite high because they have little contact with majority children that might lead to feelings of inferiority. Zirkel almost ludicrously concludes that "it is safe to say at least that ethnic group membership may either enhance or depress the self-concept of a disadvantaged child;"[28] the only remaining possibility he omits from the summary is that it may have no effect at all.

It has been suggested that the self-concept of black children who are segregated may be high because they have little contact with majority children, which might lead to feelings of inferiority. Such a possibility sounds persuasive, considering that the Soares' study was done in segregated schools, and that at least one of the others with the same findings examined self-concept among a group of black children in a very stable, segregated community in a Southern city. But in a direct test of the hypothesis, Zirkel and Moses failed to support it.[29] They selected 120 students from the fifth and sixth grades of three schools, all with black, Puerto Rican, and white students. Each of the schools had a different one of the three groups as a majority. From each school, they selected 20 representing the majority in the school, and 10 representing the minority; the groups contained equal distributions of boys and girls, socioeconomic levels, and IQ's. The only significant difference in self-concept scores was demonstrated for the Puerto Rican children whose self-image was lower than either of the other groups. Both black and white children showed a slight tendency to have lower scores when in a majority than when in a minority, but the effect was no greater than chance.

McCarthy and Yancey have recently reviewed the vast literature on the psychological state of American blacks and seriously question the general belief in a black "crisis of identity" and the existence of a persuasive sense of low self-esteem.[30] They conclude from their very interesting argument that, because different subcultures provide varying criteria for assessing success or failure, lower class blacks should have better self-concepts than lower class whites, and middle-class blacks poorer self-concepts than middle-class whites. If the theory is supported by future research, many of the inconsistencies in our present state of knowledge may be explained.

THE SELF-CONCEPT OF ACHIEVEMENT

The most reasonable explanation of these findings is probably that there is no causal link between *general* self-image and school achievement; the psychological variable is most likely a more specialized aspect of the self that educational psychologists call *self-concept of achievement*. It seems perfectly possible that a child might feel that he is an adequate and liked person, but just does not do very well at the things the school requires from him. The high school social butterfly or football hero does not, as a type, feel notably inferior, even though she or he might just be squeezing by academically.

Brookover, Paterson, and Thomas conducted a study which looked directly at the relation between the self-concept of ability and actual school achievement, using a sample of 1050 junior high school students.[31] They found a correlation of .57 between self-concept of ability and academic achievement. Other conclusions were that the student's view of his own ability is positively related to the image he perceives others to have of him; and among those others, his parents are particularly important. Finally, as one would expect, students who aspire or expect to go to college have significantly higher self-concept of ability scores than students with low educational aspirations.

The puzzling feature of all these findings is: If self-concept of ability is a reasonable if partial predictor of school performance, why is there not a difference in self-concept of ability scores between black and white children, to match the consistent school performance differences between the two groups? In the national study of Equal Educational Opportunity conducted in the midsixties by Coleman and his associates, blacks exceeded whites on their positive response to the item "I feel I can learn;" Stephanie Paton and her associates in a Chicago study almost ten years later found that black high school students also have higher self-concept of achievement scores than whites.[32]

Robert Bilby, in a study done in association with Brookover and Erickson, provide a possible answer.[33] Using the "plans for future schooling" reported by a sample of elementary school children as the dependent variable, they factored "self-concept of ability" into three separate elements: feelings about one's *capability* for successful role performance in school, *worthiness* for role performance, and the likelihood of *reward* for role performance. *All three* of these must be present in order to account for variations in future educational plans. Even the combination of any two of the elements in interaction with each other did not prove to have any explanatory value.

The writers suggest that a low level of belief in any one must be compensated for by a very high value of the others if one's self-concept of ability is to operate as a motivator.

IMPROVING MOTIVATION AND ACHIEVEMENT:
THE ROLE OF FAMILY AND SCHOOL

Almost all attempts to improve the school performance of lower class and minority children in recent years have included an effort to work with families, and to bring family and school together as partners in the program. Chapter 10 will take an extended look at the power of the school to affect existing differences among children in academic achievement; it is appropriate here to assess the possibilities of improving the motivation to succeed by changes in family behavior and school program. So far as the family is concerned, we might summarize the evidence as follows:

1. There is a clear, consistent, and moderate relationship between social class positions and both measured intelligence and school achievement.
2. There is a consistent and probably greater relationship between particular family environments and both intelligence and school achievement, notably those environments that include parental urging to do well coupled with consistent help that realistically prepares the child for the types of intellectual and linguistic performance required in school.
3. Generalized parental urging and underlying parental aspirations in themselves do not appear to operate very consistently, as witness the case of the lower class black family. Aspirations must be accompanied by parental attention—note the consistently positive factor of smaller families—and be directed to *academic* achievement instead of some other success goal.
4. Despite items 1 and 2 above, which would lead one to assume that social class status should clearly differentiate among types of family environment, since both class and environment predict academic achievement, the correlation of these two variables is not a consistent one, appearing in some studies and only weakly, if at all, in others.

One explanation of the anomaly is in the sample variation among different studies. It is perfectly possible to find a sample of lower class children almost all of whom are in the stable working class and whose family environments do not greatly differ in range from that of a sample of middle-class children, particularly if these latter do not come from upper-middle professional families. Wolf's study of family educational process variables, for example, used a sample that admittedly underrepresented lower-lower-class families.

Another possibility is that we are simply dealing with a good deal of overlap between two causal variables (*see* Figure 9.1). If 20–25 percent of the variations in intelligence and school grades can be explained by social class, a good deal remains to be accounted for. Suppose that there are sizable numbers of families technically designated as lower class that provide helpful environments for their children, because the parents happen to be better educated than their station would predict or for any number of other possible reasons. Then the relationship between family environment and school achievement would be larger than that between social class and school achievement, because *some* of this latter relation depends on differences in family environment. So, the prediction on the basis of family environment includes some of the already explained variation due to social class. The variability of the third relationship, between family environment and social class, is probably due to differences in sampling; higher when representative numbers of lower-lower-class children are included, lower when they are omitted.

To return to the earlier discussion of teacher predictions: The further away one gets within the lower class generally from the absolute bottom of the social scale, the riskier it becomes to predict a particular kind of family environment for a lower-class child, and consequently how well he may do in school. If ethnic factors are involved, using aspiration as a cue to school achievement becomes particularly unreliable on the present evidence.

Finally, one must at least consider the possibility of increasing the lower-class family's *skills* for providing help to their children in school, since aspiration without know-how seems of little use. It is difficult to assess the

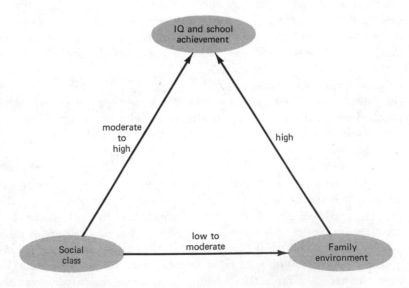

FIG. 9.1   General relationship between social class, family environment, and achievement.

degree to which such a program might be useful. There are several modest plans aimed at training parents to establish the most positive home environments for school achievement, though the evidence for their success is purely anecdotal.

But it is unlikely that intervention at the family level can crucially affect the environment of those homes which account for the most difficult problems of the urban schools, as a controlled study of the multiproblem family demonstrates.[34]

The study was done in New York State in a nonurban county and gave special, intensive service for thirty-one months by a team of highly trained social workers to fifty multiproblem families. An equal number of similar families were used as a control and were given normal public assistance service. The families were assessed both before and after the experiment on a numbr of variables that are relevant to the issues examined in this chapter: family relationships, individual behavior, care and training of children, social activities, economic practices, household practices, health conditions, and relation to worker and community resources.

The major finding was that while the demonstration group attained a slightly better degree of family functioning, its progress was not sufficiently greater than the control group's to be significant. Indeed, "a subsidiary finding indicated that the more often the problem family saw its caseworker, the less progress it showed," a result that was understandably termed "unsettling" by the director of the agency which conducted the study.

It is unsettling from the viewpoint of the school as well. If almost three years of consistent effort by trained social workers fails to change the environment of this kind of family, the school is unlikely to do much better, although there are a considerable number of educators who feel hopeful about the prospect.

THE SCHOOL AS MOTIVATOR

One of the most severe and vocal critics of the ghetto school has been Kenneth Clark, formerly a professor of psychology at the City University of New York, and member of the state Board of Regents. He has insisted, for over a decade, that the poor school performance of black children in the city is primarily a response to a failure of the system's teachers. Their belief that these children will do poorly, he argues, results in low motivation in the children to achieve. Clark has offered as evidence for his thesis the results of a number of experimental efforts, both his own and others:[35]

1. At his Northside Center for Child Development in New York, Clark operated a summer remedial reading program for several years, which produced gains of almost one year in reading level; the only difference in this program of that of the schools attended by the program's children, Clark reports, is that the Northside teachers really believed the children could

learn and communicated that belief. He further notes that his students retained their gains in the following school year, but did not exhibit similar advances in their regular classes. No comparison group data are provided, however, nor do we know how "deprived" the children were in the first place; the students were volunteers, which suggests that they were better motivated than the average.

2.   Clark points out that black children in New York attending Harlem schools in the 1920s and 1930s demonstrated at least average academic ability; assuming that they were not less economically deprived than the present population of Harlem, the blame for the current black-white achievement gap must lie with the contemporary schools.

His conclusion appears to depend on the odd notion that the teachers of forty years ago were *less* prejudiced than they are today, which is extremely unlikely considering that the psychology texts they were using taught that blacks were genetically inferior to whites. There are much more likely historical hypotheses that may account for the differences; for one thing, the blacks in New York in the earlier period were more economically stable than today's in-migrants.

3.   Clark further cites several demonstration projects of the 1960s that appeared, at least at the beginning, to have considerable effect on the motivations of black students. One of these was the Banneker Project in St. Louis; the project director told teachers to ignore mental ability scores and treat all children as superior academically, a great deal of effort was devoted to setting up reward systems to provide recognition for each student for whatever achievement he could demonstrate, and a spirit of competition among the schools was assiduously cultivated. A somewhat similar attempt was made at a junior high school in New York under the project title of Higher Horizons.

In the Banneker schools, Clark points out, the proportion of children in the top track of the schools increased from 7 to 22 percent, and the average IQ rose by 10 points. In New York, 25 percent of the students later went on to college (a rise from 4 percent earlier), the dropout rate halved, and 80 percent of the students involved in the program were judged to be more able than their earlier IQ and achievement scores had indicated.

In both cases, unfortunately, the early reported gains that Clark makes so much of (most of them admittedly subjective) faded. Higher Horizons was expanded throughout much of the junior high school system in New York until an evaluation of the Board of Education several years later found the program a failure.[36] Five years after the Banneker project had begun, the U.S. Commission on Civil Rights reported that the schools included in it were doing no better than other black schools in St. Louis.[37]

Early excitement and later disillusionment over such demonstration projects has become the norm in educational efforts of this kind. Part of the explanation undoubtedly lies in the tendency of school innovators to "cream" the available pupil population, and to accept the best motivated

PANEL 9.4   The "Doll Studies"

The negative evidence from a variety of actual school programs is unlikely to dampen the hopes of educational idealists, nor should it bring to a halt further attempts to find ways for the school to influence positive psychological growth in children. It is possible that the child's age may be a critical factor, as a recent experiment by Crooks perhaps demonstrates.[38] He tested a number of white and black four- and five-year-olds who had just been through a special preschool program in which teachers, both black and white, attempted to create an atmosphere of racial understanding and self-respect. Similar children who had not had the experience were selected as controls. The test used duplicated the procedure developed by Clark in the forties in a famous set of experiments:[39] the children were presented with four dolls, alike in every respect except hair and skin color; two of the dolls were brown with black hair, and two were white with blond hair. The children were asked to select the doll they would like to play with, the one that is "a nice doll," the one that "looks bad," and so on. As in the earlier study, control group black children tended to choose the white doll, as did the white children, and tended also to reject the brown doll significantly more. The black children who had experienced the special program, however, more frequently chose the doll of their own color, and the white children showed significantly greater brown-doll preference than the control white children. A change may be taking place in this racial preference effect, without educational intervention. Hraba and Grant did a straight replication of Clark's experiment in five public schools in Lincoln, Nebraska, with 4- to 8-year-old children and got strikingly different results. A majority of black children preferred the black doll, a preference that increased with age. Fox and his associates generally confirmed these findings, and also discovered that the Chinese children included in their doll experiments appear to be responding as black children did a generation ago.[40]

children as volunteers. There is also a very understandable habit of issuing euphoric, subjective reports based on a few cases, in order to justify further funding for a pilot project. "Novelty" effects and the Hawthorne Effect undoubtedly also play a role. In any event, Clark's thesis was later the subject of a prolonged series of well-controlled studies of what came to be called the Pygmalion hypothesis which will be described in Chapter 11.

As for achievement motivation, McClelland has reviewed the results of a series of attempts to change children's motivation to achieve by direct training programs, and reports success to be at least variable.[41] The most effective effort was by Richard de Charms who trained a group of St. Louis teachers to train their own children; the best results were from a program spread through the entire year. Several other experiments have reported successful results in changing external attributions to internal ones, with accompanying achievement gains,[42] and Seymour Spilerman has resurrected the idea of using financial rewards to increase academic motivations of lower class adolescents, suggesting that such a system, in combination with attempts to develop group competitiveness, should be effective.

The Black Studies Movement

Perhaps the most extensive educational effort to influence the self-concept of black youngsters has been through the development of special black studies programs. The introduction of materials on black history and literature began in the mid-sixties and intensified toward the end of the decade as the strains of black nationalism and separatism in the civil rights movement became more marked. As large numbers of black youth entered college, they demanded special black studies courses, and later black studies departments.

The movement has been extensively described and debated. Vontress, a black educator, has listed the following objectives that, as he puts it, one can sort out of the rhetoric:[44]

1. To enhance the black self-concept that has been damaged as the black child has grown up acquiring the attitudes of the white society toward the black. "Thus a significant goal of black studies is to make persons of African descent 'black and proud.' The objective implies that black studies is designed to be therapeutic, that it will somehow remediate the damaged self-concept."[45]
2. To train black leaders. Though colleges *have* been training black leaders, "collegians perceive the present cadre of so-called leaders to be too 'white-washed' to relate to the black masses."[46]
3. To combat discrimination among both black and white. The assumption here is that the black cannot be compared with other racial and ethnic groups that have come to the U.S., because he was brought here by force and stripped of his social heritage of language, religion, and culture. One of the basic purposes, then, is to communicate information about black history as it really was and help both races accept one another.
4. To develop black nationalism. Vontress notes that this concept is often misunderstood and misinterpreted as an effort to train revolutionaries. He argues that "it simply refers to the belief of a group that it possesses, or ought to possess, a country; that it shares, or ought to share, a com-

mon heritage of language, culture, and religion; and that its heritage, way of life, and ethnic identity are distinct from other groups."[47] Its most common expression among blacks is "soul," a feeling of shared difference from others.

As the concept of black studies has grown and moved downward into the high school and even the elementary school, criticism, particularly among black educators, has also increased in volume and severity. In his review, Vontress summarizes the critics:

1. White college faculty and administrators have quickly given in to the demands for black studies only because they want to avoid trouble, and because they don't really care about the education and welfare of blacks.
2. Although some courses have some reasonable academic content (black history, black literature, black personality), there are many one can raise serious questions about—such as, "Relevant Recreation in the Ghetto" and "The Selection and Preparation of Soul Food."
3. There are not enough scholars who are knowledgeable in the field generally, and the black intellectual who applies for a post in a black studies department is caught in an impossible situation. Unlike other departments, where he is interviewed by his peers, he finds himself before an undergraduate screening committee, and must "look black, talk black, and act black." Trained in academic objectivity, he is expected by students to provide propaganda.
4. The general result of the programs has been a self-imposed segregation that appears to be further polarizing, dividing the races and preparing black students badly to function in a society where broad training is a requisite.

More recently, Wilson Record has described black studies in the university as having had an adverse impact on academic freedom; students and some faculty members have militantly rejected any criticism of blacks or black policy, with college administrations showing little stomach for a showdown with the militants on such issues.[48] His survey of colleges indicated that in many places marginal students regard black studies programs as a convenient way of offsetting poor grades in their regular courses, and only a few schools insist on equal rigor in grading. Fully a third of the 150 sociologists he surveyed reported a fear of being labeled "racist" for giving black students low grades, and tried to discourage them from registering in regular courses in sociology. "Those I can't get rid of I give B's to," said one, "I can't stand all the hassling if I don't give them a higher grade."[49] Many white sociologists, Record discovered, simply ignore black studies departments, regarding them as "academic ghettos."

It is unlikely that these programs will wither away in the near future;

they are in many cases firmly entrenched in academic structures and faculty careers. Record believes that a two or three track curriculum for some black students may develop, but that it is also possible for the situation to improve. A national association is attempting to set standards, and there are at least the beginnings of pressures from other parts of the university in some cases. Over the years, perhaps, black intellectuals may succeed in eliminating their faults and shaping them into scholarly programs that stand for the best of what the university has to offer.

CHAPTER NOTES

1 Edward Zigler and Kevin L. Child, "Socialization," in Gardner Lindzey and Elliott Aronson (eds.), *Handbook of Social Psychology*, 2d ed. (Reading, Mass.: Addison-Wesley, 1969), 450–489.

2 J. D. Nisbet and N. J. Entwhistle, "Intelligence and Family Size," *British Journal of Educational Psychology*, 37 (June 1967), 188–193.

3 Seymour M. Lipset and Reinhard Bendix, *Social Mobility in Industrial Society* (Berkeley: University of California Press, 1964), p. 241.

4 John N. McCall and Orval G. Johnson, "The Independence of Intelligence from Family Size and Birth Order," *Journal of Genetic Psychology*, 121 (1972), 207–213.

5 B. C. Rosen and R. C. D'Andrade, "The Psychosocial Origin of Achievement Motivation," *Sociometry*, 22 (1959), 185–218.

6 Zigler and Child, p. 551.

7 Zigler and Child, p. 549.

8 Eva E. Sandis, "The Transmission of Parental Educational Ambitions, as related to Parental Socialization Techniques," American Sociological Association, 64th Annual Meeting (September 1969).

9 Denise B. Kandel and Gerald S. Lesser, "Parental and Peer Influences on Educational Plans of Adolescents," *American Sociological Review*, 34, no. 2 (April 1969), 213–223.

10 Kandel and Lesser, p. 218.

11 Richard M. Wolf, *The Identification and Measurement of Environmental Process Variables Related to Intelligence* (Ph.D. Dissertation, University of Chicago, 1964).

12 Doris R. Entwistle, "To Dispel Fantasies about Fantasy-Based Measures of Achievement Motivation," *Psychological Bulletin*, 77 (1972), 377–391.

13 Daniel Solomon, "The Generality of Children's Achievement-Related Behavior," *Journal of Genetic Psychology*, 114 (1969), 109–125.

14 Trevor Williams, "Dimensions of Family Environments," *The Generator*, Division G of AERA, 6 (1975), 2–5.

15 Irwin Katz, "Academic Motivation and Equal Educational Opportunity," *Harvard Educational Review*, 38, no. 1 (Winter 1968), 57–65.

16 Katz, 63–64.

17 Katz, p. 64.

18 Dorothy Rubin, "Parental Schemata of Negro Primary Grade Children," *Psychological Reports*, 25 (1969), 60–62.

19 J. C. Diggory, *Self-Evaluation Concepts and Studies* (New York: Wiley, 1966).

20 Arthur J. Jersild, "Emotional Development," in L. Carmichael (ed.), *Manual of Child Psychology*, 2d ed. (New York: Wiley, 1954), p. 142.

21 Jonathan Kozol, *Death at an Early Age* (New York: Bantam Books, 1968), 60–61.

22 Anthony T. Soares and Louise M. Soares, "Self-Perception of Culturally Disadvantaged Children," *American Educational Research Journal*, 6 (1969), 31–45.

[23] Anthony T. Soares and Louise M. Soares, "Difference in Self-Concepts of Disadvantaged and Advantaged Students," XXth International Congress of Psychiatry, Tokyo, Japan (August 1972).

[24] Barbara H. Long, "Critique of Soares and Soares' 'Self-Perceptions of Culturally Disadvantaged Children,'" *American Educational Research Journal*, 6, no. 4 (November 1969), 710–711.

[25] Anthony T. Soares and Louise M. Soares, "Critique of Soares and Soares' Self-Perceptions of Culturally Disadvantaged Children—A Reply," *American Educational Research Journal*, 7, no. 4 (November 1970), 631–635.

[26] Perry A. Zirkel and E. Gnanaraj Moses, "Self-Concept and Ethnic Group Membership among Public School Students," *American Educational Research Journal*, 8, no. 2 (March 1971), 253–265.

[27] Perry A. Zirkel, "Self-Concept and the Disadvantage of Ethnic Group Membership and Mixture," *Review of Educational Research*, 41 (June 1971), 211–226.

[28] Zirkel, p. 220.

[29] Zirkel, 264–265.

[30] John D. McCarthy and William L. Yancey, "Uncle Tom and Mr. Charlie: Metaphysical Pathos in the Study of Racism and Personal Disorganization," *American Journal of Sociology*, 76, no. 4 (January 1971), 648–671.

[31] Wilbur B. Brookover, Ann Petarson, and Shailer Thomas, *Self-Concept of Ability and School Achievement*, Cooperative Research Project #845 (East Lansing, Michigan: Office of Research and Publications, Michigan State University, 1962).

[32] Stephanie M. Paton, Herbert J. Walberg, Elaine G. Yeh, "Ethnicity, Environmental Control, and Academic Self-Concept in Chicago," *American Educational Research Journal*, 10 (1973), 85–99.

[33] Robert W. Bilby, Wilbur B. Brookover, and Edsel L. Erickson, "Characterization of Self and Student Decision-Making," *Review of Educational Research*, 42 (1972), 505–524.

[34] "Casework Found No Poverty Cure," *New York Times*, September 19, 1968, p. 55.

[35] Kenneth B. Clark, *Youth in the Ghetto* (New York: Harlem Youth Opportunities Unlimited, Inc., 1964).

[36] Wayne J. Wrightstone, *et al.*, *Evaluation of Higher Horizons Programs for Underprivileged Children* (New York: Board of Education, 1964).

[37] *Racial Isolation in the Public Schools*, A Report of the U.S. Commission on Civil Rights (Washington, D.C.: U.S. Commission on Civil Rights, 1967).

[38] Roland C. Crooks, "The Effects of an Interracial Pre-School Program upon Racial Preference, Knowledge of Racial Differences, and Racial Identification," *Journal of Social Issues*, 26 (1970), 137–144.

[39] Kenneth B. Clark and M. P. Clark, "Racial Identification and Preference in Negro Children," in T. M. Newcomb and E. L. Hartley (eds.), *Readings in Social Psychology* (New York: Holt, Rinehart and Winston, 1947).

[40] Joseph Hraba and Geoffrey Grant, "Black Is Beautiful: A Reexamination of Racial Preference and Identification," *Journal of Personality and Social Psychology*, 16, no. 3 (1970), 398–402; David J. Fox and Valerie B. Jordan, "Racial Preference and Identity of Black, American, Chinese, and White Children," *Genetic Psychology Monographs*, 88 (1973), 229–286.

[41] David C. McClelland, "What Is the Effect of Achievement Motivation Training in the Schools?" *Teachers College Record*, 74 (1972), 129–145.

[42] K. B. Mattheny and R. C. Edwards, "Academic Improvement through an Experimental Classroom Management System," *Journal of School Psychology*, 12 (1974), 222–232.

[43] Seymour Spilerman, "Raising Academic Motivation in Lower Class Adolescents: A Convergence of Two Research Traditions," *Sociology of Education*, 44 (1971), 103–118.

[44] Clemmont E. Vontress, "Black Studies—Boon or Bane?" *Journal of Negro Education*,

39 (Summer 1970), 192–201.
[45] Vontress, p. 193.
[46] Vontress, p. 193.
[47] Vontress, p. 194.
[48] Wilson Record, "The Black Studies Movement in Higher Education," *Equal Educational Opportunity*, III (1973), 1–16.
[49] Record, p. 7.

PART II

The Schools and Their Communities

Chapter 10

Compensatory Education

This second major section of the book turns from the economic and social background influences on the urban school to focus on the school itself. We begin with the almost two-decade experience with efforts to close the social class and ethnic achievement gaps by applying remediation. The chapter:

Describes the major components of most compensatory education programs.

Provides illustrations of significant compensatory efforts in preschool programming and in a special elementary school project.

Summarizes the status of compensatory education and the terms of the debate over its effectiveness.

Describes the current trends in the field, as exemplified in mastery learning and intervention in infancy.

Some of the questions readers might address are:

What seems to me the most plausible explanation for the mostly marginal achievement gains that compensatory programs seem to produce?

Do I agree mainly with those who argue that the benefits outweigh the costs, whatever those costs may be? Or with the critics of the effort?

Looking at the evidence on recent trends in programming, is an optimistic view of compensatory education a reasonable one? To what extent would I temper the optimism with caution?

Up to this point we have looked primarily at the influence on levels of school achievement of factors that in the main are not under the control of the educational institution. We have seen how massive social determinants such as class and ethnicity, migration and urban milieu, affect family environment in ways that appear to account for a very considerable part of the variations in academic achievement between the mainstream schools and those of lower class city children, particularly those in ethnic ghettos. In this chapter we turn to a concentration on what the school itself can do to modify the results of these social forces, the concern of the remainder of the book.

One might well ask, after reading the preceding chapters, whether such powerful forces *can* be modified by a single institution, particularly if it is a relatively weak one. Family and culture appear to account for so considerable a proportion of the variation in school achievement that, in the view of some educators, there is not enough left to matter. Others, more optimistic, argue that even if one accepts the upper possible limits of early environmental influences there is still much left to be accounted for; still others take the position that the correlation between background factors and school success is high only because the school does little to change the odds for those children who come to it with background handicaps.

This chapter and the succeeding ones will examine this last possibility in detail, in a review of the influence on urban school achievement of remediation, teachers, administration and organization of the school, school population mixture, and school–community relations.

THE COMPENSATORY MOVEMENT

By the last half of the decade of the fifties, the population changes in the central cities, combined with the growing strength of the civil rights movement, turned national attention to the urban schools' difficulties. In the early years of the sixties, a great many academic conferences were held and reports written about what must be done. During this period, the term "compensatory education" was coined, its meaning clearly implying a diagnosis as well as a remedy for the problem (*see* Chapter 7 for a discussion of cultural deprivation). If the lower class child, and particularly the lower class black and other minority children, did not do well in school because of environmentally induced deficits in training and language, then the school must compensate for those deficits with special programs aimed specifically at overcoming them.

The major source of funds for such programs came from the first federal grants to the public schools, made possible by the Elementary and Secondary Education Act of 1966. Title I of the act, with an appropriation of over one billion dollars, was aimed at the education of children of low-income families, and provided grants to all school districts with a particular percentage of low-income families and a sizable proportion of ADC families. As a result, a large number of compensatory programs went into effect in many of the urban school systems throughout the country. The review below of the most common features of these efforts to compensate is summarized from Gordon and Wilkerson's survey of existing programs:[1]

1. *Reading and language development.* This constitutes perhaps the major emphasis in most programs; it includes the use of specially trained reading teachers; the extension of time devoted to reading instruction; the development of special materials presumed to be of interest to the disadvantaged child; and, for those youngsters who do not speak English, the use of special methods and materials for developing bilingualism.

The development of special reading instructional materials has proceeded at an extraordinary pace. There is a wide variety of programmed exercise series that permit children to proceed at their own pace, a proliferation of word and grammar games, audiovisual equipment that the child himself can manipulate, including widely used gadgets that permit him to project the pages of children's books on a TV-like screen, and tape recorders that encourage him to listen to his own language production efforts.

A great deal of money has been devoted to the effort of making reading materials less alien for the minority-group child. One of the most widespread early criticisms of the urban ghetto school had been that reader illustrations gave the black child little opportunity to identify. Almost without exception, they pictured white, blond children who lived in suburban homes or in the country, occasionally visiting granddaddy's farm. Not only were they offensively and misleadingly one-sided racially—implying the nonexistence of anyone with brown, black, or yellow skin—but they presented a remarkably innocuous image of life, devoid of trouble, fear, passion, pain, or reality. Many new reading series have since appeared, of widely varying quality; some of them, unhappily, have merely colored the skins of a few of the children without much other change, but there are some very good new readers as well.

2. *Changes in teacher allocation.* A wide variety of practices have been developed to deploy teaching resources more effectively, among them team teaching and the ungraded class. The first of these, by assigning two or three or four teachers to a class, permits a more flexible use of teacher time and encourages individualized or small-group instruction for children needing special help, while other members of the teaching team are supervising activities appropriate for a large group.

Some systems have adopted an ungraded primary plan that eliminates the self-contained classroom restricted to a single grade in the early years. In such a system the first two or three grades are considered as a block of years undivided by separate grade levels; the child progresses toward mastery of required skills and knowledge at his own pace. For each subject he works with a group of other children at his own level of mastery. Thus, the wide variations in ability among children are taken into account without the stigma of "being left behind a grade" or of having to compete against unfair odds.

3. *Recognition of minority contributions.* New curriculum materials have been developed that emphasize the contribution minority groups have made to American life and that describe their cultures. The most notable area of such development is in black history and culture; some urban high schools have introduced courses in black literature as well. The movement is not without its problems; some historians fear that in the attempt to redress the prejudiced treatment of the black role in American history, found in most school textbooks, equally bad history will be written, distorting the black image in the opposite direction. There is some question, too, about the usefulness of treating the role of the black as a separate subject. Far better, some social-studies experts argue, is an approach that would include the description of that role fairly and in perspective as part of general history texts and courses.

Field trips and guest speakers have also been used to help the minority-group child see that there are roles that he can play other than those for which the society at large stereotypes him.

4. *Extracurricular innovations.* These include a wide variety of efforts to extend the influence of the school into nonschool time. New York City has long provided an All-Day Neighborhood program for selected children in a number of schools. An extension of the school program, combined with supervised recreation, is offered for children who need it throughout the afternoon. Neighborhood study centers, staffed with volunteer tutors, have appeared in many city slum sections; these often operate on Saturdays as well, and increasingly extend their activities into the summer months.

5. *Parental involvement.* Almost all large programs of compensatory education recognize the need to involve parents in the project. Visits by teachers and other project staff to the homes of pupils are encouraged, and a wide variety of methods are developed to bring the parents into the school for informal activities. Some schools now have "parents' rooms," where mothers can drop in for sewing or cooking lessons or for a chat with neighbors.

The "new careers" movement has provided opportunity for many special programs to hire members of the school community, often parents of the children in the school, as extra resources to perform helping roles. They may be employed as teacher aides in the classroom or as family aides, acting as liaison between the school and other parents. Many schools now employ professionals, too, who spend all of their time working on parent and community problems, explaining school goals to parents and helping teachers understand the community.

6. *Teacher recruitment and training.* The variety of special programs in their area are described in Chapter 12.

7. *Guidance.* Almost every project school has instituted special guidance and counseling services or increased already existing ones. Observers

note a change in the traditional definition of the guidance role from one that emphasizes the special-problems child or the misfit to one that gives services to all the children in project schools. Counselors not only provide vocational information on a more intensive basis than before, but also are using group counseling techniques aimed at improving the children's self-image and school motivation.

All of these compensatory devices have been employed in a number of mixtures in both preschool programs like Head Start and in the regular school program. The following section considers at length their effectiveness in several cases where many devices have been used together within total programs. But even if a program of that kind were to be successful, it would be impossible to tell what part of the compensatory effort was responsible for success. Because such information is of obvious strategical importance, it is useful to consider the evidence that exists on the isolated effectiveness of several of these approaches.

One would suppose from the proven influence of family environment that working with parents and with the community should have a substantial impact on the achievement of the child. Most programs that have worked with parents, however, have not evaluated that effort in any controlled sense. There is some evidence from Brookover's experimental work on the achievement self-concept (cited in Chapter 9) that training parents to relate in specific ways to their sons as achievers is far more effective than anything the school is apparently able to do. It is important to note, though, that Brookover's experiment involved a fairly prolonged, structured series of training sessions for the parents, a situation unlikely to hold for the really multiproblem families.

The relative failure of school counseling in that experiment is not surprising, in view of the previous evidence from a variety of experimental studies that counseling is of little empirical value either in reducing dropouts or raising achievement levels. A good example is the report of a five-year program, called Project Able, instituted in a number of New York City high schools.[2] These schools were permitted additional counseling staff and the services of psychologists and social workers. At the end of four years, an evaluation found no measurable effect in the way students were selecting courses, in course loads, in term averages, in attendance, or in dropout rates.

Such findings are puzzling and subject to several different interpretations. One possibility is that although counseling helps people feel better about their problems, it is not powerful enough in the school setting to influence a change in behavior. Another is that our measurements are too rough to pick up the real differences in attitudes that actually occur. A third possibility is that the evidence accurately indicates that school counseling simply is not at all helpful to children, a conclusion that most educators are reluctant to adopt in view of the anecdotal evidence from counselors and counselees that it *has* helped.

COMPENSATORY PROGRAMS—SOME EXAMPLES

Thousands of programs have been established across the country in the past decade, and it is impossible to generalize about them all. Instead, two major programs are described below, as illustrations of the general ideas behind compensation and of the controversies that are often ignited about it. The first is Head Start, a national program; the second, New York City's More Effective Schools Project, which was selected by the Office of Education as one of the twent-five best compensatory programs in the country.

Head Start and the Early Childhood Movement

As one of the earliest programs of the Office of Economic Opportunity, the agency that Congress created to fight poverty, Head Start was an immediate popular success. It was much influenced by the work of Martin Deutsch and others during the late fifties and early sixties, in applying the fundamental idea of compensatory education in the most direct possible fashion—which is to compensate for early deficiencies *before* the child gets to school in special preschool programs.[3] Though such an attempt would sooner or later have been made in any event, the OEO's early start on it can in some measure be attributed to the fact that Congress had instructed that agency to conduct no educational programs during regular school hours for children in school.

Head Start was much more than nursery school training for disadvantaged children. Originally, at least, it included medical and dental treatment (many of the children, it turned out, had never been seen by a doctor or a dentist), social work intervention if necessary to help the family, and strenuous attempts to bridge the gap between the school program and the community. Much use was made of "indigenous" aides, women who lived in the poverty areas who were hired by the program to serve as liaison with the families of the children or in the classroom as teacher aides. It was in the best educational sense a program for the whole child.

The curriculum of Head Start was developed by early childhood experts to conform to the best of modern preschool practice, particularly shaped to provide an environment that stressed experiences assumed to be lacking in the lower-class home and neighborhood—such as free play with a great variety of materials of different shapes, colors, and textures; there was also an emphasis on verbal experiences of many types—listening to stories read by the teacher, talking into a tape recorder and listening to one's own voice, becoming familiar with the shapes of the letters of the alphabet, and so on.

Head Start was so successful that popular accounts of the first summer programs gave the impression that the problem of the disadvantaged school child had once and for all been solved. Many of the children in the summer preschools made astonishing gains over the period of a few months in measured verbal skills and even in IQ; *group* averages in many cases were impressively higher than on pretests. Experts were more cautious, but even they were enthusiastic, as in this report from an observer of the early trials:

> Fortunately, the majority of teachers did capitalize on the small group and did make the transition to preschool type of curriculum. Activities included art, stories, science activities, creative play and visits to various community facilities. These programs were designed to stimulate children's thinking—but, in contrast to situations mentioned earlier, the curriculum was geared to the interests and abilities appropriate to the children of this age.
>
> I feel much of the success of the program was due to the factor of class size. For years educators have asked for small groups and Head Start has demonstrated the values of such class size. The most consistent comment from teachers was in terms of class size and their feeling that substantial gains were possible since they could provide each child with maximum individualized instruction. Whether or not communities will ultimately bear the high cost of small group instruction is another matter. However, this may be the price we must pay for earlier deprivation.
>
> I also believe that the program will ultimately affect the entire educational field in another way. Everywhere I went, school administrators were discussing ways to extend school downward.[4]

But even as the first Head Starters entered school, some educators began to have doubts about the lasting nature of the summer gains. Annie Butler, in an article prophetically entitled "Will Head Start Be a False Start?" warned that the schools would have to change if the preschool progress were to be maintained:

> It has been predicted that Head Start and other preschool education programs will result in some of the most revolutionary developments in elementary education this country has ever known. A tremendous corps of teachers has been helped to understand concepts of child development which are important in working with young children, including the deprived; further, they have had experience in planning programs for them. If we now forget what has been learned this summer and expect Head Start children to "adjust" to existing school programs, these children will have made a "false start." If these children really are to have a head start, changes will have to be provided by many schools.[5]

Within a few years, though Head Start programs in many instances had been lengthened to extend through the entire school year, controlled studies that took the place of earlier informal observation confirmed fears of a regression in gains made in preschool experiences once the child enrolled in school. The amount of regression varied, depending probably on the original degree of retardation in the particular group of children and on the quality of the program, but it almost always occurred.

The results of hundreds of separate evaluations of Head Start programs were, however, uneven enough to suggest the desirability of a full-scale national study of its effectiveness; and OEO commissioned such a study in

1968, to be undertaken by the Westinghouse Learning Corporation. The study included Head Start graduates of both summer and full-year programs for the years 1965, 1966, and 1967; at the time, these children were entering the first, second, and third grades. By the terms of this mandate, a true experiment could not be done, since experimental and control groups could not be set up in advance of the Head Start experience.

Westinghouse selected a random sample of Head Start centers across the country, including both summer and full-year programs. In the "target areas" served by these selected centers, lists of children who had attended Head Start were drawn up, and a random sample of such children was taken. Another list of all children in the area who had been eligible to attend Head Start but had not done so was compiled, and control samples were drawn from that list. Tests of psycholinguistic ability, reading readiness, and primary grade achievement were then administered at appropriate grade levels to both groups of children. In addition to these cognitive measures, a self-concept measure, an attitude test, and a classroom behavior inventory were also completed. The conclusions of the study were that:[6]

Summer Head Start programs do not produce either cognitive or attitudinal gains that persist into the elementary grades.

Full-year programs, though not affecting the attitudinal dimensions studied, produce gains that are marginally apparent in the elementary years.

The program is most effective in Negro centers in some of the central cities and in the South.

In the elementary grades studied, Head Start children's readiness scores (in the first grade) approach national norms, but they are below national norms on the Standard Achievement Test and the Illinois Test of Psycholinguistic Ability in the later grades.

The publication of the Westinghouse study was greeted with outrage in many quarters; Head Start is a very popular program, and the environmentalist leanings of most educators disposed them to a suspicion of any such findings.

Subsequent reviews of evaluations of Head Start and other early childhood programs, cited in a report to Congress by the Comptroller General, support the Westinghouse findings; gains in neither achievement nor IQ persist beyond the third grade. However, some early reports of several studies that have traced children into later grades indicate a reappearance of differences between experimental and control children. The issue is still an open one.[9] The two articles cited in Panel 10.1 constitute a remarkably interesting example of the growing body of controversy over large-scale educational research, and the interested reader will find it useful to consult them himself. The controversy itself demonstrates the difficulty of conducting research in a politically sensitive area, an issue that has been thoughtfully dissected by Walter Williams and John Evans in *The Politics of Evaluation*.[10]

PANEL 10.1   The Head Start Research Controversy

Of the many critical attacks on the study's validity, the most extensive probably is that of Smith and Bissell, who argued that the design of the study made its findings suspect:[7]

1.   A simple, random sample of only one hundred centers, they pointed out, produced a sample that was unrepresentative. Since programs vary considerably, centers should first have been classified by type, then sampled; as it was, many kinds of centers remained unexamined. Further, since a number of centers refused to cooperate and had to be substituted for by additional selections, it is difficult to tell whether the sample was even a good random one.
2.   In the selection of individual children, the population sampled were those children who had been eligible for Head Start in the designated years, and who still lived in the area. Smith and Bissell noted that this eliminated from the experimental group those families who might have moved from the area *because* of the Head Start experience of their children, and gone to more advantaged neighborhoods with better schools and more opportunities. Although the mean income, education, and occupation of parents of experimental and control children were about the same, these critics showed that the correlation between income and the child's Metropolitan Readiness scores was lower for the experimental group than for the control group; the same was true of parental education and occupation. This suggests that, for one reason or another, the two groups of children were not really equivalent.
3.   Smith and Bissell did a reanalysis of part of the Westinghouse data, focusing on the full-year programs and on the first-grade sample, using a somewhat different statistical treatment. They found a significant difference in Metropolitan Readiness scores favoring the experimental children. They further analyzed for the subgroup of black, urban centers, and found a difference of roughly 7.5 score points between the two groups.

In a detailed rebuttal, Cicirelli and his associates point out that the reanalysis of data, which was based on a selection of the *most* favorable portion of the data, is largely meaningless. Even with a different statistical procedure, they note, Smith and Bissell's finding of a difference of 7.5 points in readiness score is not appreciably different from their own results for that special group of urban black children; they further note that the number of the cases in the subsample is very low, and that the difference itself is "so small that it requires heroic assumptions to imagine that it is going to improve the life chances of these children or indeed their performance in school."[8]

Cicirelli and his colleagues defend their sampling procedures by noting that the absence of information about the centers made it impossible to group them by important characteristics before sampling, but that they are at least representative of the regional distribution of the centers. As for the selection of individual children, they had early noted the problem of migration out of the area, and had done a special supplemental study of it. Their conclusion was that a total of only 12 percent of the target population had moved out of their areas, which were roughly equivalent to school districts, and that these moves included a large number to nearby locations outside the school district but within the same general poverty area.

As a final point, it must be noted that whatever the flaws of the Westinghouse study, it does confirm the findings of the majority of hundreds of small separate studies that followed up Head Start children—particularly those that were carefully enough designed to include control groups.[11]

There is some evidence for the possibility that preschool training simply does not have any lasting effect for children of any background, whatever their degree of cognitive retardation. A longitudinal study of a large number of Toronto children found that by the end of four years in school the earlier advantage shown by children who attended some form of preschool disappeared; to put it perhaps more accurately, what seems to happen is that the children without such training manage to catch up after some years of schooling.[12]

The response from experts to the disappointment of earlier hopes that an answer had been found for the learning retardation of the disadvantaged child took several forms. One was to argue that most of the Head Start programs were based on early childhood theories that work very well for middle-class nursery schools but are inappropriate for children who are seriously retarded linguistically. At the University of Illinois, Bereiter and Engelmann began experimenting with a highly structured program, far from the relaxed, playful atmosphere advocated by early childhood experts. Their theory of early childhood training for the disadvantaged is based on the following logic:[13] Most middle-class children grow up in small families with few siblings to interact with, and in a general environment characterized by close adult supervision and consequently a great deal of verbal interaction with adults. As they begin to move out of the family orbit, preparatory to beginning school, the middle-class nursery milieu is an excellent one for them. It emphasizes social interaction with other children, sharing, and opportunity to explore without close adult supervision and direction, and a great deal of physical as opposed to verbal manipulation.

The lower-class child, on the other hand, tends to grow up with many other children, siblings as well as peers, and with considerably less inter-action with adults than is available to the middle-class child. He is far more accustomed to physical activities than verbal ones; and because he is much less supervised, he has ample opportunity to explore the world about him. The traditional nursery school, say Bereiter and Engelmann, is pre-cisely what he does *not* need; instead, he requires experience with language in a highly structured form—*i.e.*, to be drenched with language—in order to learn how to conceptualize the world of experience. It is noteworthy that the most successful of the groups in the Perry Preschool Project cited earlier were subjected to the kind of experience proposed by Bereiter and Engel-mann:

> To summarize other findings from the three waves taken together, the instruc-tional method found to be effective is "verbal bombardment," which means that the teacher maintains a steady stream of questions and comments to draw the child's attention to aspects of his environment. The "bombardment" does not necessarily demand answers on the part of the children. It is continued in re-warding the child for good performance, in disciplining him, and in presenting academic material, and the complexity of the language is increased as the child's verbal ability develops. It is this "bombardment" that seems to produce dramatic growth in intelligence.[14]

In a long-range study of the effects of these methods, Karnes has tenta-tively found that the more highly structured nursery school gets better results, though she suggests that even these higher gains are unlikely to be maintained without further intervention once the child has entered school.[15]

In its most radical form, a call for reconstructing the school itself (see Panel 10.2) instead of trying to prepare children for the school-as-it-is, results

---

PANEL 10.2 The Critical Attack on the Bereiter-Engelmann Method

Many early childhood experts have been horrified by the Bereiter-Engelmann approach to the preschool child; they are, almost without exception, committed to a humanistic orientation, and have criticized the program in unscientific terms that range from "cruel and inhuman" to "mechanistic." Even so thoughtful a critic as Brian Crittenden uses the phrase "The Child As Pavlov's Dog" as one of his subheads. His critique is one of the more balanced attacks on the approach, however, and worth examining:[16]

1. Bereiter and Engelmann, he argues, completely separate the cognitive from the affective use of language. They ignore "the determining influence which forms of language have on personal relations, emotional responses in various situations, attitudes, immediate versus delayed satisfaction, sense of guilt, a person's perception of his environment, and so on."[17] As an example, he cites the passage involving the generic term "weapon," which he considers "quite macabre" in places.

2. The methodology, with its emphasis on drill, does not teach children to raise relevant questions about something they want to know or do.

3. Schooling is treated as a phenomenon isolated from life. For Bereiter and Engelmann, "Education becomes a purely formal, complex initiation ceremony. It employs a special language which plays a very significant part in the ritual. Those who perform the ritual successfully are admitted to the land of the privileged. Thus, to give culturally disadvantaged children a chance of surviving the initiation, the preschool coaches them in the rudiments of the ceremonial language."[19]

4. On the most general level, Bereiter and Engelmann accept school as it is, without questioning either its structure or the values it enforces, and adopt a purely technological approach, finding a better way to engineer what it perhaps should not be doing in the first place. This is much the same point that Frank Riessman so vigorously argued in his attack against what he calls "the preschool mythology." What we are doing, he says, is attempting to prepare children for presently inadequate educational systems; the emphasis is not on changing educational institutions but on changing these youngsters to fit into existing programs."[19]

in experimentation with "alternative schools," a movement discussed in a later chapter. In a more moderate form, the demand results in significant amounts of compensatory intervention in the school program itself. If children who grow through Head Start programs fall back when they enter school, then the obvious answer is to step up the intensity of the effort in the school itself. We turn now to look at one of the most intensive attempts to do just that with Title I funds.

NEW YORK CITY'S MES PROGRAM

In 1964, a planning committee for more effective schools (MES), established by the city's superintendent of schools, submitted a report recommending policy guidelines for producing more effective education for children of the city's slum areas. The recommendations involved basic changes in four aspects: pupils and curriculum, personnel, school plant and organization, and community relations; and included such specifics as selecting schools for the program to maximize integration, setting a maximum class size of twenty-two, providing teacher specialists, grouping classes heterogeneously, instituting team teaching, and emphasizing positive school-community relations.

The program was established in 1964 in ten schools; in 1965 eleven additional schools were designated for the experiment. In the evaluation data cited below,[20] the first group is referred to as "old ME schools," the second group as "new ME schools." The program has been subjected to five different assessments at various points in its history. The fourth evaluation study is reported here; the old MES had been in operation for three years, the new MES for two. By the mid-seventies, the program had been abandoned.

The data for this study was gathered primarily through observational visits of a team of two educational experts who: (a) rated the quality of class functioning in visits to classes that were selected randomly as well as to classes elected by the principal; (b) interviewed staff to obtain their appraisals of the school's effectiveness; (c) arranged to have the children fill out simple rating instruments that measured their perceptions of themselves and of the school; (d) obtained data on arithmetic and reading test scores throughout the period under study. A total of 300 classes in the middle grades were observed, and sixty-eight early childhood classes were visited by specialists in that field. Similar data was collected for a group of control schools.

The findings were contradictory in ways that educational experimenters find relatively common:

1. There was considerable variation in effectiveness from school to school, suggesting that a fruitful direction for follow-up research is to examine the reasons for the differences. Although a possible assumption is that a special combination of school factors accounts for the greater effectiveness of some schools, it is, of course, equally plausible that the explanation lies in different characteristics of the student bodies.
2. As perceived by the staff, the climate of the experimental schools was enthusiastic, hopeful, and interested. The parents were enthusiastic, and even the observers, in their overall ratings of the schools, agreed that they were places to which they would willingly send their own children.
3. Despite considerable administrative and organizational change, how-

ever, there was litte curriculum innovation or instructional adaptation to smaller classes. The report notes:

> Observers noted that a majority of lessons they saw could have been taught to larger classes with no loss of effectiveness. When asked about changes in "method of instruction," administrators and teachers alike pointed to the small class and the use of specialists and cluster teachers which we would consider administrative changes rather than changes in method of instruction. All levels of staff noted that the basic weakness of the program, or their major disappointment with it, centered about the functioning of teachers, which they attributed to inexperience and lack of preparation. All of these comments combined to a general agreement that in the absence of specific preparation, teachers have not revised techniques of instruction to obtain the presumed instructional advantages of the small class and the availability of specialized instruction. In view of this, the lack of academic progress is not surprising.[21]

4. Both in comparison with the control schools and in general progress within the ME schools, the children showed little overall difference in attitudes or achievement. Because the focus of this book is on the academic retardation of large city slum children, the data on this point are worth a more detailed look.

First, the children's functioning in the classroom was rated on the basis of an assessment of five observable behaviors: the children's verbal fluency, their interest and enthusiasm, the amount of overall participation, the proportion of children volunteering, and the number of children who raised spontaneous questions. Measures of the first four of these variables showed no difference between ME and control children. On the fifth, ME children were significantly better; but the absolute number of children who raised spontaneous questions was, in any case, very small.

Second, the children's perception of their class was measured by having them respond to twenty statements about it—for example, "Everyone can do a good job if he tries," and "Good class, except for one or two children." The results were compared not only to control group children but to responses from a previous study of a busing program that had used the same instrument. MES children showed slightly more positive perceptions of their classrooms than controls, but were no more positive than the broader sample of children in sending schools. An interesting sidelight is that between 70 and 80 percent of the children in these slum schools checked positive responses to such items as "Do interesting things in class," and "Can have a good time in class."

Third, the findings on both arithmetic and reading achievement are open to some variable interpretation:

Compared to urban norms of arithmetic achievement, third graders in old MES schools in 1964 were five months behind, a loss of two months;

fourth graders were one year and one month behind in 1964, and only 7 months behind in 1967, having gained on the norms by four months.

In new MES schools, fourth graders went from one year and one month behind to only six months behind, but fifth graders remained one year and two months behind the norms.

In reading, an analysis of second, third, and fourth grades in all the schools over three years showed a regression for two of the grades of four to five months, with the fourth grade remaining the same, nine months behind.

Some initial gains were made in the first year, but in more cases than not, they were lost in the succeeding years.

The report concludes that no consistent effect on achievement can be demonstrated for the ME schools, and suggests that early gains for some groups probably were due to a Hawthorne effect. It does, however, note that for *some* children ME schools were indeed more effective; when the reading scores for (a) those children who had never attended any other school *and* who had a full three years of ME schooling were compared to (b) those who had the full program but had a history of school mobility and to (c) those who had less than the three years and a history of mobility, the first group did somewhat better. The comparison consistently favored those with a consecutive educational history and full MES, though even these remained behind the norm by a half a year.

This important finding was confirmed by a later study of MES by Forlano, who separated for examination those children who had an unbroken record in MES, comparing their reading scores with a matched sample of other slum school children.[22] A year after the Fox study these children were reading almost at the level of national norms. For this most stable group of children, then, the schools were more effective.

HAS COMPENSATORY EDUCATION FAILED?

By the end of the sixties, only five years after the first massive funding of a compensatory education policy, a prolonged debate began over whether or not it must be judged a failure. Below is a discussion of the two major positions that appear to have attracted most of the partisans in the argument.

Most spokesmen for ethnic minorities, the Department of Health Education and Welfare, and some educational policy experts, notably Henry Levin of Harvard, take the position that the effort to raise lower class minority children's academic achievement levels has simply been mismanaged or has not been massive enough.

The NAACP, for example, has sharply criticized the Title I program for spreading funds too thinly and for not ensuring that the available resources reached the appropriate children.[23] Their report cited a number of instances in which the funds were spent on educational hardware that bore little direct relation to the instruction of poor children, or for resources that the local school districts should have themselves paid for.

The Follow Through program is also cited as a typical example of the tendency to starve a program and then call it a failure. Follow Through was intended as a test of the possibility that Head Start children stopped progressing upon entering school because the educational enrichment provided by the preschool activity was not continued in the normal classroom. Instead of providing the 120 million originally called for, however, the appropriation was for only 15 million. HEW therefore decided to use the funds as a vehicle for developing field tests of a variety of alternative approaches to improving elementary school instruction for the disadvantaged; 173 sites around the country were designated, each of them assigned several of the selected approaches in such a way that a particular approach could be tested under a variety of conditions. Unfortunately, the rigorous evaluation at each site that would have justified such a rational scheme proved to be too expensive and had to be scaled down. It turned out to be impossible to select adequate controls, and difficult to retain the cooperation of that many schools.[24]

Advocates point to the generally positive HEW report in 1972 that summarized and reviewed the evidence on the effectiveness of compensatory education.[25] Although it concluded that there is no guarantee of success, and that some very expensive programs have failed, the report claimed that any program succeeding in helping disadvantaged children gain better than their average of .7 of a grade equivalent per year was worthy, and that, in general, compensatory education was a sound investment. This conclusion was based primarily on the California experience over a four-year period, during which time 54–67 percent of the children receiving compensatory service at an average cost of $300 per child showed reading gains greater than the usual maximum gains associated with such groups.

If such reading gains in particular studies are put in the form of a predicting equation, as Herbert Kiesling has done, it is possible to calculate costs for raising achievement levels attributable to given inputs.[26] Instruction by reading specialists, for example, is estimated as contributing .076 of a grade equivalent per month of instruction for each ten minutes of instruction per pupil per week. An extra $100 invested in that resource will thus contribute .09 of a month's gain, and $300 per pupil per year will bring the average disadvantaged child to normal reading levels. Why don't large scale survey results show such gains? One answer: because they depend on matching program children with superior control groups, since children who need remediation most are selected for Title I groups, leaving only the somewhat more able children as comparisons.

Henry Levin has incorporated these views into what one might almost call a theory of compensatory education.[27] It is possible, he argues, to estimate the value of the human capital that is invested by families and the society in the superior academic abilities of the middle-class child; the availability, for instance, of a highly educated mother during the first five years of life, or the opportunity to experience a wide range of cultural stimuli. We should be prepared to invest an equal amount in raising the achievement of the lower class child who did not have access to those resources.

From this perspective the figure of $300 per year per child currently taken as a reasonable investment in compensatory education, Levin says, is far from satisfactory. We must define the student population that needs remediation, do the necessary research to discover the most effective treatments and their costs, and calculate the dollar costs associated with closing the gap. He hypothesizes that $300 a year may take as long as 14 generations to do so, but we might find that $5000 a year would reduce the gap in 16 years, and $15,000 a year may do it in eight years. Thus, equalizing opportunity is primarily a matter of politics, the issue of what we consider important to spend money on.

Those who see compensatory education as a failure include a number of politicians who have grown dubious about what they describe as "throwing money at social problems," and a growing number of policy analysts and educators who have followed closely the results of a considerable variety of evaluation efforts. Although they concede that compensatory funds have in some cases been misdirected, they point out that in most cases they have been allocated fairly and spent for programs which even the NAACP presumably would agree were useful, but with only minimal results.

The optimistic report by HEW on the effects of compensation is widely regarded by members of this group as an exercise in public relations, a biased reading of the evidence in an attempt to justify continuance of a program that Congress was beginning to question. A similar Rand Corporation review of the evidence is quite gloomy throughout.[28] Even Levin criticized the HEW report as an exceedingly poor job from the research point of view; the California data on which it principally bases its conclusions were unreliable, and the report ignored the much less encouraging results of other state evaluations.[29]

To the advocates' accusation that the successes of compensatory programs are unfairly ignored, and that inappropriate comparison groups are used, the critics reply that the only success stories are newspaper and magazine puffery without any comparisons at all. In 1972, for example, *The New York Times* frontpaged a story about the "astounding" success of a new reading method developed by a teacher in a largely black district on Long Island.[30] Kenneth Clark immediately was quoted as recommending that "this is the way every child in the country should be taught to read," and officials of the state department of education began an immediate study of the method that raised reading scores in one year from the bottom quarter in the state to the top quarter. Several days later it turned out that the pupils had been coached for the test, had been given extended time limits for completing it, and the story was given a deecnt burial. However, most such magical cure stories never receive such a followup.

Reasonably well-controlled studies conducted by objective evaluators, as in the MES case, provide little support for optimism. Philip Jensen and his associates studied the Victoria Plan in Newark for a number of years, and followed one class of graduates into junior high school.[31] The Plan embodied every major suggestion ever proposed for compensatory education, from supplementary teacher resources, new methods and materials, to full-time social workers and a school psychologist; what marginal effects they observed disappeared by the second year of junior high.

Recognizing the difficulty of providing good comparison groups for Title I programs, some state evaluations use each child as his own control by comparing his performance after a remedial year with the average of his gains during the preceding years in school. Although such a procedure tends to show that gains exceed those of preceding years, the differences are seldom very substantial. The question, argues the critics, is not whether compensatory education is effective *at all*, but whether the average gains are worth it. The use of predicting equations to estimate costs of bringing children up to grade equivalents by projecting gains from a single month assumes a consistency of relationship for which there is no evidence. There is, in fact, reason for assuming the opposite, that whatever gains can be made are the result of very minimum effort, after which they hit a ceiling.[32]

Levin's justification for enormously increasing the resources put into compensation in order to close the achievement gap in eight or ten years might, in practice, founder on just such a ceiling effect. Even if it did not, spending $10,000 a year on a child for ten years, as he notes, requires $100,000 which, if invested carefully, would yield him about $8000 a year in income, considerably more than any amount of schooling would be likely to provide by anyone's estimate. If the target population consisted of 4 million children, we would have to provide 400 billion in order to satisfy his goal of wiping out the achievement gap in a period of ten years. And any way, would the next group of children be any less in need of compensation?

Many of the suggestions and experiments that have become part of the compensatory effort are characterized by an apparently total disregard of the cost/benefit relationship. We have already noted the central issue in MES of class size. In a city with over a million pupils, the reduction of average class size by even a very small number costs millions of dollars, with little evidence that it is likely to have an effect on achievement.[33] Or, to take an extreme example, one experimental summer program concentrated on twelve children, and used twelve teachers, twelve black assistants who had been trained in human relations, and twelve counselors, providing a team of three adults for every child.[34] The end result was that each child was able to make some sort of oral presentation to the assembled children and adults—an achievement that is, in itself, a little difficult to evaluate. If the results *were* useful, how could one possibly apply them to the real world? It is no wonder that critics like Sternlieb become acid when commenting on the apparently aimless way that school reform has proceeded:

> If the 1960s demonstrated anything, it was that the social sciences had not yet arrived at the point of being able to design programs that could be counted on actually to accomplish what they were supposed to accomplish. It is true that social scientists themselves were often quick to recognize the failure of a given program and would attempt to design a better one in light of that failure. But the new programs usually did not arise from any strong theory or experimentation; they were rather the complements of past failure. One simply took apparently salient parameters of the failed program and reversed them. The façade of intellectual rationalization was produced *post hoc*. Schools don't work because classes are too large and lack the personal touch? Make classes smaller. If smaller classes don't work, what is left? Ah! Skin color, the teacher's doesn't match that of the student; change the skin color. That doesn't seem to be working as well as one would have anticipated? It must be the supervisor's color—paint principal black. Principal black doesn't seem to provide the answer? Paint the board of education an appropriate hue. And when this entire mountain of stratagems brings forth nothing but mice, bring the parents in. Parents don't want to come in? Pay them, we'll call them paraprofessionals. And so it has gone. The rationalizers of these programs dutifully turn out Ph.D. theses and proposals without end to justify the programs.[35]

Even in the absence of theory, one might well ask for a greater consideration of the balance between costs and benefits in educational innovation. But many would argue that this kind of analysis is irrelevant to social policy, that the kind of reasoning that makes sense when applied to a decision about the design to be selected for a military plane hardly makes sense when applied to matters of education. It would be difficult to calculate the benefits derived from these programs, they suggest, even if only a minority of the children involved were helped. From this point of view, the values of our society look topsy-turvy: The social benefits of a new military plane justify spending billions, but the relatively small cost of special educational programs for underprivileged children is questioned because educators have not triumphantly succeeded in wiping out the problem.

As attractive as this view appears to be for most educators, it obscures the very real advantages of a cost/benefit approach, which requires a critical look at the actual payoff for social programs and some hard evidence for the relative effectiveness of alternative solutions. In this case, it would force us to examine the social benefits of concentrating on raising the academic achievement levels of lower-class minorities; if the ultimate aim is to insure everyone a good chance at a stable and adequately rewarding occupation, the cost of trying to achieve it through educational intervention may be far greater than the cost of subsidizing employers to expand their employment and training opportunities. Even if the benefits of greater success in school should appear large enough to justify very sizable costs, it might turn out that some strategy quite different from compensatory approaches is more effective and justifies much bigger costs.

PANEL 10.3   Compensatory Education as Imperialism

A third view of compensation that is articulated primarily by those who identify themselves with the "cultural difference" thesis described in Chapter 8 is that the compensatory idea itself is morally and practically wrong. As Richard Davis puts it, it is a "kind of cultural imperialism in the guise of melting-pot democracy."[36] His statement of the thesis is included here to add a necessary dimension to the discussion of compensation; an examination of the implications of the approach may be found in the chapter on culture.

Davis (and other "difference" theorists such as the Baratz's) attack compensatory education for the following reasons: (a) it assumes that there are norms of values and aspirations that everyone must share, and imposes those norms on those who are not part of the dominant culture; (b) those who fail to meet those norms are assumed to be deficient —they are implicitly or explicitly told that they are not worthy, that the range of experience the student brings from his own culture is inferior; (c) compensatory education assumes further that the student can only be brought up to the norms, never that he can exceed them, never that his own experience might be more valuable and richer than that of WASP culture; (d) it fails to recognize that educational programs in American schools were not designed for the needs of third-world persons and that the American middle-class skills and values they are forced to learn may not be relevant for them in the future world.

He concludes that it is the schools that must change, and the programs that must be redesigned, not the children. On the practical level, the most basic problem with compensatory education is that it does not work, and thus sets children "on the track of failure by reinforcing the myth of their own incapacity."[37]

TRENDS IN COMPENSATORY EDUCATION

Some moderates, Robert Havighurst among them, now believe that drastic educational intervention is no longer necessary, that the general economic and social situation of lower class blacks and other minorities is slowly improving, and that this trend will in the long run close the gap.[38] Parents of the poor are better schooled, and he sees a slow decrease in the degree of economic and racial segregation, a gradually decreasing gap in life style and social values between the lower and middle class, and an improvement in cognitive skills among minority students. The necessary preparation for school life will thus be taken over by families of the contemporary poor in the same way that it has always been by midddle-class parents.

In this process the school can help children best by finding ways of presenting the normal curriculum more effectively. Havighurst sees no evidence for claiming that what should be taught must be made more flexible, or that the lower class child must be given freedom in the classroom to seek his own cultural ends. Indeed, if his analysis is correct, what is required is more effective methodology in the form of more careful structure, a major trend that has come to be known as "mastery learning."

Mastery Learning

Although by no means a new concept (earlier in the century teaching was influenced by a "teach-test, teach-test" methodology), the interest in learning to mastery is presently associated with Benjamin Bloom, a University of Chicago educational psychologist.[39] Bloom is critical of the basic expectations of most teachers that for any given course of instruction about a third of the students will master the skill or the material; about a third will learn a good deal, but not enough to be regarded as good students; and a third will fail or "just get by." In justification of such an attitude, when the teacher tests a class, he distributes the results on a normal curve and assigns appropriate grades. The explanation is that aptitude for any particular learning task is normally distributed; and if the same instruction is provided, the end result will be a normal distribution of achievement. Generally speaking, the correlation between aptitude and achievement can be expected to be high, about .70 or higher.

Bloom's suggestion for mastery learning is based on the different assumption that students' aptitudes are normally distributed, but if the type of instruction and the time devoted to a particular task is made appropriate to levels of aptitude, the majority should be able to achieve mastery:

> Most students (perhaps over 90 percent) can master what we have to teach them, and it is the task of instruction to find the means which will enable our students to master the subject under consideration. Our basic task is to determine what we mean by mastery of the subject and to search for the methods and

materials which will enable the largest proportion of our students to attain such mastery.[40]

For this purpose, a substitute definition of aptitude is needed; and it has been proposed by John Carroll as: *the amount of time required by the learner to attain mastery of a learning task.* Bloom is convinced by his study of aptitude distributions that there is a considerable difference between an approximately 5 percent of students who have some special talent for a subject and the remainder of the population; there may be another 5 percent at the bottom of the aptitude distribution who have just as special disabilities (as in the case of dyslexic students in reading classes). But for the 90 percent in between:

> We believe [as does Carroll] that aptitudes are predictive of rate of learning rather than the level (or complexity) of learning that is possible. Thus, we are expressing a view that, given sufficient time (and appropriate types of help) 95 percent of students (the top 5 percent plus the next 90 percent) can learn a subject up to a high level of mastery. We are convinced that the grade A as an index of mastery of a subject can, under appropriate conditions, be achieved by up to 95 percent of the students in a class.[41]

The abandonment of the normal curve of achievement can be justified on several grounds, Bloom argues. Though it may be appropriate as a means of identifying those with the greatest talent in a society that can use only a limited number of highly educated persons, a society such as ours, which requires an increasingly skilled labor force, must find ways of increasing the proportion of the well-educated of any age group. Secondly, the normal curve is an appropriate statement of chance activity, of randomness; but educators are engaged in purposeful activity, and the distribution of achievement should be very different from the normal curve.

An ideal strategy for learning mastery, presumably, would be to supply a tutor for each student. In the absence of such an expensive ideal, some form of the ungraded school would be necessary, with children grouped according to their instructional needs. Bloom stresses the importance of getting students concerned with levels of performance instead of grades. In one informal experiment, he permitted the instructor to work normally (on the assumption that teaching behavior is the most difficult of the variables to change in the situation), but provided extensive feedback on progress to the students and the teacher. Where supplementary instruction for some seemed necessary, that also was supplied.

Bloom suggests that mastery has far-reaching consequences for the individual and his view of the world:

> The student desires some control over his environment, and mastery of a subject gives him some feeling of control over a part of his environment. Interest in a subject is both a cause of mastery of the subject as well as a result of mastery.

> Motivation for further learning is one of the more important consequences of mastery. At a deeper level is the student's self-concept. Each person searches for positive recognition of his worth and he comes to view himself as adequate in those areas where he receives assurance of his competence or success . . . Mastery and its public recognition provide the necessary reassurance and reinforcement to help the student view himself as adequate.[42]

Bloom's recently published book describes a wide variety of mastery learning experiments in classes ranging from elementary school to college, and claims a considerable degree of success for the method. In one predominantly black community college in Chicago, for example, a class in which two-thirds of the students did not achieve mastery on the first unit only one-third required special work by the end of the year. And 88 percent of this class earned a grade of A or B at the end of the semester in contrast with only 35 percent of a control class taking the same final examination.[43]

Evidence available from other sources includes a very well-designed and controlled study by Charles Burrows and James Okey,[44] who randomly assigned students in a math class to four treatments: a control group that worked on a series of programmed units on geometry, receiving only help from the teacher; a second group was given the list of performance objectives in advance; a third that, in addition, was provided with sample test items to practice on; and a fourth that was given diagnostic tests after each skill book was completed and directed to further instructional units covering the items they had missed. Each of the four groups contained high and low aptitude students, and the fourth, mastery, group was the only one in which low aptitude students did as well as the high aptitude controls in the final examination. Merely providing the student with the performance goals in the second group, thought by some to be of major importance to mastery learning, did not prove effective, however; the crucial difference appears to lie in diagnostic testing and in providing further instructional aid in working on the revealed deficiencies, which is supported in other findings, particularly those of William Rohwer.[45]

Mastery learning is not without its critics. Patrick Goff and others have suggested that a claim for overcoming individual differences as demonstrated in past learning achievement for all levels of education is rather hard to swallow,[46] and only future rigorous evaluation of the approach can prove the critics right or wrong. What is perhaps more troubling is the potential effect of mastery education on the school curriculum. Although Bloom himself argues that almost all children can be taught "everything that the schools have to offer," enthusiasts like Rohwer put the problem differently: Schools should teach only what is teachable. One of his criteria for the selection of any skill to be taught by the schools is the extent to which a substantial majority of adults possess that skill. The clear implication from his work is that only those skills over which we can expect everyone to attain mastery are worth teaching. The adoption of this view would appear to many educators to be a sure prescription for driving out of the urban schools those middle-class children who are still attending them.

Intervention in Infancy

A second major trend in compensation embodies an approach taken by those who conclude from the relative lack of persistence of the effects of preschool programs that the four-year -old is already too old to constitute a productive starting point. Their answer is to begin intervention much earlier in the child's life—as early, if possible, as six months.

Although there was some early interest expressed in the Kibbutz model in Israel, in which children lived apart from their families, early childhood experts came to be convinced that a more moderate amount of training, if it comes early enough, will overcome the deficits engendered by impoverished family and community life. A wide variety of suggestive research underpins the approach; one of the most convincing examples may be found in the very careful research of Burton White.[50]

PANEL 10.4   The Kibbutz as a Model for Early Intervention

In the beginning phases of this movement there was considerable interest in the model provided by the Israeli kibbutz of the children living from infancy in a residential center staffed by professional child care personnel. Child-rearing in the kibbutz, the communal form of life adopted by some of the earlier settlers in Israel, took such a form to free women from family chores so that they could make an equal contribution with men to the task of nation-building. Although only about three percent of Israelis now live in kibbutzim and there is no very convincing general evidence of the superiority of their child-rearing patterns,[47] the residential, communal children's center appeared to have produced some positive results in overcoming the deprived family backgrounds of non-Western immigrants into Israel.

Bruno Bettelheim, whose book *Children of the Dream*[48] became widely known as a thoughtful and positive examination of kibbutz rearing, does not agree that it is a viable alternative for the American welfare mother. He points out that the circumstances that led to the kibbutz mother's ready acceptance of communal child-rearing were very particular ones; she feared that she might damage the child herself because of her limited background, and also that mothering would interfere with her deep desire to live and work as freely as a man. For the American welfare mother to give her child over to others, on the other hand, would be a deprivation, because the baby is often her only available emotional satisfaction. Furthermore, though she wants her child to have a better life, handing him over to educators may well mean that as he grows up he will leave her behind or look down upon her.

The Israelis, in the course of time, themselves moved away from early childhood intervention as an approach to their own disadvantaged population. A variety of programs in that country are experimenting with approaches that are much closer to American compensatory ones.[49] One, for example, uses real-life, inductive ways of teaching mathematics, another emphasizes classroom integration of Oriental immigrant children with native Israeli children (though not including the top or bottom 15 percent in ability), a third concentrates on repairing "overall intelligence" rather than specific skills.

White began by studying six-year-old children in an effort to identify those child behaviors that, taken together, attest to his *competence*. His general categories include: (a) social abilities; for example, getting the attention of adults, using them as resources, expressing both affection and hostility to both peers and adults, expressing pride in self, etc.; (b) linguistic competence, including the ability to sense dissonance and note discrepancies, the ability to anticipate consequences, the ability to deal with abstractions, etc.; and to plan and carry out multistep activities, etc.; (c) executive abilities, for example, to carry out multistep activities, use resources effectively, etc.

In a second stage of the study, White sought out a number of families that seemed to be doing a great job of producing highly competent children, and a contrasting group that seemed to develop children with low levels of competence. Where the families identified had new babies at home, the investigators requested permission to watch the baby develop. Some of the findings thus far: Differences in competence begin to show up as early as 14 months, clear differences are visible from two years of age; the 12 to 15 month, and the 18 to 21 month periods appear to be most interesting and crucial; overall competence correlated .40 with social class, but the relationship was due only to linguistic and executive competence, with none at all observed between social class and social competence measures.

White concludes from his careful observational data that the more effective infant caretakers are themselves competent as designers, consultants, and authorities. They protected the child from the dangers of the home, and the home from the child, and then provide maximum access to the living quarters. They made themselves available to assist and excite, usually responding "promptly even if only to delay action. They would pause to consider the baby's *purpose of the moment*. They would provide what was needed *with* some language, on target and at or slightly above his level of comprehension. They would add a related idea or two and they would not prolong the exchange longer than the baby wanted."[51] Finally, though they were loving and encouraging, they were *firm,* and no matter how young the infant, they set clear limits. But the twenty-or-so experimental programs in early intervention that have incorporated at least some semblance of research control have produced very mixed and inconclusive results, as the following examples demonstrate: In a two-year study, Karnes and associates worked with twenty infants between one and two years of age by training their mothers in two-hour weekly sessions.[52] They were instructed in principles of teaching that emphasized positive reinforcement, and trained to use a sequential educational program at home with their babies. Compared with a matched group who did not receive training, the experimental children were sixteen points higher on the Binet IQ. Six of the children who could be compared with their own siblings scored an average of twenty-eight points higher.

Painter worked directly with children, eight through twenty-four months old, using tutors who spent one hour a day, five days a week, for a year on language and concept training, body image, and number and time concepts.[53] The children's IQ scores were significantly higher than those of a control group; and on twenty-five subtests composing a number of standard language tests, the experimental children did better than controls, although in only eight of the twenty-five did the difference exceed chance.

One of the more ambitious of the studies is Gray and Klaus' Early Training Project. Their seventh-year report was able to follow some of the children through the fourth grade.[54] Group 1 attended, over a period of three summers, a ten-week preschool; in addition, they had three years of weekly meetings with a specially trained home visitor. Group 2 began a year later, and received two years of the same treatment. Group 3 was a control. Although Gray and Klaus report that the results are encouraging, it is difficult to see why they do. Both treatment groups show a pattern of rising IQ during the training period, then a leveling off and decline; the control group shows a similar pattern, except that the increase comes with entrance into first grade. But, in 1962, the IQ of Group 1 was 87.6; in 1968, it was 86.7. For Group 2, the comparable figures are 92.5 and 90.2. The control group showed, if anything, a somewhat smaller decline from 86.7 to 84.9. Results on the achievement batteries showed no superiority for the experimental children.

THE MILWAUKEE PROJECT

The experiment that received the greatest public attention and that appears to have achieved the most extraordinary results was developed outside the mainstream of such early childhood studies. The project grew out of the work of a group established to study the problems of mental retardation, the University of Wisconsin's High-Risk Population Laboratory.[55] In search of a method for early detection of the population, the Laboratory surveyed an area of Milwaukee that had been identified as having an extremely high rate of retardation. The area contained only two percent of the city's population, but contributed fully a third of all children diagnosed as "educable mentally retarded." The survey itself showed that depressed maternal IQ was strikingly associated with child retardation: 45 percent of the mothers with IQs below 80 accounted for almost 80 percent of the children with IQs below 80. The infants of these mothers did as well as other infants, but after infancy the children of mothers with IQs above 80 progressed fairly evenly, while those with mothers with IQs below 80 showed a marked decline in intellectual level (see Fig. 10.1).

From a population of mothers with newborn babies, a sample was drawn of those with IQ below 75 (all were blacks). The children were randomly assigned to an experimental and control group. Beginning with the first

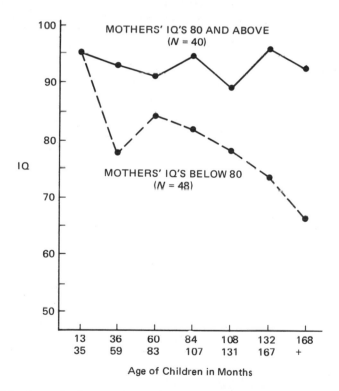

FIG. 10.1   IQ change in the offspring of disadvantaged mothers as a function of maternal IQ.

Source: Howard Garber and Rick Heber, *The Milwaukee Project: Early Intervention as a Technique to Prevent Mental Retardation* (Connecticut University, Storrs National Leadership Institute, 1973), p. 3.

few months of life, the experimental children became part of a massive intervention program, with the following major components:

They were transported daily to an educational center where teachers worked with them first on a one-to-one basis, later in groups of two or three. Early cognitive stimulation activities were followed, as the children grew, by a strongly language-oriented curriculum, highly structured and prescriptive.

Their progress was closely monitored with an intensive schedule of measurements, also applied to the control group children, including assessments of physical maturation, infant adaptive behavior, standardized tests of general intelligence, learning, motivation, and social development.

At the same time the Laboratory carried out a maternal rehabilitation program aimed at helping the mothers of experimental group children obtain training and work and deal with other problems in their life.

Figure 10.2 summarizes the results at a little over five years of age. (The Contrast group represents the IQ scores obtained in the original survey of

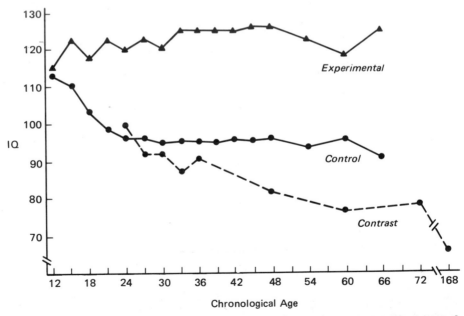

FIG. 10.2   Mean IQ performance with increasing age for the experimental and control groups in comparison to the high risk survey contrast group.

Source: Howard Garber and Rick Heber, *The Milwaukee Project: Early Intervention as a Technique to Prevent Mental Retardation* (Connecticut University, Storrs National Leadership Institute, 1973), p. 10.

children with mothers below 75 IQ.) The mean IQ of the experimental group based on scores taken at each major age interval was 123.4; the mean of the control group, 94.8. The conclusion: "The present standardized test data, when considered along with performance on learning tasks and language tests, indicate an unquestionably superior present level of cognitive development on the part of the Experimental group. Also, the first 'wave' of our children are now in public schools. *None* have been assigned to classes for the retarded and we are collecting data on school performance generally."[56]

The Milwaukee Project certainly provides some reason for optimism on the early infancy training theory, but it should be mixed with caution. That infant intelligence scores of the babies of lower and higher IQ mothers are relatively equal, but diverge later, is hardly proof of the Laboratory's assumption that the decline in IQ is due to interaction with the retarded mothers; *infant* IQ measures very different behavior from that tested by scales administered when the child has acquired language. Indeed, according to Michael Lewis and Harry McGurk, the concept of intelligence does not apply to the infancy period, and should not be used at all to judge the effectiveness of programs.[57] Furthermore, the instructional program of the early childhood center included many of the skills which form the basis for tests of IQ of young children; the teachers were, in some sense, teaching the test. The scores of the control group are puzzling, too; if none of the experimental children were assigned to classes for the mentally retarded, with an average score of 90 there is little reason to expect the schools to assign the control children to those classes either. The gains of the experimental group, nevertheless, do seem far too large to be ephemeral. Even should there turn out to be some regression later, it is doubtful that they would regress to the level one would expect for a group of children of mothers with IQs below 75.

So, in one way or another, compensatory education as a policy is still very much alive, though attention has critically shifted to a number of other efforts to change the schools in more fundamental ways, a series of approaches to be examined in the following chapter.

CHAPTER NOTES

[1] Edmund S. Gordon and Doxey A. Wilkerson, *Compensatory Education for the Disadvantaged* (New York: College Entrance Examination Board, 1966).

[2] Joseph Reswick, *The Effectiveness of Full-time and Coordinated Guidance Services in the High School* (Project Able 4th Report, New York City Board of Education, January 1966, mimeo).

[3] Martin P. Deutsch, "The Disadvantaged Child and the Learning Process," in A. Harry Passow (ed.), *Education in Depressed Areas* (New York: Teachers College, 1963), 168–178.

[4] Keith Osborn, "Project Head Start—An Assessment," in Harry L. Miller (ed.), *Education for the Disadvantaged* (New York: Free Press, 1967), p. 135.

[5] Annie L. Butler, "Will Head Start Be a False Start?" *Childhood Education* (November 1965), p. 166.

[6] Victor G. Cicirelli, *The Impact of Head Start* (Washington, D.C.: Office of Economic Opportunity, June 12, 1969).

[7] Marshall S. Smith and Joan S. Bissell, "Report Analysis: The Impact of Head Start," *Harvard Educational Review*, 40 (February 1970), 51–104.

[8] Victor G. Cicirelli, John W. Evans, and Jeffry S. Schiller, "The Impact of Head Start: A Reply to the Report Analysis," *Harvard Educational Review*, 40 (February 1970), p. 124.

[9] *Project Head Start: Achievements and Problems.* Report to the Congress by the Comptroller General, May 20, 1975; *Report on Educational Research*, Vol. IX, June 15, 1977, 2–3.

[10] Walter Williams and John W. Evans, "The Politics of Evaluation: The Case of Head Start," *Annals of the American Academy of Political Science*, 385 (September 1969), 118–132.

[11] See, for example, M. A. Krider and M. Petsche, *An Evaluation of Head Start Preschool Enrichment Programs as They Affect the Intellectual Ability, Social Adjustment, and the Achievement Level of Five Year Old Children Enrolled in Lincoln, Nebraska,* Nebraska University, 1967; S. B. Chorost, *An Evaluation of the Effects of a Summer Head Start Program* (Staten Island, N.Y.: Walcott Research Center, June 1967); *A Study of the Full Year Head Start Program* (Washington, D.C.: Planning Research Corporation, 1967); Douglas Hommes, *et al., An Evaluation of Differences among Different Classes of Head Start Participants* (New York: Associated YM-YWHA's of Greater New York, 1966).

[12] Judith A. Palmer, *The Effects of Junior Kindergarten on Achievement* (Toronto: Toronto Board of Education, 1966).

[13] Carl Bereiter and Siegfried Engelmann, *Teaching Disadvantaged Children in the Preschool* (Englewood Cliffs, N.J.: Prentice-Hall, 1966).

[14] David P. Weilcart, *et al., Perry Preschool Project Report,* Ypsilanti Public Schools (June 1964).

[15] Merle B. Karnes, *A Research Program to Determine the Effects of Various Preschool Intervention Programs* (University of Illinois, Institute of Research in Exceptional Children, 1968).

[16] Brian S. Crittenden, "A Critique of the Bereiter-Engelmann Preschool Program," *School Review*, 78 (February 1970), 145–167.

[17] Crittenden, p. 155.

[18] Crittenden, p. 156.

[19] Frank Riessman, "The New Preschool Mythology: Child-Centered Radicalism," *American Child* (Spring 1966), p. 19.

[20] David J. Fox, *Expansion of the More Effective School Program* (New York: Center for Urban Education, 1967, mimeo).

[21] Fox, p. 122.

[22] George Forlano and Jack Abrahamson, *Measuring Pupil Growth in Reading in the More Effective Schools* (New York: Board of Education of the City of New York, 1968).

[23] *Title I: Is It Helping Poor Children?* National Association for the Advancement of Colored People, 1970.

[24] Garry L. McDaniels, "The Evaluation of Follow-Through," *Educational Researcher*, 4 (1975), 7–11.

[25] *The Effectiveness of Compensatory Education, Summary and Review of the Evidence,* U.S. Department of HEW, 1972.

[26] Herbert J. Kresling, "Reading Performance of Disadvantaged Children: Cost Effectiveness of Educational Inputs," *Education and Urban Society*, IV (1972), 91–103.

[27] Henry M. Levin, "Some Methodological Problems in Economic Policy Research," *Education and Urban Society*, 7 (1975), 303–349.

28 *How Effective Is Schooling? A Critical Review and Synthesis of Research Findings* (Santa Monica: Rand Corporation, 1972).

29 James Welsh, "Compensatory Education: Still More Funds," *Education Researcher*, 1 (1972), 13–15.

30 David A. Andelman, "New Plan Raises Reading Levels," *New York Times*, March 9, 1972, p. 1. See also stories following during that week.

31 Philip K. Jensen, James M. O'Kane, David Graybeal, and Robert W. Friedricks, "Evaluating Compensatory Education," *Education and Urban Society* (February 1972), 211–233.

32 The HEW report cited in footnote 25 itself suggests the probability of a ceiling effect.

33 Bruce M. Mitchell, "Small Class Size: A Panacea for Educational Ills?" *Peabody Journal of Education* (July 1969), 32–35.

34 Barbara R. Carkhuff, "The Development of Effective Courses of Action for Ghetto School Children," *Psychology in the Schools*, VII (July 1970), 272–274.

35 George Sternlieb, "The City as Sandbox," *The Public Interest*, no. 25 (Fall 1971), p. 18.

36 Richard H. Davis, "The Failures of Compensatory Education," *Education and Urban Society*, IV (1972), p. 255.

37 Davis, p. 240.

38 Robert J. Havighurst, "Curriculum for the Disadvantaged," *Phi Delta Kappan* (March 1970), 371–373.

39 Benjamin S. Bloom, "Learning for Mastery," *Evaluation Comment*, 1 (May 1968), Center for the Study of Evaluation of Instructional Programs, University of California at Los Angeles.

40 Bloom, p. 1.

41 Bloom, p. 4.

42 Bloom, p. 11.

43 Benjamin S. Bloom, *Human Characteristics and School Learning* (New York: McGraw-Hill, 1976).

44 Charles K. Burrows, James B. Okey, "The Effects of a Mastery Learning Strategy on Achievement." Paper presented at the American Educational Research Association, Washington, D.C., March 30–April 9, 1975.

45 William D. Rohwer, "Decisive Research: A Means for Answering Fundamental Questions about Instruction," *Educational Researcher* 1 (1972), 5–12.

46 Patrick Groff, "Some Criticisms of Mastery Learning," *Today's Education*, 63 (1974), 88–93.

47 Benjamin Schlesinger, "Family Life in the Kibbutz of Israel: Utopia Gained or Paradise Lost?" *International Journal of Comparative Sociology*, XI (December 1970), 251–271.

48 Bruno Bettelheim, *Children of the Dream* (New York: Macmillan, 1969).

49 Sol Weiss, "Educating the Disadvantaged Israeli Style," *Urban Education*, July 1972, 181–197.

50 Burton L. White, "Critical Influences in the Origins of Competence," *Merrill-Palmer Quarterly*, 21 (1975), 243–265.

51 White, p. 264.

52 Merle B. Karnes, James A. Teska, Audrey S. Hodgins, and Earladeen D. Badger, "Educational Intervention at Home by Mothers of Disadvantaged Infants," *Child Development*, 41 (December 1970), 925–935.

53 Genevieve Painter, "The Effect of a Structured Tutorial Program on the Cognitive and Language Development of Culturally Disadvantaged Infants" *Merrill-Palmer Quarterly*, 15 (1969), 279–294.

54 Susan W. Gray and Rupert A. Klaus, "The Early Training Project: A Seventh-Year Report," *Child Development*, 41 (December 1970), 909–924.

55 Howard Garber and Rick Heber, *The Milwaukee Project: Early Intervention as a Technique to Prevent Mental Retardation* (Connecticut University, Storrs National Leadership Institute, 1973).
56 Garber and Heber, p. 10.
57 Michael Lewis and Harry McGurk, *The Evaluation of Infant Intelligence* (Princeton, N.J.: 1972) Educational Testing Service.

Chapter 11

School Reform Movements

While compensatory programs were trying to improve school effectiveness by supplying "more of the same," a series of efforts were being made to reshape the schools themselves. This chapter:

Reviews those reform ideas that stem from the humanist tradition emphasizing freedom of the child, and assesses the impact of their "alternative" school programs.

Describes the trend toward adapting those approaches to the education of lower class minority children.

Examines a variety of proposed reforms that can be categorized as part of an "accountability" movement, including voucher systems, performance contracting, and statewide assessment programs.

Tests the basic assumption of all these reforms (that changing the school can significantly improve pupil achievement generally), by reviewing the evidence available on school impact.

Some questions readers might address are:

The author clearly finds little to admire in the more extreme forms of alternative schooling. If I disagree with his judgment, how would I answer him?

On the basis of my own experience with the "open classroom" in public schools, is he correct in claiming that it is now being used to describe basically traditional educational approaches?

Can I accept the data presented that appear to mean that schools and teachers cannot change predicted learning levels by very much? If I don't find it acceptable, what would be a reasonable position to take in response?

During the same period of time that compensatory education experiments and the controversy they produced were proceeding (roughly the decade from the middle of the sixties to the midseventies), American schools were subjected to the sharpest and the most prolonged attack in their history. The resulting turmoil produced an extraordinary body of literature and a sense of continuing uncertainty and ambivalence in the schools themselves; whether it also led to any meaningful change in education is a question that this chapter is primarily devoted to examining.

An outline of the reform movements is provided in Figure 11.1 in the hope that it will clarify the subsequent discussion. The humanist tradition (shown appropriately on the left) exploded in an attack on the schools and on schooling itself with a fury that approached, at times, hysteria. It led to the establishment of a number of private "free schools" around the country, and to a movement within the public schools toward the "open classroom"; the conceptual bedrock of this movement was the freedom of the child.

The rationalist tradition, whose central interest was producing improvement in academic achievement, found compensatory education wanting in this area, and spawned a number of reforms aimed at making the school "accountable" for its educational results. Educational voucher proposals sought to do so by making the school accountable to parents; performance contracting introduced the accountability practices of business and industry;

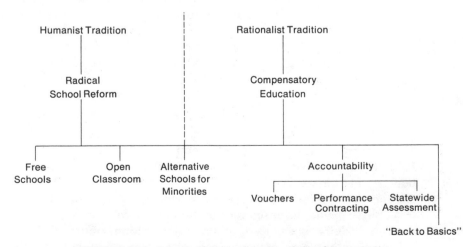

FIGURE 11.1   School reform movements of the 1960s and 1970s.

and statewide assessment schemes gave managerial control responsibility to state departments of education.

The curious hybrid in the center of the diagram is the alternative schools established for minority group students; some are private schools, others are minischools within the public system, and they draw their inspiration from both ideological streams. They are an attempt to wed humanistic and cultural concerns to an emphasis on the development of basic academic skills.

RADICAL SCHOOL REFORM: THE VISIONS

The godfather of the contemporary radical reformers is probably A. S. Neill. His book, *Summerhill*, which described his British school for disturbed children, created widespread early interest in the idea of giving children complete freedom in a school setting.[1] In the burgeoning literature of the sixties the most extreme antischool position was taken by writers such as Paul Goodman, Edgar Friedenberg, Everett Reimer, Paolo Freire, and Ivan Illich;[2] a somewhat more moderate stance is represented by those who thought it possible to reform the school as it was, including John Holt, Herbert Kohl, Jonathan Kozol, Neil Postman, and James Herndon.[3]

All of them shared the basic values of the movement, which recapitulate the fundamental upper-middle-class ideas noted in Chapter 3:

1. The basic theme is liberation from external restraint. Man is born free and good and, unrestrained, will be naturally curious and creative. Children are interested in learning, but only in what genuinely interests them when given freedom to choose. Creativity, spontaneity, and the development of the authentic self are the central concerns of education; institutional demands and social role requirements are its enemy.
2. The shared view of society is strongly antibureaucratic and antitechnological; all institutions and technology they regard as oppressive and inhibiting forces that attempt to mold children into mechanical, "plastic" beings.
3. The teacher ideal is that of a nurturing, loving guide. The teacher must be as open and spontaneous as the child ideal that is sought and as the context of learning must be. The line between adult and child status is blurred, in the relation between teacher and pupil as well as in the child's own development; the child's present stage is what must be attended to, not his future.
4. Political reformers, particularly socialists, have complained that the movement, in its concentration on the individual, lacks the kind of structure that might lead somewhere in terms of real social reform. That gap has been recently filled, perhaps, by a book called *Schooling in Capitalist America,* by Samuel Bowles and Herbert Gintis, which

blames capitalism for the schools' "hostility to the individual's need for personal development."[4]

Illich is perhaps the most widely admired of the more extreme radical reformers, and his ideas may serve as an example.[5] American culture, Illich argues, employs a "hidden curriculum;" its institutions may have originally been established to achieve human values, but in time (a) have become dehumanizing and resistant to change; (b) have done everything possible to "hook" people on the consumption of their services; and (c) have thus brought about an enormous inflation of institutional malfunctioning. Thus addicted, Americans rely more and more on institutions to which they subordinate their will and their freedom to develop.

Illich divides institutions into "left-wing" and "right-wing" types. The former ("convivial" institutions like subway lines, public markets, hand laundries, music teachers, hairdressers, etc.) are unbureaucratic, unadministered, somewhat "unpredictable and spontaneous," "self-activated and self-employed," rich in "personal encounters and free choice," and foster "self-help" and "a recognition of the joy and beauty" that man ought to experience. Right-wing institutions (health care, agriculture, orphan asylums, family life, churches, the military, large industry, the schools, etc.) are "manipulative," "culturally reinforcing," "bureaucratic," "rigid," and inclined to frustrate the search for "alternative ways."

We must, counsels Illich, do away with compulsory education laws and thus "disestablish" the schools. Once they are eliminated we can develop a genuine educational system that will provide everyone who wants to learn access to available resources throughout their lifetime, empower those with knowledge or skills to share them with those who wish to obtain them, and make available to all who want to present an issue to the public the opportunities to do so. Illich envisions a vast network of "skills exchange" relationships enabling all citizens to acquire fundamental skills. A communication network would bring learners into contact with one another so that those with similar interests could seek resources together. They would have available in their search a directory to independent, freelance teachers, whose skills would be evaluated by polling previous clients.

At the other extreme within the radical reform movement is a set of much more moderate ideas imported from the British Infant School experience and generally referred to as "the open classroom." Unlike Illich's notions, which he admitted were framed for a society that does not exist, open classroom advocates proposed reform within the system. The ideas were first popularized in this country in a book by Charles Silberman, *Crisis in the Classroom*;[6] a New York Times reviewer summed up the book's view of American schools in a classic paragraph: "Mr. Silberman has sailed up the shallow creek of American education, surveyed the landscape and pronounced it joyless, mindless, barren. The natives, he says, are pinched and crabbed, and stand before their children mumbling empty incantations; the children stare back silently, hollow-eyed, and pick their scabs."[7]

Silberman had visited the British Infant Schools (kindergarten and first grades of the elementary schools) and returned with a vision: The educational system must be transformed by sweeping but peaceful change. Since the ills of education reinforce those of a nation in deep crisis, the society will thus be transformed. The classroom must be redone, with self-directed, self-disciplined children pursuing thir own interests, enjoying their activities rather than working at tasks. The teacher provides a stimulating and encouraging environment, maintains informality and lets the children explore and find what interests them.

Silberman's book was followed by a rash of others, written by teacher educators and enthusiastic laymen, a sympathetic teacher education establishment began a prolonged period of workshop training for teachers, a number of school systems around the country established open schools in at least a few sites, and most of the 600-odd educational journals devoted to education became devoted to "open education." In a relatively short period of time, in the curious fashion of American education, it appeared that a peaceful revolution had been accomplished overnight.

ALTERNATIVE SCHOOLS: THE REALITIES

Enormously stimulated by the flood of ideas and publications of the radical school reformers, an alternative school movement rapidly took shape by the late sixties. In the belief that everything from the dropout rate and academic retardation of the poor to the rebelliousness of some upper-middle-class students could be traced to standardized curricula and authoritarian teachers, participants in the movement, both parents and educators, began to set up schools that would represent alternatives to the public school system.

Most of these schools were established by and for upper middles; some typical names: Knowplace, World of Inquiry, Student Development Center, All Together New Free School, Involvement Education. Typical statements of their objectives include: "We believe that in a loving, accepting environment in which emotional needs are met, children will feel free to grow; and that feeling free, they will grow; they will follow their natural curiosity, will do whatever they find necessary to meet their needs." "We believe in the right of every individual to be free to experience the world around him in his own way." "We encourage kids to live their own lives."[8]

Harvey Haber, who founded the *New Schools Exchange,* estimated that in the early years of the decade "two or three new alternative schools are born everyday and everyday one dies or gives up its freedom."[9] His exchange published a directory of experimental schools and acted as a clearinghouse for information and teaching jobs, a service also performed by a number of other newsletters. The number of free schools at that time was estimated to be somewhere between 700 and 1000; by the middle of the decade it had not increased, so Haber's estimate of the failure rate appears to be somewhat optimistic. Their average life span seems to be, at a guess, about eighteen months.

For a time urban school systems were much interested in the free school idea; Philadelphia's experimental high school, "The High School without Walls," was the object of a steady pilgrimmage of visitors from school systems in other cities.[10] In that school students spend their time out in the city—in museums, businesses, factories, courts—and come together only a few times a week to meet with a faculty member. There is little indication, however, that the model was emulated in very many other places.

Another type of alternative school is rather more relevant to the focus of this book, the schools founded to serve the special needs of the poor, minority youth who performs poorly in the standard school. They originated partly in the school reform movement but also in the civil rights movement of the fifties and sixties; some of them are indeed referred to as "freedom schools," an echo of the terminology of civil rights. They have been established in storefronts and church basements, often include a strong strain of black nationalism and a rhetoric of "self-determination," and emphasize strong ties to the community. At the secondary level they are likely to call themselves street academies, or if administratively part of a public high school, satellite schools.[11]

The aims of these alternative schools generally include a strong emphasis on academic achievement and individual self-esteem, along with attempts to improve school attendance and to produce better attitudes toward school; they seek to improve these factors in part by attaining the greatest possible parental participation.

The alternative school movement is exceedingly difficult to evaluate. The upper-middle-class parents and teachers who run the free schools often indignantly reject the very idea of measurement; the street academies and dropout centers generally have good political reasons for being wary about releasing hard data. Harlem Prep, for example, a nationally known secondary school for dropouts in New York City, claimed an extraordinary success rate in getting their graduates into college; it was not generally known for some time that the only students the school actually "graduated" were those who had been accepted by a college, nor that the school was highly selective in its admission policy.[12] Most such schools discovered quickly that students who lack self-discipline and motivation do no better in a setting in which they are given freedom and independence. Once the initial period of enthusiasm dies down, staff turnover increases and administration becomes unstable. The New School for Children, part of the Federation of Boston Community Schools, went through just such a typical cycle and reported six years after its establishment that "the parents weren't interested in community controlled schools."[13]

Where the "free school" idea was enthusiastically picked up by a regular urban public school system, as happened occasionally, the results proved disastrous. The Louisville public schools decided in 1969 that it needed what it called "a system renewal" and bravely eliminated throughout their schools any semblance of structure; they liberated everyone. What is barely manageable in a private free school with fifteen to twenty children turned into a chaos in the Fall of 1970 when they made the change. Even a pair of sympathetic reporters on the experiment concluded that "while it probably would be an exaggeration to say that the chaotic situations that resulted brought Impact and Focus schools to the brink of dissolution, dissatisfaction and disorder in several of the schools apparently reached an explosive level. As one would expect, the greatest difficulties seem to have been manifest in the secondary schools, where size of school and hostility among alienated adolescents tend to compound and complicate problems arising from lack of structure."[14]

The free school paid for by public funds is more likely to be evaluated, and the interested reader may now be able to find at least a scattered literature of evaluation, as, for example, A. Gaite and Richard Rankin's study of a satellite high school;[15] James Baines and William Young's account of New Jersey street academies;[16] and Terence Deal's attempt to develop a theory of alternative secondary school failures.[17] There are a few relatively objective accounts of some private free schools, among them Bruce Cooper's comparative study of seven of them,[18] and Steven Singleton and associates' study of the structure crisis in a school called Xanadu.[19]

THE RISE AND DEMISE OF THE OPEN CLASSROOM

Because open classroom advocates aimed at reforming the public schools directly, rather than merely presenting an alternative to them, this more moderate movement must be taken more seriously. Any assessment of its significance and its success at reforming the public system must take account of its historical context because, although the antihistorical bias of the reformers created the impression that their ideas were new, the open classroom movement represented their fourth appearance in American education.

During the first half of the nineteenth century the schools in the largest cities were organized around the monitorial system. Originated by a British military man for schools in India, the approach replicated the army's platoon structure; classes were very large (up to 1000) and divided into manageable groups each headed by a student monitor who carried out the teacher's instructions; discipline was maintained by a corps of student ushers who noted and reported infractions of the rules.

Such a system was functionally useful for a time in which trained teachers were in short supply and enrollments were rapidly rising; it was extraordinarily inexpensive and, at least as measured by the expectations of the era, very efficient. Although the structure itself disappeared, what has survived into a more affluent and child-conscious era are the fundamental premises of the method: the school, not the child, determines what is to be learned; the teacher is a directing figure of authority; learning requires work, sometimes drudgery; the school's priorities, and the teacher's, are the acquisition of cognitive skills and moral character.

The first challenge to this tradition came in the midnineteenth century from the ideas of Johann Pestalozzi, a Swiss educator primarily interested in early childhood teaching. Charles Brauner, on whose excellent historical account of educational ideas this discussion is based, classified Pestalozzi's approach as "object method," because of its basic stress on contact with real objects for an understanding of the abstract concepts that must be mastered.[20] Learning begins with sensory experiences that arouse feelings within the child and that establish a variety of particular understandings on which future learning can draw. The child himself is metaphorically perceived, much as Rousseau perceived him, as a plant that grows naturally with the proper nourishment. As the leaf draws resources for growth from the sunlight, so the child grows in understanding from sensory contact. The classroom is much like the home, with the teacher giving sympathy and acceptance to stimulate interest and inquiry and making clear the connections between objects and abstract concepts.

By the end of the century a second assault on the monitorial tradition appeared: *the child study movement*. Its insistence that children must be closely observed in order to understand them and that observations must be reported in behavorial terms, has a very modern ring of scientific objectivity. But, as Brauner observes, such objectivity was negated by the movement's concern with attitudes and feeling states that are, to a very considerable degree, unobservable. "The worst external chaos in the classroom might be a reflection of the most peaceful internal order within the child. Appearances would not be trusted. Committed to the principles of beginning with careful, objective, diversified observations, child study nullified this by petitioning teachers not to be deceived by simple accounts of what they had seen."[21] The movement believed that freedom for self-expression would lead to self-control, that the child, like a flower, needs the right climate and soil. It stressed physical activity and creativity, especially in the arts, permissiveness, and a totally autonomous teacher to tend to the unfolding petals.

Experimentalism, the third wave of reform and the basis for the progressive educational movement in the nineteen thirties, saw the child's motivations in much the same way as these earlier movements but added a new element, the social context of self-guided growth. Cooperative planning and decision-making in the course of project activity was perceived as crucial because the rebuilding of a democratic community was central to John Dewey's thought, and the school was to be a miniature democratic order. In fact, as Dewey himself complained, progressivism ignored the complexities of his ideas and in practice emphasized the simple-minded precepts of freedom and self-expression of the earlier movements.[22]

Finally, the open classroom movement. Its identification with the ideas of preceding reforms may be most simply noted by listing some of the statements in a long catalog proposed by Barth as ideas that British and American open educators would agree with strongly:[23]

Children are innately curious and will explore their environment without adult intervention; exploratory behavior is self-perpetuating.

Children have the competence and the right to make significant decisions concerning their own learning.

If a child is fully involved in and is having fun with an activity, learning is taking place.

Children pass through similar stages of intellectual development, each in his own way and at his own rate and in his own time.

Verbal abstractions should follow direct experience, not precede or substitute for them.

The best way of evaluating the effect of the school experience on the child is to observe him over a long period of time; objective measures may have a negative effect on learning.

The best measure of a child's work is his work.

Little or no knowledge exists which it is essential for everyone to acquire.

The question of whether the first three of these historical reform moments failed is easily disposed of; the advocates of the open classroom during the sixties declared them a failure by finding nothing good at all about the schools in that era. To Silberman's view, noted earlier, one could add endlessly from a voluminous literature that described the schools as rigid, oppressive, authoritarian, over-competitive, little better than prisons in which small, wan ghosts of children crept about fearfully, like Dickens characters, or, in other accounts, in a Dantesquerie of tormented boredom.

It is beside the point that none of these descriptions even vaguely approximate the reality that most parents and many professionals perceived in the same schools. If any of the reform movements of the century-and-a half preceding the sixties had left an imprint, it is clear that the contemporary reformers of the same theoretical persuasion did not themselves see those traces.

A good case can now be made that the basic ideas of the current open classroom movement have achieved as little success as the preceding three attempts. Some of the prime movers have themselves given up; John Holt has confessed to a New York Times reporter that each of his six books published after the very successful *How Children Fail* has sold less well than the one before. Holt is convinced that he is addressing himself to a very small minority, and as for the reform movement generally, was quoted as saying that for the most part it was nonsense, foolishness, based on the mistaken idea that schools really did wish to be better and freer.[24]

Of far greater importance than such reports of internal disintegration is the decided trend toward applying the term "open classroom" to schools and classes that are essentially traditional in operation and philosophy, gradually emptying the words of their earlier meaning. Press reports of such "innovations" as California's Early Childhood Education Plan, for example, describe it as an instance of open education, though any reading of the scheme's details provides abundant evidence of its philosophical kinship to basically traditional ideas.[25] Educators now commonly refer to any classroom in which children are sometimes permitted to work at their own pace as "open," although the individualization that is mistakenly so called is, oddly enough, a return of sorts to the monitorial system. What intervenes now between the teacher and pupil is not a monitor but sets of carefully structured commercial materials; teachers no longer have to spend so much time directing pupil activities because an SRA booklet does it for them. The end result is clearly the same.

Much the same transfer of meaning occurred during the preceding progressive movement, whose "project method" originally referred to any planned activity chosen, developed, and carried out by the child, or by a group of children in cooperation. Over the years it turned into carefully pre-planned projects assigned by the teacher. As Little Red Schoolhouse and some other private schools for the affluent upper middle class survived as relics of that progressive era, some genuine open schools will probably survive the seventies, but they are as unlikely to influence the public school mainstream as Little Red did.

Although there would be some disagreement with the thesis that the open classroom is dead, most educators would probably agree that its original philosophical thrust is dying out. Nor does one have to look far for an explanation of its lack of viability. There is very little consonance between the vision of the innocent child, all good, all loving, unfolding like a flower in the gentle sunshine, learning all he needs to know impelled only by his own curiosity and his unerring perception of his own needs, and the reality of the public schools as an enormous institution that absorbs about 7 percent of the gross national product and must instruct over 40 million children of widely varying talent, inclination, temperament, and mental health.

The early suspicions of the doubters that the open classroom must trade off basic skill achievement now appears also to have the support of some hard evidence. A major difficulty in evaluating the impact of the open classroom has been that parents of open school children tend to self-select themselves into that type of school; differences observed between pupils in open versus non-open settings were thus explainable by family differences. In this country Robert Wright solved the problem by finding several such contrasting schools whose pupils had been assigned to each by administrative allocation rather than parent selection; he found that differences favoring the *traditional* school were sizable and significant in academic skills achievement, and that on such measures as self-concept the open school children exhibit no advantage.[26] A study of English schools by Neville Bennett, who identified teachers rather than schools as "formal," "informal," or "mixed," found much the same result; in language arts the best results were achieved by formal approaches, the least by informal ones, with a difference of three to four months' progress in a school year; in reading, the mixed approach was best, followed by the formal; in math, the formal was far more effective than either of the other two.[27]

Finally, it is possible that the enthusiasm of the educational Establishment for the open classroom has worsened the relations between the schools and the majority of parents who have never shared the upper-middle-class values embodied in this historical thread of school reform. Perhaps there is a message in the fact that when the Pasadena school system offered its parents an alternative school that emphasized a return to fundamentals—academic skills and firm discipline—3000 applications were received for the 950 places available.[28] In the rising tide of concern over the inability of some high school graduates to read at an acceptable level, and over the writing deficiencies of college entrants, and the steady decline over the past decade in college entrance examination scores, it seems clear that, for the immediate future, the "back to basics" movement will be paramount.

THE ACCOUNTABILITY MOVEMENT

Accountability—making schools responsible for the achievement of specified objectives—appears to be the new educational battleground, supplanting the arguments over the liberation of the classroom. Unlike the liberation issue which, as we have seen, was a more extreme expression of a humanistic tradition with deep roots in the past, important elements in the current demands for accountability seem very new, and one must dig hard into the history of the American school to find only a few scattered efforts to base teacher salaries on results, or discover advocates of the idea of subjecting schooling to the forces of the market. The examination below of the major forms in which the movement has appeared begins with educational voucher proposals because they represent, in a sense, a transition between alternative school policies and the much more limited accountability policies grounded in ideas of efficiency.

Educational Vouchers

In the middle of the sixties Christopher Jencks advanced the idea of giving parents an educational allowance for each child and allowing them to choose the school at which to spend it, much as the federal government hands out food stamps to be used at whatever grocery store the recipient chooses.[29] The idea was not a new one; Milton Friedman, a conservative economist, had already suggested it as a way of creating a free market in education. But Jencks began actively campaigning for it, and for different reasons.

The urban public school system, he argued, through a bureaucratic hardening of the arteries, has amply demonstrated that it is incapable of dealing adequately with the learning needs of lower-class and ethnic minority children; and the system is too cumbersome and hard to move to offer much hope that it can change itself into an institution that can do the required job.

If the system were abandoned and all parents were given an educational allowance for their children, they would at least have free choice in selecting schooling. The assumption of the argument is that in a free-market situation people will spend their money in ways that maximize the achievement of their own self-interests. Jencks has elaborated the idea by suggesting that in such a situation a vast array of private schools will spring up, whose continued existence will depend on their proven ability to help children learn; if a parent is dissatisfied with his child's program, he need merely enroll him in another school. Experimentation with ways of improving the achievement of socially retarded children will be widespread, as schools compete with one another for pupils instead of being bogged down in red tape.

The federal bureaucracy was interested in the idea, and provided Jencks with several planning grants to his newly established Harvard Center for the Study of Public Policy. What emerged was a fully developed plan, generally referred to as the Voucher System.[30] Under the plan, an Educational Voucher Agency (EVA) would be established as a publicly accountable institution to administer vouchers for parents with children of elementary school age. The value of the basic voucher would initially be equal to the present per-pupil expenditure of the public schools in a particular area. The EVA governing board might be elected or appointed, but would have to be structured to reflect both majority and minority interests; it would receive all funds—state, federal, and local—that would normally be allocated to the area.

The heart of the proposal lies in Jenck's definition of "public school" and "private school." A school was to be considered public if it was open to all on a nondiscriminatory basis, charged no tuition (other than the voucher), and provided full information about itself to anyone interested. A school was to be considered private if it discriminated, charged tuition, or withheld information. Any group that operated a "public" school by this definition would be entitled to receive public subsidies. The rules for each subsidy, via the voucher system, are the following:

The school must accept the voucher as full payment, and charge no additional tuition.
It must accept any applicant as long as it has vacant places.

It must accept uniform standards established by the EVA regarding suspension and expulsion of students.

Agree to make available information about its teachers, facilities, and program to the EVA and to the public.

Maintain open accounts of money received and disbursed, and meet existing state requirements for private schools.

The system would work this way: each spring parents would inform the local EVA of the school to which it wanted to send each child in the fall; any child already enrolled in a voucher school would be guaranteed a place. If the school was some distance away, the federal government would provide transportation costs. If a particular school was oversubscribed, it could fill half of its seats as it chose from the applicants, so long as it did not use any discriminatory criterion; the other half would be filled by lottery from the remaining group of applicants. At enrollment, the parents would give the voucher to the school as payment of all tuition.

Jencks and his associates feel that such an approach would encourage freedom of choice and diversity in schooling by involving the private sector and by putting pressure on the public sector to innovate and find ways of meeting the needs of children. The proposed rules would not permit the plan to be used to support private schools as a haven for those who wish to escape desegregation; nor could it be used by the affluent to obtain public funds to add to the tuition they already pay to private schools. It would serve to provide adequate funding for some of the existing alternative private schools, some of which, in Jenck's view, are showing "spectacular results."

To the objection that ill-educated poor parents would be incapable of making competent decisions about schools, he argues that state supervision would eliminate the charlatans; in any event, middle-class parents have the freedom of movement and the financial resources to choose schools for their children, and the poor should be given the same freedom of choice. And, by assigning a higher value to the vouchers of poor parents, the government could easily increase the share of national educational resources available to the disadvantaged.

Other criticisms cannot be so readily dismissed, however:[31]

1. Although Jencks aims at dismantling the bureaucracy of the city school systems, the EVA's themselves, say the critics, would have a number of functions that would almost inevitably turn them into sizable bureaucracies. They would continually have to inspect the grade schools, administer the lotteries, and supervise admission procedure to guard against illegal racial discrimination. In addition, they would be charged with protecting children against unfair expulsion and suspension, a job of great complexity and one that would tangle the system in the red tape of other institutions.

2.   Ginzberg estimates that the voucher system would require an increase in government expenditure of 10 to 15 percent, or about 5 billion annually.

3.   Most existing private schools are religion-based, and are either Catholic or Jewish. Most blacks are Protestants, and it is not probable that any level of government would force a school to accept large numbers of blacks and other minorities unless they were of the same faith. Where, in the large cities, would the new and alternative schools come from? The better non-denominational private schools spend anywhere from 50 to 150 percent more per pupil than public schools, and they are unlikely to opt for a plan that would force them to reduce their expenditure.

4.   The NAACP and others condemn the plan because they fear that it would only result in worse segregation. Many of the safeguards Jencks built into the plan, they argue, could be circumvented, and there is little question that EVA's would be subjected to extreme pressures; on the other hand, black nationalists would eagerly seize on the idea to develop all-black schools with militant curricula.

PANEL 11.1   A Voucher Tryout in Alum Rock

When the Office of Economic Opportunity offered to support a tryout of the voucher idea, a number of school districts around the country agreed to study its feasibility, but only one, Alum Rock, California, has actually operated a voucher system. During the first year six schools (all part of the public system) were designated as voucher schools; each of the six was divided into minischools offering different curriculum emphases, ranging from a traditional format to one that was called School 2000, complete with television sets and a geodesic dome; another was devoted to "daily living," featuring such methods as teaching math through cooking and sewing lessons. Seven more schools joined the program for the second year. Vouchers for children who qualified for the free lunch program were worth a third more than a standard voucher, and parents could select any school, and any minischool within it.[32]

The Rand Corporation was retained to evaluate the program, and reported at the end of the first year that the major change was not in parent behavior (parents were not much interested or involved) or academic achievement, but in the roles of staff. Local administrators and teachers had more autonomy and teachers had a good deal more control over their resources.[33] A moderate storm blew up over the achievement data. In a technical appendix to the Rand report Robert Klitgaard reported that achievement scores dropped for every voucher school in every grade but one, while remaining stable in nonvoucher schools. "One of the starkest downward effects I've ever seen," he reported to an interviewer.[34] Another Rand researcher, using a different approach to the analysis found no such affect on academic achievement, although he admitted that Klitgaard's analysis was a perfectly sound one. The second year tests shunned such direct comparison of scores with local comparison groups and instead did an analysis based on predicting scores for each child, estimated from national norms of children who scored in the same range as the Alum Rock voucher children in their pretest. Using this rather roundabout method, 90 percent of the children were reported to have done as well or better than the prediction.[35]

Rand concluded that the Alum Rock test on the whole was not a test of what OEO was interested in: the effect of economic competition, the role of private schools, detailed information to parents. In a sardonic aside the report pointed out that what was achieved was a demonstration of the school superintendent's "deftness in garnering federal funds (4.5 million in two years) to carry out a school decentralization program that he wanted anyway." In the meantime, New Rochelle terminated its bid for the program after spending $40,000 on a feasibility study; Gary, Indiana; Seattle, Washington; and San Francisco, California also dropped the idea after considering it, and a part of New Hampshire, which indicated its intention of giving the voucher idea a complete tryout, submitted the proposition to its voters who voted it down. As of the late seventies the voucher plan appears to be an orphan with no offers of a home.

PERFORMANCE CONTRACTING

The voucher plan hoped to improve the performance of schools by making them accountable to parents; performance contracting revealed the essential role of *efficiency* in the accountability movement by proposing to use the techniques of business and industry in the school's instructional program. It is a cost/benefit, technological approach to improving the urban school. Blaschke and his associates[36] call it a "turnkey" system; and, in some respects, it is like the turnkey contracts used for public housing, in which a private company builds a housing project, then turns the key over to the government officials to operate.

During the sixties, a number of private corporations were attracted to education as the "new growth industry"; they concentrated primarily on the development of instructional hardware, machines for programmed instruction, new audiovisual tools, and the like. Only recently have they turned their attention to the delivery of educational services on the basis of a specific contract with a particular school district. The contracts are of two types: one of them specifies only that a specific kind of training will be delivered to a guaranteed number of persons—for example, a new reading instruction program for all second graders in the district, or an inservice teacher training program for all the teachers in several schools. The second, and more interesting, contract is one that specifies a level of pupil performance that is to be attained in a school or district. The payment that the contractor receives is pegged to that performance level; he gets paid fully for those students who achieve that level, somewhat less for those students who perform at a lower level, and nothing at all for those students who do not perform above a given level.

The programs are usually highly structured, using a good deal of hardware and providing instructors, often paraprofessionals, trained by the company. One part of the contract usually calls for training the regular teachers in the district to use the technology that has been introduced, thereby gradually phasing out the contractor's personnel. The technology itself often relies heavily on systematic positive reinforcement, either through programmed instruction or some form of "token economy."

The future of performance contracting was clouded by an early experiment in Texarkana, where authorities learned that personnel of the contracting company had taught children the answers to questions on the standardized test used to measure performance. Despite the national scandal that resulted, the Office of Education decided to continue with the experiments, exercising care to institute careful controls.[37]

Further difficulties arose in a large-scale contract for the Banneker school in Gary, Indiana. Behavioral Research Laboratories contracted for a four-year program for the school, which is in a black, working-class neighborhood. The firm set up a nongraded structure, with the day divided into 20-minute instructional modules using primarily programmed workbooks. The state department of education grew uneasy about the program, pointing out that classes were too large, state-adopted textbooks were being ignored, some of the staff was uncertified, and nothing but reading and math was being taught. The state removed its certification of the school, but reinstated it after some changes were made.[38]

The teachers' union raised strenuous objections to the teacher-pupil ratios that BRL was maintaining, to the forced transfer of thirteen teachers, the use of paraprofessionals as teachers, overtime imposed, and the operation, they claimed, of a hidden merit system. At the end of the first year the union rejected BRL's claim that over 70 percent of the children had made average or better-than-average gains in academic skills, with an average growth of 9.5 months for the year. Branding the figures as an "outright deception," the union pointed to tables in the BRL report that showed only six pupils in ten making at least a year's gain in math, and only four in ten demonstrating such a gain in reading. (The Gary contract was cancelled by the school system after a few years.)

Educators who observed other performance contracts in action point out that the promise of "individualized instruction" is seldom delivered; only a few of the systems, say Mecklenburger and Wilson, really include the personal touch and others merely individualize the *rate* of instruction.[39] They also argue that testing practices constitute a central problem; it is possible, they say, to create statistical increases even though students have learned very little.

A national assessment of the effectiveness of performance contracting was sponsored by OEO in 1972 and found very little advantage for contract pupils over controls (see Panel 11.2). Although the evaluation was attacked on technical grounds, the size of the sample used was convincing for a number of observers, and the number of performance contracts began to decline precipitously in the midseventies. It is probable that this particular variant of accountability will join the voucher plan and other very interesting ideas that just did not work out.

PANEL 11.2   A National Evaluation of Contracting

Performance contracting may have been dealt a mortal blow by the 1972 results of a year-long study conducted by the Office of Economic Opportunity, which had also been investing heavily in school contracts.[40] The OEO evaluated performance contracts in fifty-four school districts in twenty-four states; in their unusually blunt report, they concluded that "There is no evidence to support a massive move to utilize performance contracting for remedial education in the nation's schools. School districts should be skeptical of extravagant claims for the concept."[41] The experiment involved 13,000 children compared with about 10,000 controls; the largest difference demonstrated was one-tenth of a grade. In some grades experimental children did slightly better, in others slightly worse; the general conclusion was "no consistent gain."

As with most such national studies, the OEO evaluation was greeted with cries of rage and a barrage of technical criticism. Despite the fact that such an eminent educational researcher as Ellis Page called it the most impressive experiment ever conducted in education,[42] the critics have a point. As John Miller notes, the projects were not randomly selected and hence the findings are not generalizable (though the enormous sample size and representativeness are impressive).[43] The poorest achievers in each district were selected, experimental and control subjects were in different schools, and standardized tests instead of measures of specific learning were used. Miller also points out that no attempt was made to look at those contract schools in which results were far better than the others to determine whether some approaches were more successful than others.

STATEWIDE ASSESSMENT

The relative lack of success of compensatory education efforts produced in some educators a sense of frustration and a conviction that far from being incapable of closing the performance gap between minority and mainstream children, the public schools are *unwilling* to do what is necessary to achieve that goal. The causes have been variously attributed to the stifling and stingy bureaucracy of the urban systems, the racism of teachers, or their lack of skills, or their laziness, the job-protectiveness of staff unions, the ineptitude of teacher training institutions, the unfairness of civil service, or the lack of involvement of the community.[44]

Whatever the imputed cause, the reaction led in the early seventies to demands that the schools be held accountable for results, demands that were received with unexpected cordiality by state legislatures, which, notoriously slow to act on most major issues, began passing school accountability laws with what most observers regard as extraordinary speed. For their part, most state legislators were marching to a very different drum; having watched education budgets rise at a rate of between two and three times that of the gross national product in less than a decade, they argued that it was time that the schools were compelled to justify the funds spent on them.

By 1974, thirty-two states had passed some version of accountability legislation and all but four of the others were considering such laws.[45] The most consistent features of legislation include:

the setting of management goals by the system as a whole and by districts
a periodic assessment on a statewide basis of student performance, with the
    areas of performance to be specified clearly and in detail
cost/performance analysis as a justification for programs
periodic evaluation of professional personnel at all levels with about half of
    the plans requiring that student performance be considered the most important criterion for determining the competency of teaching staffs.

On the surface, at least, such a program makes a great deal of sense. The public surely should have the right, through its representatives, to set educational goals for the schools it finances, to require them to produce evidence that the goals are being met, and to set performance standards for the agents it employs to run the system. The political and technical obstacles that must be overcome in pursuit of the public will, however, can turn out to be formidable.

A detailed account of one state's experience with accountability, Jerome Murphy and David Cohen's description of the Michigan story, points up some of the difficulties:[46]

1. Different motivations among the advocates of accountability may produce confusion; reform minded officials are interested in equalizing the distribution of school resources and improving decision-making, whereas many state legislators see accountability as a way of holding down the rise in school expenditures.

2. Publication of statewide test data and other pupil information can set off political explosions and set a variety of groups interested in education at one another's throats.

3. Tests of school achievement involve a number of technical issues not suitable to public debate. In the case of some objectives the schools are interested in, the state of the art is not up to reliable measurement.

4. A state effort to hold school districts accountable for improvement in pupil achievement is likely to founder on the rocks of politics. The test results for the 1972 to 1973 school year in Michigan showed that some districts, particularly in Detroit, would lose several millions in extra funds because they had demonstrated no improvement in the year past. But the legislature yielded to pressure and waived the requirement. The chances that a Michigan legislature will ever take the politically unpopular step of depriving Detroit of available funds are dim indeed, but without such a penalty how can a system of accountability work?

THE IMPACT OF SCHOOLING

The humanist critics and the advocates of accountability, whatever their other differences, agree on one assumption: changes in school organization, teaching, or curriculum will have a direct and powerful impact on the child's learning; indeed one often finds educators talking about the school as a "molder" or "shaper" of children, as if they were formless putty in the hands of teachers.

The issue of whether that *is* the nature of the child is as old as philosophy; what has added current fuel to the controversy are the results of relatively recent efforts to determine empirically the school's real ability to make a difference in what the child is and can do. Some of these we have already reviewed in Chapter 9, in the discussion of self-concept; a later chapter will examine the sizable body of evidence on the impact of integration. What is of interest here is the question of whether different school characteristics actually produce differences in student achievement. One might argue that the weakness of the school's effect on self-concept, for example, is explained by the fact that it is not set up to influence such psychological characteristics. But the school *is* intended to produce changes in cognitive development, and its ability to do so is surely a crucial test of the assumption that schooling has a powerful shaping influence on the child.

One of the difficulties in making sense of the contemporary widespread argument over that assumption is the muddled way in which the question is often framed. When we ask, "How much does schooling count?" we are not suggesting that there will be no differences between a child with twelve years of school when compared with one who had no school at all. Nor that we would not expect the average Japanese student, who is required to take many courses in mathematics, to be more skilled in math than the average American student who is increasingly required to take fewer courses in that subject.

Even on this question of quantity of schooling there are some puzzling data. David Wiley and Annegret Harnischfeger, in an attempt to show that schooling really does make a difference, published a study of student achievement in the Detroit area schools showing that pupils with more days of attendance in schools with a longer school year did better than those whose number of real school days of instruction was less. Nancy Karweit, however, re-analyzed the Detroit data along with similar data from other cities and found that their conclusion was valid only for central city Detroit and not for its suburbs, and that it held up for other cities either weakly or not at all.

Nor is any real light thrown on the question of school impact by such interesting studies as *The Enduring Effects of Education*, by Herbert Hyman and his associates, who used the findings of a number of national surveys to show that the more years of schooling people have, the more knowledge and information they have about politics, foreign affairs, and the world generally.[48] In suggesting that schools do succeed in general in producing more sophisticated populations, the study supports the widespread notion that schooling is good for people, but there is not, on the other hand, any very significant movement afoot except for Illich and a handful of followers to do away with school altogether.

In the context of the accountability movement the question that must be addressed is: How much of the variation in student achievement can be accounted for by differences among school resources when other sources for the variation in achievement are held constant? More specifically, *given the same quantity of instruction, with pupils of the same social class background and subject to the same parental pressures to achieve, can we predict that one kind of school resource or teaching behavior will get appreciably better results than another?*

There are three sizable streams of different evidence bearing on this question: large-scale correlational studies, evaluations of innovative curriculum materials and audiovisual instructional devices, and attempts to find more effective teaching behaviors and methods. A summary of the crucial evidence in each body of literature is provided below.

Correlational Studies

The best known of these, and the one that began the controversy over school impact, was a survey published under the title *Equality of Educational Opportunity*, conducted by James Coleman and associates for the U.S. Office of Education in the midsixties.[49]

Coleman's sample of schools was representative of the range of schools nationally, though a number of them failed to return his detailed questionnaires. It has been argued that these losses from the sample seriously affect the conclusions of the study; but Coleman is probably correct in saying that, since the nonrespondents did not differ substantially from those schools that returned questionnaires, the data is representative of the whole population of schools.

The basic idea of the study was to examine the "inputs" the school provides in the form of curriculum, facilities, teaching, pupil recruitment, and so on, and compare them with the "outputs" of the system in the form of achievement differences. As Moynihan puts it, "in effect, the Coleman study was intended to prove beyond further question two central theses of the reform establishment: first, that school facilities available to minorities were shockingly unequal; and second, that this accounted for unequal outcomes." In fact, as a later section will show, it did not find the first of these to be very strikingly true; as for the second, the data seem to indicate that nothing about the school program itself has a very great effect on the achievement of pupils. To summarize:

1.   For both white and minority group children, facilities and curriculum had least effect on achievement; teacher quality had a somewhat greater influence, but not very much greater; the educational background of fellow students had the most influence (*see* a later section for a discussion of this last finding), but even this factor showed only modest impact.

2.   Differences in any of these aspects of the school are more influential for black children than they are for whites; that is, it makes less difference if a white child attends a school with good facilities and good teachers than it does for his black counterpart.

The general conclusion of the report was not to dispute earlier findings of a relationship between school inputs and achievement results but to suggest that its influence was much less great than most people assumed. To accept the findings as valid, one would have to conclude, with Coleman, that equality of educational opportunity means much more than merely providing the same resources; it requires substantially *greater* efforts for those who come to school educationally handicapped.

A number of educators have refused, however, to accept the findings as presented. Their criticisms of the report are varied and in many cases technical:

1.   The survey was forced to use a number of indirect measures that substitute for direct observation or measurement. Forty-five measures were used, for example, that described the school itself, but there was no direct measure of such a variable as teacher quality; it had to be inferred from a variety of indirect data, such as the teacher's estimate of the quality of the college he attended, his years of experience, his highest degree received, and his score on a verbal test. Pupils were asked whether they had an encyclopedia at home, which was used as one way of inferring parental interest in the education of their children. Such indirect measures introduce a good deal of uncertainty into any final interpretation of results.

2.   A major attack has been mounted on the way Coleman analyzed his data. He began his analysis by first computing the correlation between socioeconomic status and achievement, then held the first factor constant while looking at the influence of school inputs. When the social background is controlled first, the school resources add very little predictive power to the analysis. Samuel Bowles has shown that if you control for school resources first, then look at what is contributed by social background, you get radically different results than if school resources are not so controlled. The amount of variation in achievement scores of twelfth grade black students that is explained by "teachers' verbal ability" more than doubles if one runs the analysis that way. Bowles explains why:

> Both approaches, however, give misleading results. Let me try to explain why this is so. Assume that we want to predict the weight of children on the basis of knowledge of both their age and their height. Because heights and ages of children are closely associated, we can predict a child's weight if we know only his age nearly as well as when we know both his height and his age. If we can read the analysis the other way around, i.e., first controlled for height and then investigated the additional predictive power associated with the variable age, the result would of course be reversed. We would find very little additional predictive power associated with age.
>
> A similar statistical difficulty arises in the Coleman analysis because the level of resources devoted to the child's education and the child's own social background are not independent. When we control for the social class of the student, we implicitly control also for some part of the variation in school resources . . . By choosing to control first for social-background factors, the authors of the report inadvertently biased its analysis against finding school resources to be an important determinant of scholastic achievement.[50]

A reanalysis of the Coleman data has shown,[51] however, that even taking these technical considerations into account makes little difference in the original conclusions, and a majority of educators expert in this aspect of the field appear to agree that the analysis is reasonably sound.

3. The weakness of the school's influence found by Coleman has been further attacked because it appears to contradict earlier studies of the relation between school factors and achievement, particularly as regards per-pupil expenditure and teacher experience. None of the previous studies, however, used as large and representative a sample, and many of the effects found are not very sizable. The results of Samuel Goodman's New York State study are shown in Table 11.1. Even with the usual high relationship between socioeconomic status and achievement taken into account, several school factors have significant associations with achievement, but the partial correlations are not large enough to be of very great practical significance. Henry Dyer has cited additional data from several other studies, but not all of it substantiates his thesis that such important factors as teacher experience and per-pupil expenditure really make a difference.[52] One of the studies he describes, the Mollenkopf and Melville study of 100 schools, found the influence of teacher experience to be negligible, and another one did not specifically analyze for separate school factors.

Table 11.1   Correlations of Certain School Factors with Pupil Achievement and Socioeconomic Status

| | Correlation with Composite Achievement Score at Grade 7 | |
Variable	*Raw Correlation*	*Partial Correlation (SES partialled out)*
Teacher experience	.56	.37
Per-pupil expenditure	.51	.31
Special staff per 1000 pupils	.24	.12
Classroom atmosphere*	.24	.23
Socioeconomic status of parents	.61	—

* *"Classroom atmosphere" is a measure of the degree to which a school is rated "subject-centered" vs. "child-centered," the ratings being based on an instrument known as* The Growing Edge, *by P. R. Mort et al. (New York: Metropolitan Study Council, 1957).*

Source: *Henry R. Dyer, "School Factors and Equal Educational Opportunity," Harvard Educational Review, vol. 38, no. 1 (Winter 1968), p. 43.*

PANEL 11.3   Which School Factors Make the Most Difference?

Although Dyer and his fellow critics can hardly be said to have made an overwhelming case for the faultiness of Coleman's conclusions, it is a strong enough one to merit serious consideration of the question: Suppose the Coleman study underestimates the effectiveness of school characteristics in influencing pupil effectiveness—what are the implications?

Oddly enough, two of the severest critics of the Coleman findings answer that question rather pessimistically. After his devastating attack on the statistical methodology of the study, Bowles remarks:

> The same evidence mentioned earlier suggests that were we merely to raise the quality of the teaching resources devoted to the education of Negroes to the level of that currently devoted to whites, we would significantly improve Negro achievement. Nevertheless, we would reduce the gap in Negro and white verbal achievement at grade 12 by only a little more than a quarter.[53]

Dyer answers it in a very interesting way. Since it is probable that the actual correlations between measures of school characteristics and achievement are too low, he argues that it might be useful to take a very lenient view of their significance. He proceeds by disregarding the socioeconomic status correction factor and then looking through the raw correlations between school characteristics and achievement. He accepts as significant any school characteristic that correlated .20 or better with any one or more of the three achievement measures—reading, mathematics, and general information—in any one of the eight ethnic categories at either grade 6 or grade 9. In his words: "This may seem like an excessively lenient acceptance criterion, but in view of the probable amount of noise in the basic data, a considerable amount of leniency is needed if one is to identify any school variables at all that might be worth speculating about."[54]

The procedure revealed that school characteristics, if they make a difference at all, are more influential for some of the minority children in the schools than for the white majority. Fourteen of the school variables, for example, correlate at least .20 with Puerto Rican achievement, and only two of them with achievement scores of Northern whites. Furthermore, those items that correlate at all with school achievement are the hardest to change: home backgrounds, verbal test score of the student body, verbal ability of the teaching staff, teacher attitudes toward integration. The factors that are easiest to change (hours spent doing homework, teacher experience, teacher degrees, pupil-teacher ratio, etc.) do not correlate with pupil achievement at all.

One of Dyer's major criticisms of the Coleman study, however, must be taken seriously. He points out that Coleman measured school achievement by testing verbal ability at various school levels; since this ability is difficult to change radically, he argues that "Coleman's analysis probably makes for an underestimate of the importance of factors that school systems do in fact control."[55] In support of this view, he cites Shaycroft's longitudinal study of some of the Project Talent data that uses achievement in actual curriculum areas such as literature, mathematics, art, accounting, mechanics, and electricity. Not only do students show substantial growth in these subjects through the course of their schooling, but, with socioeconomic status controlled, students in some schools learn more or improve their ability more than in other schools.

But, several years after the Coleman report appeared and the dust had cleared it is probably fair to say that most observers with research training accepted its general conclusion, that school differences did not have a substantial impact on the characteristics with which children entered the schools, that input determined output to a much greater extent than did the process of schooling itself. Five or six years later the more complex analysis of Jencks resulted in very much the same finding.

Jencks and Brown carried the analysis one considerable step forward. They did a very careful study of about 100 comprehensive high schools included in Project Talent;[57] in contrast to Coleman's data, which took a cross-section of pupils at one moment in time, Project Talent provides a longitudinal look at a sample of high school students who were tested first in 1960, retested in 1963, then followed up by questionnaire about a year-and a half and five years later. The data also included achievement data in objectives that the school might be expected to influence, social studies information, vocabulary, arithmetic reasoning, and the like.

Jencks and Brown followed a procedure based essentially on predicting how each student would perform on a twelfth grade test if he or she had attended an "average" school, then looking at whether the particular school attended actually produced a result that was better or worse than that predicted average. They also examined the years of higher education attained later by the student, and his occupational status and career plans. The conclusions:

> Some high schools are more effective than others in raising test scores. Nevertheless, the gains are never large relative to the variance of initial scores, and schools that boost performance on one test are not especially likely to boost performance on other tests. Moreover, high-school characteristics such as social composition, per-pupil expenditure, teacher training, teacher experience, and class size have no consistent impact on cognitive growth between ninth and twelfth grades. These findings imply that if we want to boost student performance, we will need drastically new methods. Our data tell us nothing about what methods might be most effective. They tell us only that more money, more graduate courses for teachers, smaller classes, socioeconomic desegregation, and other traditional remedies are unlikely to have much effect. We cannot say anything about the effects of racial desegregation, since we excluded schools with more than 25 percent black enrollment from our retest sample.

Much the same conclusion is true of the other variables they examined. Some schools are more effective than others in producing students who go on to obtain more years of schooling, or more effective in raising students' occupational status and career plans. Schools that are effective in one area are not effective in another. "But even when schools are unusually effective or ineffective, the reasons for these effects remain obscure. These findings suggest that neither educators nor social scientists know how to change high schools so as to raise students' test scores, educational attainment, or occupational status."[59]

CURRICULUM STUDIES

Since 1960, with the new interest in making schools better and with the availability of federal support for curriculum development, a variety of elaborate, carefully constructed, and very interesting special curriculum packages have been made available. The earliest efforts can be traced to the national uproar in the late fifties when the Soviet Union made the first successful venture into space and American schools were blamed for neglecting the scientific development of youth. It was a curious *non sequitur*; that the nation had an abundance of scientific talent and lacked only the national will to invest the tremendous resources necessary for space exploration was shown shortly afterward, but the schools set about restructuring its science curriculum just the same.

New science curricula were followed by new approaches to mathematics, social studies, and English. Many of these packages have been in use in a variety of schools for a number of years, and have been in some cases carefully evaluated. Twenty-three such studies were recently reviewed by Walker and Schaffarzik, whose first finding was that those students who studied subjects with the innovative curricula almost always did as well as or better on outcome measures than those using traditional texts and standard approaches.[60] When the authors checked for the content bias of the tests used, however, they discovered that the innovative curricula were shown to be superior only when the test used emphasized the special goals of the particular curriculum; on tests that stressed traditional knowledge and skills the advantage vanished.

During the same period a great deal of attention was also devoted to instructional media: radio, television, programmed instructional devices, and computer-assisted instruction (CAI). Dean Jamison and his associates, in an extraordinarily detailed and careful survey of the most recent batch of evaluations of these media, both as independent learning devices and as supplements to regular instruction, conclude that although many of the studies show significant effects, there is a "striking lack of uniformity concerning the significance of various variables,"[61] much the same conclusion Jencks and Brown came to about the impact of high schools. In the case of the media, advantages are likely to relate to such variables as student interest rather than to improvement in learning productivity.

John Vinsonhaler and Ronald Bass examined ten independent studies of CAI involving thirty separate experiments with a total of 10,000 students in language arts and mathematics. The best they can conclude is that "CAI plus traditional classroom instruction is usually more effective than traditional instruction alone in developing skills—at least during the first year or two."[63] But it is doubtful, they report, that CAI is more effective than less expensive methods for augmenting instruction. There is some evidence, for example, that 30 minutes of ordinary classroom drill is equivalent to 15 minutes of CAI, and quite inexpensive programmed instruction devices may, in competition with expensive computer terminals, be more effective.

This issue is a very important one for accountability, because of its implied promise to deliver the greatest educational benefit for the least cost. Leon Lessinger, one of the central figures in the accontability movement, has spelled out that promise in great detail in a book called *Accountability: Systems Planning in Education.* Ernest House, admitting that cost is a legitimate issue in education, has nevertheless pointed out some of the ironies involved in the costing-out of instructional media by Lessinger:

> Based on their cost estimates, the authors make cost projections for four types of instruction. Although their figures are somewhat biased toward auto-tutorial instruction, the cheapest course for fifty students or less is the traditional small group. For 100 students the conventional large-group is cheapest and remains competitive with both locally developed and commercially developed auto-tutorial instruction up to class sizes of 200 to 400. In other words, the authors appear to be saying that the "individualized instruction" offers economies of scale only with great masses of students. If one placed a high value on having a variety of options available for the students to choose from, one would have to conclude that traditional small-group instruction is best. Thus we are face-to-face with one of those ironies to which we have become accustomed: "individualized instruction" as defined by the authors would require masses of students plowing through the same materials while "traditional" instruction would permit greater variety and choice among individuals.[64]

TEACHING AND STUDENT ACHIEVEMENT

A very large body of research has accumulated over the past several generations that bears on the question of whether teacher characteristics or teacher behavior differentially affects student learning. In a 1971 review of the most recent findings, Barak Rosenshine and Norma Furst began their paper by saying that "this review is an admission that we know very little about the relationship between classroom behavior and student gains," but they go on to argue that one can at least look to the findings for the directions that future work might find most fruitful.[65]

From forty-two studies of teaching that employ student achievement as an outcome measure Rosenshine and Furst selected eleven teacher variables that they consider "most promising," teacher characteristics that appear to correlate with learning with some degree of consistency, and better than chance. These variables are listed below: The first five are considered to have "strong support," the last six less so:

clarity
variability (variety of methods, approaches, etc.)
enthusiasm
task-oriented and/or businesslike behavior
student opportunity to learn what is later tested
use of student ideas and general indirectness
criticism (negative correlation)
use of structuring comments (summarizing, etc.)
types of questions asked (though exactly what type is at the moment unclear)
probing
level of difficulty of instruction

It is of some interest to note the variables that, on the basis of the research, do *not* appear promising, because they include many that some advocates of accountability have in mind as crucial: nonverbal approval, praise, warmth, the ratio of all indirect behaviors to all direct teacher behaviors, flexibility, the amount of teacher talk versus student talk, student participation, number of student-teacher interactions, student absences, teacher absences, teacher time spent on class participation, teacher experience, and teacher knowledge of the subjects taught.

Although Rosenshine and Furst's conclusions seem to offer at least some modest support for believing that even if schools don't make a difference, teachers do, a more detailed and rigorous examination of the same group of studies by Robert Heath and Mark Neilson suggests otherwise. Their analysis goes well beyond the surface findings to assess the adequacy of the research and the degree of confidence one can reasonably assign to the findings (see Panel 11.4). Their conclusions are that there is little evidence for hoping that we have as yet found the key to teaching effectiveness.

Teacher Expectation and Achievement
Some accountability advocates are likely to respond to such a demonstration of the absence of an empirical basis for demanding that teachers should produce predictable outcomes by arguing that the impact of the teacher involves variables much more subtle than those ordinarily studied. The most popular of such explanations for differences in achievement between white middle class students and those from lower class minority groups is contained in the hypothesis of the self-fulfilling prophecy, or the Pygmalion Effect.

The thesis asserts that teachers, prophesying low achievement levels for

PANEL 11.4   How Much Difference *Do* Teachers Make?

In a detailed analysis of the studies reviewed by Rosenshine and Furst, Heath and Neilson[66] found that nearly a third of the definitions used by observers to rate the 11 teacher variables did not correspond to variables cited in research conclusions, as, for instance, a classroom rating of "difficulty of the lesson" is cited later as a measure of "clarity." More often than not the studies themselves did not claim to find significant relations between the variable cited and student achievement; for many of the variables negative, or clearly nonsignificant results are reported. Almost none of the forty-two studies tested their data for a number of technical, but important, characteristics that have bearing on their adequacy. Finally, they note that two important variables that might well have influenced the relationships cited were not controlled:

> . . . Though the studies reviewed here were concerned with everything from aircraft mechanics to reading, no effort is apparent in identifying the possible interactions between teacher-behavior variables and content. It seems unlikely that one set of teaching behaviors is most effective for teaching everything. If there is an important interaction between type of content and teaching behavior (given cognitive achievement as criteria), then the conclusion about which teaching behavior is effective may be determined as much by content as by teacher behavior . . . Despite persistent evidence that variables such as socioeconomic status and ethnic status are more important determinants of average achievement level than teacher behavior, the research on teacher-behavior variables largely ignores the differences among students. Similarly, the studies cited by Rosenshire and Furst cover a wide student age range (preschool to adult), yet the idea that effective teacher behavior might be different for different age groups is ignored when conclusions are drawn from such collections. It seems unlikely that one set of teacher behaviors is more effective for teaching everything to everybody.[67]

Heath and Nielson also provide a valuable service in collating the conclusions of a number of earlier reviews of research on teacher characteristics and student achievement. Brim: ". . . show no consistent relation between any characteristics, including intelligence, and teaching effectiveness."[68] Dubin and Taveggia: ". . . demonstrate clearly and unequivocally that there is no measurable difference among truly distinctive methods of college instruction . . ."[69] Mood: ". . . at the present moment we cannot make any sort of meaningful quantitative estimate of the effect of teachers on student achievement."[70] Getzels and Jackson: ". . . very little is known for certain about the nature and measurement of teacher personality, or about the relation between teacher personality and teaching effectiveness.[71] Wallen and Travers: ". . . the best one might hope for would be slight differences in teaching effectiveness within narrow aspects of the learning process, and this is roughly what is found by empirical research."[72]

Commenting on the findings of his own review, Stephens makes the following acute observation on the meaningfulness of the evidence:

> The fact is, insensitive as the tests may be and over-controlled or under-controlled as some experiments probably are and exacting as standards undoubtedly are, a great deal of growth does appear and does meet the standards. The investigations cited do not fail to reveal growth. They merely fail to reveal differences in growth attributable to the administrative (teaching) variables. If we use other variables, such as background factors, moreover, marked differences in growth also come through. If the tests, and the designs, and the criteria of significance permit such differences to appear, it is difficult to see why they should not also permit differences in administrative (teaching) factors to come through if these were present.[73]

their minority pupils, not only act on that prophecy by failing to try to get them to achieve, but also communicate to their pupils a sense of inevitable failure. The argument was widely disseminated by Kenneth Clark in a number of speeches and articles and given empirical support by a dramatic and extensively publicized study by Robert Rosenthal and Lenore Jacobson.

Rosenthal and Jacobson administered a mental ability test to all the children in a San Francisco school; the school's teachers, however, were told that the test being given was devised to discover which children were achieving below their true ability and could be expected later to "spurt ahead" academically. The testing was done during the spring, and when the teachers returned to work the following fall they were given the names of the children who, on the basis of the test, could be expected to better their performance dramatically during the ensuing school year. These children were, in fact, selected at random from the roster of each classroom.

The very ingenious research design aimed, of course, at finding out whether the children whom teachers had reason to *expect* would do better actually *would* do better. Retests on the original mental ability test were administered during the winter and at the end of the school year. For two of the grades, those who had been in kindergarten and first grade in the preceding year, the retests demonstrated a significant rise in scores; for the other grades no differences beyond chance occurred.

Although Rosenthal, Clark, and a number of other firm believers in the strength of teachers' expectations made much of this study, the inconsistent results hardly provide much support for the thesis. When Robert Thorndike,[75] perhaps the most respected expert in educational measurement in the country, subsequently pointed out that the pattern of class scores on the pretest demonstrates that the test was obviously unreliable for the youngest children, confidence in the Pygmalion study decreased even further.

So fascinated were educators with the concept, however, that a flood of investigations by a number of researchers around the country followed. Panel 11.5 reviews these efforts. It would be difficult to conclude that there are any better empirical grounds for asserting a teacher expectancy effect on student achievement than there is for claiming superior results for a particular teacher style or set of teacher behaviors. The best one can say for either of the assumptions is that there is little supporting evidence for it.

PANEL 11.5   Pygmalion Revisited—The Later Studies

Interest in the self-fulfilling prophecy continued and within a period of five or six years after the Rosenthal and Jacobson study approximately sixty research efforts had been made to establish its existence.

1. A number of such attempts follow the Rosenthal and Jacobson model—teachers are given in some plausible form information that they should expect a higher level of achievement from a particular group of children who have in fact been selected at random. Eleven such studies employing outcome measures that at least approximate school goals and in regular classroom situations are cited by Jere Brophy and Thomas Good in their book on teacher expectations.[76] Of the eleven, only one (using Air Force cadets in mathematics sections) reports results that are any better than chance. Brophy and Good attribute these negative findings primarily to the difficulty of persuading teachers to accept false data about their students when they contradict their own experience with them, and the diagnosis is undoubtedly correct. The era of designing studies based on falsely inducing teacher expectations is probably over.

2. An alternative to that design, the study of *natural* teacher expectations, poses very considerable difficulties of another kind. The problem, of course, is that most of the time teacher expectations of a child's performance are realistic assessments of a child's ability to achieve. Any measurement of a discrepancy between those judgments and how

well children actually perform at some later time may simply be normal error of judgment; one cannot expect teachers to be any less fallible than other groups of professionals who are required to make complicated estimates of human qualities.

As an example, a British study by J. Douglas is nominated by Brophy and Good as the "most definitive and compelling" evidence on the effect of teacher expectations.[77] Douglas reports a three-year follow-up study of children who had been assigned to academic tracks at the age of eight. Some of these children had been "misplaced" into either upper or lower tracks, if "correct" placement is defined by their performance on standardized tests. Three years later Douglas found that some of those who had been misplaced into higher sections improved, some of those misplaced into lower sections deteriorated. This finding is interpreted as showing that "labelling" children by putting them into a section that is known to be for "better achievers" will induce them to live up to their label, and vice-versa. It may equally or even more plausibly be interpreted as a tribute to the prediction ability of teachers who, thoroughly familiar with individual children, were able to take into account a wider range of information than that provided by a standardized test.

There is no way of knowing which of these interpretations is correct, which is precisely why the study of teacher expectations in natural settings is bound to be inconclusive.

3. Another way of getting at the issue is to establish a link between teacher expectation and teacher behavior, that is, to find whether teachers interact differently with students from whom they expect good performance than with those from whom they expect poor performance. If such a link cannot be proven, the entire self-fulfilling prophecy hypothesis falls apart. (It should be noted that Rosenthal and Jacobson found no evidence of such differential interaction in classroom observations conducted during their original study.)

Most direct studies of selective teacher behavior yield inconsistent results; some find, for example, that teachers pay more attention, or give more praise to, or interact more with, high expectancy students; others find no difference or even the opposite state of affairs. Brophy and Good performed two carefully designed studies of this type, by asking teachers to rank their students in the order of expected achievement, then selecting six of the highest rank order students and six of the lowest rank order for observation during regular classroom periods. In the first study of four classrooms they found that high expectancy children were praised more often for the correct answer, criticized less often for incorrect answers, and given more cues by the teacher to help find the right answer or the solution to a problem. Their second study, this time of nine classrooms, found no such discrimination in teacher behavior, and "if anything, the opposite was true"; teachers attempted "to compensate by calling on lows more frequently and especially by frequently initiating work-related contacts with them."[78]

<hr>

THE FUTURE OF ACCOUNTABILITY

If differences in school resources do not consistently affect achievement, and if curriculum design, instructional curriculum hardware, and teacher behavior explain differences in achievement no better, a simple approach to school accountability appears doomed to failure. Such an approach, if applied to medicine, would demand equal curative powers for a given treatment applied by a doctor whatever the state of his patient.

The Michigan experience suggests that political pressures will mediate between reality and the absurdity of pressing such a policy. It is also likely that accountability practice will slowly shift to a process that operates within the well-established boundaries of predictable achievement levels for different groups of students. Such a model has been adopted by New York City schools. The accountability program, developed by the Educational Testing Service, groups schools in the system with reference to student characteristics and backgrounds, and the environmental conditions of the home and community. Predictions based on input variables are then projected and compared with the actual achievement levels in schools within each group. Those schools which either exceed the group norm noticeably, or fall below the group norm by more than one would expect, are to be subjected to detailed examination. One might learn from the first of these types what accounts for their unusual success, and from the second what changes should be made to improve them.

Few educators could object to such an eminently sensible procedure and, indeed, the model was developed in cooperation with the city's teacher union. The adoption of accountability approaches of this kind might well lead to modest, but genuine, improvements in urban school effectiveness.

CHAPTER NOTES

[1] A. S. Neill, *Summerhill: A Radical Approach to Child Rearing* (New York: Hart, 1960).

[2] For typical works, see Ivan Illich, *DeSchooling Society* (New York: Harper & Row, 1971); Paul Goodman, *Growing Up Absurd* (New York: Random House, 1960); Paolo Freire, *Pedagogy of the Oppressed* (New York: Seabury Pub., 1971).

[3] For typical works, see Herbert Kohl, *Thirty-Six Children* (New York: New American Library, 1967); Jonathan Kozol, *Death at an Early Age* (New York: Bantam Books, 1970); George Dennison, *The Lives of Children* (New York: Random House, 1969); Neil Postman and Charles Weingartner, *Teaching as a Subversive Activity* (New York:

Delacorte, 1969); James Herndon, *The Way it Spozed To Be* (New York: Simon & Schuster, 1968).

4 Samuel Bowles and Herbert Gintis, *Schooling in Capitalist America* (New York: Basic Books, 1976).

5 Illich, especially Chap. 4.

6 Charles Silberman, *Crisis in the Classroom* (New York: Random House, 1971).

7 Christopher Lehman-Haupt, "Review of *The Open Classroom*," *New York Times,* October 8, 1970 p. 45.

8 Donald W. Robinson, "Alternative Schools: Is the Old Order Really Changing?" *Educational Leadership,* 28 (1971), 604–606.

9 Quoted in Robinson, p. 605.

10 John Bremer and Michael von Moschziker, *School without Walls* (New York: Holt, Rinehart and Winston, 1971).

11 Allen Graubard, *Alternative Education: The Free School Movement in the U.S.,* An ERIC Paper, Stanford University (September 1972).

12 Albert Shanker, "Harlem Prep: Success or Failure?" *New York Times,* March 17, 1974, Section E, p. 7.

13 *Matters of Choice: A Ford Foundation Report on Alternative Schools* (New York: The Ford Foundation, 1974).

14 Daniel U. Levine and Russell C. Doll, *Systems Renewal in the Louisville Public Schools* (Center for the Study of Metropolitan Problems in Education, University of Missouri, Kansas City, undated).

15 A. J. H. Gaite and Richard J. Rankin, *Evaluating an Alternative School: Theory, Practice, and Outcomes.* Paper presented to the Annual Meeting of the American Educational Research Association, Chicago, 1974.

16 James Baines and William H. Young, "The Sudden Rise and Decline of New Jersey Street Academies," *Phi Delta Kappan* (December 1971), 240–242.

17 Terence E. Deal, "An Organizational Explanation of the Failure of Alternative Secondary Schools," *Educational Researcher,* 4 (1975), 10–16.

18 Bruce Cooper, "Organizational Survival, A Comparative Case of Seven American 'Free Schools,' " *Education and Urban Society,* 5 (1973), 487–508.

19 Steven Singleton, David Boyer, and Paul Dorsey, "Xanadu: A Study of the Structure Crisis in an Alternative School," *Review of Educational Research,* 42 (1972), 525–531.

20 Charles J. Brauner, *American Educational Theory* (Englewood Cliffs, N.J.: Prentice-Hall, 1964).

21 Brauner, p. 250.

22 John Dewey, *Experience and Education* (New York: Macmillan, 1938).

23 Roland S. Barth, "So You Want To Change to an Open Classroom," *Phi Delta Kappan,* 53 (October 1971), 97–99.

24 Richard Flaste, "Embittered Reformer Advises: Avoid School," *New York Times,* April 16, 1976, p. 35.

25 California State Task Force, Report of the Task Force on Early Childhood Education (Sacramento: California State Board of Education, 1971).

26 Robert J. Wright, "The Affective and Cognitive Consequences of an Open Education Elementary School," *American Educational Research Journal,* 12 (1975), 449–468.

27 Neville Bennett, *Teaching Styles and Pupil Progress* (New York: Open Books, 1976).

28 F. McLaughlin, "Back to Basics," *Media and Methods,* 11 (1974), 8–10.

29 Christopher Jencks, "Is the Public School Obsolete?" *The Public Interest* (Winter 1968), 18–27.

30 J. Areen and Christopher Jencks, "Educational Vouchers: A Proposal for Diversity and Choice," *Record,* 72 (February 1971), 327–335.

31 Robert A. Lekachman, "Vouchers and Public Education," *The United Teacher Magazine* (November 14, 1971), 1–4; Robert Dentler, "Vouchers: A Problem of Scale," *The Record,* 72 (February 1971), 383–387; Eli Ginzburg, "The Economics of the Voucher

System," *The Record,* 72 (February 1971), 373–382; David Selden, "Vouchers—Solution or Sop?" *The Record,* 72 (February 1971) 366–371.

32 *A Public School Voucher Demonstration: The First Year at Alum Rock.* The Rand Corporation, June, 1974.

33 A Public School Voucher Demonstration.

34 Quoted in "Report on Education," *Educational Researcher,* 3 (1974), p. 6.

35 Joel M. Levin, "Alum Rock after Two Years," *Phi Delta Kappan,* 56 (1974), 201–204.

36 Charles Blaschke, Peter Briggs and Reed Martin, "The Performance Contract—Turnkey Approach to Urban School System Reform," *Educational Technology* (September 1970), 45–48.

37 "U.S. Plans Test of Teaching of Pupils by Private Contractors," *New York Times,* July 15, 1970.

38 John A. Wilson, *Banneker: A Case Study of Educational Change* (Champaign: University of Illinois Press, 1973).

39 James A. Mecklenburger and John A. Wilson, "Learning C.O.D.: Can the Schools Buy Success?" *Saturday Review* (September 18, 1971), 62–65 ff.

40 *Evaluation of the Office of Economic Opportunity's Performance Contract Experiment,* Comptroller General of the U.S. B130515, 1973.

41 *Evaluation of the OEO's Performance Contract Experiment,* p. 92.

42 Ellis Page, "How We All Failed at Performance Contracting," *Phi Delta Kappan* (October 1972), 115–117.

43 John K. Miller, "Not Performance Contracting but the OEO Experiment Was A Failure," *Phi Delta Kappan* (February 1973), 394–396.

44 Kenneth Clark, *Dark Ghetto* (New York: Harper & Row, 1965).

45 Phyllis Hawthorne, *Legislation by the States—Accountability and Assessment in Education,* Department of Health, Education and Welfare (August 1973).

46 Jerome T. Murphy and David K. Cohen, "Accountability in Education—The Michigan Experience," *The Public Interest,* no. 36 (Summer 1974), 56–81.

47 David E. Wiley and Annegret Harnischfeger, "Explosion of a Myth: Quantity of Schooling and Exposure to Instruction, Major Educational Vehicles," *Educational Researcher,* 3 (1974), 7–12; Nancy Karweit, "Quantity of Schooling: A Major Educational Factor?" *Educational Researcher,* 5 (1975), 15–17.

48 Herbert Hyman, Charles Wright, and John Reed, *The Enduring Effects of Education* (New York: Wiley, 1975).

49 James S. Coleman *et al., Equality of Educational Opportunity,* HEW, 1966.

50 Samuel Bowles, "Toward Equality of Educational Opportunity?" *Harvard Educational Review,* 38 (Winter 1968), 92–93.

51 Frederick Mosteller and Daniel P. Moynihan (eds.), *On Equality of Educational Opportunity* (New York: Random House, 1972).

52 Henry R. Dyer, "School Factors and Equal Educational Opportunity," *Harvard Educational Review,* 38 (Winter 1968), 38–56.

53 Bowles, p. 95.

54 Dyer, p. 50.

55 Dyer, p. 46.

56 Christopher S. Jencks, *et al., Inequality: A Reassessment of Family and Schooling* (New York: Basic Books, 1972).

57 Christopher S. Jencks and Marsha D. Brown, "Effects of High Schools on Their Students," *Harvard Educational Review,* 45 (1975), 273–324.

58 Jencks and Brown, p. 320.

59 Jencks and Brown, p. 321.

60 Derek F. Walker and Jon Schaffarzik, "Comparing Curricula," *Review of Educational Research,* 44 (1974), 83–111.

61 Dean Jamison, Patrick Suppes and Stuart Wells, "The Effectiveness of Alternative Instructional Media: A Survey," *Review of Educational Research,* 44 (1974), p. 19.

62 John F. Vinsonhaler and Ronald K. Bass, "A Summary of Ten Major Studies in CAI Drill and Practice," *Educational Technology* (July 1972), 29–32.

63 Vinsonhaler and Bass, p. 31.

64 Leon Lessinger and associates, *Accountability: Systems Planning in Education* (Homewood, Ill.: ETC Publications, 1973); Ernest House, "Essay Review," *American Educational Research Journal,* 11 (1974), 275–279.

65 Barak Rosenshine and Norma Furst, "Research in Teacher Performance Criteria," in B.O. Smith (ed.), *Research in Teacher Education* (Englewood Cliffs, N.J.: Prentice-Hall, 1971), p. 37.

66 R. W. Heath and Mark A. Neilson, "The Research Basis for Performance-Based Teacher Education," *Review of Educational Research,* 44 (Fall 1974), 463–484.

67 Heath and Neilson, p. 476.

68 O. G. Brim, *Sociology and the Field of Education* (New York: Russell Sage Foundation, 1958).

69 R. Dubin and T. C. Taveggia, *The Teacher-Learning Paradox: A Comparative Analysis of College Teaching Methods* (Eugene: Center for the Advanced Study of Educational Administration, University of Oregon, 1968).

70 A. Mood, "Do Teachers Make a Difference?" in *Do Teachers Make a Difference? A Report on Recent Research in Pupil Achievement* (Washington, D.C.: Bureau of Educational Personnel Development, Office of Education, 1970).

71 J. W. Getzels and P. W. Jackson, "The Teacher's Personality and Characteristics," in N. S. Gage (ed.), *Handbook of Research on Teaching* (Skokie, Ill.: Rand McNally, 1963).

72 N. E. Wallen and R. M. W. Travers, "Analysis and Investigation of Teaching Methods," in Gage, p. 800.

73 J. M. Stephens, *The Process of Schooling* (New York: Holt, Rinehart and Winston, 1967), 83–84.

74 R. Rosenthal and L. Jacobson, *Pygmalion in the Classroom* (New York: Holt, Rinehart and Winston, 1968).

75 Robert Thorndike, "Review of *Pygmalion in the Classroom,*" *American Educational Research Journal,* 5 (1968), 708–711.

76 J. E. Brophy and T. L. Good, *Teacher-Student Relationships* (New York: Holt, Rinehart and Winston, 1974).

77 J. Douglas, *The Home and the School* (London: MacGibbon and Kee, 1964).

78 Brophy and Good, p. 104.

79 Henry S. Dyer, "Toward Objective Criteria of Professional Accountability in the Schools of New York City," *Phi Delta Kappan,* LII (1970), 206–211.

Chapter 12

Urban Teachers

From curriculum and program we now turn to what has always been viewed as the crucial component of the school structure—the teachers. This chapter:

Examines the problem of classroom control, one that teachers in the urban schools see as their most difficult one, and describes models proposed to deal with it.

Reviews the major issues involved in selecting and training teachers for the urban schools, including recent competency-based efforts.

Looks at the influence on staffing patterns of teacher attitudes and career cycle, turnover rates, ethnic identification, and unionization.

Describes the development of the paraprofessional role, and its impact in the classroom.

Assesses the influence of administrative behavior on teacher morale and effectiveness.

Some questions readers might address are:

Faced with the often turbulent classroom of the urban school, which of the two control tendencies described as extreme models would I find most comfortable?

Competency-based training for teachers is a highly rational approach to the problem. What strikes me as the most plausible reason for its not working as well as anticipated?

Would I like to teach in an urban school in the slums? What kind of advice can be distilled from the chapter for a teacher preparing to enter such a school?

This chapter considers one of the most sensitive and poorly understood aspects of urban education; sensitive because it touches on arguments over the competence and attitudes of large numbers of professionals who run and staff the schools, poorly understood because it is difficult to get hard evidence about the real impact of school personnel on their pupils.

Some critics of the urban schools, particularly those with large proportions of poor minority group children in them, have damned the administrators and teachers who run them as "awful people . . . tyrants . . . silly and malicious . . . who have a lot of faith in punishment, manipulation, and taking orders."[1] Others, who view the problems of the urban schools as stemming primarily from the children's environments and homes, consider such criticisms irresponsible.[2] Hundreds of books and articles on teaching the urban slum child counsel teachers on the one hand to keep instructional goals clear and take them in small steps, to plan and organize and be efficient, and on the other hand, to be interested first in the child's emotional needs and in whatever interests and motivates him.

Whatever the emphasis, most people who have talked with many teachers in the urban schools agree that teachers perceive the major problem to be that of classroom control. Confirmation of this truism, and a look at how a variety of both new and experienced teachers handle the problem, is contained in a well-conducted study by Gertrude Moskowitz and John Hayman,[3] who polled students in three junior high schools in a low income area in Flint, Michigan, to find a group of "best" teachers (those teachers students "liked a lot" and from whom they "learned a lot"). A comparison group of typical teachers was selected by asking principals to nominate their fifteen best teachers and eliminating them as well as those the students selected from the pool of teachers; the typical group was then selected randomly from the remainder. A third group consisted of first-year teachers at the beginning of their first full-time teaching year. Classes were observed and described by a variant of the Flanders teacher-pupil interaction system, during the first period of teacher contact with the class, later during the first week, twice during the second week, and once each during the third and fourth weeks.

Figure 12.1 reproduces some of the comparisons, beginning with the differences in disorderliness. It suggests that all teachers had control problems, as indicated by a rise in teacher critical comment, but the rate of increase was greatest for beginners. The best teachers apparently use humor a good deal at first, then drop to the same level as the typical teacher. The best

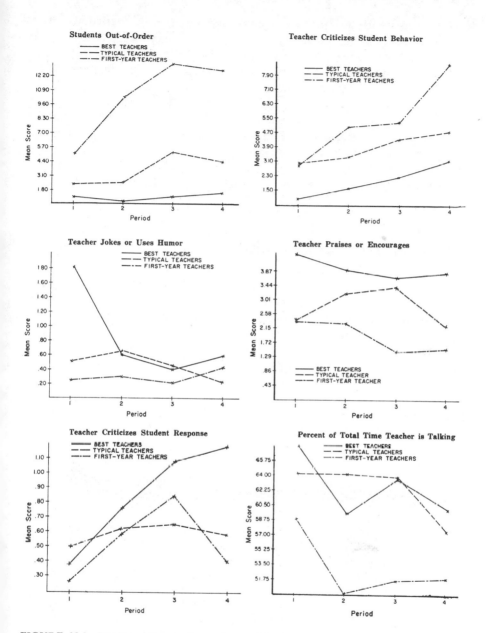

FIGURE 12.1   Pupil reaction to inner-city teaching styles. From Gertrude Moskowitz and John L. Hayman, "Interaction Patterns of First-Year, Typical, and 'Best' Teachers in Inner-City Schools," *Journal of Educational Research*, 67 (1974), 226–229.

teachers consistently use praise and encouragement, with particularly high levels at the beginning, but use criticism very sparingly at first, then permit the level to rise. (They criticize student behavior less than the other two groups, however.) The final diagram shows that the best teachers are hardly the model of current "indirect" fashions in teaching.

Moskowitz and Hayman conclude that the very early period of the year is obviously important, and that when they first met a class, the best teachers exceeded the other groups in time spent dealing with students' feelings, joking, and giving students suggestions that would benefit them. They also began by setting expectations and standards relating to subject matter, in contrast with the new teachers' concentration on administrative and routine matters.

THE TREND TO THE EXTREMES

What is most interesting perhaps about the question of how teachers should establish a reasonable degree of order in the classroom, when faced with more volatile children than most people can handle, is that in recent years a noticeable trend toward two extremes has emerged. One of them belongs to the child-liberation wing of the school reform; one of the most highly praised and widely read examples of this humanist model is a book by James Herndon, *The Way It Spozed To Be*.[4] Friedenberg called it "the most valuable of all" the works on the slum school; John Holt said it was "honest, profound, concerned"; others offered equally impressive accolades. The book describes Herndon's first year of teaching in a California slum school whose students were 98 percent black. It is clear that his teaching style was not learned there, for his special educational philosophy is evidenced in the first faculty meeting in his lack of interest in the principal's talk about "order in the classroom."

> My lack of interest wasn't simply naive, at least not in the way which springs immediately to mind, that of the imaginary progressive educator who imagines, or has been popularly supposed to imagine, that given a nice, friendly teacher and lots of freedom of action and very little planning, the students will always be good-natured, orderly, interested, motivated, well-behaved, and studious, in short, nice themselves. I didn't doubt that there might be noise, disorder, anarchy, chaos and all that in my classroom; I just didn't see that this constituted a "problem" any more than a quiet, studious class was a "problem." Perhaps they were both problems, put it that way.[5]

The school divided its classes by IQ into eight groupings, assigning the letters A to H to the classes. Herndon was assigned two B classes, about which he talks very little, a 7H class, and a 9D class, to whom he devotes major attention in the book. Both classes provide him with considerable amounts of "noise, disorder, anarchy, chaos," but Herndon is convinced, when another teacher takes his classes for a time, that they learn little when traditional order is maintained anyway, so he seldom bothers.

> He comes finally to the conclusion that the problem with 9D was that they had rejected the ordinary avenues of activity which had been offered them, but hadn't come up with any alternative of their own. In fairness to them, it didn't seem likely that the possibility of making up their own alternatives had been often granted them. No, they had been presented year after year with an offer of certain things to either do or not do, which is alternative enough in itself. I remember reading, from some novel or other, about two kids talking about class, this last alternative wasn't being offered. What to do? I wish school would start, said one kid, so we'd have something to do. What would we do then, man? asked the other. Then we could cut school! said the first.
>
> They could not-go. Not-do it. It was something. Now, in our class, this last alternative wasn't being offered. What to do? They had never gotten the idea that they might be doing something else and call it school.[6]

Herndon considers what *he* wants them to do: to learn something about English, about writing. But his attempts at discussions with them, and at getting them to write about what they thought as a result of the discussions, had failed. "The problem of 9D was to find out what they wanted done which needed the classroom, the school situation to do, which couldn't be done otherwise."[7]

His solution was simply to let them do what they wanted. In 7H, he imported some tape recorders, into which the kids took turns orating; suggested reading groups for those with the slightest interest in improving their reading, with the somewhat better readers acting as monitors; and provided word games for any one to choose from when they felt like it. Class 9D's favorite activity was Friday movies; they played a number of educational films over and over, while munching popcorn and potato chips. They also settled into a routine on other days of distributing the parts of a dramatized version of Cinderella, and acting it out time after time.

Since all of these activities were accompanied by incessant arguments, screams, and fights, it is not surprising that at the end of the year Herndon was not rehired. And it is easy for the reader to be swept along in the wave of his resentment at his dismissal, unless he stops to consider whether Herndon's own objectives were met. There was very little in any of the students' activities that would suggest that they could improve either their reading or writing, because the activities were simply irrelevant to those skills; one nonreader did learn to read, but it was undoubtedly because he was one of the few who plugged away in a reading group. The major question is whether the classes had indeed discovered something they wanted to do that needed a classroom or a teacher; what they chose to do seems, on the face of it, just as feasible in any setting, nor does Herndon make any claim to making a contribution to their activity.

At the opposite pole from this trend toward providing absolute freedom for the pupil is a rapidly growing body of experimentation with shaping behavior in the classroom; more technically, it is called "applied analysis of behavior."

These principles are extensions and applications of Skinner's work on operant conditioning, which led first to a very sizable body of experimental laboratory work with animals in the fifties, and more recently to a number of behavior modification experiments with retarded children and with delinquents. Application of the principles to autistic children, so withdrawn and unresponsive that they generally resisted being taught to feed or dress themselves, resulted in a number of astonishing successes. Work with delinquent children in institutions followed; in some cases, elaborate "token economies" were developed, with children being given a plastic disc for each instance of an approved behavior on the understanding that they could turn in the discs for some set value at the commissary. The successful results in these settings sparked a number of experiments with normal children in classrooms.

The principles themselves are simple: A behavior that is reinforced (rewarded) has a greater probability of recurring than one that is not. It is a principle that most teachers have learned, and that most probably think they apply. But, as one psychologist notes, "If given a test on the principles so far discussed, most people would score very high. It is not a lack of reinforcement or lack of knowledge about how to use them. The difficulty can be primarily traced to the failure to systematically apply what is known. It is not only that operant principles are not systematically applied, they are if applied at all, sporadically applied."[8]

The experimentation with behavior modifications is often far more rigorous and controlled than most classroom research. The description of one of these studies below is representative of the field, and will provide a specific view of the teaching technique as well as of the research methodology.[9]

The experiment was conducted in a demonstration school for disadvantaged children, in a classroom of twenty children and two teachers. Two seven-year-old girls were selected for study, both of them of average IQ, both difficult for the teachers to handle. One of the children spent about 90 percent of her time on some days in disruptive behavior, throwing a basketball at the ceiling, going about the room pulling workbooks away from other children, running into the hall, etc. The other child specialized in responding "I won't" or "I ain't" when given a direction by the teacher; and, if the teacher insisted, the girl would kick and hit at her.

Observers were trained to categorize the behavior of both the children and the teachers. Children's behavior was classified as *desirable, inappropriate,* and *unacceptable*; teacher interactions were classified as *positive* (anything that encouraged or approved the behavior of the child), *neutral* (statements that referred to academic work or set limits for the child), *question, redirection* (a statement with which the teacher tried to redirect a child from an inappropriate to an appropriate behavior), and *negative* (any statement disapproving of the child's behavior).

The experiment consisted of four stages: First came the baseline period, during which, for ten days, observations of both children and teachers were collected. Second, the Modification I period, during which the teacher was trained to respond in particular ways to the children's behavior. She was to give praise and attention to either child when she exhibited desirable behavior, and was instructed to withhold reinforcement by turning away from the child when her behavior was inappropriate or attention-getting. When the child was aggressive or resistive, the teacher was to first try redirection ("You are supposed to be doing . . ."), then a warning, and finally, after fifteen seconds, to remove the child from the room.

Modification I came to an end when for five successive days both children's desirable behaviors exceeded 75 percent of all behavior, and averaged 90 percent. The third period, Postmodification, required the teacher to return to her baseline behavior; and during the fourth period, Modification II, teachers were instructed to return to the experimental procedures of Modification I.

In the case of one child, Dianne, during the baseline period there are several days when she exhibited *no* desirable behavior at all. In the Postmodification period, when the teachers returned to their normal interaction patterns, Dianne's appropriate behaviors remained high. The teachers were then instructed to give her as little attention as possible, and though there was a decrease in appropriate behavior, the former disruptive behavior did not reappear. A followup three months after the study was completed found that the desirable behavior of each child remained high, ranging from 85 percent to 100 percent.

In a field in which behavior change in response to experimental situations tends to be modest at best, these are startlingly effective results, although there are some mixed findings in the very substantial body of literature that is now accumulating. In one inner-city junior high school, for example, James Long and Robert Williams found that a token economy in a class of children selected as being most disruptive did not work at all, though the use of free time as a reward managed to maintain satisfactory levels of behavior.[10] The results are more consistent than one usually finds, however, and even the criticism directed at behavior mod's tendency to use the experimental group as its own control has been answered—Marion Thompson and his associates tested behavior shaping with control classes in an inner city Atlanta school and report considerable differences between the experimental and control groups.[11]

The humanistically inclined do tend to be horrified by what they see as dehumanization in the approach. Richard Winett and Robin Winkler sum up the critical attack in the title of an article: "Current Behavior Modification in the Classroom: Be Still, Be Quiet, Be Docile."[12] They argue from a review of behavior mod studies that the method emphasizes the status quo and petty law and order in the classroom, to the detriment of learning itself. If we intend to reinforce "appropriate" behavior, they say, how are we to define *what* is appropriate?

K. Daniel O'Leary replies that Winnett and Winkler are merely setting up a straw man Model Child, that there is no instance in the articles they reviewed of a demand for such extreme behavior.[13] In fact, he claims, teachers and researchers employing the approach aim primarily at the reduction of disruptive behavior of only a minority of children to manageable levels.

It is important to note that most behavior mod experiments focus on classroom behavior rather than on academic achievement. O'Leary and Drabman offer a reasonable explanation for that phenomenon:

> If token programs serve as a priming or incentive function, one would certainly expect academic behaviors to be more difficult to change than social behaviors, since children in token programs frequently have the appropriate social behaviors in their repertoire but not the academic skills necessary to progress without considerable instruction.[14]

TEACHER SELECTION

There is so much controversy about what makes an effective teacher that any efforts at preselection at the point of entry into teacher training are unlikely to be successful, not that there have been many attempts to do so. For almost a generation, in fact, the attempts of city schools to cope with a teacher shortage that decisively ended only at the beginning of the decade of the seventies discouraged any selectivity. Many school systems were happy if they succeeded in finding enough "warm bodies" to put into their burgeoning classrooms.

The shortage was due to several very different trends. The one that affected most schools was the birth-rate leap that followed the end of World War II, resulting in a population cohort that traveled through the school system like a large rabbit progressing through the body of a snake. The second developed from the demographic trends discussed in Chapter 5, drawing more experienced, and possibly more able, teachers to the suburbs as middle-class whites left the central cities and built more attractive school systems. As the effects of the population explosion peter out, this second movement may still persist.

By 1972 it was very clear that the shortage had ended and that a period of oversupply had begun, a switch that was quietly predicted earlier from the declining birth rate of the sixties. Figure 12.2 displays current projections of teacher supply and demand based on two different assumptions about school populations and educational expenditures. Even if the more optimistic assumption for both supply and demand is adopted it is obvious

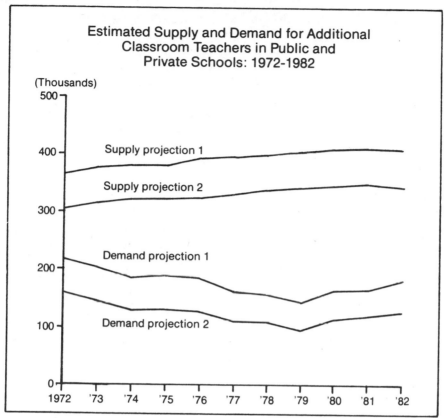

FIGURE 12.2   Estimated supply and demand for classroom teachers, to 1982. From *Conditions of Education*, National Center for Educational Statistics, Department of Health, Education and Welfare. Washington, D.C.: Government Printing Office, 1975, p. 74.

that an oversupply of about a hundred thousand teachers may be expected into the 1980s.

Many educators argue that, considering the educational tasks to be done, the oversupply of trained teachers is illusory. Allan Ornstein has listed the following opportunities now open to us:[15] the extending of the kindergarten movement to all school systems, cutting class size, tackling adult illiteracy, increasing the inadequate supply of high school counselors, and developing a system of lifelong learning for all adults. He argues further that the oversupply provides teacher training institutions with the opportunity to be more selective and thus upgrade the quality of teaching staffs nationwide; we might also release more of the time of teachers now on the job for inservice training.

Those who make such suggestions recognize at the same time their unfeasibility. Most of them require very substantial increases in public support and one must consider not only the financial troubles of urban areas but a public mood reflecting a feeling that the schools are already getting more than a fair share of resources.

Does the termination of the teacher shortage present an inexpensive opportunity to develop a teacher selection policy? The great demand for teachers in the past several decades encouraged a high level of teacher turnover. Any occupation that employs large numbers of young women must expect a high turnover rate as they leave to raise a family; but the costs of elaborate training programs for teachers, many of whom stay in the profession only one to three years, were probably excessive. Because the job market overwhelmingly influences turnover rate, the schools may now face the opposite problem of a static labor force, growing increasingly older and more tenured, and with even less of an opportunity to develop a selection policy.

Recently, the issue has become more complicated in urban areas by the growing demand for the hiring of a representative proportion of black teachers and administrators in city schools whose pupil populations are increasingly black. Cities like New York, which supplements the requirements for a state license with a special entry examination, are now castigated for making an effort to be more selective on the grounds that the examination is unfair to minority group candidates. Whether it is or not is a matter of some dispute. There is no doubt that the examination stresses verbal performance and an acquaintance with the world of middle-class culture, areas in which Southern born and educated blacks are likely to be deficient. The New York Board of Examiners, however, argue that black and Puerto Rican candidates succeed or fail in about the same proportion as whites who take the examination, and that the reason for the strikingly low proportions of these groups among the city's teachers is the small number of blacks and Puerto Ricans available with the educational background required even to take the exam.

Any such selection device is likely in the near future to become a target for similar political conflicts on the urban scene, and cannot, therefore, be considered very seriously. Whether the alternative currently most strongly advocated—*i.e.*, leaving the selection process to interviews with principals and local boards—will result in higher overall quality of teaching is a question that only the future can answer.

PANEL 12.1 Predicting Teacher Effectiveness

In view of the difficulties involved in applying any of the traditional methods of selection, it would be useful to have a body of tested, empirical predictors of teacher quality in urban schools, but it is difficult to develop. In general, the verbal ability of teachers (perhaps a proxy for IQ) and teacher experience correlate modestly with pupil achievement. Henry Levin has found that teacher verbal ability has a slightly larger effect on pupil achievement than does teacher experience for both black and white urban children; to the extent that experience matters at all, it is more important for black children than for whites.[16] He also estimates that hiring a teacher with an additional year of experience costs a school system three times as much as hiring one with an additional point of verbal score, so the more effective characteristic is also less expensive to acquire. Unfortunately, it is the youngest teachers, with the highest dropout rate from the profession, who exhibit the highest verbal ability.

Most prediction studies of teacher effectiveness, unlike Levin's, attempt to predict performance from personality measures, and have done so with indifferent success. To cite one such study, Strom and Larimore found a surprisingly high correlation for a few personality measures with classroom performance of a group of teachers in Columbus entering slum classrooms for the first time.[17] The performance measure was the rating given each teacher by the college supervisor (not children's learning achievement), and of the battery of personality tests used, only three measures predicted the performance level very efficiently: one that indicates a high degree of efficiency, organization, responsibility, and persistence; a second that describes a person who is appreciative, patient, helpful, gentle, and accepting of others; and a third that indicates a high level of achievement drive. Although a combination of the three scales predicts performance with a correlation of .94, which is very high indeed, the sample is small and the performance ratings are based on only one person's judgment. It is possible that the Columbus teacher-rating scale emphasizes as desirable some of the very qualities that appear in the personality scales. Like all studies of teacher effectiveness, this one must inevitably confront the wide variations in criteria for teacher effectiveness.

TEACHER TRAINING

Although the evidence cited here and in the preceding chapter suggests that the intellectually able, emotionally stable, and well-organized teacher is probably the best bet for staffing the urban schools, most of the teacher-training institutions seem, since the late sixties, to have moved toward a stress on the human relations aspect of the teaching role. The general mood of professional educators in the seventies can be sensed by picking up almost any of the professional journals and leafing through them; a recent symposium on teacher education for inner city schools in the *Journal of Teacher Education* condensed all its aspects very well:[18] the sweeping and largely unsupported generalizations about urban systems and teachers, a considerable amount of moral agonizing and revolutionary fervor, and very little in the way of concrete programs with actual results.

Among the range of current attitudes and convictions, four appear as dominant themes:

1. One current emphasis is on attitude change, particularly sensitivity training—a logical extension of the theory that poor school performance is a direct outcome of the child's feeling of alienation and of being misunderstood.

Many recent programs have concentrated on developing among entering teachers more positive attitudes toward teaching in inner-city schools and toward the children and families they encounter there. There is a general trend toward seeing the summer after graduation and just preceding the teacher's first classroom experience as a crucial period of time for specific preparation for the slum school assignment. Strom's Preface Plan is a good example of the general program design:[19] a six-week summer session that included a variety of lectures on poverty, the lower-class family, self-concept and motivation, and so forth; a two-week team teaching experience with eighteen children from a disadvantaged area; visits with welfare workers and to a juvenile court. During the following school year, the participants were visited by project staff and were brought together for conferences once a month in a continuing inservice program.

At the end of the school year and before the beginning of the program only eight of Strom's twenty-one teachers expressed a preference for teaching in the neighborhoods to which they had been assigned; by the end of the first year of teaching and of the program, twenty of them indicated such a preference, a very considerable shift in attitude. Unfortunately, such effects seldom last; generally speaking, 80 to 90 percent of student teachers in experimental inner-city programs of this kind do take jobs in slum schools, but most of them leave within a three-year period.[20]

Other programs have succeeded in inducing apparently more profound changes in trainees. One fifteen-week spring and summer graduate program for a group of students who had just completed their teacher training at Western Michigan University was divided into (a) a period including work in a guidance clinic and detention home, field trips to social and community agencies, and weekly therapy meetings in addition to standard lectures; and (b) a period of paid internship working with migrant children or in a summer camp for the disadvantaged.[21] Attitudes toward lower class children and parents improved substantially, and there was also a significant increase in the students' self-rating scores on a personality inventory, showing movement toward greater self-realization.

Findings of attitude changes such as these are far from rare. It is striking, however, that the amount of effort expended on a program does not consistently correlate with results. A Penn State program, for example, went so far as to assign students for periods of ten weeks to live and work in the homes, communities, and jobs considered typical of working-class youth.[22] They lived with poor families, assuming the role of older sister or daughter, worked eight hours a day in restaurants or on assembly lines, and shared their free time with the families. One would expect such an experience to have a sizable impact on attitudes; but pre and post comparisons show only small, if any, gains in self-actualization, flexibility, or knowledge and attitudes about teacher relationships to the community.

Carolyn Stern and Evan Keislar, in a review of such "immersion" programs, conclude that reported experimental program gains do not hold up in those programs in which control groups are used.[23] Neither do the "encounter group" methods that have become popular in recent years; the literature on these sensitivity approaches intended to "get to the gut level" is replete with accounts of dramatic changes in attitude and behavior, but more rigorously designed evaluations indicate only limited gains and some indication of negative effects.

Even if these programs were uniformly effective, the question of the effect of the human relations approach on pupil learning remains unanswered. One very interesting and at least partially controlled study of this central issue suggests that the answer may be in the negative.[24] The experiment was conducted in a Montreal slum school by a psychiatrist from a local community mental health center. Each teacher from the ten classrooms that covered the third to seventh grades selected four children she considered most disturbed in general conduct and learning, and two control children who were well-behaved and optimally working. Of the disturbed children, twelve were from multiproblem families, twenty-eight from more stable working-class families.

In consultation with the teachers, the children were divided into *treatment* and *nontreatment* groups; the authors wryly observe that they could not assign them randomly because of the pressure to put the most seriously disturbed children into the treatment group, a tendency they could not avoid. Baseline observations of the children's behavior were collected in the three to four weeks after the program began, and observations were made one month, three months, and one year later. Treatment was carried out by a team of two psychiatrists, a social worker, and sometimes by the school nurses. The psychiatrist had almost daily meetings with the classroom teachers, discussing the children's behavior and remedial methods, to a total of 300 psychiatric hours. In addition to 1500 hours of tutoring, the treatment group also were given 200 hours of the time of the principal, the social worker, and the nurse. At the end of the year, they found no appreciable change in the children's functioning, either in behavior or in performance.

2. A second major trend, illustrated also in some of the programs noted above, is the demand to shift teacher training from the university to the school. This development stems from a variety of considerations: Trainees

have always seen the reality experience of student teaching as the most valuable part of training; the culture shock for middle-class teachers facing the
different milieu of the slum school can be dealt with in a supportive training situation; in-school training forces the trainers in the university to confront reality, instead of depending on academic generalizations.

The problems of logistics involved in such a move to the field can be
formidable, and it is more than a little contradictory to involve to an even
greater extent in teacher training school personnel whom teacher trainers
are publicly berating as incompetent and corrupting, but the training rationale is powerful enough to overcome these hurdles. The most recent
trend is toward an adaptation of a British in-service training approach, the
Teacher Center. These consist of fairly informal, small locations in the field
at which teachers in neighboring schools can meet to discuss their problems,
help one another, and perhaps formulate training needs with which they
can then approach a nearby college.

A typical, if somewhat elaborate, model for university teacher training
that illustrates many of these trends was developed in Chicago by the Cooperative Program in Urban Teacher Education.[25] The plan is built around
the development of learning centers in individual schools, each of them
featuring:

an advisory committee drawn from the community, the school, and the
    training university.
a working committee composed of university personnel, the school-commu-
    nity coordinator, and representative students training.
a program for five student teachers who spend their junior year partly at the
    center, the rest of their time in academic work at the university. Sugges-
    tions are made for each trainee by the advisory committee and imple-
    mented by the working committee, which meets with her to discuss her
    teaching experiences.

The issues raised by this new direction in training, and by the two major
assumptions underlying them (discussed in 1 and 2 above), are complex
ones and not readily settled. Teaching is an applied professional field, and
an increased training emphasis on practical work in the field is welcomed
by everyone. Whether the results will stand up under a cost/effectiveness
analysis remains to be seen; the costs are sizable; and, if the teacher turnover in the early years of the career is not significantly reduced, we shall be
putting even more social effort into training people whose contribution to
the school system lasts only a year or two. The question of whether the improvement in teaching effectiveness is large enough to justify the very considerable amount of organization and coordination involved in many of
these new training designs also needs to be investigated. The answer to
such questions will probably not be available until the end of the seventies,
when sufficient experience has been accumulated.

3. Finally, and surely most controversially, there is competency-based teacher education (CBTE), closely associated with the accountability movement described in the preceding chapter. Pushed with great fervor by a loose coalition of some state boards of education, teacher training professionals, the U.S. Office of Education, and executives of some major foundations, CBTE's basic assumption is that teacher education must be held accountable for its product. Its implied assumption, given its title, is that up until now teachers have *not* been competent because their training has not made them so. CBTE programs typically include the following:[26]

1.   Both pre-service and in-service programs must be based on "competencies"—skills, knowledge, attitudes, and behaviors that the teacher must have.

2.   Competencies are defined by what teachers must actually do in the classroom (teach addition, maintain order, diagnose pupil needs, etc.)

3.   The criteria for determining competency are explicit, stated in terms of demonstrated performance, and are public. Most programs include specific statements as to the *level* of performance that is to be judged adequate.

4.   Rate of progress through the training program is to be determined by attainment of the competencies, rather than by amount of time spent, college credits, degrees, or other standards.

Some states, among them California and New York, have mandated CBTE (New York has indeed threatened to decertify any teacher training institution that does not revamp its curriculum to CBTE specifications), a number of other states have moved toward it or are studying it; perhaps half of the states have done something about it, though estimates vary.[27] There are thirteen national centers for CBTE, a number of newsletters, hundreds of books and catalogs containing lists of competencies, instructional modules for specific competencies, minicourses and other materials.

The critics are as savage as the advocates are messianic; Albert Shanker, the president of the United Federation of Teachers, calls it "quackery."[28] In a sardonic review of the state of the movement John Merrow, of the Institute for Educational Leadership, notes the following major criticisms directed at CBTE:[29]

1. Who is to determine what teacher competencies are necessary and most important? Enthusiastic list-makers have compiled competency statements that range from Cruikshank's 43 to 1000 or more produced by some major universities' departments of education. In the absence of any hard evidence linking specific teacher behaviors to pupil achievement (see Chapter 11) how are the lists of competencies to be justified?[30] In reality, no one bothers justifying them; as Shanker pointed out:

> After competency-based certification was imposed on one state last year, the State Education Department sent the form throughout the state and said that all programs must be stated in competency terms. Every institution sat down,

figured what they were doing, and got hold of somebody willing to learn the terminology of "competency" and rewrote everything they were doing already and then sent it in . . .[31]

2. The CBTE movement encourages the development of instructional modules and minicourses which the students can tackle on their own. Merrow recounts the experience of Weber State College, an early enthusiast for CBTE, which organized its curriculum into 130 objectives and into modules known as WILKITS (for Weber Individualized Learning Kits). Over 500 observers found their way to Weber to admire, and presumably, to emulate. But, "the image of hundreds of students completing their WILKITS, rapping in the 'interaction laboratory' and student teaching— all with minimal faculty attention," reports Merrow, is not accurate.[32] Like students in traditional programs, Weber's wait until the end of the term to do their work; they complain about the lack of faculty contact and group instruction, and want fewer WILKITS.

3. Critics, among them Harry Broudy, the well-known philosopher of education, complain that the movement is well-designed to produce "mindless robots" with no feeling for the art of teaching.[33] Allen Schmeider, a CBTE advocate in the U.S. Office of Education, admits that "it could become the most vicious, fascistic method imaginable," but only if institutions make mistakes.[34]

4. Merrow argues that the major drawback to the program is that it is likely to become a weapon used against teacher militancy. In a period of declining demand for teachers, economy-minded state governments can seize on CBTE as a pseudo-scientific basis for measuring teacher performance and weed out the militants as "substandard."

> The language used by CBTE's respectable supporters in the research community fit easily into the campaigns against larger education budgets and tenure. That unplanned partnership is CBTE's greatest problem. If the terminology had not existed, someone favoring accountability would have invented it . . . Those who want to cut education budgets hardly favor increased spending on educational research, but there can be no genuine CBTE until research (which is expensive) identifies the competencies a successful teacher must have . . . But questions about competency-based teacher education are no longer educational ones; they are political. And that seems to mean that judgments about the competence of teachers will be made in the same old ways, though probably more often and perhaps more harshly.[35]

THE TEACHER CORPS

Much of the substance in these trends in teacher training and their potential for incorporation into teacher education can be best examined in the experience of the Teacher Corps. A look at that experience also provides a revealing glimpse of the problems of organizational change in school systems generally.

The Teacher Corps was created by the Higher Education Act of 1965; in the social euphoria of the sixties what could seem more attractive than the notion of recruiting and training idealistic young people to go into the slum schools of city and countryside and show the educational establishment what could be done? Its original goals were: (a) to improve the learning opportunities of disadvantaged children by providing them with committed, sympathetic teachers; and (b) to reform the teacher training practices of the universities and colleges by presenting them with models of innovative training programming.[36]

The Corps' procedure was first to gain the cooperation of a number of university teacher training divisions throughout the country, help them recruit liberal young college graduates oriented toward social change and to working with the poor, and arrange cooperative links between the training center and local school districts. Training designs varied, but all included a mix of some academic work at the university and field experience in the cooperating school districts; the young interns were made part of a team that included university faculty members and a cooperating teacher in the district.

The Corpsmen's image of themselves and of the school systems in which they worked is summarized in Table 12.1. It is hardly surprising that such a set of beliefs and intentions would be viewed unfavorably, even blasphemously, by many members of Congress and school professionals. Congress only grudgingly voted appropriations for the program and kept it finan-

Table 12.1   Hawaii Teacher Corps Interns' View of Themselves
and of Their Schools

Hawaii Teacher Corps Intern	Schools
Personal Attributes	
Aggressive, free wheeling	Conforming, going through channels
"Mod" clothes, hair styles, speech	Conservative clothes, hair styles, speech
Deep personal and social conscience	"Don't make waves"
Self realization, individuality	Accept group decision
Perceived Role of Teacher Corpsmen	
To reconstruct school and society	To learn about teaching "disadvantaged"
To fight present schools	To fit into the present system
To *rescue* children by replacing incompetent and unimaginative teachers	To recruit teachers who are willing to stay in districts with high turnover rate
We are part of the "solution" to getting dedicated teachers	Interns perhaps just another "problem"?

Source: *Melvin Lang,* Cultural Shock and the Teacher Corps: The Identification of Sources of Conflict. *Paper presented at the annual meeting of the American Educational Research Association, New York, 1971, pp. 2–3.*

cially starved, and the schools gradually blunted the impact of its major thrust. In a fascinating evaluation of the Teacher Corps, a noted educational sociologist, Ronald Corwin, describes how local school districts, using a variety of political pressures, gained control of the funds and thus more control over local interns, until the program's original goals were dissipated.[37] In the early seventies the Corps dedicated itself to the promotion of competency-based teacher education, and, although local programs still use the rhetoric of "advocacy" it is clear that little remains of the original.

PANEL 12.2   Evaluations of the Teacher Corps

Did the Corps attain, even temporarily, any of its aims? A number of evaluations suggest not; the National Advisory Council on Educational Professional Development gives it a "B" but even a cursory examination of the evidence reveals that such an assessment is wildly off the mark. Most of the evaluation studies agree that the institutions of higher education involved remained unaffected; regular teacher training programs are proceeding in the traditional ways. The few studies of children's academic achievement under the Corps' interns show no evidence that they were more effective than regular teachers; six of the nine major evaluations conclude that interns make ineffective change agents.[38]

In his book Corwin considers at great length and complexity the problem of establishing an innovative program faced with opposition in Congress, unstable funding, resistance from the field, and the need to satisfy a variety of different publics, and concludes:

The national office developed a variety of goals and competing models in order to protect its major goal of achieving innovation; it used goals as bargaining counters and the result was a dissipation of effort.

An attempt was made to attain maximum visibility for the program by spending small amounts on a large number of local centers; the result was that the program remained marginal and temporary in the cooperating universities because it constituted a negligible part of their budgets.

The Corps sought to obtain leverage over local institutions by selecting less wealthy, academically mediocre colleges; this excluded from the program prestigious institutions that might have been more influential in getting others to emulate the program models.

In an attempt to husband limited resources the Corps provided only start-up funds and required institutions to carry the program on with their own resources, which few local colleges could do; either the program was abandoned or the colleges developed program variations that bore little resemblance to the original model.

The cooperating school districts received the bulk of the funds and controlled routine operations; they could and did isolate the "troublemakers," coopt team leaders, and replace interns and staff not "loyal" to the local schools.

The college-intern-cooperating teacher team was an insulated and temporary group, plagued by contradictory and overlapping roles, and no match for the self-contained classroom in a conflict over change.

Interns were supposed to be "catalytic change agents," colleagues of veteran teachers, and a means of "socializing" their professors. But the more aggressive they became, the more defensive and inflexible the schools' reactions; they threatened the teachers and irritated the professors.

The humane and liberal ideology of the interns was often pursued at the expense of scholarly virtues; they were hostile to the very idea of scholarship and discounted academic achievement for their pupils, "precisely the group of youngsters who most needed to improve their academic skills."[39]

Corwin, himself sympathetic to both social and educational change, concludes that although federal programs can probably expect to achieve only modest improvements under the best of circumstances,

the failures in this program were caused by the particular circumstances identified here, some of which are amenable to change. I have said that such programs always will be partially compromised by organizational principles, but the probability of complete failure is virtually assured as long as the nation's leadership continues to concoct program after program in complete disregard of known constraints that will vitiate the strategies and without any attempt to provide at least some of the conditions necessary for programs to survive and thrive.[40]

STAFFING THE URBAN SCHOOL

The reversal in teacher supply and demand will probably in the long run result in an aging teacher population in the schools in general, but up until the early seventies the typical teacher was getting younger (35 versus 41 years old in 1960) and less experienced (8 versus 11 years of teaching).[14]

They were also, however, better educated; by 1971 only 3 percent did not have at least a bachelor's degree, and 20 percent had a master's degree or equivalent.

It has become a truism that urban school teaching staffs are younger and less experienced than those in suburban areas, and that, particularly in the inner-city slums, the turnover rates that create that imbalance are inordinately high. It is difficult to know whether the high turnover rate creates the condition of younger and less experienced faculties, or whether the high proportion of young people in the schools leads to higher turnover rates. A statewide study of teacher mobility in Michigan in the late sixties found that, in the course of a single year, local school systems retained only four-fifths of their teachers, and that the highest percentage of dropouts were women under thirty.[42] Of these young dropouts, most left teaching altogether; only about a quarter of them migrated to other schools in the state. Such evidence suggests that even were other factors absent, the assignment patterns of the urban school systems would result in higher turnover rates. About eight years later, however, a survey in a California urban district by Annegret Harnischfeger found that school characteristics (family income, proportion of Mexican-American children, etc.) did not predict dropout rates at all, although they greatly influenced transfer rates, and that teacher dropouts tended to be middle-aged rather than young.[43] Either regional differences are at work in creating these disparities, or the teacher oversupply has already begun to affect drop out conditions.

There *are*, of course, other factors, an important one being the attitudes of teachers and their view of what constitutes a desirable school. In a classic study of the Chicago teacher's career line, Howard Becker found that she typically begins in a less desirable school, then takes one of two paths.[44] The first of these consists of an adjustment to the situation, a resigned acceptance of professional problems with which she either does or does not learn to cope adequately. The alternative path is a restless transfer from one school to another, searching for the best possible combination of tractable children and satisfactory administration.

Becker reports that perception of the problems the teachers are likely to encounter varies directly with the social class composition of the school. Their ideal is the child who responds well to discipline and is consequently easiest to manage. The slum child is viewed as uncontrollable, as well as morally unacceptable in a variety of ways, from his physical cleanliness to his sexual mores. The upper-middle-class child, on the other hand, though easy to teach, is viewed as spoiled and as not showing sufficient respect for his elders. The lower-middle and upper-working-class child seems to these teachers most ideal in response to discipline as well as in morality.

The characteristic youth and inexperience of urban slum school staffs may thus be viewed as a result of large-scale mobility patterns which are themselves part of the general mobility of teachers; Pedersen notes, in the Michigan study, that the urban region of the state attracts more of the younger teachers, while older women tend to gravitate to the less urban areas.

But differences in the allocation of teaching resources are probably more important *within* cities, between different socioeconomic areas, than between cities and other types of community. James Guthrie and his associates found no differences in credentials, experience, or degrees between urban and suburban teachers in California; rural districts turned out to be the have-nots.[45] On the question of within-city differences, John Owen's study of large American cities is instructive.[46] Owen found that an increase of $1000 in family income in a city was associated in the sixties with $18 in per-pupil expenditure on teacher salaries. A school serving an affluent area with 50 percent greater income than the families in another school employed teachers with an average of 30 percent higher experience. Teachers with the most experience, earning maximum salaries, were likely to be in the more affluent and white areas of cities.

Differences in educational resources between white and black area schools, however, are not as clearcut. Although teachers in nonwhite sections were less experienced, earned somewhat lower salaries, and had lower verbal ability scores, Owen found that these differences were wholly explained by the presence in those schools of larger proportions of black teachers, who tend to be younger, hence less experienced and lower on the salary scale, and who test at lower levels in verbal ability.

It is commonly assumed that the consequences of these patterns for the urban slum school are unqualifiedly bad, but the case is by no means clear. For school systems generally high teacher retention rates mean spiraling costs as they pay for greater experience with higher salaries. Less turnover also results in a lower infusion of younger and, Pedersen suggests, possibly more vigorous and more creative teachers into the system. For pupils, the varying payoffs discussed earlier associated with experience versus verbal ability should have some weight, though the higher levels of verbal skill among younger white teachers may be offset by the lower ones of black teachers in ghetto areas.

Nor is there a simple and direct relation between the urban teacher mobility pattern and her attitudes. To conclude that those who leave the slum school do so because they are less professionally oriented than those who stay, or that those who stay are more altruistic or dedicated, is a mistake in view of the evidence from William Wayson's study of teacher motivation (see Panel 12.3).

PANEL 12.3   A Study of Teacher Transfers

Of the sixty-two women teachers Wayson interviewed in a midwestern city school, twenty were transferring. The following analysis of results present a very mixed picture indeed:[47]

Two-thirds of the white teachers who had remained in the slum school indicated that they either feared making a change (inertia) or enjoyed freedom from interference by parents or the scrutiny of superiors (autonomy). Several of these respondents expressed other reasons for remaining in the school, but it appeared that their staying was due to these two factors and that other satisfactions were secondary. The autonomy in the slum school did not seem to stimulate efforts to change the curriculum or to improve the learning situation. Rather, the type of autonomy sought by these respondents resulted in their withdrawal from the community and reliance upon bureaucratic defenses against pressures from outside the school.

Pupils were the most important referent group for stayers. Nearly sixty percent of the white stayers and one-third of the Negro stayers expressed the motive to be personally liked and appreciated by their pupils. Stayers who sought personal esteem stayed in the school because they receive warm, affectionate, highly personalized responses from pupils. They doubted that schools in better neighborhoods would afford them such esteem or would afford close personal relationships with pupils.

Closely related to the desire for personal esteem were the altruistic responses given by one-fifth of the white stayers (but none of the leavers). Altruists spoke more of contributing to the personal needs of the pupil than of his contributions to teachers. Altruistic teachers seemed to fulfill their own felt needs through beneficent and maternal ministry of their pupils.

About one-fifth of the white stayers expressed an attachment to an accommodating principal who created an organization and interacted with teachers in ways that maximized their comfort and convenience. He was generous with materials and supplies, and he restrained disobedient children or belligerent parents. These reasons for staying seemed related to the motives categorized as inertia and autonomy.

Nearly 40 percent of the white leavers said that they gained most satisfaction from having the principal or a supervisor give them a positive professional appraisal. They gained little satisfaction from interacting with pupils. Although leavers recognized the bureaucratic attractions of the school, those attractions were not sufficient to make leavers want to remain there.

Almost equal percentages (about one-third) of stayers and leavers, white and Negro, expressed missionary zeal. They stressed ethical relationships to other persons, "the good life," occupational mobility, or religion. Stayers tended to generalize from their successful converts feeling that even one success was worth all their efforts. Leavers tended to be frustrated by the relative infrequency with which they succeeded in their missions. Stayers felt successful when former pupils demonstrated adherence to the values espoused by the teacher. Leavers, generally younger than stayers, had not had many former pupils return to see them. Leavers sought more immediate evidence of having been successful. Responses from which these data are drawn indicated that missionary zeal is not sufficient motive to keep a teacher in the slum school and that those missionaries who stayed revised downward their aspirations in the mission field.

About one-fourth of the white leavers and a similar percentage of the Negro stayers expressed satisfaction in being affiliated with the faculty in the school. Young leavers sought belongingness as a tangible mark of professional status and were not strongly attached to the group. Negro teachers, on the other hand, seemed to gain personal status from membership in clearly defined, cohesive friendship groups that persisted even outside school.

In most other comparisons the motives expressed by Negro teachers were like those expressed by white stayers. Negroes much more than whites felt constrained to remain in the slum school.[48]

CLASS AND ETHNIC DIFFERENCES

It is hardly surprising to find such a variation in turnover between white and black teachers; what is surprising, so rapidly has the school situation changed, is the absence among the expressed motivations of a new kind of missionary zeal among black teachers. Until recently, one could with reasonable adequacy account for the attitude patterns in the urban school by reference to social class variations between teachers and pupils—*i.e.*, a clash of life styles and moralities. But the accelerating polarization of the larger society around the issues raised by ethnic, and particularly black, militancy has markedly invaded the school.

In the past black teachers have generally shared the middle-class attitudes of their white colleagues; many come from solidly middle-class families and others, having achieved that status by becoming professionals, tended to emphasize the separation between middle- and lower-class values even more than those born into the class.[49] The greater significance of class in contrast to race in determining teacher attitude is now becoming reasonably well-established. Tom Freijo and Richard Jaeger, using data from a national teacher sample, analyzed teacher ratings of over 8000 fourth-grade pupils on a number of behaviors, seeking evidence for the degree to which the ratings of an individual child showed a tendency to stereotype him, rather than providing separate judgments on different dimensions.[50] They found that: (a) ratings of high SES pupils were less stereotyped than those of lower class children; (b) social class had a greater effect on the tendency to stereotype than the race of either pupil or teacher.

Some city school systems, however, show signs of a shift to greater racial identity. In the late sixties many middle-class blacks and especially profes-

sionals, were swept up in the increasing militancy of the civil rights movement; for many, group identification began to transcend class identification.
At the same time, many urban systems in the north set about actively recruiting black teachers to staff the inner city ghetto schools. The resulting situation has not yet been systematically studied, but there are clear evidences of
changed attitudes.

It is instructive, for example, to compare a recent informal study of the
turnover rates of two different schools with Wayson's, done five years previous to it.[51] Vesey and Turner are two elementary schools in Chicago, only
a mile apart, serving the same type of poor, black neighborhoods. They have
about the same pupil load, both are overcrowded, and the student bodies
in each case are highly mobile. Five years after the opening of the schools,
McPherson noted that their turnover rates were very different: Only 44 percent of the original faculty at Turner remained, but at Vesey 85 percent of
the original faculty were still there.

Of immediate interest is the fact that of the nine white teachers in Mc-
Pherson's sample, seven had left; of the forty blacks, fourteen had left.
The significant question is why a lower percentage of black teachers left
Vesey. McPherson concludes that the answer lies in differences in teacher
selection and induction *before* the schools opened. The Turner principal
simply waited for the system to assign teachers to the school, and provided
no induction period for them. The principal at Vesey spent the eight months
prior to school opening actively searching for teachers throughout the system. He began with a core group of teachers who committed themselves to
transferring to Vesey, and worked with them on the job of recruiting. They
brought the names of potential staff members to the principal, who made his
own judgment, but one that often agreed with the recommendations.

At Turner, the principal placed a high value on orderliness and conven-
tionally measured academic progress, and a low value on relations with the
community. Given the recruiting method she used, teachers who did not
share these values could find it out only after joining the staff; if they did
not share them, they tended to leave, thus accounting for much of the
turnover. The stayers, however, says McPherson, "expressed complete
accord with the purposes of the school and with the methods employed."[52]

Vesey's principal shared the first two of the values of the principal at
Turner, but was also committed to community involvement in the school.
Teachers who did not agree presumably did not join the faculty in the first
place. Those who did, stress the importance of their induction period, a
period in August during which they were encouraged to help in getting
the school ready to open. The principal made them feel needed and appreciated, helped them get organized, and built a sense of unity and common
commitment to the purposes of the school.

During the fifth year at Vesey, sharp conflict broke out between a group
of militant black teachers and the rest of the staff; the militants argued that
the children would continue to fail as long as the values associated with the

school were those of the middle class rather than the black lower class. Some white and less militant black teachers left, but most of the moderates and militants remained. McPherson reports that many stayed because of the way the principal handled the conflict, sharing with his staff the tasks of formulating purposes and programs. He quotes one moderate black teacher on another source of satisfaction:

> The comments of the parents are most important. And my fellow workers' feelings toward me. My black-thinking sister says to me, "Eloise, I respect you because you are a good teacher, but you're lost." But her respect—that's what I want. You don't ask people for love.[53]

McPherson concludes that because the process of selection and induction brought people together as a group originally, later conflict did not result in significant turnover.

The story suggests the possible forms of turbulence already on the increase among urban school staffs. Other factors may influence the emerging pattern; as school integration in the south squeezes out many black teachers, they are likely to move north into the urban schools where hiring practices, reinforced in some areas by court orders, are more in their favor. If the number of black teachers increases substantially to match the rise in the proportion of black children in urban schools in the larger cities, we may well see another of the ethnic shifts in urban school staffs that most cities have been through in the past as one group or another on its way through the class system has dominated a particular school system. Historically, the stage appears to be set for a shift to black domination of the school staff in many northern cities and such a shift appears to be consciously a part of some black educators' political strategy.

THE ROLE OF TEACHER UNIONS

Teacher associations were initiated very early in the historical experience of the American school; the earliest recorded is in 1794. By the mid-nineteenth century state associations were formed and then a national organization. By 1974 the National Education Association had a million and a half members, but in its long history it had concentrated primarily on the professionalization of the field, committed to gentlemanly negotiations over salary and working conditions and an anti-strike policy.[54] Its traditional style changed drastically during the sixties; in competition with the growing strength of the American Federation of Teachers, it turned militant and abandoned its position on teacher strikes.

The AFT had its small beginnings around the turn of this century, concentrating its efforts in the large cities where the NEA was weakest. It affiliated with the American Federation of Labor and in the decade of the fifties began its strikingly successful militant career, winning a number of urban teacher strikes in the following decade and increasing rapidly in size and power. By 1974 its membership was over 400,000.[55] The most recent trends involving both of these teacher organizations include the following:

> Increasing militancy has pushed far in the background the issue of whether teachers, as professionals, should use the strike weapon, an issue that was taken very seriously only ten years ago. Despite numerous state laws specifically forbidding teachers to strike, the number of such actions is substantially rising from year to year. Teacher militancy should not, however, be overgeneralized, as Richard Porter has demonstrated in an attitude study of urban teachers in California.[56] Although educationally change-oriented, his large sample of teachers were generally conservative on most social issues, including the desirability of racial mixing in the schools.
>
> Both have emerged as potent political forces at all levels of government. During the 1974 elections it was claimed that 80 percent of teacher-backed Congressional candidates had won their races. A major political goal is an increase in federal aid to education; the NEA aims at having as much as a third of all education costs covered federally (which would require an increase from about 8 billion to 40 billion).[57]
>
> The long-discussed merger of the two organizations was stalled by the mid-seventies, although it certainly remains a future possibility. Strong disagreements over policy remain (the NEA, for example, has ruled for itself that a specific proportion of places on all its committees must be set aside for black members), and the sharing of power has proved a difficult issue to resolve.

Still concentrated in the urban areas, the union has played a signficant role in the growing conflicts over the urban school; an important aspect of that role will be discussed in Chapter 14, in the context of the movement toward community control. But the union also has influenced the staffing of the urban school in a number of ways. Trade unions are in the business of defending members against management, and not of insuring the development of the most competent staffs, which is, in any sensible view, a management interest. In a period of rising attack on urban school teachers, the union has played a defensive role very adequately though perforce indiscriminately. That the attack has been widely over-generalized is undoubtedly true; but there is little doubt that there are *some* incompetent and prejudiced teachers in the inner city, and the union must defend them, too.

Some union leaders who recognize the problem argue, at least in private, that they would welcome a more vigorous attack on the part of administrations against incompetent teachers. The union must defend them, they say; but if an administrator was forceful enough in insisting on his prerogatives, he would win often enough. Whatever the merits of this argument, it is certainly undeniable that urban school administrators for a variety of reasons seldom press hard for dismissal of tenured slum school teachers who should not, by anyone's standards, be in a classroom.

The existence of a strong union is also likely to alter the historically normal course of a new ethnic takeover of large city teaching positions. Teachers can no longer be dismissed at administrative or political whim without vigorous union retaliation, and what was previously accomplished over a long period of time and almost went unnoticed is now likely to provide a variety of confrontations.

The other side of the coin is that, as black and other minority group membership grows, unions must also present their interests and defensive needs. After decades of setting up segregated chapters in the south and refusing to defend the job rights of black teachers, the NEA has done a complete about-face and now insists, as noted, on black representative quotas. It is possible that in the northern cities where unions are responsive to their members, the form of future conflict may pit unionized black teachers against black community militants, as in Newark in 1971. Much depends on which set of values black teachers in the mass adopt: the traditions of the profession and of the union, or those of the community militants. In the long run union membership and identification may well mitigate considerably the trend toward racial identification and militancy discussed earlier.

PARAPROFESSIONALS IN THE CLASSROOM

One of the most promising proposals for dealing with the special problems of the slum school is to provide auxiliary personnel, themselves members of the lower-class community, who will help the teacher. There are a sizable number of possible advantages in the employment of such auxiliaries in the classroom

The child benefits by having an adult present from his own social background, to interpret his needs and his behavior; the children who need individual attention are more likely to get it, if the aide is deployed for occasional tutoring or small group instruction.

The teacher has a chance to play a more professional role by delegating routine clerical tasks to the auxiliary, and should thereby improve her status not only in her own eyes but in general.

The auxiliary has gained a job that is meaningful, relatively well-paid, and one that opens up the opportunity for a career; most such "new careers" programs provide for training and certification along a career ladder that ultimately leads to full licensing as a teacher.

Because the auxiliaries either are or will become parents, a long-range positive influence on family life may accrue as they learn, both in training and in practice, some basic principles of child development.

In the early stages of the program, a number of difficulties arose. Among the teachers, there was concern that (a) professional standards might be lowered; (b) the auxiliaries might try to "take over" professional functions; (c) the administrators might assign auxiliaries to professional duties without supervision; (d) there might be insufficient time for team planning; and (e) there might be insufficient leadership among teachers. Among the auxiliaries, there were anxieties about the differences between their own and the professionals' background and values.[58]

There were about 80,000 paraprofessionals in the schools in 1968, a number that increased to 255,000 by 1973.[59] In the years since that early study the specific apprehensions have abated; now there is a widespread acceptance of the idea and the reality. But a number of new issues have arisen:

1.   The reduction in tension about the role of the paraprofessional has in part been achieved by agreement among teachers and administrators on a relatively restricted one. Thus, one recent study found both of these groups expressing preference for the role of "educational materials assistant" over that of "instructional assistant"; they wanted paraprofessionals "to perform a variety of tasks including clerical assignments, preparation of instructional materials, and assistance with routine classroom and school duties such as supervision of bus loading of children."[60]

The original hope of the new careers movement, however, was to provide an opportunity for genuine career-ladder movement to ghetto residents whose lack of schooling locked them into dead-end jobs. There is a fairly strong movement toward combining inservice training with junior college attendance to provide an opportunity for paraprofessionals to move toward teacher certification within a reasonable time; but if it is to succeed, it is obvious that paras must be given a meaningful role to play in the classroom. The problem is complicated by the fact that many of them are content with an aide's job, and do not want to undertake a career. It is likely that some division must sooner or later be made in paraprofessional roles that will separate the ambitious from those who merely wish a good job.

2.   A related issue involves the question of how paraprofessionals are to be recruited. Bennett and Falk provide an illuminating contrast between St. Paul and Minneapolis.[61] The former city has centralized recruiting in a city-wide office, and applies fairly high standards in selecting from those who apply. The end result is a group of paras, then assigned to schools throughout the city, who look a good deal like the normal group of "volunteers" one finds in hospitals, social agencies, and other helping organizations: relatively well-educated women with working husbands, looking around for a socially useful way of spending their time, and with no desire for a career. Minneapolis, on the other hand, recruits from the school neighborhood and is "open entry"—that is, it does not stress educational or other background factors in selection. Bennett and Falk note that the latter system is subject to abuses; if the principal recruits from the neighborhood, he can

"co-opt" critics of the school and thus blunt community disaffection. But the open entry, decentralized pattern of recruiting is clearly more appropriate to the thrust of the new careers movement. The basic question is: to "cream" or not to "cream"; to select the most middle-class and ambitious, who will get along most smoothly with the professionals they must work with, or to undertake the strenuous effort necessary to train the more difficult lower class, a problem exactly analogous to those discussed in Chapter 2. Bennett and Falk's estimate is that nationally the majority of programs are both centralized and selective.

3. The *credentials* controversy is still alive in another guise. The new careers program originally intended to provide semiprofessional jobs for the poor who were barred from them by the fact that they lacked the proper paper credentials in the forms of education credits and diplomas and who were prevented from getting those credentials by social and economic handicaps. But, if they are to move up from para- to full-professional status, should they be required to obtain the educational credits along the way? The debate is now on between those who argue that they should—with the aid of paid tuition, time off for study, and credit for some work experience—and those who would like to mount an all-out attack on the credential system generally, using the paraprofessional movement as one way of destroying that system utterly. If the route to attaining a teacher's certificate, or a social work license, for that matter, is merely to be a specified number of years of practical experience for some, not very many would choose the more arduous route of five or six years of higher education. But neither would teaching be regarded any longer by most people as a profession; the likelihood of victory by the foes of credentialism is dim at best.

PANEL 12.4   The Impact of Paraprofessionals in the Classroom

Although school paraprofessionals have not been around long enough to permit any hard and fast estimate of the program's success, there are a few indicative studies. The effects on the aides themselves appear to be spotty and inconsistent. Bennett and Falk studied self-concept change in both "regular aides" and "new careerists" and found a consistent and positive shift in self-concept among the first, but not among the latter.[62] They speculate that the strains for the new careerists were greater, and they were in much greater danger of encountering negative and deprecatory behavior from professionals. The same study got inconsistent results in an attempt to find out whether the new careerists had become more oriented to the professional role, nor could it determine much change in their aspirations for mobility, though this can be explained by the fact that their aspiration level was very high in the first place.

The evidence is clear, however, that the great majority of teachers and principals regard aides as valuable, though it is difficult to tell whether the findings relate to regular aides or careerists. Bennett and Falk report from the Minneapolis study an 80 percent majority agreeing that the aide program was worth continuing. Natzke and Bennett compared responses from urban teachers with aides, urban teachers without aides, and suburban teachers to a scale of job satisfaction and morale; they found that those with aides perceive a wide range of problems with "less intensity" than do either of the other two groups.[63] There was no difference, however, between the two urban groups on job satisfaction, on which scale the suburban teachers exceed both groups.

Evidence for teacher-aide effects on pupil achievement is tenuous at best. Gartner and Reissman[64] note that, in a study conducted by the U.S. Office of Education, only twenty-three of the 1000 programs for the disadvantaged studied yielded measured educational benefits of cognitive achievement; and of those twenty-three, ten involved the use of paraprofessionals. To be sure, when that study was made in 1967, there were not many schools employing paraprofessionals. Still, it is not very convincing evidence; the schools that did employ paraprofessionals at the time are likely, by the same token, to be most determinedly at work at the problem. Bennett and Falk report a more direct experiment on this issue, using nine kindergarten classes—three with no aides at all, three with one aide, and three with five aides.[65] The criterion measure was the Metropolitan Readiness Test, administered both before and after the kindergarten year. There were no differences on number readiness among the groups; but on reading readiness, the group of classes with *one* aide exceeded *both* of the others. In fact, the classes with *no* aides did a little better than those with five aides. Although the researchers attempt to justify these odd results by suggesting that five adults in the classroom probably posed special problems in supervision, it is best to conclude that readiness tests for kindergarten-aged children are likely to be too unreliable to compare small samples very meaningfully.

The Bureau of Research and Evaluation of the New York system has attempted persistently in its evaluations of Title I programs to isolate the effects of paraprofessionals on achievement gains, with no success, although most of the teachers in the system feel that there are other kinds of advantages in having the aides in the classroom.[66]

ADMINISTRATIVE CLIMATE AND THE TEACHER

In a classic study of school administrative leadership, Gross and Herriott found a strong link between a particular pattern of principal behavior and teacher morale.[67] Principals who stress their obligation to improve the quality of staff performance and who treat teachers as professional workers were most likely to have staffs with high morale. A striking subsidiary finding was that in urban slum schools, though not in schools generally, the heightened teacher morale connected with that type of leadership correlated with somewhat higher pupil achievement.

More recently, the study of the principal's leadership role has expanded to include what Halpin and Croft call "administrative climate."[68] Most of this analysis confirms the earlier Gross and Herriott work, suggesting that principals create different climates for their schools by their emphasis either on Person or System. Ignatovich studied seventy-eight Iowa schools and found these types of principal:[69]

> Type One appears to be a "potent" principal-leader who maintains a balance between "freedom for teachers" and "order for the system" and does it *with teachers*. Type Two appears to be a "potent" principal-leader who maximizes "order in the system" and minimizes "freedom for teachers" and does it *by directives*. Type Three appears to be a relatively less "potent" principal-leader who allows maximum freedom for teachers and provides relatively little order for the system and does it *by abstention*.

In the Iowa sample, the majority of principals were Type One, and only 10 percent were Type Three; higher levels of teacher morale was associated with Type One principals, in consonance with earlier studies.

Ignatovich's categories greatly resemble the leadership styles developed from small group research a generation ago: democratic, authoritarian and laissez-faire. We may again be in danger of stereotyping leadership in ways that become misleading. "Administrative climate" studies, it should be noted, seldom find very substantial effects of climate on employee behavior in either industry or education; one recent study of school climate found practically none at all.[70] What may be far more important than whether an administrator gives more or less freedom to his teachers is whether he pays significant attention to their situation and their problems. To put the matter in the context of the earlier discussion of urban teachers, would only a Type Two principal be likely to fire a teacher like James Herndon? A look at the real behavior of some Type Ones may throw some light on the most effective administrative styles in inner-city schools.

Russell C. Doll became interested in what he calls "deviant" schools in the slum areas of Kansas City.[71] A deviant school is the occasional "better" school in a cluster of schools in the same severe problem area, or the really chaotic "worse" school among such a cluster. His nonsystematic study of their principals is revealing, because they fall at the extreme ends of a continuum. The successful principal in these schools:

1. showed a willingness to move independently and decisively in matters affecting the faculty or school.
2. had a genuine empathy for the teaching staff and the residents of the neighborhood as well as an ability to show this empathy in a non-condescending manner.
3. had a perception of the principal's role as one whose primary task is to assist the teachers to teach, even if it meant clashing with the wishes of the administrative hierarchy.[72]

Doll found that the largest difference between the successful and unsuccessful principals in the first of these areas was that the successful ones backed their teachers on discipline problems, including suspensions and parental complaints. They were willing to risk disapproval from both their administrative superiors and from parents in order to handle the problems that teachers felt unable to handle.

They also risked disapproval in other areas they considered important:

> A good neat school has a beneficial effect on teachers and pupils, and when they (the district office) told me they had cancelled our repairs and painting, I hit the ceiling. I got on the phone and politely asked the district, and downtown, what was up. They gave me some runaround. Well, I would call about twice every week. They didn't like it, but before long we got what we needed.[73]

One teacher, in talking about a "successful" principal, told Doll about the time she had decided she couldn't teach with movable desks in her classroom. She had an overage group with many discipline problems, and the children would not only make all the noise they could with their desks, but would also inch them forward; by the end of the day, they were crowding the blackboard. Though movable desks were district policy, the principal hunted up thirty-five stationary ones and had them installed in her room. Following a visit by the district superintendent, the principal was reprimanded for having installed them; but he told the superintendent that it had been *his* idea to have them put in, instead of blaming the teacher.

Another successful principal said:

> I run my school on the assumption that the teacher is the most important part of the school system, and that every one and everything in the system exists only to help that person in the classroom.

By contrast, Doll notes the case of one of the "unsuccessful" principals and the action he took when a directive was issued stating that the minutes of a certain meeting of the Board of Education were to be read to teachers during their meeting.

> The investigator was re-visiting this very chaotic school on that day. During the teachers' meeting, the principal read the minutes "as ordered" for one hour and 30 minutes. After the investigator and the faculty shook off their drowsiness, one wag asked the principal, "Could you read that again? I missed some sections." The principal glared at the teacher and said, "There was a directive that I read this, and I've read it."[75]

On the same day, Doll called two "successful" principals in the same high problem district and asked if they had read the minutes to their faculty. Neither one had. One said:

> The hell I did! What do you think I am? Some kind of an idiot? Just because some nut with a screw loose thinks the teachers have nothing to do but listen to me, I'm not going to prove *I* have a screw loose too. With all the work my teachers have to do on record day, do you think I'm going to waste their time with that? Sure, I'll tell the Super I did—but—come now—.[76]

The "successful" principals maintained contact with their communities, went to meetings, and joined organizations; but it is clear that they would, if necessary, defend their teachers from community and parental pressures. One or two occasionally are quoted as mentioning the need for the principal to be democratic, but it is far from the dominant theme in the interview material. What comes through is their preoccupation with the need to help their teachers with a difficult and frustrating task.

CHAPTER NOTES

[1] Edgar Z. Friedenberg, "Requiem for the Urban School," *Saturday Review*, 50 (November 1967), 94.

[2] Robert J. Havighurst, "It's Time for a Moritorium on Negativism," *The United Teacher* (September 1968), 18, 19.

[3] Gertrude Moskowitz and John L. Hayman, "Interaction Patterns of First-Year, Typical, and 'Best' Teachers in Inner-City Schools," *Journal of Educational Research*, 67 (1974).

[4] James Herndon, *The Way It Spozed To Be* (New York: Bantam, 1967).

[5] Herndon, p. 9.

[6] Herndon, p. 99.

[7] Herndon, p. 100.

[8] L. Homme and D. Tosti, "Some Considerations of Contingency Management and Motivation," Unpublished manuscript, quoted in Edward M. Hanley, "Review of Research Involving Applied Behavioral Analysis in the Classroom," *Review of Educational Research*, 40 (December 1970), 598.

[9] Barbara H. Wasik, Kathryn Senn, Roberta H. Welch and Barbara R. Cooper, "Behavior Modification with Culturally Deprived School Children: Two Case Studies," *Journal of Applied Behavior Analysis*, 2, no. 3 (Fall 1969), 181–194.

[10] James D. Long and Robert L. Williams, "Comparative Effect of Group and Individual Contingent Free Time with Inner-City Junior High School Students," *Journal of Applied Behavioral Analysis*, 6 (1973), 465–474.

[11] Marion Thompson, William R. Brassell, Scott Persons, Richard Tucker and Howard Rollins, "Contingency Management in the Schools: How Often and How Well Does It Work?" *American Educational Research Journal*, 11 (1974), 19–28.

[12] Richard A. Winett and Robin C. Winkler, "Current Behavior Modification in the Classroom: Be Still, Be Quiet, Be Docile," *Journal of Applied Behavioral Analysis*, 5 (1972), 499–504.

[13] K. Daniel O'Leary, "Behavior Modification in the Classroom: A Rejoinder to Winett and Winkler," *Journal of Applied Behavioral Analysis*, 5 (1972), 504–510.

[14] K. Daniel O'Leary and Ronald Drabman, "Token Reinforcement in the Classroom: A Review," *Psychological Bulletin*, 75 (1971), 379–398.

[15] Allan C. Ornstein, *Teaching in a New Era* (Champaign, Ill.: Stipes Publishing Co., 1976).

[16] Henry M. Levin, "A Cost-Effectiveness Analysis of Teacher Selection," *Journal of Human Resources*, V, no. 1 (Winter 1970), 24–33.

[17] Robert D. Strom and David Larimore, "Predicting Teacher Success: The Inner City," *Journal of Experimental Education*, 38, no. 4 (Summer 1970), 69–77.

[18] "A Symposium on Teacher Training," *Journal of Teacher Education*, XX, no. 4 (Winter 1969).

[19] Robert D. Strom, *The Preface Plan*, Project no. 6-1365, Washington, D.C.: U.S. Department of Health, Education and Welfare, August 1967.

[20] Carolyn Stern and Evan P. Keislar, *Teacher Attitude and Attitude Change*, vol. 2 (University of California at Los Angeles, Teacher Education Laboratory, 1975).

[21] Gilbert E. Mazer, "Attitude and Personality Change in Student Teachers of Disadvantaged Youth," *Journal of Educational Research*, 63, no. 3 (November 1969), 116–120.

[22] Julia Boleratz and Marjorie East, "A Cross-Cultural and Cross-Class Experience for Pre-teachers," *Journal of Teacher Education*, XX, no. 4 (Winter 1969), 435–439.

[23] Stern and Keisler, p. 72.

[24] Klaus K. Minde and John S. Werry, "Intensive Psychiatric Teacher Counseling in a Low Socioeconomic Area: A controlled evaluation," *American Journal of Orthopsychiatry*, 39, no. 4 (July 1969), 598–608.

[25] Harriet Talmage and George E. Monroe, "The Teacher as a Teacher Educator: A Self-Regenerating System," *Educational Leadership*, 27 (March 1970), 609–13.

[26] John G. Merrow II, *Politics of Competence: A Review of Competency-Based Teacher Education*, U.S. DHEW, National Institute of Education, 1975. See also *David A. Potter, PBTE: Problem-Solver or Problem-Maker*. Paper presented at the Annual Meeting of the American Educational Research Association, Washington, D.C., 1975; David C. Berliner, *A Status Report on the Study of Teacher Effectiveness*, DHEW, National Institute of Education, Washington, D.C., March, 1975.

[27] Merrow, p. 13.

[28] Quoted in Merrow, p. 18.

[29] Merrow, 16–28.

[30] Merrow, p. 23.

[31] Merrow, p. 24.

[32] Merrow, p. 25.

[33] Harry S. Broudy, "CBTE/PBTE—Do They Mean What They Say?" in *Upheaval in Teacher Education*, Office of Teacher Education, The City University of New York, 1973, 55–73.

[34] Merrow, p. 30.

[35] Merrow, 34–35.

[36] *Teacher Corps: Past or Prologue?* National Advisory Council on Education, Committee on Professional Development (July 1975).

[37] Ronald G. Corwin, *Reform and Organizational Survival* (New York: Wiley, 1973).

[38] Testimony quoted in *Teacher Corps: Past or Prologue*, p. 13.

[39] Corwin, p. 375.

[40] Corwin, p. 394.

[41] *American Education*, July 1972, p. 37.

[42] K. George Pedersen, "Teacher Migration and Attrition," *Administrator's Notebook*, Midwest Administrator's Center, University of Chicago, XVIII, no. 8 (April 1970), unpaged.

[43] Annegret Harnischfeger, *Personal and Institutional Characteristics Affecting Teacher Mobility: Schools Do Make a Difference*. Stanford Center for Research and Development in Teaching, Stanford University (May 1975).

[44] Howard S. Becker, "Social Class Variation in Teacher-Pupil Relationship," *Journal of Educational Sociology*, 25 (1952), 451–465.

[45] James W. Guthrie, Douglas A. Penfield, and David N. Evans, "Geographic Distribution of Teaching Talent," *American Educational Research Journal*, 6 (1969), 645–659.

[46] John D. Owen, "The Distribution of Educational Resources in Large American Cities," *Journal of Human Resources*, VII (1969), 1–38.

[47] William Wayson, "Expressed Motives of Teachers in Slum Schools," *Urban Education*, 1, no. 4 (1965), 223–238.

[48] Wayson, 231–232.

[49] Nat Hentoff, *The New Equality* (New York: Viking, 1965).

[50] Tom D. Freijo and Richard M. Jaeger, "Social Class and Race as Concomitants of Composite Halo in Teachers' Evaluative Rating of Pupils," *American Educational Research Journal*, 13 (1976), 1–14.

[51] R. Bruce McPherson, "Teacher Turnover in the Inner City," *Administrator's Notebook*, Midwest Administrator's Center, University of Chicago, XIX, no. 4 (December 1970), unpaged.

[53] McPherson.

[54] T. M. Stinnett and Raymond E. Cleveland, "The Politics and Rise of Teacher Organizations," in Allan Ornstein and Steven Miller (eds.), *Policy Issues in Education* (Lexington, Mass.: Heath, 1976), 83–94.

[55] *Conditions of Education*, DHEW, Washington, D.C., 1975.

[56] Richard D. Porter, *Dimensions of Teacher Militancy: A Factor Analysis of Teacher Attitudes*, ERIC Document ED 103 359.

[57] Stinnett and Cleveland, p. 88.

[58] Garda W. Bowman and Gordon J. Klopf, *Auxiliary School Personnel: Their Roles, Training, and Institutionalization* (New York: Bank Street College of Education, March, 1967).

[59] *Conditions of Education*, p. 125.

[60] John T. Seyfarth and Robert L. Canaday, "Paraprofessionals in Search of an Identity," *The Clearinghouse* (December 1970), p. 222.

[61] William S. Bennett, Jr., and R. Frank Falk, *New Careers and Urban Schools* (New York: Holt, Rinehart and Winston, 1970).

[62] Bennett and Falk, p. 160.

[63] John H. Natzke and William S. Bennett, Jr., "Teacher Aide Use and Role Satisfaction of Inner-City Teachers," *Education and Urban Society* (May 1970), 295–314.

[64] A. Gartner, and Frank Riessman, "Paraprofessionals: The Effect on Children's Learning," *Urban Review*, 4 (October 1969) 21–22.

[65] Bennett and Falk, p. 185.

[66] Henry M. Brickell, *Paraprofessional Influence on Student Achievement and Attitudes* (New York: Institute for Educational Development, 1971).

[67] Neal Gross and Robert Herriott, *Staff Leadership in Public Schools* (New York: Wiley, 1965).

[68] Andrew Halpin and Don B. Croft, *The Organizational Climate of Schools* (Chicago: Midwest Administration Center, University of Chicago, 1963).

[69] Frederick R. Ignatovitch, *Types of Elementary School Principal-Leaders: A Q-Factor Analysis*, A paper presented to the annual meeting of the American Educational Research Association, New York, 1971 p. 16.

[70] Robert J. Coughlan, "Social Structure in Relatively Closed and Open Schools," *Educational Administration Quarterly*, VI (1970), 14-35.

[71] Russell C. Doll, *Variations Among Inner City Elementary Schools* (Kansas City: Center for the Study of Metropolitan Problems, 1971).

[72] Doll, p. 13.

[73] Doll, 14–15.

[74] Doll, p. 17.

[75] Doll, p. 20.

[76] Doll, p. 20.

Chapter 13

Urban School Desegregation

Segregation of black and white school children has been a sore issue for American society since the Civil War. The 1954 Supreme Court decision declaring segregated schools unconstitutional brought it sharply to the forefront of public attention, where it has remained ever since. This chapter:

Reviews the history of the schooling of black children before 1954.

Describes the course of desegregation efforts that followed the 1954 decision, first in the South, then in northern schools, and provides a picture of the present status of desegregation.

Describes the range of positions on school desegregation taken by a variety of groups on the current scene.

Reviews the research into the effects of desegregation on school achievement and aspirations of black children.

Summarizes some of the dilemmas now facing the desegregation movement.

Some of the questions readers might address are:

Which of the variety of positions presented on desegregation is closest to my own? Have I ever changed my mind on the issue, and if so, what influenced the change? Do any of the arguments described in the chapter make me rethink my position?

How far should the courts go in insisting on desegregating the cities? To the point of imposing black/white percentages for each school? If not, what arguments against that tendency of the courts do I find most persuasive? If I agree that they should order such desegregation plans, on what grounds?

Almost a quarter of a century after the historic Supreme Court decision that struck down state-sanctioned segregation in schooling the great majority of the public has come to agree that enforced segregation of any group on the basis of race is incompatible with the professions of a democracy. So complex, however, are the problems involved in undoing the effects of hundreds of years of overt and covert segregation policies, separating social class from racial issues, and maintaining gains in the midst of large-scale movements of people, that basic agreement on the principle of a desegregated society is of little import. Although it is a national problem, it is a particularly difficult one for urban areas, which present legal and social dilemmas that seem singularly intractable.

Understanding the story of school desegregation is impossible without a clear picture of the role the courts have played in interpreting constitutional doctrine, and the chapter will trace that intervention in detail. Education has traditionally been the responsibility of the states in our federal system and, with the exception of a few landmark cases that found their way to the Supreme Court during the nineteenth and early twentieth century, state supremacy over school matters has remained largely undisturbed. The conflict over desegregation represents the first consistent and long-range instance of federal intervention in education; the next chapter, which looks at trends in educational power relationships, will suggest that it is not likely to be the last.

THE EDUCATION OF BLACK AMERICANS

Until the epic migration north of the past generation, the schooling of blacks was primarily a southern issue, since that is where the great majority of blacks lived. The struggle for educational opportunity took place within a broader context of various movements toward civil rights and equality of treatment.

The first of these began with the Reconstruction and ended in 1896, a period characterized by considerable militancy.[1] Several Reconstruction governments in the South immediately after the Civil War legalized mixed schools, and all emphasized the value of schooling as a crucial means for overcoming the legacy of slavery. Northern abolitionist organizations subsidized southern schools for blacks and sent teachers to staff them. Movement toward a unitary school system was, however, evanescent; with the departure of federal troops from the South and the recapture of state governments by southern whites, a dual school system—one for whites and the other for blacks—became firmly fixed as the southern norm. By 1896 two events on the national scene brought the era to a close: the coalition of forces that fought for Negro civil rights, among other populist causes, suffered final political defeat in the election of that year; and in *Plessy vs. Ferguson* the Supreme Court turned back legal efforts to dismantle the southern system of segregation generally.[2] In considering whether segregated facilities required by state law violated the constitutional requirement of equal protection under the law, the Court ruled that equal protection could be satisfied by the provision of equal, even if separate, facilities.

During the following period, from the turn of the century to World War II, most blacks remained in the South; their segregated schools, despite the separate-but-equal doctrine of *Plessy,* deteriorated miserably. As late as 1931, the expenditure per pupil in the South as a whole for white schools was three times that spent for black schools. Nevertheless, in the face of a fever of anti-Negro sentiment that reached heights of hatred and fear at the end of the century, the dominant black leadership counseled moderation and compromise. Booker T. Washington, their chief spokesman, was above all a pragmatist, and derided the post-Civil War craze among blacks for "Latin and Greek learning." Believing that social equality, though desirable in the future, was impractical in the present, he advocated as the wisest course training in the manual skills. In a famous speech delivered to a white audience at the Atlanta Exposition of 1895 he declared that "the agitation of questions of social equality is the extremist folly," and went on to argue:

> . . . to those of my race who depend upon bettering their condition in a foreign land, or who underestimate the importance of cultivating friendly relations with the Southern white man who is their next-door neighbor, I would say, "Cast down your bucket where you are"—cast it down in making friends, in every manly way, of the people of all races by whom we are surrounded.
>
> Cast it down in agriculture, mechanics, in commerce, in domestic service, and in the professions. And in this connection it is well to bear in mind that whatever other sins the South may be called to bear, when it comes to business, pure and simple, it is in the South that the Negro is given a man's chance in the commercial world, and in nothing is this Exposition more eloquent than in emphasizing this chance. Our greatest danger is that in the great leap from slavery to feedom we may overlook the fact that the masses of us are to live by the productions of our hands, and fail to keep in mind that we shall prosper in proportion as we learn to dignify and glorify common labor, and put brains and skill into the common occupations of life; shall prosper in proportion as we learn to draw the line between the superficial and the substantial, the ornamental gewgaws of life and the useful. No race can prosper till it learns that there is as much dignity in tilling a field as in writing a poem. It is at the bot-

tom of life we must begin, and not at the top. Nor should we permit our grievances to overshadow our opportunities. As we have proved our loyalty to you in the past, in nursing your children, watching by the sick bed of your mothers and fathers, and often following them with tear-dimmed eyes to their graves, so in the future, in our humble way, we shall stand by you with a devotion that no foreigner can approach, ready to lay down our lives, if need be, in defense of yours, interlacing our industrial, commercial, civil, and religious life with yours in a way that shall make the interests of both races one. In all things that are purely social we can be as separate as the fingers, yet one as the hand in all things essential to mutual progress.[3]

As a compromiser Washington satisfied neither the rabid white supremacists nor such integrationists as W. E. B. DuBois, by whom he was blamed for neglecting the intellectual advancement of blacks and for accepting the caste system. The drift of blacks into the north and west, a process that began with World War I and enormously accelerated with World War II, revived a spirit of militancy that was to climax in the elan and excitement of the civil rights movement of the late fifties and sixties.

This third period began with efforts by black rights groups to chip away at the *Plessy* separate but equal doctrine in a series of federal court suits. How could a state, for example, claim that it was offering equal educational facilities to blacks when, though a separate college for them existed, no law school except a segregated white one was available? A number of favorable decisions on such specifics[4] offered encouraging evidence that the federal courts might be willing at last to overturn the *Plessy* doctrine. In 1954 the Supreme Court consolidated a number of lower court cases directly attacking school segregation under the title of one of them, *Brown vs. the Board of Education of Topeka,* and took that historic step.[5]

Agreeing with a lower court order asserting that school segregation, particularly when it has the sanction of law, is interpreted as denoting inferiority, the *Brown* decision concluded:

> . . . that in the field of public education the doctrine of "separate but equal" has no place. Separate educational facilities are inherently unequal. Therefore we hold that plaintiffs and others similarly situated for whom the actions have been brought are, by reason of the segregation complained of, deprived of the equal protection of the laws guaranteed by the Fourteenth Amendment.

DESEGREGATION IN THE SOUTH

Having overturned the *Plessy* doctrine, the Court turned its attention in a series of hearings to the question of how its decision was to be implemented. It was urged by some to reverse its ruling and turn the issue over to Congress; by others to order district judges to require the submission of desegregation plans by the various states, to be accomplished in gradual steps; by still others to order immediate desegregation by a specific date.

The Court chose the second of these alternatives, remanding the cases it had considered to district judges so that local difficulties could be solved at the local level "with all due deliberate speed"; it was a move regarded by civil rights forces as a clear concession to the South.

In a review of the southern desegregation process, Marian Wright Edelman has characterized the five years that followed as a period of massive southern resistance and weak federal response:

> By 1957, well over one hundred new laws and constitutional amendments designed to delay or prevent desegregation were on the books. The most common device was "the pupil assignment law" giving local school boards power to establish criteria for assigning students to schools. Other resistance devices included prohibitions on expenditures of state funds for desegregated education, authorization for transfer of public school property to racially exclusive schools, modification of compulsory attendance laws, weakening of teacher tenure provisions, school closing bills, interposition resolutions, and a variety of attempts to curb the activities of the National Association for the Advancement of Colored People (NAACP), the leading advocate for black schoolchildren. These segregationist attacks, arrayed against a proponent force consisting only of private litigants and the courts, made progress almost impossible.[6]

Aside from the courts, the federal government did little in the face of southern resistance. It was not until Governor Faubus defied a court order by calling out the National Guard to prevent a group of black students from entering a school in Little Rock that President Eisenhower ordered federal troops to enforce a court decision. In the Little Rock case the Supreme Court ruled that community opposition was not grounds for postponing compliance with a court order,[7] by 1964 in a ruling on the Prince Edward County case it noted that "there had been entirely too much deliberation and not enough speed" in desegregation.[8]

With the election of John Kennedy as President, the period of 1960–1964 was one of increasing federal intervention. Kennedy endorsed the Brown decision, and though he used his executive power little in promoting desegregation, a sympathetic presence in the White House was helpful. A major issue involving the use of federal power was resolved during these years. It focused on whether the government should cut off federal funds to school districts that continued to segregate. After a sizable Congressional battle, a nondiscrimination clause was added to the National Defense Education Act withdrawing federal funds from colleges that discriminated racially, and the precedent was set.

During this period a dramatic confrontation between blacks led by Martin Luther King, Jr. and the police in Birmingham created a major shift in public opinion and made possible the passage of a strong civil rights bill in 1964. The law authorized the attorney general to sue discriminating school districts, and provided for federal assistance to districts preparing for desegregation.

One of the sections of the bills, considered of only minor importance at the time, provided that federal financial assistance could not be granted to schools that discriminated. It turned out to be a very powerful federal weapon indeed, because within a year Congress passed the Elementary and Secondary Act, the first time in the nation's history that substantial federal support was given to the public schools. As of 1966, only 14 percent of black children were attending desegregated schools; the Department of Health, Education, and Welfare (HEW) ruled against the voluntary desegregation plans being used by southern districts and required comprehensive plans to eliminate dual systems, and by 1968 the number rose to 20 percent.

Although the executive branch under President Nixon tried to slow up the process, the Supreme Court, in *Swann vs. Charlotte Mecklenburg Board of Education,* restated the "affirmative constitutional duty" of the states to dismantle the dual school system, and approved of the use of busing as an instrument.[9] The legal battle over the dual system of the South had been won, and more blacks now attend desegregated schools in the South than in the North.

DESEGREGATION IN THE NORTH

In the North and West the problems were different and in many ways much more difficult, despite the somewhat more favorable climate for blacks outside the South. In legal terminology, segregation in the South was *de jure,* the result of positive legal action taken by governments; in the North and West, and particularly in the large cities, it was *de facto,* a consequence of housing patterns that surely were caused by prejudice but had not been imposed by law.

Many smaller communities outside the South, under pressure from local groups and in response to the sentiments of their own Boards of Education, made good-faith and often successful efforts to desegregate their schools, using a variety of procedures available in particular situations.

Open Enrollment

Probably the most popular plan in the early years of desegregation, because it involved no coercion at all, open enrollment simply involved relaxing the school attendance zoning rules to permit students to attend any underutilized school of their choice. In many cases free transportation was supplied so that even young children could attend a distant elementary school. The effectiveness of the procedure depended on a number of circumstances: Where the open enrollment privilege was restricted to black children the effect on school segregation patterns was greater than in general open enrollment schemes; the opportunity had to be widely publicized and parents urged to take advantage of it. Even when it worked fairly well, the policy was by no means a cure-all because although it might reduce overcrowding in the ghetto-sending schools, it left them no less segregated;

furthermore, the children whose parents were most likely to respond to the opportunity tended to be among the less economically deprived and most socially mobile. In the larger cities that tried out the policy in the sixties seldom more than a few thousand children were involved, and a number of cities such as New York abandoned it.

Princeton Plan

Sometimes called "school pairing," this procedure involves locating two schools, one mainly black and the other white, that are close enough to each other to exchange parts of their pupil populations. Some grades are assigned to be taught in one of the schools, the remaining grades in the other; for example, one school might have only grades K–3, the other grades 4–6. The schools are automatically desegregated, since all first graders in both attendance zones go to one school, all sixth grades in both zones attend the other school, and so on. The obvious difficulty is that the procedure works only where two schools happen to be in a fringe area between racially different neighborhoods; and in large cities, where black areas stretch for miles, school pairing is of little use. It *can* be effective in small communities, however, and even in some small cities where black neighborhoods are small and scattered.

Rezoning

In many cities attendance districts for elementary and junior high schools have generally been drawn to conform to the boundaries of coherent neighborhoods. In many cases some degree of desegregation can be achieved simply by redrawing the lines separating attendance zones. As in the case with school pairing, however, the procedure is effective only in fringe areas.

Educational Parks

By far the most expensive proposal for desegregating the cities, this idea has been discussed for many years but never implemented on a large scale. The plan would bring together all the children from a large section of a city, or from an entire small city, into schools clustered on a sizable campus. As a novel application of the consolidated rural school district, in which all children from an area consisting of many square miles are bused into a central town for their schooling from kindergarten through high school, it would certainly solve the problem of segregated schools in one stroke. However, it would also involve losing all the capital invested in present school facilities and require investing an enormous amount of new capital in building new ones; very few cities would care to underwrite such a cost, even if it were politically feasible to decide to do so.

Magnet Schools

A considerably more modest plan for attracting students from widely separated parts of a city has occasioned some recent experimentation—

providing one of the high schools in a black community with a special curriculum so desirable that white students from other areas will make an effort to enroll in them. Such schools usually specialize in a theme or in an attractive occupation such as communications, oceanography, aerospace, the health professions, or urban planning. Such a policy may have educational advantages quite apart from its use as a desegregation device, but many courts considering urban desegregation plans have approved them for the latter purpose. Their effectiveness as tools of integration is much in doubt, however; although they have not been systematically studied, informal reports from a number of cities indicate that attendance of white students, after an initial spurt, tends to fall off. The President of Detroit's Board of Education, after four years of effort devoted to a magnet school program, declared them "utterly and completely a failure."[10]

Metropolitan Schools Concept

Not only are large cities faced with the difficulties already cited but the availability of the extensive suburban rings that surround them are magnets for the middle-class whites in the central cities resulting in rising proportions of blacks in central city schools. In thirteen of the largest twenty cities in the nation, blacks now represent a majority of the school population, and the proportion is up to 97 percent in Washington, D.C.[11] The most extensive remedy for segregation in these metropolitan areas was proposed by Robert Havighurst in the 1960s: the creation of metropolitan school districts including both the central city and the nearby suburbs. Administrative and curriculum decisions would be left to local boards, but the area-wide authority would have the power to plan and construct schools and certify teachers. A mix of the desegregation devices described above could then be used to integrate the white students of the suburbs with the black students of the central city. The proposal would require a radical shift in the attitudes of most metropolitan residents and a profound change in their political structures, and seemed visionary at the time. But, as we shall see, some federal courts now seem disposed to go at least part of the way down that road.

THE NORTHERN LEGAL BATTLE

The NAACP began to press the legal fight on northern school segregation in the early sixties. The *Brown* decision had given them two weapons: *de jure* segregation was outlawed, so if actual official discriminatory intent could be proven a community could be compelled to desegregate; second, the decision had recognized the importance of psychological factors involved in separation of the races. NAACP lawyers hoped to avoid the expensive process of proving discriminatory intent in city after city and so adopted the tactic of demanding desegregation on the grounds of racial imbalance itself, whatever the reason for its existence.[12]

For almost a decade, then, the legal fight involved arguing that discrimination in facilities and low achievement scores of black children, buttressed by psychological testimony, justified a finding of unequal treatment. A number of state and federal courts in the east agreed with them, and ordered the implementation of desegregation plans; but in the Midwest more often than not the argument was dismissed.

A major difficulty turned out to be that, outside the South, school facilities in majority black schools, contrary to what educators long believed, were by no means consistently poorer than those in majority white schools. The first hard evidence on the question appeared in Coleman's report on equal educational opportunity released in 1966.[13] Although the study found a massive amount of segregation in the North and West, it also reported, for example that:

> for the nation as a whole, white children attend schools with a smaller average number of pupils per room than do many of the minorities (29 vs. 30–33), but there is a reversal of the pattern for some regions (nonmetropolitan sections of the North, West, and Southwest);
>
> there are definite and systematic differences, which tend to be rather small on the national scale, quite large in particular regions such as the South, and fluctuating in other regions: 95 percent of black and 80 percent of white high school students in the Far West have access to language laboratories, compared with 48 percent and 72 percent respectively in the metropolitan South; in the metropolitan Midwest the average black student shares his classroom with 54 pupils, compared with 33 per room for whites.

The psychological argument adopted in the original decision, that separation mandated by law or by pervasive official discrimination induced feelings of inferiority, was also open to question. The Court had footnoted in its original decision a number of psychological studies that supported its conclusions. Among them was a well-known series of experiments (see Chapter 9) by Kenneth Clark in which young black children were given the choice of white and black dolls to play with; their tendency to choose white dolls over black ones was interpreted as a rejection of their blackness.[14] But, Clark's own data demonstrated that this tendency was *greater* among integrated children than among segregated ones, hardly support for the negative psychological impact of separation.

On the other hand, to pursue a strategy of emphasizing *de jure* segregation, aside from its expense, led to other problems; even if, for example, one could prove that in a particular case a school district had drawn a district line deliberately to separate black from white children, a court might merely order that the specific act be undone, without providing general relief in the form of a total desegregation order. "Unless the plaintiffs could show that the school boards' decisions were generally permeated by racism or bad faith, the expensive and time-consuming effort to prove intentional discrimination might leave black children ensconced in black schools."[15]

In 1970 the NAACP legal staff began a new drive. Since the courts refused to recognize explicitly that the mere presence of *de facto* segregation posed communities with an "affirmative duty" to require racial balancing, they sought to persuade judges that *any* discriminatory act by an official in relation to the schools required system-wide desegregation. In a number of major cases they succeeded dramatically in that effort.

In Denver, a federal court not only agreed that a finding of discriminatory intention in one district must trigger city-wide desegregation, but it came very close to adopting the NAACP's hope for establishing the doctrine that *de facto* segregation was in itself justification for legal action.[16] The judge found black schools to be unequal in achievement, morale, and teacher experience and turnover. Since the plaintiffs also convinced him that compensatory education was unlikely to equalize black schools on these measures, the only way to equalize was to integrate, he declared. In essence, while declaring that there was no legal duty to racially balance *de facto* segregated schools, there was no legal way to equalize them *except* by balancing them.

In Detroit the federal courts took an even greater step toward *de facto* doctrine. In that city a liberal majority on the Board of Education had tried hard to integrate the schools by ordering an extensive busing program; angry citizens retaliated by holding a recall election, sweeping most of the liberals off the Board, and the state legislature then nullified the busing program. The court declared that even if the original integration plan had not been court-ordered, the state and city could not nullify it and return the situation to a neutral one; once the intention to integrate had been indicated, it must proceed.[17] In effect, not only was intentional discrimination unconstitutional, so also were "knowledgeable omissions" on the part of officials which perpetuate segregation, or a return to neutrality after a declared intention to integrate.

By the midseventies, then, lower court actions had succeeded in establishing a doctrine fairly close to an affirmative duty to desegregate on the show of almost any inequality, *de jure* or *de facto;* in the southern *Swann* case, as earlier noted, busing as an instrument of desegregation was affirmed, thus providing a legal means as well as duty. One major obstacle now remained: How could the larger cities with high proportions of black pupils in the schools be desegregated without involving the suburbs?

Detroit provided the first major test of the courts' willingness to take that final step. Judge Stephen Roth, in finding for the NAACP, recognized that a busing program restricted to the city would do very little to desegregate the schools, and ordered tricounty busing between Detroit and several of its suburbs. But, on appeal to the Supreme Court, the plan was rejected.[18] The majority ruled, first, that "the metropolitan remedy would require, in effect, consolidation of fifty-four independent school districts historically administered as separate units into a vast new super school district. Entirely apart from the logistical and other serious problems attending large-scale transportation of students, the consolidation would give rise to an array of other problems in financing and operating this new school system"; it refused to make the district court "a de facto 'legislative authority' to resolve these complex questions." Secondly, it pointed out that no proof had been submitted showing that the suburban districts involved were responsible for *de jure* segregated conditions; there was evidence of it only in the Detroit schools.

Although the Detroit decision represented a considerable setback, efforts to desegregate on a metropolitan scale may well succeed on a piecemeal basis within the limits set by that decision. An order requiring Richmond to bus across suburban boundaries on the grounds that it already bused children to the suburbs in order to avoid desegregation was reversed, to be sure.[19] But in the fall of 1975 Louisville was ordered to institute suburb-city busing, setting off a year of violent confrontation in that city, and Wilmington is under a later court order (upheld by the Supreme Court) to desegregate with its suburbs. The next northern city test is likely to be in Cleveland, where the NAACP believes that they can show a state obligation to desegregate; such a showing would compel the suburbs as well as the city to become involved in an effort to desegregate.[20] A recent suit in Kansas City will test the possibility of imposing interstate remedies as well as city-suburban ones.

By 1977 many of the uncertainties about the extent to which the high court will back up the stream of lower federal court orders in the cities of the north and west had been resolved. In summary:

The court has shown no disposition to retreat on the requirement of busing, where it appears necessary to remedy school segregation. The battle on that issue has shifted to the Congress, where a variety of efforts have been made to forbid the executive branch to encourage busing or to cut off federal funds to school districts that refuse to adopt large-scale busing programs.

It has upheld desegregation plans that require exchange of students between central cities and their suburbs, where evidence of official acts leading to segregation in the specific suburb can be shown.

It has consistently rejected the efforts of some lower courts to establish the *de facto* doctrine, that a finding of segregation is in itself sufficient cause for remedy; discriminatory *intent* is a constitutional sin, but not, apparently, discriminatory *effect*.

Despite the Denver ruling, the court majority has questioned the broadness of desegregation rulings in some cities (notably Dayton) and returned some cases to lower courts for reconsideration. Specific findings of broad, illegal segregation must be presented to justify broad desegregation remedies.

It has upheld the intervention of federal courts in educational programming, specifically in Detroit where it approved the action of a lower court in ordering compensatory education programs to help children recover from the disadvantages of having attended illegally segregated schools.

PRESENT STATUS OF SCHOOL DESEGREGATION

For a look at the general situation in the midseventies it is useful to consider first as benchmark data the state of the schools a decade earlier when the first national surveys were reported. In 1966 Coleman found, in his study of equal educational opportunity, that "the great majority of American children attend schools that are largely segregated, that is, almost all of their fellow students are of the same racial background as they are."[21]
Specifically:

Over 80 percent of southern black students were in schools with a high saturation of blacks (80–100 percent); nationwide, 65 percent of all first-grade black pupils attended schools that had an enrollment of 90 percent or more black; 77 percent of all first-grade white students attended schools that were 90 percent or more white.

in the largest metropolitan areas, 80 percent of the nonwhite enrollment was in central city schools, while almost 70 percent of the white enrollment was suburban, outside the city itself

within the 75 central cities of largest population, 75 percent of the black elementary students were in schools that were almost all black; 83 percent of the whites were in nearly all-white schools

although the proportion of black children was growing in the school populations of many large cities, that proportion did not necessarily determine the degree of segregation; blacks made up only 25 percent of elementary school enrollment in Milwaukee and almost 60 percent of Philadelphia's, yet in both cities about three out of four black children attended nearly all-black schools.

Figure 13.1 shows the progress made between 1968 and 1972. Note the very sharp drop in high levels of segregation in the southern states within that four-year period, and the very considerable rise in students in integrated settings in the same states. In contrast, desegregation declined minimally in the border states and almost not at all in the North and West. Data based on sampling studies by HEW in 1974 showed little change from these 1972 figures, a few percentage points at the most, and in the case of the Northeast a small rise in segregation.[22]

During the decade there was a growing awareness of the isolation of minorities other than the blacks. Table 13.1 shows the percentage of Latino children (the designation is HEW's) in schools of varying degrees of segre-

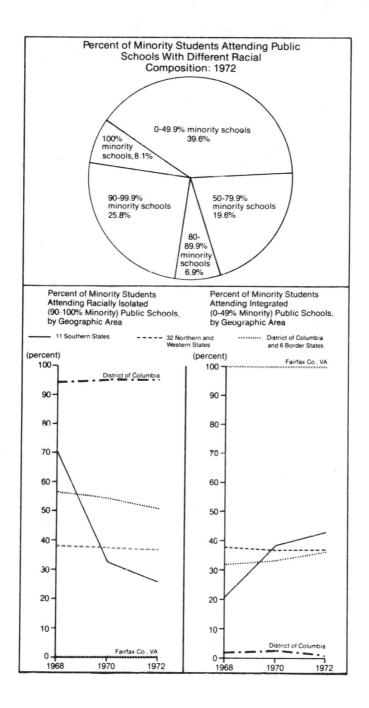

FIGURE 13.1   From *Conditions of Education*, National Center for Educational Statistics, Department of Health, Education and Welfare. Washington, D.C.: Government Printing Office, 1975, p. 70.

Table   13.1

(A)—Percentage of Latino children in predominantly
minority schools, 1970–74

	1970	1972	1974
National	64.2	65.2	67.4
Northeast	84.2	83.1	84.2
South	72.6	72.3	72.8
Midwest	52.6	53.4	57.1
West	48.5	51.4	56.3

SOURCE.—HEW Office for Civil Rights, May 1976.

NOTE.—The statistics in this and the following tables are based on enrollment figures from districts estimated to contain 74 percent of the nation's Latino students at the time of HEW's last universe projections, covering the 1972–73 school year. The data covers an estimated 87 percent of Latino enrollment in the Northeast, 82 percent in the South, 66 percent in the West, and 62 percent in the Midwest.

(B)—Percentage of Latino children in intensely segregated
schools (90 to 100 percent minority enrollment)

	1970	1972	1974
National	29.0	29.2	30.0
Northeast	50.0	50.5	53.8
Midwest	11.7	15.0	20.9
West	14.6	14.2	15.7
South	36.1	35.5	34.1

(C)—1974 enrollment (percentage) of Latino children in
schools with 70 percent or more minority children

	1974
National	50.0
Northeast	71.7
South	56.8
Midwest	40.8
West	34.9

SOURCE.—HEW Office for Civil Rights, May 1976, in *Report on Educational Research*, June 30, 1976, p. 5.

gation; where time comparisons are shown it is clear that instead of declining segregation appears to be slowly on the rise in most regions of the country.

Federal agencies have been reluctant to use their major weapon, the withholding of federal funds from segregated school districts, for a number of good political reasons. For one, the pressure from Congress to restrict the use of busing, which is the only feasible desegregation instrument in most northern cities, has been sizable, and in 1974 HEW was ordered to refrain from requiring busing plans that take children any further than the closest, or next closest school, and in any event to require busing only as a last resort;[23] a year later Congress made the ban even stiffer.[24] A second consideration that the Department must weigh is the consequence of withdrawing federal money; since most of it goes to districts with concentrations of poor and minority group children the decision to cut off funds may hurt primarily those whom desegregation orders are aiming to help.

The NAACP brought suit against the Department in 1975 demanding an end to desegregation in northern and western states or the termination of all federal school aid to those states.[25] It is questionable whether, even with a more liberal executive branch as a result of the 1976 elections, the Department will be able to play a much stronger role than in the past, however, unless the political cross-pressures to which it is subject materially change.

In addition to the deep divisions among the public on the issue of *de facto* segregation which are sketched below, some earlier victories of the civil rights forces are beginning to come apart. In Little Rock, the scene of the earliest dramatic confrontation over school desegregation in the South, large-scale shifts of population have created racial islands—white in the suburbs, black in the central city—that have led to resegregation. Central High School, the old "white school," was integrated by court order in 1957; until 1970 its black students constituted 35 percent of the whole, but the 1970 tenth-grade class was 55 percent black, presaging a black majority in two years or less.[26] Twenty years after the *Brown* decision against the Topeka Board of Education, that city was back in the courts.[27] Its dual system was gone, but with blacks constituting only 10 percent of the school population some schools are overwhelmingly black because the board assigns to schools by neighborhood. In Inglewood, California, a suburb of Los Angeles, five years after a court order requiring massive cross-town busing, the courts permitted the community to drop its desegregation plan, the first school district in the country to be permitted to do so.[28] The concentration of minority students in that city of 90,000 had risen from 38 percent in 1970 to 80 percent in 1975 and black students were being bused from predominantly black schools to other predominantly black schools.

THE POLITICAL DIVISIONS

The fairly clear liberal versus conservative split on desegregation in the early 1950s at the time of the *Brown* decision dissolved twenty years later into a number of positions that make the attitude spectrum uncertain and ambivalent. The following description is not intended to represent clear-cut categories of opinion, but rather major emphases that seem to attract sizable numbers of people often cutting across traditional political lines. The confusion is primarily created by the issue of "forced busing" rather than the desirability of school desegregation itself, but since further progress toward integration is overwhelmingly conditioned on an acceptance of busing as an instrument, the important question is no longer where one stands on integration but where one stands on busing.

1.   The core of strongly pro-integration forces remains the NAACP and its legal staff, which has managed most of the court strategy described earlier, and appears to have the support of most black liberals. In their view any kind of racial separation in the schools is patently unconstitutional and whatever the resistance or the consequence it must be eradicated. Marian Edelman states the quiet determination of this position in an earlier cited article:

> It is to be hoped that the present national uncertainty over the false issue of school busing will not let us ignore the thousands of black and white school children in scores of southern school districts that are successfully desegregated and who are pointing the way for the rest of us. They, and the nation, have a right to be free of the shameful blight of public school segregation. Strong national and local leadership must come forth in support of Brown's promise for one nation.[29]

White liberals, on the other hand, appear to be in a state of disarray. Congressional liberals can no longer be expected to vote on the "right" side of the issue; even in the negotiations that led to the passage of the Civil Rights Act of 1964 many liberals joined forces successfully with southern and northern conservatives to keep out of the bill language requiring "racial balance" in the schools. For years afterward southern senators tried to pass a resolution requiring that the provisions of the Act be applied uniformly in all regions of the country "without regard to the origin or cause of such segregation." Their reasoning was that if the government moved on northern segregation with the same force they used in the South, northern members of Congress would join the southern cause. In a strikingly ironic scene in 1970 a group of the most liberal Senators broke with their colleagues and voted with the South on its latest attempt to pass the resolution. In declaring that he would side with Senator Stennis of Mississippi, Senator Ribicoff of Connecticut declared, "The North is guilty of monumental hypocrisy"; but his more moderate colleagues, voting with northern conservatives, succeeded in killing the resolution.[30] As pressure on northern *de facto* segregation mounted, so has the ambivalence of liberal Congressmen caught in the cross-fire between their principles and pressure from their districts.

In the executive branch, the U.S. Civil Rights Commission (not to be confused with the Office of Civil Rights of HEW) takes the most fervent probusing stance, possibly because the Commission plays no regulatory role and is free of the normal political pressures on federal agencies. The commissioners have issued a number of influential reports, including one setting out to prove that compensatory education has failed, leaving desegregation as the only instrument for equalization, a position which, as earlier noted, some courts seemed inclined to adopt. In a more recent report issued in 1976, the Commission provided evidence from a two million dollar study showing that 82 percent of the nation's schools have desegregated without violence and only 10 percent report a decline in educational levels.[31] In its eagerness to demonstrate sporadic headlines describing resistance to desegregation have created a false impression, however, the commission has sacrificed a good deal of its own credibility. One of its own researchers and several state advisory committees protested that the study was based on rigged evidence, that the Commission had instructed its field offices in collecting data to emphasize only those districts in which desegregation plans were working.[32]

Some white professional liberals, notably leaders in organizations such as NEA, many university professors, such as Thomas Pettigrew of Harvard, and the staffs of federal agencies, have remained loyal to desegregation as a first priority, but there has been a considerable if unmeasured dropping off of enthusiasm as the complexities and contradictions in the northern desegregation process become apparent. A sense of betrayal is noticeable in much pro-integration literature, as in the following statement by Ivor Kraft, a social work professional:

> We must dig in, defend our gains, and oppose any effort to sell out integration. The youth of the nation are with us, many of the courts are with us. And the responsible, forward-looking citizens—not the defeatists and silent minorities— are also with us. In the long run we shall prevail . . . we can never abandon the task of providing ever more satisfactory basic American services in a multi-racial open society.
>
> It is this rock-bottom premise in the American way that is being challenged and crippled by the Nixon administration. Its minions will make use of any who will aid them in their work of spoilage. Careerist and defeatist liberals, visionary if misled black nationalists, Southern bourbons, tired schoolmen, the always mysterious "silent majority" . . . the decision to all but abandon the struggle for school desegregation, when we are just on the verge of making real headway in that struggle, is a piece of that work of spoilage. But the alternative to racial integration is the destruction of America.[33]

2.   The public's position is unequivocal: a rapid *rise* in support for integration generally over the past several decades, and a clear *decrease* in support for school busing as an instrument of integration.

There is still a significant difference of opinion among blacks and whites about the pace of integration. A national study of attitudes by Conant found a wide gap between the two groups on the question of whether integration was going too fast or not fast enough, a gap so wide that there was no overlap between the most liberal whites and the most conservative blacks. But Conant's analysis suggests that long-range prospects are good. "The most resistant whites are the older, nonhigh-schoolers who have had little or no contact with blacks. Stronger support among whites for a quickened pace of change derives from the younger, high school and college educated who have black friends. High economic status tends to reinforce these liberal attitudes."[34]

A study conducted by National Opinion Research Center several years later confirms the existence of a rapid shift in white attitudes.[35] The expressed support of whites for integration of schools, parks, restaurants, hotels, etc., has risen to 75 percent from about 30 percent in the 1940s. Only the issues of neighborhood integration and mixed marriages are still of concern to a majority.

On the other hand, in 1971 a Harris poll found 47 percent willing to have their children bused for desegregation, with 41 percent opposed; a year later, only 25 percent accepted busing, with 60 percent opposed, and by 1975 the percentage had dropped to 20 percent (though 80 percent of parents whose children were bused for all reasons expressed themselves as satisfied with busing).[36]

3.   The more militant black leaders, committed during the midsixties to integration, have moved away from that position. As early as 1966, Livingstone Wingate, a New York civil rights leader, put it this way.

> The greatest need today is the immediate establishment of *quality education* in the ghetto. We must no longer pursue the myth that integrated education is equated with quality education. Busing a disadvantaged and isolated child out of Harlem on a segregated bus to an "integrated" classroom downtown will not give him quality education. Once in a classroom downtown, the disadvantaged Harlem pupil would find himself below the achievement level of his white classmates and suffer a more demoralizing experience of frustration than he had in the ghetto inferior school. Moreover, he would return at night to the same ghetto conditions he left in the morning.[37]

Since then, the more militant of the black leaders have displayed little interest in integration; in fact, many of them have developed an active hostility to it, arguing that it is demeaning for blacks to agree that sitting in the classroom with whites could possibly help the black child. The road to quality education, they have come to believe, lies in the control of the ghetto school by its own community, an issue we shall examine in greater depth in the last chapter.

4.   A relatively new position has developed among a number of intellectuals who, while favoring integration as a general goal, believe that the federal courts are not the proper instrument to decree and administer it. In this view, the courts represent the least democratic political forum in which to seek the resolution of an issue that so sharply divides the country no matter how desirable the ideal that is being sought. The massive resistance to busing can be found not only in the street confrontations that have attended some busing orders, not only in the public opinion polls, but in Congress. As noted earlier, in 1975 an anti-busing majority managed to pass an amendment restricting HEW's (but not the courts')) authority to re-

quire busing remedies, and came close to getting approval for a constitutional amendment to forbid school busing altogether.

For the courts to go beyond their constitutional duty to remedy specific *de jure* instances of desegregation involves them in creating social policy, then legislating and administering it; in Nathan Glazer's words, "a damaging and unconstitutional revolution."[38] The terms of the indictment include the following arguments:

a. Most critically, the *Brown* decision outlawed pupil assignment by race; the courts have gradually moved to a position in which they require the reassignment of pupils by race to fulfill quotas that are increasingly set by the courts themselves, and children are moved about on the basis of whether they are black or white. Can the constitutional duty to be "color blind" be enforced only when motivations are "bad" but not when they are "good"?

b. The *Brown* decision rested on two arguments: that the law cannot treat some citizens differently than it treats others, and that separation generates feelings of inferiority among black children and hence affects their motivation to learn. Only the psychological effect justifies going beyond the eradication of legally-enforced segregation to require racial balance in all schools. But the psychological argument rested largely on Kenneth Clark's studies that in fact showed that the presumed harm is greater in more integrated settings.

c. The increasing tendency of the courts to rely on such social science data is viewed generally with considerable concern by those who take this position. Many desegregation cases have featured elaborate hearings in which expert witnesses produce and discuss a wide variety of social science data, often of doubtful quality and just as often contradictory. Eleanor Wolf, in a detailed examination of the way in which such data were assessed in one desegregation case, clearly reveals the difficulties: the courts' ignorance of quantitative methods; their misunderstanding of the logic of scientific inquiry; their acceptance of "pop" sociology; and the injurious effect of the legal adversary method on the consideration of conflicting evidence.[39] The tendency of judges to pick and choose among the data to confirm already established opinions is demonstrated by Judge Roth in the Detroit case; he ruled inadmissible a deposition by David Armour analyzing the evidence on the effect of busing on achievement because it represented in his view "a new rationale for a return to the discredited 'separate but equal' policy."[40]

d. Some federal judges have gone beyond policy-making to ordering far-reaching changes in municipal activities or to taking over the schools themselves. In order to desegregate one city school in Brooklyn, Judge Jack Weinstein in an extraordinary example of what Glazer calls judicial imperialism ordered housing officials to provide a plan to undo the racial imbalance in public housing in the area, the Metropolitan

Transportation Authority to rearrange bus schedules, the Police Commissioner to produce a plan for adequate protection of children in the school's vicinity, and the Parks Department to do something about the children's use of nearby parks.[41] And even *The New York Times*, a strong editorial supporter of school busing for integration, was shaken by a decision of a federal judge (W. Arthur Garrity) in Boston to assume administrative control of the system. He held hearings to determine individually which temporary teachers could be laid off (and disallowed most of the dismissals), ordered the city to provide more funds for a system that many experts think wastes a good deal of money already, and eliminated the use of admission tests for Boston's two prestigious academic high schools ("the glories of an otherwise ramshackle system" said William Shannon, *The New York Times* editor) in order to attain exact racial balance in them. "Could there be an act more racially provocative," asks Shannon, "or better calculated to divide white and black parents? Can such manipulation be defended as merely the neutral working of the law?"[42]

e. Finally, many observers are now concluding that however desirable school integration may be, attempts to enforce it by moving students around will merely increase the flow of whites from central cities to suburbs and defeat the original purpose of court orders. That sense of futility was beginning to emerge in the early seventies in such statements as the following by Alexander Bickel, a widely respected and generally liberal professor of law:

I have argued that integration is, under present circumstances, impossible of achievement on a national scale; that attempts to impose it, in the South as elsewhere, often produce the perverse result of resegregation; that a rising segment of Negro leadership no more wants it imposed than do many whites; that it often amounts to the mixing of the black lower class with the white lower class, which is educationally useless, so far as we know, even though the mixing of the lower and middle classes might have some uses; and that, therefore, integration ought not to have the highest priority in the allocation of our human, political, and material resources.[43]

Such fears may or may not be based on reality (see Panel 13.1). Predic-

PANEL 13.1   Does Segregation Increase "White Flight?"

Bickel's fear that it would exploded as an issue into national awareness in the midseventies when James Coleman, whose study of equal educational opportunity had been used for years as a justification for desegregation efforts, announced that he now could provide evidence that desegregation in the larger cities led to an increase in the movement of whites out of the central cities.

Coleman studied the rate of loss of white students from nineteen large city school districts between the years 1968 and 1973. He took as a benchmark the rate of loss for 1968 and found that:[44]

Eleven of those cities experienced little desegregation activity between 1969 and 1973; based on their 1968 loss one could expect a loss of 15 percent between 1969–1973. Their actual loss was slightly greater, 18 percent.

Eight cities in the sample had some desegregation activity, ranging from moderate to considerable; their expected loss was 17 percent during 1969–1973, but they actually lost 26 percent of their white students.

The apparent relation between desegregation and white flight did not appear among middle-sized cities.

A sizable uproar ensued in the press and in educational journals. Some of the response to Coleman was not very relevant; the citation by a national columnist of a study in Pasadena showing that the decline in white students after desegregation was no greater than the regular annual rate took no account of the fact that Coleman himself had found no effect in cities of that size. Much of the criticism was useful:[45]

Coleman used no direct measure of white families moving out of the city, only the percent of change in school enrollment of whites. His inferences about "white flight," consequently, overextended his data.

In only two of the nineteen large cities included in the study did any substantial degree of desegregation occur during the period he examined.

Studies such as Christine Rossell's did not come to similar conclusions about a relationship between desegregation and white flight, though Pettigrew noted that she used a different sample (omitting southern cities) and counted only desegregation efforts that resulted from government action.

It is hazardous to infer a long-run effect from an initial impact; an immediate reaction to desegregation might well fall off as people adjusted to it.

When the dust had cleared there turned out to be rather more agreement among all sides than might have been expected. Coleman agreed that his original announcement of findings had overstated the case. Reynolds Farley, who had criticized Coleman at a 1975 scholarly meeting, announced at the 1976 session that on the basis of more recent data he could confirm that in large central cities in which blacks made up more than a third of school enrollment a substantial loss of white students (double the normal rate) is associated with desegregation. Everyone agreed that there is some evidence that such loss rates drop after the initial spurt, though how long the adjustment takes is not clear. In Boston, which experienced a prolonged controversy over desegregation and several years of violent confrontation in the midseventies, 40 percent of the white students left the public schools in the period from 1970–1975, a decline that continued into the 1976–1977 school year.[46]

tions on such a volatile issue are easy to find but difficult to substantiate by either side. Pro-integration forces were fearful and unhappy at the beginning of the school year in 1975 as violence flared in both Louisville and Boston, but optimistic and buoyant a year later as schools opened quietly. It is possible that nothing much changed in the slow pace of national desegregation in the interim except the presence or absence of headlines.

EFFECTS OF DESEGREGATION ON ACHIEVEMENT AND ASPIRATION

A major source of confusion in the tangle of arguments over school desegregation lies in the different interpretations people make of a mass of research data available on the effects of racial mixture in the schools. It is possible to come to different conclusions as degrees of advocacy and sophistication vary. Those who view desegregation as an important positive measure read the data one way, those less interested, or antagonistic, another; the less sophisticated, including most of the mass media, are likely to accept data at face value, while the scientifically trained tend to evaluate the results much more cautiously. The purpose of this section is to clarify these differences, using a few important studies to illustrate the difficulties.

The available evidence is of several kinds: studies of change in groups of children who have undergone some shift from a segregated to an integrated situation, and studies that are cross-sectional in that they look at different groups of children who are in different conditions of integration at a given time. The problems of evaluating the conclusions are different, but almost equally formidable.

Before/After Studies
Much of the early evidence for the claim that desegregation significantly improves the academic performance of black pupils was derived from southern cities that desegregated in the late fifties and early sixties, and

consisted of system-wide comparisons between achievement scores pre- and post-desegregation. In Louisville, for example, two years after desegregation median scores for all pupils had risen with black pupils showing the greatest gains. It turned out, however, that much of that gain occurred in schools where black children were still segregated.[47] The same rise was noted in Washington, D.C. during the same period, but by 1960 that system was so predominantly black that integration could hardly account for the differences.[48] As with Louisville, the most reasonable explanation for the modest rise in achievement levels lies in the upgrading of curriculum and instruction that occurred at the time of desegregation.

Most southern data are subject to this ambiguity. Southern schools for blacks were generally so far below the standards of white schools that desegregation inevitably meant a very sizable jump in school quality. Even if, in general, the impact of school factors on achievement is minimal, it is difficult to believe that there is not some point of school inferiority beyond which the school begins to contribute substantially to educational retardation. Most southern schools for blacks in the fifties and early sixties probably *were* beyond that point.

The data from Northern cities, then, is particularly important, not only because the differences between ghetto schools and middle-class white schools are not so great as in the South, but also because it is clear by now that integration in the large cities, as noted earlier, must involve busing large numbers of children, and Northern before/after studies are largely evaluations of busing programs.

Differences in interpretation are particularly evident here, depending on how much attention one pays to the question of control. A typical case is that of New York City's busing program. Fox found that bused children were somewhat more favorable about their receiving schools than their former classmates were about the schools from which they were being bused, but not overwhelmingly so.[49] Observers found that in their new schools, hearteningly, the children were not being stereotyped by the resident children and were readily accepted into friendship relationships. But studies of reading gains are contradictory. In the first study of the program, a group of open enrollment pupils were found to be superior in reading to the median reading levels of the schools from which they came. In the second year study groups of bused children were instead compared to a *matched* group in the sending schools, that is, the two groups were roughly equivalent in social class, earlier reading achievement, etc. In this second evaluation no gains in reading achievement were found for the bused group. These differences can most reasonably be explained by supposing that the bused children represented a superior ability group in their sending schools, rather than by attributing their higher scores to the effects of busing. Fox substantiated the first of these conclusions by finding that the majority of principals involved agreed that the bused pupils were indeed a select group.

Matthai critically reviewed data on achievement change from fifteen cities that had instituted busing programs, including such widely publicized ones as Project Concern in Hartford and METCO in Boston. His conclusion:

> It is readily apparent that a dissonant theme runs through almost all of the studies discussed in this paper: small numbers, lack of control of significant variables, equivocal or even unwarranted conclusions based on often flimsy data. The only findings in common are that white students' academic performance seems unaffected by the presence of bused students, and that bused students perform well below the level of receiving school students.
>
> While it cannot be concluded from the research results discussed in this paper that bused students do worse academically that their non-bused counterparts, neither can it be concluded that they do better.[50]

The METCO busing program is of particular interest because in addition to reading scores and other achievement data a number of self-concept and attitude measures were administered at the beginning and end of the school year to a group of bused children. David Armor, in a detailed analysis of these findings, found little evidence that the program resulted in improvement in either academic achievement or self-esteem, and some indication that it induced among black students a greater desire for racial separation and an increase in their acceptance of black nationalist ideology.[51] The article drew a sharp, critical response from Pettigrew, who found no reason at all for confidence in the study's methodology, sampling, instrumentation, or intepretation. The exchange, which is well worth reading, amply illustrates the tone of barely controlled fury that one often finds in the arguments in this area, as well as the tendency to select from an enormous number of studies of desegregation and achievement those that most confirm one's own position. In a later article Pettigrew, for example, cites seven studies which show that desegregation does have a positive influence on black children, none of them freer from methodological flaws that those reviewed by Armor.[52]

Because of the difficulties involved in controlling by finding really equivalent groups in these studies, the few longitudinal studies that get baseline data about children before they are bused and then follow them into their new schools are particularly useful. One such attempt was made in Ann Arbor by Patricia Carrigan, who had the opportunity of making pupil assessments during a pretransfer year before busing program began, selecting a control group, and observing changes during the first post-transfer year.[53] A follow-up study three years later was done by Aberdeen. Carrigan concludes:

> School attendance patterns were similar in both groups during the pre-transfer year; over the post-transfer year the absence rate increased in the transfer group.
> Academic performance for the transfer group, which was lower than the nontransfer or the receiving school population, was also lower during the

post-transfer period. Pre-transfer scores were reasonably good predictors for all groups. The increasing gap between white and black children as they progress through the grades was not erased; though some children showed unexpected improvement, others demonstrated little or none.

Motivation and interest in school remained relatively stable, decreasing slightly for white and black boys, increasing slightly for white girls, unchanged for black girls. Black boys showed significant gains in need-achievement scores, and a reduced tendency to over aspiration.

Except for reading achievement, the greatest gains tended to occur among pupils with low pre-transfer scores; changes in reading achievement showed the least relationship to change in other measures (self-concept, motivation, etc.).

The three year follow-up study found little change in the psychological measures, and a slight decline in reading levels.

Cross-Sectional Studies

This kind of investigation compares schools with a varying proportion of *already existing* racial mixes, to compare the performance of black children in each milieu. Whatever differences they find, however, are always subject to different interpretation; they may be due to racial mix or to the fact that different kinds of families live in neighborhoods that exhibit various patterns of school mixture.

Coleman's national survey has on this account become the focus of a considerable amount of controversy. Although school resources themselves accounted for little in the variation in achievement among minority group children, he did find that the composition of the student body did make a difference. A reanalysis of the data later by McPartland showed that the important variable appears to be the mix of children *in the actual classroom*, rather than in the school generally.[54]

These conclusions were widely assumed to be a direct support for racial integration, and Coleman himself for a number of years made that argument from his study. But, as he more recently pointed out, the student body mix that the study was describing had to do with *social class*, not race. That is, "children from disadvantaged backgrounds did somewhat better in schools that were predominantly middle class than in schools that were homogeneously lower class." Since a high proportion of blacks come from disadvantaged backgrounds, one can by inference argue that "if they are to receive the kind of educational resource that comes from being with middle-class schoolmates, it must be primarily through racial integration."[55]

The difficulty with cross-sectional research, however, is that even that inference is questionable. It is easy to suppose that disadvantaged children already living in school districts that are middle class belong to upwardly mobile parents who have gone to considerable trouble to provide better schooling for their children.

Other studies are subject to the same difficulty, as an examination of

Alan Wilson's Berkeley research indicates.[56] In his first study, Wilson collected data on sixth-graders in Berkeley who attended schools in one of three distinct parts of the city: the Berkeley Hills, where most of the students are from professional or executive families; the Flats, where most of the black population is concentrated; and the Foothills, which is between these extremes both geographically and in terms of social composition. The Hills schools were overwhelmingly white; the Flats schools had 62 percent black students; and the Foothills comprised 71 percent white and 14 percent black (the remainder was Oriental).

An examination of achievement test scores of the students, grouped by their father's occupation, indicates that, as one might expect, the differences are mainly due to differences in the backgrounds of the children attending schools in various areas of the city. Wilson's question is: Are there differences in the achievement of children *from the same occupational level* who are attending different schools? Taking reading achievement as a crucial test, he compared children whose fathers were in roughly the same occupations with the same grouping in other schools; the results are reported in Table 13.2. These data strongly suggest that the school itself has an "homogenizing" effect on students, and seems to confirm a belief in the potency of the peer group. Indeed, Wilson collected data on boys' peer groups in the Berkeley schools which indicates that in the Flats schools the boys who are not interested in going on with their education are well-integrated among their classmates and are overrepresented among the leaders of the school.

There are some significant objections to this interpretation, however. It is possible that the heavy concentration of black students in the Flats reduces the average reading scores. To test the effect of a number of variables within each occupational grouping, Wilson performed a complex analysis that resulted in a series of weights indicating how much each variable contributed

Table 13.2   Mean Reading Achievement-Test Scores of High-Sixth-Grade
Students Classified by Sex, School Strata, and Father's Occupations

	BOYS			GIRLS		
Father's Occupation	*Hills*	*Foothills*	*Flats*	*Hills*	*Foothills*	*Flats*
Professional and executive	107	100	—*	107	108	—*
	(94)	(21)	(2)	(93)	(15)	(1)
White-collar and merchant	106	93	81	102	99	81
	(46)	(31)	(18)	(55)	(38)	(16)
Manual and artisan	—*	91	71	103	93	84
	(3)	(55)	(72)	(11)	(46)	(87)

* Means are not reported for cells containing fewer than ten cases.
SOURCE: Alan B. Wilson, "Social Stratification and Academic Achievement," in A. Harry Passow (ed.), *Education in Depressed Areas* (New York: Teachers College, 1963), p. 223.

to reading scores. In Table 13.3, the weights for each of the variables is a measure of how much the variable *independently* contributes, holding all other factors constant.

One can predict the average reading score for any particular group by adding or subtracting the appropriate effects to the total mean of 97.7. Thus, the predicted reading achievement of black working-class boys in Flats schools is $97.7 - 1.7 - 12.7 - 4.3 - 4.4 = 74.6$. But the prediction for the same boys in Foothills schools is only 4.2 more, or 78.8. Although Wilson has produced evidence that the schools have *some* effect, it does not seem to be a very substantial one.

Furthermore, there is an alternative explanation for the fact that boys of the same class and race do better in schools in areas outside the ghetto. As Wilson himself points out:

> It is doubtless true that one of the reasons manual workers choose to live in the Hills is to obtain greater educational and social advantages for their children. Very likely they place an emphasis upon the value of school success which is more comparable to other residents of the Hills than to their educational compeers in the Foothills and Flats.

In a San Francisco study, Wallin and Waldo tested this possibility by gathering data on parental educational aspiration for their children.[57] The

Table 13.3   Estimates of the Main Orthogonal Effects of Sex, Race, School Strata, and Fathers' Occupations upon Reading-Test Scores

Source of Variation	Main Effect
Sex	
Male	−1.7
Female	+1.5
Race	
White	+3.0
Oriental	+0.9
Negro	−12.7
School Stratum	
Hills	+2.3
Foothills	−0.1
Flats	−4.3
Father's occupation	
Professional and executive	+3.7
White-collar and merchant	+1.1
Manual and artisan	−4.4
Mean	97.7

SOURCE: Alan B. Wilson, "Social Stratification and Academic Achievement," in A. Harry Passow (ed.), *Education in Depressed Areas* (New York: Teachers College, 1963), p. 226.

sample included about 2400 eighth-grade boys and girls, of whom 135 were black boys and 133 were black girls. The researchers found a sizable association between school climate (based on the proportion of students from middle-class families in the school) and student's level of aspiration. But, when the parents' aspirations for the child (reported by the child himself) were controlled, the relation between school climate and the child's educational aspirations was considerably reduced. The children in the schools with greater numbers of middle-class pupils tended to have parents with high aspirations for them. Although Wallin and Waldo did not investigate achievement levels, their findings suggest that parents of lower-class children in mixed schools have higher aspirations for their children and probably exert more pressure on them to achieve.

Thus, the claim that an integrated school climate has any substantial effect on black student achievement seems at best unproven, and the likelihood that it independently influences aspirations is not very great. A later study by Wilson of high school climate does suggest that the social class composition of secondary schools may influence the aspirations for higher education of its students, but the proportion of black students did not permit a separate analysis by race.[58]

Although we have been examining here only a few studies for the purpose of clarifying the difficulties of generalizing and interpreting the data in the field, there have been over the past fifteen years several thousand research attempts to provide evidence for a relationship between desegregation and achievement or aspiration. Reviews of this literature, by strong proponents of integration in several recent instances, conclude that there is little empirical basis for arguing that equalization of the results of schooling will result from desegregation. Nancy St. John comes to that conclusion in an extensive review, *School Desegregation: Outcomes for Children*, in which she reviewed over 120 studies, finding contradictory evidence to be the norm, with the best-designed studies showing no difference in achievement; black children in predominantly white schools were fairly often found to have lower self-esteem scores than those in segregated schools.[59]

Patricia Lines similarly found "little basis to support beliefs about educational gains or losses resulting from busing."[60] She nevertheless goes on to say that busing should be required because "this nation has not yet paid off past debts" to black citizens. The present state of the argument over the research can perhaps best be summarized by two additional comments. McAdams, in response to Lines' remark, notes that "one might be forgiven for wondering how a nation can pay off its debts to black citizens with a policy which does not seem to benefit them;"[61] Robert Crain, a Rand researcher, dismisses the research in general: "When research has asked whether desegregation was good or bad, it has almost always asked the question in the wrong way—namely, in terms of short-run achievement tests rather than long-run effects on students or the impact of desegregation on the whole community . . . (researchers) have been far too quick to conclude that desegregation has not been beneficial."[62]

SOME POLICY DILEMMAS

One might reasonably conclude from all this that the advocacy of school integration might be better based on sound democratic principle than on the shaky grounds of improved school performance. The demands of civil rights advocates on the courts, however, and the response of some courts, seem increasingly to involve equality of results rather than equality of conditions. General democratic principles by themselves can hardly be invoked to justify enforcement of racial balance quotas; as Coleman has pointed out, it is "not a constitutional matter of equal protection that all segregation must be eliminated. Just as it is not the case that all segregation between Irish and Italians must be eliminated. The goal of eliminating all segregation is not only not realizable but not desirable; indeed, it is improper."[63]

The relation between race and social class poses another dilemma. If the data say anything at all, it is that whatever benefit might accrue academically to desegregated minority children derives from a social class mix. Yet, in Boston, the worst excesses of the battles over desegregation resulted from a court order that sent black children into lower class white schools that were by everyone's estimate the least academically oriented in the city. And in doing so the order violated most profoundly the sense of community of a working class group whose life is built on neighborhood cohesiveness.

Finally, there is growing evidence that civil rights advocates will seek far more than mere physical proximity and that the urban schools will increasingly face demands to shape themselves to fit the visions of the advocates. Nathaniel Hickerson argues:

> If we reject *de facto* segregation as inimical to American democracy, then we must reject mere physical integration of Negroes and whites in schools as inimical to the best interests of Negro children . . . we must decide that this integration is to be more than placing of Negro and white children in the same school building.[64]

Hickerson proposes nine basic steps that must be taken to improve education in the integrated schools of the North:

1. A realistic proportion of Negro teachers, counselors, and administrators, should serve in the public schools, particularly integrated schools.
2. Teachers, both white and Negro, with special interests and training in education of minority groups should be employed whenever possible in integrated schools.
3. Teacher training institutions must offer courses in minority-group education, and should sanction for employment in schools with an integrated student body only those teachers who have successfully completed these courses.
4. Race-minded and bigoted faculty members, employed in integrated

schools should be identified and ruthlessly removed wherever possible. Perhaps expressions of racial hostility could be grounds for immediate dismissal as a violation of policy of the board of education . . .

5. All schools, but particularly those that are integrated must place emphasis upon the historical contributions of Negroes to the development of man's culture and American institutions . . .

6. Business, professional, union, civic and sports leaders, both white and Negro, should be encouraged to come to the school in the community to discuss with students the kinds of employment opportunities available for those who do well in school and who plan to continue in advanced training . . .

7. Schools, through home visits by faculty personnel, should encourage Negro parents to attend school functions and to become identified with the school and its problems.

8. Negro students (together with whites) in junior high and high schools should be sent as missionaries into the lower grades of the elementary schools to talk with children and impress upon white and black alike the necessity of taking school seriously . . .

9. Special programs such as Compensatory Education and Operation Head Start should be used always by school districts in integrated situations.

Although some elements of this prescription are innocuous, others seem almost designed to create sharp community and school conflicts, further alienate the white middle class from the urban public schools, and serve ultimately, perhaps, to create in our largest cities school systems with no vestige of integration at all.

CHAPTER NOTES

1 David B. Tyack, *Turning Point in American Educational History* (Xerox College Publishing, 1967).

2 *Plessy v. Ferguson*, 163 U.S. 256, 89 S.Ct. 509 (1896).

3 Booker T. Washington, "Atlanta Exposition Address" (delivered at the opening of the Cotton States' Exposition, Atlanta, Georgia, September 1895), in *Selected Speeches of Booker T. Washington*, E. Davidson Washington, ed. (New York: Doubleday, 1932), 31–34, 35.

4 *Sweatt v. Painter*, 339 U.S. 629, L.ed. 114, 70 S.Ct. 848 (1950).

5 *Brown v. Board of Education*, 347 U.S. 483 (1954) L.ed. 98, 876–882.

6 Marian Wright Edelman, "Southern School Desegregation, 1954–1973: A Judicial-Political Overview," *Annals of the American Academy of Political and Social Science*, 407 (1973), 32–42.

7 *Cooper v. Aaron*, 358 U.S. 1, 18, 19 (1958).

8 *Griffin v. County Board of Prince Edward County*, 377 U.S. 218, 264 (1964).

9 *Swann v. Charlotte Mecklenburg Board of Education*, 402 U.S. 1 (1971).

10 Leonard Buder, "Magnet High Schools in City Are Pulling," *New York Times*, July 3, 1975, p. 13.

[11] Diane Ravitch "Busing: The Solution That Has Failed To Solve," *New York Times*, December 21, 1975, Section E, p. 3.

[12] Robert L. Herbst, "The Legal Struggle To Integrate Schools in the North," *Annals of the American Academy of Political and Social Science*, 407 (1973), 43–62.

[13] James S. Coleman, *et al., Equality of Educational Opportunity* (DHEW, 1966).

[14] Kenneth B. Clark, *Effects of Prejudice and Discrimination on Personality Development*, Midcentury White House Conference on Children and Youth, 1950.

[15] Herbst, p. 52.

[16] *Keyes v. School District No. 1, Denver*, F. Supp. 61, 313 F. Supp. 90 (1970).

[17] *Bradley v. Milliken*, 433 F. 2d 897 (6th Circuit, 1970).

[18] *Milliken v. Bradley*, 418 U.S. 717 (1974).

[19] *Haycroft v. Board of Education of Louisville*, 510 F. 2d 1358, 1361 (6th Circuit, 1974).

[20] William K. Stevens, "Cleveland Is Likely To Be the Next Battleground," *New York Times*, March 17, 1976, p. 21.

[21] Coleman, 10–13.

[22] *Report on Educational Research*, June 30, 1976, p. 5.

[23] "Data Show HEW Is Curbing Busing," *New York Times*, November 10, 1975, p. 36.

[24] Richard L. Madden "Senate Votes To Forbid HEW from Ordering School Busing," *New York Times*, September 26, 1975, p. 42.

[25] Anthony Ripley, "U.S. Court Acts to Bar Court Order Forcing Action on Integration," *New York Times*, January 9, 1973, p. 46.

[26] "Resegregation a Problem in Urban South," *New York Times*, September 28, 1970.

[27] William E. Farrell, "School Integration Resisted in Cities of the North," *New York Times*, May 13, 1974, p. 24.

[28] "Both Races Distressed 5 Years After Coast Integration Order," *New York Times*, June 18, 1975, p. 22.

[29] Edelman, p. 42.

[30] "Challenge to the North on School Segregation," *New York Times*, February 15, 1970, p. 54.

[31] *Fulfilling the Letter and Spirit of the Law, Desegregation of the Nation's Public Schools*, U.S. Civil Rights Commission Report (August 1976).

[32] "Rosy Reporting," *Time*, November 29, 1976, p. 51.

[33] Ivor Kraft, "1970—The Year of the Big Sellout on Integration," *Phi Delta Kappan*, 51 (1970), p. 526.

[34] Ralph W. Conant, Sheldon Levy, and Ralph Lewis, "Mass Polarization," *American Behavioral Scientist*, XII (1969), p. 259.

[35] "Study Finds Steady Rise in Whites' Acceptance of Integration," *New York Times*, December 8, 1971, p. 34.

[36] Edelman, ft. p. 42.

[37] Livingston Wingate (from an address to the 25th Annual Work Conference for Superintendents, Teachers College, Columbia University, July 9, 1966), in Harry L. Miller (ed.) *Education for the Disadvantaged* (New York: Free Press, 1967), p. 220.

[38] Nathan Glazer, "Toward an Imperial Judiciary?" *The Public Interest*, no. 41 (Fall 1975), p. 104.

[39] Eleanor Wolf, "Social Science and the Courts: The Detroit Schools Case," *The Public Interest*, no. 42 (Winter 1976), 102–119.

[40] Thomas F. Pettigrew, "Another Look at the 'Evidence on Busing,'" *Equal Educational Opportunity*, III (1973), p. 16.

[41] Morris Kaplan, "Housing Officials Here Told To Integrate Schools," *New York Times*, January 29, 1974, p. 1.

[42] William V. Shannon, "The Boston Affairs," *New York Times*, June 24, 1976, p. 33.

[43] Alexander M. Bickel, "Desegregation: Where Do We Go from Here?" *Phi Delta Kappan*, 5 (1970), p. 522.

[44] James S. Coleman, "Recent Trends in School Integration," *Educational Researcher* (July-August 1975), 3–12.

[45] Pettigrew, 10–15; Gregg Jackson, "Reanalysis of Coleman's 'Recent Trends in School Integration,' " *Educational Researcher* (November 1975), 21–25.

[46] Ravitch, p. 3.

[47] Irwin Katz, "Review of Evidence Relative to the Effects of Desegregation on the Intellectual Performance of Negroes," *American Psychologist* (June 1964), 371–389.

[48] Katz, p. 376.

[49] David J. Fox, *Expansion of the Free Choice Open Enrollment Program* (New York: Center for Urban Education, September 1967), mimeographed.

[50] Robert A. Matthai, *The Academic Performance of Negro Students: An Analysis of the Research Findings from Several Busing Programs* (Harvard Graduate School of Education, June 1968), p. 48.

[51] David J. Armor, "The Evidence on Busing," *The Public Interest*, no. 28 (Fall 1972), 90–126; see also the Winter issue following for a rebuttal of his analysis.

[52] Pettigrew, 6–7.

[53] Patricia M. Carrigan, *School Desegregation via Compulsory Pupil Transfer: Early Effects on Elementary School Children* (Ann Arbor Public Schools, 1969).

[54] James McPartland, "The Relative Influence of School and of Classroom Desegregation on the Academic Achievement of Ninth Grade Negro Students," *Journal of Social Issues*, XXV, no. 3 (Summer 1969), 92–103.

[55] Walter Goodman, "Integration Yes; Busing, No," *New York Times Magazine*, August 24, 1975, p. 10.

[56] Alan B. Wilson, "Social Stratification and Academic Achievement," in Harry Passow (ed.), *Education in Depressed Areas* (New York: Teachers College, 1963), p. 223.

[57] Paul Wallin and Leslie C. Waldo, *Social Class Background of Eighth Grade Pupils, Social Composition of Their Schools, Their Academic Aspirations and School Adjustment* (Washington, D.C.: U.S. Office of Education, Cooperative Research Project No. 1935, 1964).

[58] Alan B. Wilson, "Residential Segregation of Social Classes and Aspirations of High School Boys," in A. Harry Passow, *et al.*, *Education of the Disadvantaged* (New York: Holt, Rinehart and Winston, 1967), 268–283.

[59] Nancy St. John, *School Desegregation: Outcomes for Children* (New York: Wiley, 1975).

[60] Cited in John McAdams, "Can Open Enrollment Work?" *The Public Interest*, no. 37 (Fall 1974), p. 86.

[61] McAdams, p. 87.

[62] Robert L. Crain, "Why Academic Research Fails To Be Useful," *School Review*, 84 (1976), p. 337.

[63] Goodman, p. 13.

[64] Nathaniel Hickerson, "Physical Integration Is Not Enough," *Journal of Negro Education*, XXXV (1966), 115–116.

Chapter 14

The Struggle for Control of Urban Schools

Who shall control the schools of American cities, and the system level at which control shall be placed, has been an issue since publicly supported schools were established. This chapter:

Describes the growth of influences external to the city and state, as both the federal bureaucracy and the federal courts take an increasing hand in education.

Discusses the controversy over the nature of power in American cities, and the resulting arguments over central control vs. neighborhood control of institutions.

Describes the struggle over community control of the schools in five major cities.

Assesses the impact of community control in those districts where it has gained a foothold.

Some questions that readers might address are:

The author clearly sees a great deal to worry about in the prospect of increasing federal influence on the schools. Do I agree with him? If not, what reasons could be argued for a more benign view of the consequences of the federal presence?

The stories of various attempts to institute community control are very different in action and results. What conclusions do I draw from this diversity?

Historically, in this country the association between the school and the community it serves has always been assumed to be a close and mutually supportive one. The substantial power given to local school boards in general assumes that in a very real sense the school belongs to and should serve the community in which it is located.

Such a generalization conceals the occasional surges of conflict that have occurred even in rural and small town America over the past century, as definitions of "the community" have changed. A prolonged and often savage battle was fought in the last century to consolidate the small one-room schools of the rural areas into more efficient and better equipped central district schools to which children from a wide area could be bused. Most city systems, at about the same time, were also centralized as part of reform efforts aimed at breaking up political machines based in small city wards.

Although it will tell some of that earlier story, this chapter is mainly concerned with two major contemporary trends in urban school control. One is the vigorous attempt to decentralize control over schools to the local community; the second, and less visible movement, is the growth in the influence of forces outside the school districts themselves.

In either case, the central question is: Who decides how the resources that are available to the school districts get allocated? What kind of curriculum shall we invest in? How much will teachers receive in salary, and who decides which of them shall be hired? Where shall the school building be placed, and how lavishly shall it be equipped? Who contracts for outside services and selects the texts to be ordered? Which children can be excluded from school, and on what grounds?

City school systems spend tens of billions of dollars annually and the decisions that govern their allocation are no small matter. Of greater importance is the fact that the decisions in many cases must resolve conflicts in value and interest that are often sharp and frequently bitter, the seemingly inevitable accompaniment of an open society.

EXTERNAL CONTROL

In the political division of responsibility within the federal system education was left to the states; legitimate authority over school policy was thus ultimately in the hands of the state legislatures, to be administered by the state executive. Traditionally, the autonomy of the local school district was widely encouraged; it raised its own school taxes and was governed by locally elected boards within general guidelines set by the legislature and supervised by a state department of education. Until recently tradition also dictated a policy which kept the reins very loose; except in times of crisis legislatures paid little consistent attention to school matters and departments of education were small and weak, attending to such matters as teacher certification and the like.

The federal government maintained a hands-off policy for well over a century and a half, restricting itself in educational matters to a number of supportive actions aimed at strengthening higher education. The federal office of education until the sixties was a small bureau that busied itself mainly in collecting educational statistics and took so much time in publishing them that they did no one very much good.

The tradition is fast eroding. In the past generation, as states began to contribute a sizable share of school funding, state departments took their supervisory mandates more seriously and rapidly expanded in size and complexity. When the Congress enacted the Elementary and Secondary School Act in the mid-sixties, most of the funds made available were funneled through the states, which further increased state-level activity in education. Federal education operations were consolidated into the Department of Health, Education, and Welfare; the Office of Education, formerly in control of a few hundred million dollars a year, was within a decade spending seven billion.

Will control inevitably follow funding? In the case of control by the states themselves, one could argue that if it is inevitable, it is also appropriate, since the school districts are legitimately creatures of the state. If the desire to maintain local control is strong enough, the public can curb an excessive state appetite for power at the ballot box.

The problem of federal control is different and more complicated. The National Education Association is campaigning for a much larger federal contribution to educational costs, something on the order of a third of the total, which would represent a five-fold increase in its present contribution. The possibility of Congress putting up an additional 25 to 30 billion a year is exceedingly remote, but even if it were not, many educators would see it as an open invitation to a federalized education policy, and most of them would regard the even remoter possibility of full federal funding as a nightmare.[1] As cautious as HEW may have been about invading state and local educational policy prerogatives, it cannot avoid the need to set priorities and program standards when the number of requests for grants in a particular area exceeds the funds available for it. Nor have federal education officials been reticent in their public declarations about their views of desirable directions for education generally, though they have failed often enough to start intended bandwagons, as in the case of the educational voucher plan described in Chapter 11.

Whatever the potential for administrative federal control of education, it is now being rapidly exceeded by another branch of government, the courts. For most of the history of the American school the courts, and particularly the federal courts, were called upon to intervene in education mostly on issues arising out of the separation of church and state. As noted in Chapters 5 (equalization of school expenditures) and 13 (desegregation), an increasingly activist judiciary seems now very willing to exert a substantial degree of control over the schools in a number of ways.

INTERVENTION BY THE COURTS

Of the many movements created during the social activism of the sixties one of the most vigorous and articulate concerned itself with the legal rights of children. Different parts of the movement have variously championed due process rights for juvenile delinquents, including the right to have legal counsel when needed; the right to treatment for the mentally ill and mentally retarded; and the right to education for the emotionally or mentally handicapped child, in the least restrictive setting.[2] Although a number of private organizations have worked toward most of these goals for many years by putting pressure on various legislatures, contemporary child advocates have chosen a strategy that emphasizes court actions, and particularly efforts to establish various rights as constitutionally mandated.

Because the school is the only public institution intended to serve all children, it is the natural focus for child advocates whose overwhelming preference is to have all "special children" in the freest and most natural setting, that is, the regular classroom. Much of the current legal attack, consequently, consists of attempts to force school districts to deal adequately with mentally retarded children and to retain disruptive emotionally disturbed or delinquent children. The run-of-the-mill school, on the other hand, is organized precisely on the assumption that its children fall within certain ability limits, allowing at least some standardization of instruction, and the hope that only relatively mild forms of deviant behavior must be handled. To restructure all public schools on a different set of assumptions, with teachers trained to deal with the retarded and the emotionally disturbed in classes small enough to make instruction possible even for appropriately trained teachers, would require raising taxes to far higher levels than any state legislature has been willing to do.[3]

The issue now appears to be whether child advocate groups, through court action, can force the states to do what they are unwilling to do. One major thrust of that legal effort was an attempt to have the courts declare education itself a constitutional right. If education were found to be a right guaranteed by the Constitution, it would be necessary to provide it equally to all children; the full weight of the federal government could then be brought to bear on the states to obtain compliance with the judicial mandate. But, in a landmark case originating in Texas, *Rodriguez vs. the School District of San Antonio,* the Supreme Court upheld a lower court ruling that rejected a constitutional basis for education.[4]

Other federal and state courts, however, have found narrower grounds for granting much the same remedy which the *Rodriguez* court denied. One of the most significant of these cases is described below, to provide a concrete example of how the courts can influence educational decision-making, and the impact on a school system when they do. It may also be an augury of things to come, as local school districts grapple with the demands imposed by the Handicapped Children Act more recently passed by the Congress.

THE *MILLS* CASE

Mills vs. the District of Columbia Board of Education was an action on behalf of a number of children who, for one reason or another, were excluded from the District schools. At the end of 1971 the District Board, instead of contesting the suit, signed a consent decree agreeing to take a census of all children excluded because services were not available to them, including the retarded, physically handicapped, and the emotionally disturbed who had been suspended or expelled. The Board, pleading lack of resources, failed to comply with the order, and during the following year the court ordered it to submit a proposed implementation plan. Failure to produce that on time resulted in a summary judgment by the court, based on the following argument:

District of Columbia law requires all parents to see that their children attend school; the District's law itself, therefore, presumes that educational opportunity must be available to all children. It also provides for an appraisal of the mental and physical condition of children, and assignment, where necessary, to special instruction; hence, the Board has an obligation to provide specialized classes. The judge further cited constitutional grounds, both equal protection and due process. He quotes the *Brown* decision (see Chapter 13) as requiring that education must be made available to all on equal terms; since the District has promised educational opportunity, it is constitutionally required to provide it to everyone. Further still, expulsion from school or reassignment among programs without a hearing were forbidden on the grounds that they violated the constitutional right to due process.

The District Board argued that the Congress (which provides the District of Columbia's budget) had already appropriated funds for special education and that to improve those services the Board must divert funds intended by Congress for general educational services, and thus violate an act of Congress. The court swept this reasoning away, arguing that the Board's failure to provide education for these "exceptional children cannot be excused by the claim that there are insufficient funds:"

> If sufficient funds are not available to finance all of the services and programs that are needed and desirable in the system, then the available funds must be expended equitably in such a manner that no child is entirely excluded from a publicly supported education consistent with his needs and ability to benefit therefrom. The inadequacies of the District of Columbia Public School System, whether occasioned by insufficient funding or administrative inefficiency certainly cannot be permitted to bear more heavily on the "exceptional" or handicapped child than on the normal child.[5]

In a comprehensive series of orders the court directed the Board to notify all parents of the order, carry on a media campaign to identify children in need, evaluate and tentatively place children in programs, notify parents of the placement and arrange for hearings for any parent wishing to protest the placement, and institute an elaborate series of procedures for any suspension or expulsion action against any child.

The court thereupon set up a system under which parents could demand a hearing before special court-appointed masters to challenge any decision made about a child by school personnel, and kept the case under its jurisdiction to consider any future actions brought before it, taking, in effect, control over the schools' special education program.

As a result of the order the special education staff increased from 50 in 1972 to 700 in 1975.[6] Such an enormous personnel increase is inevitably disruptive to any system, and it was not easy to get qualified people; for a time people were drawn from "here and there" to augment the special education staff, thus reducing staff resources in other parts of the system. The number of children served has increased from 550 to 14,000, slightly over 10 percent of the public school population, and from a budget of 4.5 million to almost 13 million in 1976.

In attempting to meet the requirements of the court order the system has developed a multistage organization within each school. Each has at least one special education teacher who does crisis intervention and acts as a resource for other members of the instructional staff, performs diagnostic assessments, and consults with parents. Any child in the program might spend up to one hour a day with this teacher. A child who cannot be stabilized at that level becomes part of a "learning center" for as long as a semester, spending up to four hours a day in various assessment and prescription processes. If the child does not improve at this level, the special education staff try to work out placement in a private school.

The very substantial extra funding required for the program has not only proven difficult to acquire, but has created severe conflicts. The court had declared that education is a municipal function, hence the city's social service department is as responsible for handicapped children as the school board. A long wrangle developed among the special education department, the Board of Education ("which has thirty other priorities"), the social service department of the city, and the Mayor's Office of the Budget. The city told the Board of Education that there were no extra funds available and that Congress would have to supply what was necessary. School officials then brought their need for funds to satisfy the court order to Capitol Hill and were told, "cut it out of other parts of the budget, make some hard political choices."

A particularly difficult funding problem arises from the payment of tuition and maintenance costs to special private schools for those children the system cannot handle itself, costs that can run as high as $27,000 per year. School people feel that social services should cover part of these costs; social services does not agree. A number of middle-class parents are involved in the program and might be able to contribute, but the court order appears to prohibit the application of a needs test.

The court order also regarded justice as incomplete if it were not immediate, creating additional difficulties. If a hearing results in a recommendation for an expensive private school placement for a child, that placement must be made within a matter of weeks. But school budgets are written and funded at some time prior to a given school year and private facilities will not take a child unless the money to cover his tuition is in the budget. Under these circumstances one would expect the system to run out of funds very easily, which it did. By 1974 there was a deficit of one million dollars, with a backlog of children waiting to be placed, and with the special education director refusing to place them until additional funds were provided. The city's Office of the Budget was furious, and the Board was faced with a contempt-of-court action on behalf of forty children caught in the shortfall.

The potential for expansion under the iron logic of the court order seems almost infinite; some observers suggest that an industry has been created and that the Board of Education appears to be turning into a Board of Special Education. Families are moving into the District from Virginia and Maryland, attracted by the opportunity of getting children for whom they are spending substantial sums on private tuition into facilities paid for by the District's school system. Nor is there any agreement on the upper age-limit of children for whom the Board must be responsible. The court set the age limits as 7–16, but federal legislation on the handicapped often recognizes a limit of 25 years; the Board's own limit is 21. Since the judge involved tends to operate on the basis of federal guidelines, he may yet move to the higher age level.

Still another potential for expansion lies in the vagueness of the definition of some disabilities. Medical definitions of speech and vision handicaps can be fairly exact, but the special education department itself changed one admissions requirement from "emotionally disturbed" to "emotionally disabled and behavioral problems." The Director hoped, in making the change, that expansion could be controlled by stiffening the assessment process and demanding precise definition of behavior problems, but that hope seems unrealistic. In fact, the schools cannot control the entry process through its evaluations because the parents can contest them before special outside consultants acting as hearing masters. The masters are not supposed to dictate the actual placement, but in reality they appear to do so; determination of entry into the program has, in effect, been placed outside the system.

At the hearings themselves parents are entitled to counsel, though the Board is unrepresented by counsel. Wealthy parents hire lawyers, the poor are approached by advocacy organizations and, in some cases, get legal assistance from private facilities for the handicapped, which are booming and prosperous.

The advocates who brought the suit may indeed feel considerable gratification; there is little question that the system has been forced to take care of the handicapped child. The most troubling aspect of the issue is that everyone would agree with the humaneness of the goal. Critics of such judicial activism argue, however, that the proper mechanism for setting priorities in allocating resources should rest with those given authority by the public to do so, local legislators who are faced with the difficult problem of deciding among a great number of needs. The *Mills* case amply illustrates the potential dangers of judicial intervention for creating system imbalance and ambiguities of control in an institution already subject to many conflicting political pressures.

INTERNAL CONTROL

The issue of external influences on the control of the schools may well become the great educational controversy of the future. The major current conflict over control lies within the urban systems themselves on the issue of decentralization of decision-making power from professional school bureacracies to the local subcommunities within the city.

The roots of the issue lie far deeper than the schools and the question of who should control policy for them. The demand for local control is part of a much broader conflict over varying identifications of the source of power generally, and over who should make municipal policy in particular. The examination below of the contemporary "grass roots power" movement provides a necessary context for the detailed look at the school movements that follow.

Populism and Pluralism—Where Does Urban Power Lie?

Two general theories of social power are presently applied by social scientists to explain the patterns of influence in urban communities. One of these is often referred to as the "power elite" theory, after a popular book of that title by C. Wright Mills.[7] Most social scientists who take this position are influenced by Marxist ideas of class struggle and the approach in general ties variations in power in one way or another to social-class position.

The view emphasizes the existence of a pyramid of power in American communities, with a power elite, the upper class, at the top, controlling all important decision-making. It is also generally assumed that the upper class may be defined most importantly by control over the major economic resources in the community. At the national level Mills has argued that a small group of people, including the President, the presidents and board chairmen of the largest corporations, and the military leadership corps, constitute a national power elite.

The upper-class elite, the theory goes, rules in its own interest and in response to its conscious need to perpetuate its existence as a class. Although mid-level leaders in the local communities appear to make important decisions as mayors, councilmen, heads of associations and institutions, they are subordinate to the local elite and do its bidding. Conflicts within communities may appear to exhibit a variety of interests at work, but the only important source of conflict is that between the elite and the lower classes, whose economic interests are fundamentally in conflict.

Although this view of the reality of urban politics is treated as a new insight in some of the literature (Floyd Hunter's studies of power structure, for example, show little insight into its historical roots),[8] it is solidly anchored in a long tradition of American populism. In an essay tracing the outline of that tradition, James Nuechterlein points out that the model of social conflict as an unending struggle between the People and the Interests has long been a part of the tradition of American democracy.[9] In a democracy the People is supposed to rule, thus, only those who speak for the people are legitimate; those parties and movements that oppose the People's spokesmen must then represent the Interests, who oppose the will of the People. "Since at least the era of Andrew Jackson," Nuechterlein writes, "American liberal democracy has typically argued that the People not only have the right to rule, but that they are necessarily wise and virtuous. Such a view encounters difficulty explaining how things in American democratic society so often and so badly go wrong. Recourse to the People-Interests model offers a convenient solution: when the society acts unjustly or unwisely, it is not the wise and virtuous majority who are at fault, but the selfish Interests who by corruption, conspiracy, or subtle manipulation have somehow led the nation into wrongdoing."[10]

In the second half of the nineteenth century the Populist Party saw the nation divided starkly between the rich and the poor, the evil and the virtuous. Since the party had an agrarian base, the Interests were defined as the farmers' enemies—the banks, the railroads, the trusts. The successors of the Populist Party, the Progressives of the early twentieth century, "pictured the People much more broadly as including the great middle class and even the rich, if they were imbued with the proper concern for the public interest."[11] Their view of the Interests was also broader; to the trusts and those whom Teddy Roosevelt called "malefactors of great wealth" were added the evil Interests at the bottom, some early labor unions and the urban political bosses and their machines.

The thirties' depression and the great political coalition forged by Franklin Roosevelt of the "common people" brought back the duality of early populism with a vengeance; ". . . that great majority coalition that for a time, as indicated by FDR's unprecedented landslide in 1936, seemed to include almost everyone except the officers of General Motors and the DuPont Corporation."[12] But by the fifties, populist fervor had abated. Mills published *The Power Elite* in that decade, but his was a lonely voice in a period in which the liberal view of American society became increasingly one that emphasized complexity, ambiguity, the conflict of many interests.

That view in turn distintegrated in the bitterness and violence of the sixties, and the existence of a power elite was again argued forcefully. But, Nuechterlein points out, the old People-Interests model was no longer satisfactory. The People, the mass of workers and farmers, no longer seemed virtuous; organized labor supported an immoral war in Vietnam and beat up peace marchers, farmers had become agricultural businessmen. The Interests had previously always been found among the conservatives, but now it was a liberal Democratic government that refused to grant racial justice and maintained forces in Indochina.

The liberal intellectuals in the new Left thus, he concludes, were forced to redefine the old model. The People now became not the majority, but a minority of virtuous, authentic People, the very poor, the minorities, students, and those liberated members of the middle class who were their advocates. As for the Interests, they were not alone to blame—it was America itself ". . . an inchoate and diffuse evil that had permeated virtually all groups and institutions in American society. The enemy was everywhere and nowhere."[13]

The terms in which Nuechterlein writes of populism almost themselves define the second position on power in the society—"pluralism."

> In strictly analytical terms, the [People-Interests] model has little to recommend it. American observers since at least James Madison have understood that the idea of the People is based on the myth of the monolithic majority, when in fact the majority is simply a term of convenience designating that always shifting and usually unstable combination of interests making up the largest part of the electorate at a given time or on a specific issue. In the real world of democracy, political conflict is always between the Interests and the Interests, and the position of those Interests over against each other rearranges itself from time to time and frequently from issue to issue.[14]

Indeed, in the larger cities, Edward Banfield suggests, the problem is not that there is too much centralization of power, but that there is too little concentration of power to get important things done.[15] There is no doubt, he says, that there exist top leaders in any city who, together, could exert enough influence to run the city; but there is considerable question that they *want* to, or could agree among themselves on what is desirable to do. In his study of five major public conflicts in Chicago during the fifties, he found the most important economic figures in the city conspicuous by their absence.

The explanation, Banfield argues, is fairly clear. There are fundamental conflicts of interest and opinion among the top group, different conceptions of public interest and judgment of the probabilities governing various courses of action. Even if there were no such conflicts, the coordination required in order to maintain concerted action would swamp their organizations; even a single complex organization has difficulty in maintaining adequate communication channels. The Chicago businessmen themselves, Banfield reports, believe that local government should be able to do what they themselves cannot do, and attribute the weaknesses they perceive to defects in organization or defects in character.

Studies by other pluralists, Robert Dahl and Nelson Polsby,[16] support Banfield in finding a plurality of power figures, with influence in only one or two areas of municipal decision-making. But the research is of little help in resolving the conflict between the two positions, for they employ very different techniques. The power elite theorists generally do "reputational" research; they ask a wide variety of people in a community, "Who really has a lot to say about what things are done here?" The names of those who are most frequently mentioned are then assumed to be members of the power elite. Such an approach might produce a group of those with high visibility or status as well as those with actual power, and no way of identifying which is which. Pluralists study the process of decision-making itself, and identify the various actors that are involved in the process. If there is covert manipulation, it might not surface in any observable way.

Curtis and Petras have suggested that, in fact, the research methods employed by community researchers *determine* the results they obtain.[17] If one approaches a power research with a particular theoretical assumption, that assumption dictates a choice of methodology that leads logically to the desired "right" answers, thus confirming the theory. If Curtis and Petras are correct, and their review of community power studies is very persuasive, we are unlikely to resolve the issue of where power lies in American communities until someone comes up with a new research approach.

URBAN POLITICAL DECENTRALIZATION

Fueled to a considerable degree by the surge of neopopulist feeling, and supported by a separate, potent stream of black nationalism described in the section following this one, a very substantial movement is now under way toward the decentralization of public services in American cities. Political scientists point to two different types of decentralization, and the distinction is an important one:

> *Administrative decentralization:* refers to the delegation of authority from a central department to some lower unit within the organization, or to a geographically separated field office; this merely involves the expansion of decision-making power of administrators closer to the action.
> *Political decentralization:* the sharing or surrender of decision-making power by a legitimate authority to persons outside the institution or agency; this may range from the establishment of citizen advisory boards with a few limited powers, to the development of community boards empowered to make policy decisions in a number of areas.

A number of cities are experimenting with the first of these in the form of "little city halls" which duplicate in various regions of the city a number of centralized municipal services; others are splitting the city into a number of "coterminous" service areas, and decentralizing all important public services to them, with locally elected citizens' councils as overseers. An example of the second type, political decentralization, may be found in the local planning boards of some cities, with real power to accept or reject plans for new buildings, public institutions, or highways.

Richard Nathan suggests that the arguments for decentralization particularly of the political type, may be based either on *ideology, social theory,* or *efficiency*. In the first case, people tend to be for or against decentralization depending on which power center they perceive as most likely to promote the ends they seek. So, if one is interested in racial justice and believes that people at the grassroots are more likely to be concerned about achieving it, one might opt for decentraliaztion. If, on the other hand, central government appears to be a better bet, decentralization may appear to be a threat. Many teachers feel more secure with the impersonal rules of a city school bureaucracy than with the possible personality clashes of local control, and they tend to be against decentralization.

The social justifications for decentralization are summarized by Nathan as: (a) concentration of power poses the danger of tyranny; (b) each local area presents somewhat different needs and faces different problems for which standardized solutions are inappropriate; (c) local control permits experimentation with innovative approaches to public problems and trains local leadership; (d) local control reduces alienation by giving everyone a real voice in the decisions that affect his day-to-day life.

The efficiency argument asserts that the closer services are to the people for whom they are intended, the more accountable to their needs they must be and the more responsive to demands they will become.

In spite of the wide popularity in urban circles of the catch-phrases associated with the movement—self-determination, democratization, citizen participation, representativeness—real change in municipal government has been slow in coming, and the many critics of decentralization have been far from silent. The major criticisms may be summarized as:

1. The hopes for increased efficiency as a result of putting service delivery closer to the people appear to be based on nostalgic images of small town life rather than on the urban realities. What is commonly proposed for the large cities are local units containing 150,000 to 300,000 people, hardly very promising for the improvement of local access. Douglas Yates found that even when a government center exists in a small neighborhood only a tiny percentage of local residents will be aware of its existence.[19]

    It is likely, critics claim, that efficiency in fact will decrease with decentralization, and costs will go up. The duplication of effort, with everyone doing his own thing in many units rather than in a few of them, is bound to reduce overall effectiveness, and the development of an entirely new layer of administration will be unquestionably more expensive. Wallace Sayre estimates that to carry out the Little City Hall plan in New York would require 300 local councilmen with staff support at no less than 10 million annually; an executive and managerial staff of about 1000, at an additional 25 to 35 million; and with construction and maintenance costs added, a total of 100 million at least.[20]

2. The idea that smaller political units encourage greater participation and hence are more democratic, say the critics, is a myth which all previous urban experience contradicts. Participation requires a great deal of commitment of time, energy, and other resources, and the incentive for the citizen to spend them must be clear and concrete. Historically, the smaller the constituency the lower has been the level of participation of voters. One reason for this phenomenon is that the flow of information at the neighborhood level is inadequate at best, and usually nonexistent. The mass media provide information only about the issues and leaders on the city or regional level; ". . . the politics of small constituencies is word-of-mouth, rumor, and gossip, misinformation, or half-baked information."[21]

3. Neighborhood politics usually features either tight control by a few, or relatively constant conflict among unreconcilable factions. Not only will decentralization create inevitable battles between the neighborhood and City Hall, therefore, but it will increase conflict at the local level. A large number of community organizations already exist at that level in the large cities, and Daniel Bell and Virginia Held have suggested that the problem may be that there is too much participation—necessary decisions cannot be made with so many groups holding effective veto power—[22] not that there is insufficient participation. There is little evidence to suggest that neighborhood government will be any more effective than larger units in getting the cooperation of these existing organizations, or reconciling the various ethnic factions and vested interests that are at odds in the local communities.

4. Once beyond the relatively simple problems of garbage delivery or housing inspection there are very few issues in the improvement of urban life that do not involve much broader areas of authority at the state, regional, and federal level. As Donald Haider puts it, "The principal feature of the American federal system has been and continues to be the mutual interaction of national, state, and local governments to solve problems that steadily increase in complexity and scope. All levels of government significantly participate in all activities of government."[23]

Although some decentralizers speak of "sharing power," Haider argues that the concept of shared power is extremely subtle and very difficult to implement as the number of people involved increases. Merely giving local groups a consultative role in decisions that affect them is already a major feature of the system as it now exists and one that no one objects to; but the more extreme decentralizers consider it far too modest a goal.

5. Finally, while attention focuses on creating centers of power on lower levels, an opposite trend—toward increasing the centralization of authority for many functions at even higher levels of metropolitan region and the state—continues. The arguments in both school financing and desegregation for metropolitan solutions have been noted earlier, and there are persuasive arguments for transferring many functions from the city to the metropolitan areas as cities face a worsening fiscal situation.

A number of political scientists would agree with Haider, however, that the modest moves thus far taken, largely in administrative decentralization, may have some benefits.

> Such activities will probably not solve general urban problems any more than local governance will. They may, however, have a salutary effect upon pent-up grievances by neighborhood groups, provide an outlet, channel, and target for these demands. After all, greater citizen participation in local governance may have little to do with improving services. Little evidence can be found supporting or refuting this proposition.[24]

BLACK NATIONALISM: "RUBBING RAW THE SORES OF DISCONTENT"

In the century of civil rights struggle since Emancipation, the policy of black groups engaged in that struggle has been dominated by the goal of integration on equal terms with the white majority. But, in counterpoint, there has also been a strain of nationalism, sporadic movements featuring sometimes a return to nationhood in Africa, at other times the establishment of a black nation in the American south. In a period of agitation for local community control the nationalist theme has appropriately adopted as a major aim the control by blacks of their own communities, the ghettos of American cities.

A number of forces converged in the sixties to create and consolidate the black nationalist position on "black power" and black control over their separate communities and their institutions, including the schools. One such force was provided by the "war on poverty" initiated by President Johnson, in which the idea of community action formed a central part. The fascinating story of how the concept was introduced into the legislation that was to implement the war-on-poverty rhetoric is too complex to detail here; the interested reader can pursue it in Marris and Rein's *Dilemmas of Social Reform* and Moynihan's *Maximum Feasible Misunderstanding.*[25]

The new idea of community power developed as a merger of a number of different strains of thought and belief. One of these originated in the community programs of the Ford Foundation, which had discarded its rather traditional approach of the fifties and was now determined to support radical social reform. Men like Paul Ylvâsaker of the foundation reacted to a rising sense of urban crisis with frustration at the slow pace of reform. Pushing against the entrenched and organized power of the establishment, from political parties to labor unions, seemed futile to one filled with a sense of desperation at the plight of the poor and the minorities. That mood was matched among another set of liberal figures, a group of academics and intellectuals who had been brought into government by President Kennedy; many of them still served in high posts under Johnson.

The alternative that emerged seemed a simple one: If the establishment was unresponsive to the needs of those at the bottom of the social scale, then why not redistribute power by giving some decision-making power to the poor and the objects of discrimination. Although the idea was in one sense a radical one, it was at the same time profoundly conservative. It was a rejection of a long, liberal tradition, for it meant taking power away from such allies of the liberal coalition as the labor unions, the Democratic Party (that ran most of the cities), the social work establishment that ran welfare, and the liberal intellectuals that ran the schools. It was also a rejection of the cardinal liberal tenet that centralized power was the best road to reform, that local power (as exemplified particularly in such institutions as the state legislatures) was inevitably conservative. It signaled the end of the love affair between the working class and the liberal intellectual noted earlier in this chapter in the discussion of neopopulism.

Written into the legislation of the War on Poverty, then, were a number of requirements for the "maximum feasible participation" of the poor in the development of policy for, and operations of, community-based programs. As a means of coordinating these programs the Office of Economic Opportunity provided for the establishment of community action agencies in poverty areas.

At the same time a colorful community organizer, a radical populist by the name of Saul Alinsky, contributed a strategy that became nationally popular among ghetto leaders active in developing community programs, a strategy he called "rubbing raw the sores of discontent."[26] The Alinsky model encouraged setting up an umbrella organization, to which all existing neighborhood action groups sent delegates, and training them in stimulating conflict; during the first year of the strategy the groups initiate abrasive confrontations with the "power structure," and follow up with "negotiated agreements" with the targets of the confrontations during the second year.

According to the theorists of the movement, participation in such confrontations would teach the poor to overcome their orientation to the present
and replace their hostility toward the system with cooperative and collabo-
rative attitudes.

The combination of federal support for organizational efforts and the
ideology of confrontation produced a predictable period of bitter conflict
in the larger cities, between local communities and city-wide political
organizations as well as within the communities themselves. Some observers
regarded the entire movement as an elaborate put-on by ghetto leaders to
frighten liberal bureaucrats into giving them grants; Tom Wolfe's description, in his *Mau-Mauing the Flak Catchers,* of the tactics of the San Francisco community action program leaders is biting:

> There was one genius in the art of confrontation who had mau-mauing down
> to what you could term a laboratory science. He had it figured out so he didn't
> even have to bring his boys downtown in person. He would just show up with
> a crocus sack full of revolvers, ice picks, fish knives, switchblades, hatchets,
> blackjacks, gravity knives, straight razors, hand grenades, blow guns, bazookas,
> Molotov cocktails, tank rippers, unbelievable stuff, and he'd dump it all out on
> somebody's shiny walnut conference table. He'd say "These are some of the
> things I took off my boys last night . . . I don't know, man . . . Thirty minutes
> ago I talked a Panther out of busting up a cop . . ." And they would lay money
> on this man's ghetto youth patrol like it was now or never.[27]

There has been considerable criticism, too, of the raising of expectations
beyond any possible satisfaction by the real programs available. Aaron
Wildavsky puts it:

> A recipe for violence: Promise a lot; deliver a little. Lead people to believe
> they will be much better off, but let there be no dramatic improvement. Try a
> variety of small programs, each interesting but marginal in impact and
> severely underfinanced. Avoid any attempted solution remotely comparable in
> size to the dimensions of the problem you are trying to solve. Have middle-
> class civil servants hire upper-class student radicals to use lower-class Negroes as
> a battering ram against the local political systems; then complain that people
> are going around disrupting things and chastise local politicians for not coop-
> erating with those out to do them in. Get some poor people involved in local
> decision-making only to discover that there is not enough at stake to be worth
> bothering about. Feel guilty about what has happened to black people; tell
> them you are surprised they have not revolted before; express shock and dismay
> when they follow your advice. Go in for a little force, not enough to discourage.
> Feel guilty again; say you are surprised that worse has not happened. Alternate
> with a little suppression. Mix well, apply a match, and run. . . .[28]

But, to those who urged more "pluralist participation," as Jon and Sally
van Til call it, the major lesson of the War on Poverty was that real citizen

participation was frustrated by the elites in the cities, who did not trust the poor to make decisions in the public interest. The van Tils concluded:

> The cycle of citizen participation, we believe, must be moved off its direction toward stalemate by the development of a fully democratic urban pluralism. We do not think it necessary to conclude, as have some social scientists, that democracy does not work among the poor because it is inefficient and raises conflicts. Rather, we believe that the experience with citizen participation in recent social policy demonstrates the critical importance of the development of new institutional forms that will represent the interests of the poor and will build those interests into the larger political and social structure such that these purposes can be achieved.[29]

Even so severe a critic as Moynihan accepted the reality of the issue. "It remains to be seen whether it can do what is promised for it, just as we may discover to our sorrow that 'participatory democracy' can mean the end of both participation and democracy. But the spirit of the times will not be stayed: These are the issues of this moment."[30] And, although recent evidence suggests that the stereotype of the deep alienation of the ghetto resident does not conform to reality,[31] the fact is that the modern, liberal forms of urban political life do not well accommodate themselves to contemporary minority groups.[32] The disappearance of the old local ward organization, which linked the poor to the larger political and social structures, left a vacuum that must be filled.

Into the vacuum, as a result of the struggles over community action programs in the late sixties and early seventies, the black nationalists moved. J. Kenneth Benson points out that not only did these conflicts have a considerable effect in pressing black groups to think through more coherent formulations of black problems, but they clarified the differences between moderate civil rights organizations and the militant black power groups.

> Militant leaders could point to the moderates' position on the Community Action Programs as evidence for their contention that the established organizations were oriented to the concerns of middle-class Negroes and to the maintenance of their dominance over other Negroes and of their privileged relationship to the white majority . . . The proponents of the positions were locked in battle for control of a concrete set of stakes—programs, jobs, bases of power, and influence.[33]

By the midseventies these ideological differences were firmly jelled. In a singularly well-balanced article for a national audience, Charles Hamilton, one of the most prominent black nationalist theorists, pointed out that the basic difference in approach between the integrationists and the nationalists is that the former take an essentially moral position.[34] To oppose integration is basically immoral and unethical; to support it puts people "on the side of justice, goodness, and God."[35] Moralizing the race issue, argues

Hamilton, means "that blacks were viewed as unfortunate victims, persons to be pitied and helped . . . almost perpetually dependent on the good will of others."[36] From the nationalist perspective, then, the integration movement is a "pleading-beggar" movement.

The nationalist program, on the other hand, "if they were able to work their will and have their way," would range from starting a new African Republic carved out of the South, to flying the black nationalist flag over every black school. All institutions in black communities would be controlled by blacks, so that "no final decisions affecting their operations would be taken by any but black people acting in an official capacity,"[37] and they would be staffed with blacks. Electoral representation would be based on the proportion of the blacks in the population; there should be a minimum of sixty-six black Representatives and fifteen Senators in Congress, and similar proportions for state and local legislatures. Federally funded authorities must be established, under black control, aimed at developing industry for rural areas in the Black Belt, and at the creation and development of new models for black education at all levels.

The reaction of black moderates to this agenda, and to the tactics of confrontation that accompany it, has been summarized by Bayard Rustin, who has accused the nationalists of fragmenting the civil rights movement into "a powerful legacy of polarization, division, and political nonsense."[38] Many white intellectuals, such as Allan Ornstein, agree:

> What can the blacks gain by resorting to a black nationalist strategy? At best, they can and will gain control of their community, even the large and medium-sized cities of the nation. This they can do, however, without resorting to anti-white slogans, terror tactics, violence, and the rejection of compromise, tolerance, and individualism. The population trends keenly illustrate their growing strength; they need not polarize the county and risk white reaction, which is often oversimplified as racism.[39]

But white liberal neopopulists have given the movement enthusiastic support. Jason Epstein typically argued:

> It was not after all Malcolm X's plan to destroy the American middle class but to build a black version of it from the proceeds of black dry cleaning stores and service stations. The flaw in Malcolm's vision was its modesty. (And, by implication, the vision of most blackpower advocates.) The necessary goals of Black Power are the fundamental institutions of the city itself. If these goals are not met, it is impossible to see how the schools can transmit their language and their culture to tens of thousands of ghetto children and then what would be left of the city.[40]

Whatever the final impact of black nationalism on the urban communities that represent its targets, there is little question of its crucial influence on the battles over community control of the schools, to which we now turn.

URBAN SCHOOL DECENTRALIZATION: THE PEOPLE VERSUS THE BUREAUCRACY

In the second half of the decade of the sixties all of these background movements converged on the issue of school control in several of the country's largest cities. There already existed a tradition of local control in education; parents were more highly motivated to participate than citizens in general because of their personal stake in the school's performance; and the centralized school bureaucracies in the large cities were obviously failing to bring lower class minority children's performance up to mainstream norms.

For a number of historical reasons (to be detailed later) urban schools were at the time controlled by large-scale organizations staffed by educational professionals who were largely immune from political control, and much of the early attack on these systems under the banner of local community control was made in terms of "anti-bureaucracy" slogans, a championing of decentralization versus centralization. But these terms mistake the nature of bureaucracy and there was thus introduced a considerable amount of confusion that has persisted throughout the battles over the schools.

ORGANIZATION AND BUREAUCRACY

All organizations consist of patterned efforts to get something done, to fulfill some necessary social purpose by coordinating the actions of a number of individuals. All must cope with the problem of ensuring that the behavior of each individual is predictable, that when a doctor in the middle of an operation holds out his hand for a necessary instrument, a nurse will have it ready. In primitive types of organization, a small town volunteer fire brigade, for instance, coordination and predictability can be maintained informally, by ties of mutual loyalty and trust. But as organizations increase in size, and the complexity of the task grows, an authority structure is developed to enforce rules and coordinate effort, and systems are instituted to keep track of the rules, to socialize the members into the expectations held for them, and administer rewards and punishments. At this point, efforts to ensure predictability come in conflict with individual needs for spontaneity, self-determination, and the sense of personal accomplishment. Organizations can be viewed as a ceaseless conflict between these forces, which can never be entirely reconciled, between the organization's need for predictability and the individual's need for self-determination.[41]

In his brilliant analysis of complex organization, Max Weber argued that modern bureaucracies, unlike those that control behavior by invoking the traditional power of the leader, are "rational," in achieving predictability by developing principles connected to the task the organization must accomplish. These principles, which govern the behavior of the individual members of the bureaucracy, include:[42]

Specialization
Tasks are divided into a series of specific duties assigned to persons most competent to perform them, and are clearly defined to prevent overlap and confusion. In the long run this principle ensures the greatest possible efficiency, though critics point out that it also leads to isolation of specialized parts of the system and conflict among units protecting their own turf.

Hierarchy
The principle that each office should be under the control and supervision of a higher one is intended to achieve accountability; each official receives his orders from a superior level, and is responsible for carrying them out. An opportunity, say the critics, for endless buck-passing, making it difficult to pin responsibility for action at any particular level.

Rules
The behavior of all personnel is standardized by abstract rules which individuals must apply to particular cases. This principle applies equally to guide the behavior of the lowly file clerk in deciding where to put a particular piece of paper, and the Supreme Court justice applying the Constitution to a specific case. It is a principle that protects the individual official from pressures of all sorts, infuriates those for whom a specific rule is disadvantageous, and accounts for many of the accusations that bureaucracy is rigid.

Impersonality
"The ideal official," said Weber, "conducts his office in a spirit of formalistic impersonality without hatred and passion and hence without affection or enthusiasm."[43] In a rational public organization such a principle asserts that partiality to one person or group is not in the public good, and impartiality demands impersonality, coolness. If we permit affection, we open the gates to hatred and prejudice. The principle leads critics to see bureaucracy as cold and insensitive, as indeed it is.

Personnel Protection
Because such an organization asserts such a high degree of specialization and control over its personnel, Weber reasoned, it must offer them something in return, in order to prevent too great a turnover. The major reward the bureaucracy has fashioned is security; people are protected from arbitrary dismissal, and can depend on promotion through a combination of seniority and merit. Promotion by examination further depersonalizes the system and protects its efficiency by guarding against the nonrational influence of personal bias in selection and promotion. In so doing, say the critics, it also guarantees mediocrity by rewarding the routine drudge who is interested in security and is able to work his way slowly to the top simply by staying in the system.

There is nothing in this model that assumes the necessity of centralization; Weber specified a hierarchial structure but at no point did he suggest that it must be centralized. Although lower offices are responsible to higher ones, the higher authority is not allowed simply to take over the business of his subordinates; indeed, bureaucratic rules not only give legitimacy to the power of the higher authority, but limit the extent of that authority.[44] The point that many critics of bureaucracy consistently miss is that decentralization ensures *greater* control over local activities because it puts someone with real authority in a position to monitor daily operations.

Nor is large-scale bureaucracy necessarily an enemy of innovation, as the advocates of local community control of the schools have charged. It can, and usually does, specialize the innovative role by creating departments charged with paying attention to new developments; it is thereby able to identify and experiment with new ideas much more quickly than small, local unit organizations.

THE CASE FOR COMMUNITY CONTROL

What the advocates of community control really objected to in the school bureaucracy was its standardization and its requirement to be even-handed. The new wave of ethnic consciousness, strengthened by black nationalist doctrines, demanded the expression of diversity and the assertion of differences among local needs. In the school system standardization is inevitably linked to professionalism, because rules are supposed to be based on professional judgment of the best thing to do; community control inevitably, then, assumed an antiprofessional cast.

The fundamental impulse that animated the movement is one that threads through earlier chapters; in a book called *The One Best System*, a critique of American education's attempt to find such a system and thus insulate the school from the "irrelevance" of ethnic differences, David Tyack speaks for all the liberal intellectuals who have supported the move for local control of the schools.[45] The book, and the movement, is infused with a nostalgia for "the tribal school," the one-room schoolhouse of an earlier America, destroyed by consolidation and standardization. Educators have reacted to problems of immigrants and blacks, Tyack laments, not by attacking the racism of the society but by attempting to adjust children to white middle-class norms. In the name of efficiency, the urban schools have inculcated youth with the norms of bureaucracy: punctuality, thrift, industriousness, and obedience to authority.

The black nationalist wing of the movement paid little attention to such historical exercises; local control of the schools is for them merely one aspect of a broader ideological program. Stokely Carmichael and Charles Hamilton summed up their position by demanding that

. . . control of the ghetto schools must be taken out of the hands of professionals, most of whom have long since demonstrated their insensitivity to the needs and problems of the black child. These experts bring with them middle-class biases, unsuitable techniques and materials. These are at best dysfunctional and at worst destructive.[46]

The specific aims of the movement were projected onto the national scene in a number of books and articles by Mario Fantini, a Ford Foundation official, and Marilyn Gittel, a political scientist at City University of New York, whose Institute for Community Studies was supported by the Foundation.[47] Community control of the schools, they and others argued, would provide the following benefits:

1. There will be a rise in student academic achievement. In part, it is claimed, this will result from the adoption of relevant curriculum and a staff with which children can identify; the better motivation thus created will influence learning positively.[48] Most advocates further believe that community control will have a substantial effect on the children of the slums by influencing two processes that, they argue, account for his poor school performance. One is teacher expectancy; nothing in the present system can change the expectations of white professionals, but the community and parents might succeed in setting up a different climate, and they have an interest in doing so. The second is socialization; the family is now unconnected with the school, and the child must often, indeed, make a choice between the two cultures represented in them. "When parents, students, and professionals join together in the common pursuit of reform, the process itself serves to cement new relationships among them. Too, each has a stake in what has developed jointly".[49]
2. With the opportunity to participate meaningfully in the work of the schools, parents in lower class and ethnic neighborhoods will become involved in school matters and thus give a genuinely "grassroots" character to educational decisions.
3. Opening the planning process to parents and other community members will produce significant innovation in curriculum and program. The role of parent organizations will expand to include substantive matters related to the educational process; this participation, says Fantini, will lead to "an emphasis on both *cognitive* and *affective* (feeling) development . . . Humanistically oriented objectives, e.g., identity, connectedness, powerlessness."[50]

The decade of the seventies witnessed a number of battles over local control of urban schools, in New York, Detroit, Washington, Los Angeles, and Philadelphia. In most cases, as David O'Shea has pointed out, events followed a basic pattern: sizable increase in the number of children of some ethnic minority in the city's schools; debate over the gap between their academic achievement and that of mainstream children; demands for desegregation as a remedy, and an unsatisfactory response to those demands; a shift to demands for local control from a coalition of minority leaders and influential white liberals or conservatives; the adoption of some kind of decentralization plan.[51]

The fascinatingly varied events in these cities are described below. The accounts begin with New York and Detroit because the movement there came closer to achieving the goal of local policy control than in other cities; in the case of New York the historical background to the contemporary decentralization movement is also available and provides added perspective.

NEW YORK: THE COMMUNITY VERSUS THE UNION

The strident conflict in the nation's largest city during the second half of the sixties repeated in many respects a battle over local school control that had taken place 125 years earlier. Diane Ravitch, in a notable work of history, has provided us with the details of what she calls the Great School Wars of the city;[52] two of these earlier wars were fought over local control.

Irish Catholics: 1840

At the turn of the nineteenth century, New York State began to encourage support for common schools through a system of grants to towns that set them up. In New York City the money was not used to create public schools but instead was turned over to a number of existing church schools. In the earlier years of the century a group of upper-class philanthropists formed The Free School Society for the purpose of establishing a nonsectarian school for poor children, the first of many that were soon to be set up throughout the growing city. By historical accident, then, the early New York City school system was run by the Board of Trustees of a private society, though increasingly funded by public monies.

The Society adopted the Lancastrian monitorial system, in which one teacher could handle as many as 1000 pupils (see Chapter 11), and by all accounts ran an extremely effective school system under the paternalistic eyes of the Trustees, who visited and observed the schools constantly. By 1840, the schools of what was by then called The Public School Society, were widely regarded as the best in the country and had 20,000 pupils enrolled; "The system," Ravitch reports, "was a model of order and efficiency, embodying the virtues of good habits, cleanliness, thrift, and industry."[53]

But, by 1840, the city's population had dramatically changed. Not only had it almost doubled in several decades (from 120,000 in 1820 to 300,000 in 1840), but the proportion of aliens had increased sharply to about a third of the citizens; the largest group of the new immigrants were Irish. Socially

looked-down-upon by the hostile Protestants surrounding them, economically impoverished and penned in filthy slums, politically manipulated
by Tammany Hall, the local Democratic Party organization, the Irish had
little to solace them but their church. The clergy of that church, intent
upon protecting their flock from assimilation, discouraged their people from
using the schools of the Public School Society. The Society, for its part,
encouraged Irish Catholic enrollment in what it regarded as a truly public
school system open to all, but failed to recognize that the "nonsectarian"
nature of its schools was "sectless Protestantism."

The battle came to a head in 1840 as the numbers of Irish in the city,
and their conspicuous absence from the public schools, made the situation
untenable. When John Hughes, militant and aggressive, and himself an
Irish immigrant, became bishop of the New York diocese, the war against
the centralized control by the Society and for local Irish Catholic control
of their own public schools began.

Hughes' major ally in the struggle to obtain public funds for Catholic-run
schools was William Seward, then governor of the state, later to be Lincoln's
secretary of state. At the beginning of 1840, Seward proposed to the state
legislature the "establishment of schools in which they (the children of
foreigners) may be instructed by teachers speaking the same language with
themselves and professing the same faith."[54] The city's Catholic leaders
promptly petitioned for state subsidy for their church schools, and the fight
was on.

Hoping to placate the Catholics, the Public School Society began purging
its textbooks of religious references, and attempted to negotiate some form
of compromise. Hughes, who hated the idea of common schools and saw
his mission as one of saving followers' faith by maintaining separatism,
rejected compromise and fought militantly for public funding of the church
schools. When, in 1841, the issue finally reached the state legislature, it
became transformed; as presented to the legislators, the religious question
was dropped, and the broader educational question presented: Should the
school be whatever the community around it wanted it to be? On that
question the election of 1841 was fought, in a round of angry editorials
from all sides, impassioned denunciations of the Trustees of the Society,
street fights between nativists and Catholics, and the stoning of the Bishop's
palace by angry mobs.

In the midst of all the excitement and political power plays, the legislature
passed a version of the original bill that had been submitted. It promised no
public funds for Catholic schools, but it did set up a municipally run public
school system in the city, under the control of local ward boards. "The
Catholics did not win, but the Public School Society lost."[55]

The Progressives: 1896
The schools established by the Society were gradually absorbed over the
years by the ward schools authorized under the new legislation. In the half

century from 1840 to 1890 the educational scene in the city mainly featured jealous battles between the weak central board and the local ward boards over issues of authority. During one brief period, Boss Tweed and his Tammany cohorts succeeded in taking over the schools, along with most other governmental machinery, but when the Tweed ring was broken, control over the schools returned to the wards. The ward schools struggled along, under the pressure of recurrent economy drives, little less rigid than the Society's schools had been and a good deal less efficient, very much a part of local ward politics and patronage systems.

The second war was, again, initiated by a great movement of people into the city, this time the flood of immigrants, primarily Italians and Jews, from southern and eastern Europe. Their miserable conditions in the slums of the city gave rise to a powerful reform movement made up largely of socially conscious upper-class individuals, and upper-middle professionals in education and journalism, and in the emerging profession of social work. The reformers were convinced that education was the key to the improvement of the life of the immigrants; they were also impressed by the wave of new ideas in education, a ferment that proceeded from the proposals of Pestalozzi, Froebel, and Herbart, augmented by the work of such American psychologists as G. Stanley Hall and William James.

A number of educational reforms were proposed during the 1880s and pressure from the reformers on the city's central Board of Education mounted. Nicholas Murray Butler, then a young professor at Columbia University (later its fabled president), led the attack on the overcrowding in the ward schools, the lack of places for many children, the disconnectedness of the curriculum, the emphasis on memory work, the lack of training for teachers, and the ineptitude of local administration. Going beyond these flaws, Butler attacked the ward system itself and the division of power that resulted in lack of responsibility. His battlecry was *professionalism*: Educational decisions should be left to professional educators.

A long, three-cornered battle developed among the central Board (which had little power to reform the system by itself, but wanted to), the local ward trustees (with a good deal of power, but bound to tradition), and the reform movement. The teachers, whose jobs were vulnerable to local influence, and who were threatened by the cries of "professionalization," generally sided with the ward trustees.

The state of the schools was appropriated as an anti-Tammany issue by the "good government" forces in the 1890s, and again the issue of school control became a major political one. As Ravitch puts it:

> To the reformers, the issues were clearly drawn. On one side stood Tammany, local control, the ward trustee system, corruption, favoritism, nepotism, inefficiency, patronage, and backward schools. On the other were the reformers, centralized control, professional supervision, businesslike administration, scientific pedagogy, honesty, efficiency, and modern schools. The reformers saw themselves

as the guardians of progress, while their critics saw them as intolerant, self-righteous, and arrogant.[56]

In the elections of 1894 the reform movement swept to victory in state and national elections, a success of such magnitude that the reformers could scarcely believe it themselves. A school reform bill in the state legislature nevertheless failed during the following year; the reformers were split, and the ward trustees and teachers rallied in resistance to "outside interference in the schools," and managed to defeat it. But the drumbeat of Butler's attacks on the ward schools and the reformers' almost complete support by the daily newspapers proved irresistible, and during the following year the mayor signed a school reform bill that effectively centralized authority over the schools in a central Board with a staff of upper-echelon professional educators.

Community Control: 1969

At the turn of the century, and in response to similar political forces, the schools of the larger cities generally became centralized. In New York the Board of Education rapidly expanded into a very substantial professional bureaucracy, with standardization of procedures and curriculum at a high level of competency. The gradual decline in immigration and subsequent severe restrictions on the flow gave the system an unprecedented stability during the twenties and thirties. At last there were enough seats for all children and no massive group of "different" children to socialize. The city became a model for the nation, the center for admiring visits by educators from other cities and abroad.

The calm was disrupted by still another major migration, this time from the south and from Puerto Rico. Again there was the overcrowding of slum schools, the concern for poverty among the new groups, and the difficulty of coping with different cultures. A relatively new element appeared, toward the end of the 1950s. The difference between the children of the new groups and mainstream children in achievement levels was more or less taken for granted in the earlier periods; now it was expected that all children should do equally well in school, and if they did not the school was responsible. Kenneth Clark and other black intellectuals began to argue, in the late fifties, that if ghetto schools had the same resources as those in middle-class areas, and were staffed by teachers who really believed that black children *could* learn, the achievement gap would vanish.

The first period of this most recent war, then, began not as a struggle over control but over integration; if all schools had whites as well as blacks in them, black leaders perceived, the system would have the incentive to equalize resources. The Board's response to the rising demands for integration was to put into effect a voluntary open enrollment policy, which failed miserably; only a few thousand parents responded to the opportunity to send their children to underutilized middle-class schools. Mandatory busing or some other equally effective integration technique was clearly the only answer.

At the height of the national civil rights agitation in 1963, the city's integration activists launched a drive to force the Board of Education to set up a definite timetable for integrating the schools. Demonstrations were almost a daily occurrence, and several new militant organizations threatened to conduct a boycott of the schools if integration demands were not met. The superintendent and the Board resisted, not only because of enormous public opposition to forced integration, but because, practically speaking, there were not enough white pupils in the schools to go around. For several years the struggle went on; militant groups went through with their threat to boycott the schools several times, the Board proposed a number of integration plans that fizzled, the militants retaliated with attention-getting demonstrations that included taking over the Board of Education meeting room for a time.

As public tempers grew shorter, the black leadership split into militants and moderates; white liberals, who had originally supported integration, dissolved into their own factions. In 1966 the whole character of the battle shifted, and a new phase began. Some black militants concluded that integrating the schools was a hopeless goal and, in the context of the rapidly rising black nationalist consciousness, even an undesirable one. The focus of conflict dramatically changed from integration to a demand for neighborhood control of ghetto schools, with black staffs and administrators, and a curriculum infused with black culture; the boycott weapon was now put to work for a new set of goals.

There turned out to be rather more support for these new ones. White conservative opposition to, and white liberal ambivalence about forced integration was diminished; the city government had been considering some measure of decentralization, anyway, because more districts meant more state funds; and the Ford Foundation, committed to prevailing neopopulist ideas, offered to support a community control experiment in three districts in the city: Ocean Hill-Brownsville in Brooklyn, I.S. 201 in Harlem, and the Two-Bridges area in lower Manhattan.

Events in the demonstration districts very quickly identified the new focus of conflict, and the combatants. Unlike the teachers in the 1890s, the New York teachers of the sixties were thoroughly professionalized, and were organized into a strong union that had fought long and hard for a substantial degree of job security and for an accommodation with central Board authorities. A series of confrontations between the union and the local boards and administrators of the demonstration districts now ensued, the most dramatic of them in Ocean Hill-Brownsville, whose superintendent, Rhody McCoy, was a black nationalist extremist. McCoy's arbitrary transfer of a number of teachers in the Ocean Hill schools brought on two city-wide teacher strikes, one of them of extraordinary length and bitterness; because the city's teachers were mainly Jewish, the struggle resulted in a dangerous polarization of the city along both ethnic and religious lines.

It was in the context of this crisis, that seemed at times to threaten to tear the city apart, that a political compromise on a form of decentralization was finally pushed through the state legislature. Instead of the sixty districts demanded by the militants, thirty were set up; instead of complete power over all policy-making, and local boards given the authority to hire and fire their own superintendent, limited control over curriculum and some considerable flexibility in allocating their district's share of school funds were given. But control of teaching staff remained essentially with the central Board and the provisions of the union contract.

As in the 1840s, the community control forces did not win (though they gained considerably more than did the Catholics then), but the educational establishment lost. The parallels are striking in many other respects; the ethnic and religious conflicts, the charismatic and flamboyant leadership, dramatic confrontations and passionate rhetoric, the alliance between the more radical of the white liberals and the lower class ethnic leadership, and the basic issue itself: Who should control the child's education, those close to him, or the efficient professional?

DETROIT—COMMUNITY CONTROL VERSUS INTEGRATION

In 1964, a number of liberal groups in Detroit, including the powerful auto union, took control of the Detroit board of education. Committed to integration and aided by the new superintendent of schools they hired, the board in succeeding years changed school boundaries to achieve a better racial mix, increased sharply the proportions of black teachers and administrators in the schools, and adopted new minority-fair texts.

Despite all the board's efforts, however, three-quarters of the black pupils at the end of the decade were in schools that were more than 90 percent black. Some black leaders, such as Reverend Cleague, a charismatic minister, had begun turning away from integration as early as 1963; he had formed an inner city parents council, and in 1967 presented the first demands for local control of schools in the black areas of Detroit. A year later, a black Democratic member of the state legislature introduced a bill to set up sixteen autonomous school districts in Detroit; no one but Cleague supported it, and it died on the vine.

But support for the idea of decentralization grew, though not for the extreme form of community control espoused by Cleague, who declared, "The principal should have the power to hire and fire the teachers, the community the power to hire and fire the principal."[57] The NAACP announced support for "community centered schools"; and in the summer of 1969, the legislature passed a bill setting up regions within the city, with their own elected boards. The Detroit board had vacillated over whether to support it, and had had a clause inserted that made community board action subject to guidelines of the central board; and the Detroit Federation of Teachers had succeeded in adding language that protected teachers' rights.

The crucial issue now became how to draw the district lines. Blacks argued for lines that respected a sense of community and that would guarantee black control of their schools. Although 65 percent of Detroit students were black, only 44 percent of the electorate was; if regions were integrated, the schools would have black majorities but black voter minorities.

Zwerdling, the board president, wanted integrated districts, but could not command a majority. The swing vote on the board was Andrew Perdue, a black attorney who had been elected to the board with Cleague's support. If the board was serious about integration, he insisted, they would have to change the schools' feeder patterns; otherwise, they should draw lines that would give blacks power in their districts, and whites power in theirs. In order to persuade him, Zwerdling had the school administration draw up a secret plan redrawing the high school boundaries; this affected the racial composition of half of the city's schools, and required the busing of about 4,500 white students to predominantly black schools.

At a secret dinner meeting, according to Grant, the plan was discussed by the board, and won Perdue's assent. But an opposing member on the board leaked the plan to the press, and it was published a day later. The reaction was swift and devastating. Some parents kept their children home from school; a Citizens Committee for Better Education was immediately formed; and a public meeting of the board a few days later was held amid great turmoil. The board nevertheless passed the new plan for district lines, and the newly formed Citizens Committee held a rally to begin a recall campaign against the four members of the board that voted for it. In Lansing, the state capital, the legislature rushed through a bill requiring a referendum on decentralization plans, and requiring school boards to send every student to the school nearest his home. The uproar was statewide.

For the supporters of decentralization, including State Senator Young, the situation was desperate. Young, a black Detroiter, was furious at the Detroit board for accepting what he called "this chicken-shit integration plan."[58] He decided that his best tactic was to pass a new law authorizing decentralization but outlawing the integration plan, arguing, to his fellow black legislators, they they could vote for it in conscience because the anti-integration clause would not hold up in court. In order to get the bill passed, a compromise was worked out: The bill would require decentralization with boundary issues unresolved; if they could not be resolved shortly by local authorities, the governor was to appoint a three-member commission to set the district boundaries. Meanwhile, in Detroit, the recall campaign got under way and collected 130,000 signatures. At the subsequent recall vote, the four members of the board were recalled by a 60 percent majority.

The governor's commission got to work, agreed not to make integration a condition for boundary-line placing, and set up four white-controlled and four black-controlled regions for the city. The elections turned out a clear victory for the conservatives. The new thirteen-member central board included six anti-integration conservatives and only three blacks—the smallest proportion in years. Blacks won a voting majority on only two of eight regional boards. The superintendent of schools, Drachler, who had been selected for his vigorously prointegrationist position by the previous board, now resigned.

On the basis of his account, from which this description of events was summarized, Grant concludes that the results of the pressure for decentralization turned out to be wholly negative: there was severe polarization and backlash; a conservative board was elected; and those who had pressed for decentralization were the losers, ending up with less influence and power than they had before. In the fight against integration, whites who had opposed decentralization for years embraced community control as they realized that segregated regions would protect them.

WASHINGTON, D.C.: BLACKS AGAINST THE BLACKS

The idea of local control began in Washington at about the same time it was fought out in New York; in 1967 the Adams-Morgan district contracted with Antioch College to administer its two elementary schools under a locally elected school board. The experiment failed, for a number of reasons, although in its early stages the hopes of many community control advocates rode on it and they filled the education journals with articles extolling its success. Community groups could not agree on a desirable curriculum for black children, Antioch never staffed it as completely as it had promised, and finally withdrew altogether.

When it became clear that the arrangement with Antioch was unsatisfactory, the Morgan School community board successfully pressed the D.C. Board of Education to permit it to retain community control. The Morgan board went through a long period of bitter factional fighting, and the school has since been run as a "tight oligarchy" composed of the board and the school principal.[59]

The largest experiment with school decentralization in the city was the Anacostia school project. The Anacostia area represents something of a "natural" community, cut off from the rest of the city by a river; although it is a poverty area, it contained some middle-class black families who had not abandoned the public schools. To these advantages over the Morgan school, it added to its community control effort a significant interest of the federal government. President Johnson, who believed that Washington should represent a model for his attack on the urban crisis, proposed to make Anacostia a demonstration of what local participation could do to solve the ills of urban areas. The actual site for the "major model school experiment" was chosen by Office of Education officials, with the consultation of Mario Fantini of the Ford Foundation, who must surely have been the busiest education expert in the country during this period of burgeoning demands for school decentralization.

In their review of the project's history, George LaNoue and Bruce Smith note that it "offers a sobering glimpse of the difficulties involved in a federally created and managed project at the neighborhood level."[60] Johnson requested ten million dollars a year for his demonstration; Congress appropriated one million. There were frequent changes in federal officials responsible for the project, communications between the federal government, the Board of Education and the project management were bad, shifts in policy were frequent, particularly when the Nixon administration came on in 1969, elected local boards atrophied, and parental participation was so minimal as to be nonexistent.

In 1971, basing its decision on an outside evaluation, the Office of Education terminated the project; the decision, say LaNoue and Smith, was in many ways like its original one to launch it: ". . . sudden, based on unrealistic expectations, inadequately planned, stimulated by currently fashionable bureaucratic ideologies, and lacking in thorough knowledge of local conditions." Yet, they conclude, "the case that could be made for the project's continuance was weak," and the decision would be difficult to challenge.[61]

Hugh Scott, a black educator who became Washington's superintendent of schools in 1969, made clear his own opposition to community control as soon as he took over the office; "the worst thing that could happen to the city's school system" he said.[62] Scott instead advocated administrative decentralization with advisory local groups, and made some moves in that direction, but by 1973 had left a system that remains largely centralized.

LOS ANGELES: LIBERALS AND CONSERVATIVES TOGETHER

The Los Angeles school system is the second largest in the country; more significantly, it is spread over a vast geographic area encompassing sixty-nine identifiable communities. As LaNoue and Smith point out, pressures toward decentralization in such a setting are likely to be endemic under any circumstances; the unique feature of the system is that it is so diverse and sprawling that in order to develop a coherent decentralization plan one would have to centralize it first.

Throughout the sixties the city also spawned a very considerable number of citizen action groups interested in the schools; unlike New York, where such groups tended toward a coalition politics that permitted officials to identify and negotiate with important forces, Los Angeles group activity exhibited both confusion and disorder. Some of the black groups, such as Rod Karenga's Black Congress, acted for a time as a "watchdog" over the schools, seeking the removal of principals they considered incompetent, and were responsible for near chaos in some schools.

In response to these varied pressures, the central Board took a number of steps: It set up an Office of Urban Affairs to act as a cushion between community group demands and school professionals; created advisory boards to assist in allocating Title I funds; and appointed four separate minority group Commissions with access to the Superintendent and the Board. None of these, LaNoue and Smith conclude, worked as well as their proponents hoped nor as disastrously as their opponents feared, and in the peculiarly volatile atmosphere of the city they probably succeeded in keeping the situation cooler than it might have been.

In the early sixties several studies of the system emerged with recommendations for administrative decentralization, retaining a strong central Board and professional bureaucracy. The first major move was taken in 1968, when the Superintendent announced a pilot project, ultimately involving all the schools in the system, in which local planning councils for each school were to participate in revising curricula to make them appropriate to the particular school.

> It is a measure of the considerable *de facto* decentralization in the system that it was never possible to determine whether these directives had been implemented. Despite elaborate guidelines generated at downtown headquarters, there were neither adequate information systems nor staff resources to determine whether the schools complied fully with the directives. Community activists, dissatisfied with their school principals, usually sought the help of allies at central headquarters and even the school board put pressure on the local level. In this respect, decentralization required the intervention of central authority on a broader scale than before. This intervention, at least at first, encouraged a "crisis style" of decision-making. The central Board and the Superintendent's office would take little notice unless a matter had reached the crisis stage, and thus the parties to a dispute at the local school level had incentives to escalate every issue.[63]

Pressures for a more dramatic political decentralization continued, and the system considered a number of plans in 1969 to 1970. One major difficulty was that the voters turned down a school bond issue, indicating an incipient taxpayers' revolt, and any decentralization plan would require additional resources. In the midst of this irresolution at the local level, the state legislature took a hand in the issue. Two bills were introduced separately by black assemblymen from the Watts district (the scene of rioting that won nationwide attention in the late sixties). One bill, introduced by

William Greene, was modeled on the New York experimental districts, not only granting local control to the communities but giving the local boards power to contract with outside firms to run the schools if they were dissatisfied with the system. The second, Leon Ralph's, designated any school in ghetto areas that fell below established performance levels as a "self-determination" school; these would be run under the authority of local governing boards, and operated by a nonprofit educational corporation. Any parent in the district who wished to send his child to his nearest self-determination school could withdraw him from the public school and use a voucher system.

The school professionals were unenthusiastic about both bills, but indicated that they could live with the Ralph bill, except for the voucher provisions. A battle rapidly developed, however, between Ralph and Greene; the Greene forces considered Ralph self-serving and his proposal as leading away from community control. An interesting alliance formed between Greene and a conservative Republican, Senator John Harmer, whose interest in local autonomy and fiscal conservatism led him to embrace decentralization as a cause. The two bills neutralized each other, however, and neither was passed in 1969.

The following year saw a prolonged legislative battle over a bill embodying the essentials of the Greene plan. The opposition was led by the Los Angeles school system, from the Board down, but also included a number of civil rights groups who were concerned about the effect of the proposal on integration, as well as the school unions. But a coalition of liberal Democrats and conservative Republicans managed to get the bill passed. Los Angeles would now have the most extensive political decentralization plan in the country, had not Governor Reagan vetoed the bill.

School officials were now convinced that there was serious disaffection with the schools, however, and determined to do something about it. "The plan evolved," say LaNoue and Smith, "was a characteristic Los Angeles invention: A massive campaign would be launched to elicit staff, community, and group sentiment on desirable next steps in decentralization."[64] A giant referendum was planned; public hearings, a questionnaire survey of school personnel, a saturation radio and television campaign, and the distribution of 700,000 copies of an elaborate questionnaire containing a jumble of alternative decentralization ideas. Very little of this mass of information proved usable, and the Board finally voted to retain its own structure, but to offer a "local option" to each school, whose parents, staff, and community could decide what form of community advisory committee they wished to form.

Most of the Anglo majority in the city now considered that they had as much decentralization as they wanted; the issue persists in the minority areas. "The stubborn issue of improving educational performance in ghetto schools remained, and parental dissatisfaction continued."[65]

PHILADELPHIA: THE SUPERINTENDENT AGAINST THE SYSTEM

In 1967 Mark Shedd became the new Superintendent of Schools in Philadelphia, with community control high on his personal agenda. His background included graduate work at Harvard's School of Education, a magnet for students with a passionate commitment to minority group education and to revolutionary change in the schools.

The future for political decentralization in Philadelphia on his arrival was hardly propitious. According to Fred Foley, it was intensely opposed by all established groups with an interest in the schools.[66] These included: the relatively new Board of Education, whose members saw central leadership as essential to the reforms they planned to carry out; the city-wide organizations, including civil rights groups and reform movements, who trusted the Board and saw little utility in taking power away from it; the upper-echelon staff of the school system itself, who perceived a grave threat to professionalism in community control, as well as a lessening of their own power and status; and the organized parents group, the Citywide Home and School Council, who agreed with the school staff on the desirability of professional decision-making, and saw risks to their own organizational status in sharing power with fragmented community groups.

Against these forces, Shedd had very little power of his own; civil service regulations and the union contract prevented him from appointing his own people or from exerting pressure based on a control over professionals' salaries. Shedd therefore determined to mobilize a constituency of his own, people in lower income and minority communities whose children were educationally disadvantaged. His strategy was to design three experimental projects for three sections of the city, in the hope that local minority leaders would put pressure on the Board for their adoption, and that the projects would successfully demonstrate the value of community control thus neutralizing the opposition to its application to the entire system.

Two of these districts greeted Shedd's proposals with "widespread apathy and indifference," despite the fact that activists in each of the communities had been demanding school reform; what they wanted, apparently, were more and better teachers, more resources and programs, not community control. Planning meetings were poorly attended and even less well organized; black groups in both communities split for and against community control, and conflict between black and white groups polarized what remained.

The third project, the Picket Middle School, followed a different course, perhaps because the demand for community control arose from an organized community group rather than from Shedd's staff. The Ad Hoc Pickett Committee was formed when plans to build the school were announced in 1967, and demanded power over the new school's programs and facilities. Shedd, of course, acceded to these demands, and appointed a member of his staff to help present them to the Board. The Ad Hoc Committee rejected

Shedd's candidates for the principal of the school, and proposed their own choice, which he accepted.

But Shedd's obvious alliance with an aggressive local group aroused the opposition forces. Fearing the kind of conflict that occurred in New York's demonstration districts, the Board now pressured Shedd to conciliate. Negotiations among a variety of groups in 1968 finally produced a compromise; a Community Committee for the new school was created, but it was to have only advisory powers.

Shedd now shifted his strategy. He proposed the establishment of a Commission on Decentralization and Community Participation, with a membership of fifteen community control activists, to mobilize public support for community control. By the time the Board, the school establishment, and the Home and School Council finished with the proposal, the Commission had grown to sixty-eight members, representing practically every constituency in the city, and clearly had a mandate to defuse the whole issue rather than stir it up.

The Commission ultimately made its report to the Board in 1971 in the form of three decentralization options that the Board might consider. Activist members of the Commission had succeeded in including as one of those options a proposal for local boards with a considerable amount of authority, but it turned out to be a futile gesture. Public hearings on the recommendations featured almost unanimous opposition to the community control option, although there was general endorsement of some form of advisory participation at the local level. The Board quietly dropped the whole matter, and at the end of the year a new Board appointed by the incoming Mayor did not renew Shedd's contract and he departed from Philadelphia.

COMMUNITY CONTROL—AN ASSESSMENT

Detailed generalizations to be drawn from this ten-year period of struggle for community control must await a future scholarly analysis. But a few conclusions seem fairly obvious from this review of what happened in five large cities:

1   A postulated power elite seems to be remarkable by its absence. In New York, the few figures who would be considered fairly close to such an elite, Ford Foundation personnel, for example, fought for turning control over to minority communities; the major antagonists were middle-class teachers. There is far more internal conflict among minority groups than class warfare in the stories.

2.   Success or failure appears to a remarkable degree to be dependent on purely local circumstances. The existence in New York of well-organized militant forces ideologically committed to community control and supported by a sizable group of sympathetic white liberals was the key; in

Detroit, the crucial factor was the presence of a particular politician in the state legislature. The backing of conservatives in the California legislature is an almost random event, as was Reagan's veto; he apparently turned down the community control bill not because he was particularly opposed to it but to retaliate on an unrelated political issue.

3. Community control of the schools, as an issue, represents to some unestimable extent, a convenient focus for the anxiety, anger, and frustration resulting from the school performance deficits of minority group children. There is very little evidence in any of these cases that anyone had a very clear idea of any direct and supportable connection between local control and children's learning. Like many social movements it is based on a *mystique*, and it is apparent that large numbers of parents simply did not buy it.

The interesting question is: Where some degree of local control was attained, did it work? Mario Fantini is still at work advocating it, and it is possible to find in the literature such retrospective reviews as Dale Mann's claiming that the policy has splendidly achieved everything it promised,[67] though the evidence offered for such a conclusion is so thin as to be visible only by electronic miscroscope. Other advocates such as Herbert Kohl argue that, in New York, at least, it was never given a chance to succeed, with "parents tied up in combat with hostile media, a bloated and unsympathetic central administration, and a powerful union threatened with loss of power."[68]

Most evaluations, even by those with some sympathy for the policy, tend to be rather more negative than positive. Some parents do show up for community board meetings, which represent an easier avenue for the expression of grievances than any previously available. Some New York principals and supervisors feel that they have more freedom of operation.[69] There has been a rapid increase in the number of minority group educators in high level posts; almost a third of such positions are now occupied by blacks or Puerto Ricans. Their representation in principal and assistant principal posts rose from 6 percent in 1969 to 20 percent in 1975.[70] In other, and perhaps more important areas, assessments are less encouraging:

Administrative Responsibility

In contrast to the feeling of some administrators that they have more autonomy, the general picture is worrisome. Thirty of the original thirty-one community school superintendents in New York are no longer in their jobs; some of them are out of the system completely.[71] Some of the poverty area districts have had as many as three or four superintendents in a five-year period. Ralph Brande left one such district to take a position in a white middle-class area and reports, "I got tired of fighting the poverty organizations and self-interest groups down there." He still keeps a sign on his desk that says, "Looking for someone with a little authority? I have as little as anyone."

> The pressure was always there. It actually came down to a fight over who was going to control the schools. We had disruptions of public meetings, egg-throwing, sit-ins and phoned-in bomb threats. One night a couple of hundred people marched into a public meeting singing "The Battle Hymn of the Republic." Another night the militants organized a candlelight parade to support the ousting of a principal. It's interesting that whenever the parents themselves came they were usually for the jobs being filled by the best person—white, black, Puerto Rican, or anybody. They just wanted the children to learn.[73]

Alfredo Matthew, a young Puerto Rican superintendent who had staunchly supported decentralization, left his district, battle-weary.

> I think decentralization is failing miserably because it brings out the worst in people: greed, selfishness, narrowness, and discrimination. It diverts people from the main goal of education. . . . A danger of decentralization is the degrading of the professional educator. They turn you into a community whore. In my district there were very few parents involved. The word "community" doesn't always mean parents. Many of the activists in my district were well-educated professional people who sent their children to private schools.[74]

Internal Conflict

As some of this suggests, battles within districts are a fairly common feature of community control, as predicted in the earlier theoretical material on decentralization. Washington's two experimental local control districts were the scene of almost constant community in-fighting, over curriculum policy, jobs, money.[75] In one of New York's original demonstration districts, Ocean Hill-Brownsville, the echoes of the bitter fight with the union had hardly died away after the official institution of decentralization, when a new local power struggle began, this time among members of the community. Parents conducted boycotts of the several schools, protesting actions by the governing board and its president, Assemblyman Samuel Wright. Parent and community groups appealed to the school chancellor to investigate charges of illegalities and improprieties in the conduct of district affairs. The liveliness of the conflict can be illustrated by the scene at one school, where parents were boycotting to protest the governing board's action in transferring their principal, O. J. Clement, to district headquarters for duty:

> Mr. Clement—who on Thursday stood outside the front entrance to JHS 263 carrying a sign that said "Damn Sam"—and Mr. Fuentes charge that their removal was part of a "purge" being carried out by Mr. Wright and his board supporters against those in the schools who will not "play ball" politically with them. Both have refused to report to the district office.[76]

In general terms, the conflict seemed to be one between the elected officials and groups in the community who claimed that the officials did not "truly" represent the community and ignored the legitimate voice of the parents. So, a bitter conflict between community and teachers changed to a community conflict over legitimacy; the fact that the area is mixed black and Puerto Rican, and that the sides somewhat reflected that split, suggests also that an ethnic struggle for power might have been involved.

Luis Fuentes went from Ocean Hill-Brownsville to become the new superintendent of a district in lower Manhattan, where he became involved in an historic battle that lasted for years. The local board that hired him was already in the midst of turmoil. Shortly after it was elected in 1970, it split into black-white factions that fought furiously with one another. In 1971 three of the white members left the board and were replaced by nonwhites; the black and Puerto Rican majority then appointed Fuentes, and adopted a resolution calling for ethnic guidelines in hiring personnel. Though they were forced to withdraw it as formal policy, there is no question that Fuentes pursued such a policy.

A protracted struggle ensued between the teachers union and Fuentes and his board, with various factions in the community lining up on either side. Although anti-Fuentes forces won majorities in school board elections in 1973, 1974, and 1975, he managed to continue running the district for some time.

> There were continual efforts to disrupt public school board meetings through the presence of gangs, sporadic violence, and the regular shouting of obscenities and anti-Semitic epithets. Fuentes' appointees and pro-Fuentes board members have been found guilty of inciting to riot, destruction of public property, criminal assault, and embezzlement. Fuentes himself was suspended on charges of mismanagement of public funds, insubordination, general misconduct, and destruction of property, but he managed to draw full salary for his three-year term before the charges could be heard.[77]

Outside the ghettos and barrios, in the white working and middle-class areas of the system, there are few reports of such internal dissension; but where the politics of confrontation took a firm hold in the sixties it appears to be still flourishing, making it difficult to maintain the stability that, many would argue, any effective school requires.

Fiscal Accountability

The apparent trade-off between decentralized control and financial accountability has in many cases been proven to be accurate. LaNoue and Smith note in the Morgan school a variety of cases of mismanagement ranging from minor nepotism and patronage to the hiring of people never authorized on the budget. An HEW audit of Anacostia showed a misappropriation of $118,000 during one six-month period alone.[78]

In New York the central Board has at various times taken over the con- trol of five districts to straighten out financial irregularities. Kenneth Clark, an original advocate of community control, left the ideological fold in 1974 with the public declaration that it had:

> failed to improve education and so far had resulted primarily in power grabs and struggles over jobs and control of finances . . . The abuses that have been exposed so far are in districts where the people aren't even trained in sophisti- cated ways of pork-barreling. Where the board members are more sophisticated there are more sophisticated forms of financial abuses.[79]

In Fuentes' district, admittedly an extreme example but one that demon- strates the potential for abuse, the schools were found spending at a rate that, if unchecked, would result in an $800,000 deficit. The school lunch program could not account for $70,000 of its food during 1973, and over- stated lunch spending amounted to over $350,000. Telephone calls were made from district offices to most states and many foreign countries. A Youth Leadership Project spent almost a million dollars over three years to prevent drug abuse, with nothing to show for it, and a Multi-Lingual, Multi- Cultural Resource Center received one-and-a-third million from the federal government for a two-year program that could demonstrate no measurable results but did give evidence of many fiscal irregularities and misappropria- tions.[80]

Community Participation

Although the proponents of community control firmly base their position on the widening of the local base of participation, they are often vague about how much participation it actually generates. There is some evidence that, at least in districts where the issue of power over the schools has be- come salient, a sizable proportion of parents indicate a desire for more influence over the schools. Bert Swanson conducted a survey in the New York experimental districts and found that between 50 and 66 percent of parents interviewed wanted more influence.[81] It is unlikely, though possible, that the proportions would be so high in areas that had not been so dramat- ically sensitized to the issue. Nor does the figure say much about how many people actually will invest the time and energy to participate when the opportunity is offered.

Fantini quotes the unit administrator of the Ocean Hill-Brownsville dis- trict as reporting that attendance of parents at school association meetings has averaged 100 per meeting, and that attendance at the open meetings of the governing board has averaged 250.[82] He conspicuously refrains from such participatory notes for other New York experimental districts or for Morgan School in Washington. LaNoue and Smith report that few parents even visit the Morgan School, and the turnover on the local board has been 50 percent to 70 percent, with only a small activist group involved for any period of time. The Anacostia record for participation was even worse.[83] In New York, after the early excitement ended, participation has dwindled in most districts, though Melvin Zimet reports an average of 100 attending open board meetings in his study of New York's District 7, a not inconsiderable achievement.[84]

The turnout for board elections, however, is uniformly poor. The percent of eligible voters participating has declined in New York from 15 percent in the first election after the decentralization law was passed, to about 7 percent in 1977. The record in Washington is far worse. At Morgan, the high was 4 percent; in 1971 only 137 of 10,000 eligibles turned out to vote. The Anacostia vote was 6 to 7 percent after a saturation campaign that included the use of the mass media, the distribution of 60,000 flyers and the hiring of high school students as community canvassers.

School Outputs

Greater community participation in the schools, argued the advocates, would result in higher levels of performance among the children with whom the bureaucratic system has failed, and by creating an understanding and sympathetic environment, reduce antischool behavior.

In the earliest period of the movement local control proponents produced some evidence for these effects. Fantini noted a dramatic decline in suspensions: none at the Morgan School since 1967; a decline from 628 to 30 in the Ocean Hill-Brownsville schools. There was a 70 percent decline in vandalism at Morgan, and practically none in Ocean Hill-Brownsville. Pupil attendance rates in the latter district went up, while teacher absences and turnover declined to almost zero. During the 1967 to 1968 school year, Morgan was one of only six schools in Washington in which reading scores improved; in Ocean Hill-Brownsville, nearly 98 percent of the children in the seven elementary schools showed growth in reading, with an average gain of one-and-one-half years.

Even at the time, the critics found those figures a mixed bag. The decline in vandalism was certainly encouraging, but pupil suspension rates are obviously totally under the control of administrators; if a decision is made to change the definition of a suspendable offense, the rate can be reduced at will. At about the same time as these figures were being released, moreover, Rhody McCoy, the Ocean Hill-Brownsville superintendent, released a story to the press about one of the children in the district who, as a result of an intensive reading course, ended up with a reading rate of 20,250 words per minute and 100 percent comprehension. The release admitted that he attained that rate only in spurts, and it did not disclose what his normal reading rate was. Some educators developed an understandable caution about accepting any hard data issued from that district.

All available later data has justified the caution. The trend toward fewer broken windows at Morgan reversed itself and began sizably increasing. The problem of vandalism became so serious that movable equipment was kept in a locked storeroom at night. Student absenteeism settled down at only slightly above the city-wide average.[85] In New York, the attendance rate for the system was about 90 percent, and is now down to 83 percent.[86] The vandalism rate in District 7, which had dropped along with the rest of the city's schools in 1969, soared in 1970–1971 after decentralization;[87] the city as a whole has seen an alarming rise in attacks on teachers.

On the crucial issue of academic performance, the later evidence is un-equivocal. During the period of the experimental districts in New York substantial claims were made for reading improvement, particularly by McCoy, who refused to administer the city's standardized reading tests while issuing notices to parents claiming progress in reading among the district's schools. Less than a year after the dissolution of the experimental districts, however, the Metropolitan Reading Test was given at Ocean Hill-Brownsville; Ravitch reported that those schools did poorly at that point even when compared to other ghetto schools. "The highest scoring school in the district, an elementary school, had only 24.5 percent of its pupils reading on or above grade level. Junior High School 271 ranked as the next-to-lowest school in Brooklyn, with only 5.5 percent of its students reading on or above grade level."[88]

At Morgan, after some early improvement, average reading scores dropped back to where they had been for sixth graders, and fourth graders scored eight month lower than they had the year before.[89] In Detroit, achievement has improved somewhat, but the upswing began before decentralization was instituted.[90] Five years after decentralization in New York there is no evidence of a general effect on achievement and, indeed, there was a small but consistent drop in reading scores for three years following the establishment of local boards.

It is now fashionable, in fact, to deemphasize the importance of achievement as a goal of decentralization:

> The consensus is that substantive improvement in the academic achievement of New York City's students was not a stated goal. Thus, although public concern with reading scores was an initial impulse to decentralization, the delivery of educational services subsequently became a long-range goal which *might* result from structural changes. In evaluating school decentralization, therefore, we must bear in mind that educational aims were not the primary objectives of those who shepherded the final bill to passage. For them, the immediate goals were largely political and partly social.[91]

If the effect on children is not at issue, one is compelled to wonder what all the fuss is about. Perhaps, as Bernard Bard has suggested, the name of the game is jobs, the control by urban minority groups over their own patronage, from school aide positions to superintendents. The general failure of the community control movement suggests that such a shift in the ethnic composition of school staffs will occur much more slowly, and thus more peacefully, than if the movement had successfully taken off in the country generally. There is little doubt that, given the financial situation of the large cities, the pressure for local control of the schools is, for the foreseeable future, ended. As a final irony, it should be noted that in New York, where it almost achieved complete victory, the local boards are now taking the heat of parent grievance over school budget cuts, where before they would have been storming central headquarters.

CHAPTER NOTES

[1] Joel S. Berke, "Full Federal Funding: Educational Nightmare," *Current History* (August 1972), 80–90.

[2] *Harvard Educational Review* has devoted two special issues to children's rights: Part I, Vol. 43, November 1973, and Part II, Vol. 44, February 1974.

[3] Harry L. Miller, *The Child's Right to Treatment: Its Impact on Agencies and Communities*, Working Paper for a Conference on the Enforcement of Children's Right to Treatment, Institute for Child Mental Health, New York, 1975.

[4] *San Antonio Independent School District v. Rodriguez*, 93 S.Ct. 1278, 1298–99 (1973).

[5] *Mills v. The Board of Education of The District of Columbia*, Civil Action No. 1939–71 (DC 1972), p. 3.

[6] Description and opinions based on interviews by the author.

[7] C. Wright Mills, *The Power Elite* (New York: Oxford University Press, 1956).

[8] Floyd Hunter, *Community Power Structure* (Chapel Hill: University of North Carolina Press, 1953).

[9] James A. Neuchterlein, "The Peoples vs. The Interests," *Commentary* (March 1975), 66–73.

[10] Nuechterlein, p. 66.

[11] Nuechterlein, p. 67.

[12] Nuechterlein, p. 69.

[13] Nuechterlein, p. 70.

[14] Nuechterlein, p. 66.

[15] Edward C. Banfield, *Political Influence* (New York: Free Press, 1961).

[16] Robert A. Dahl, *Who Governs? Democracy and Power in an American City* (New Haven: Yale University Press, 1962); Nelson W. Polsby, *Community Power and Political Theory* (New Haven: Yale University Press, 1963).

[17] James E. Curtis and John W. Petras, "Community Power, Power Studies, and the Sociology of Knowledge," *Human Organization*, 29 (1970), 204–213.

[18] Richard P. Nathan, "Essay on Special Revenue Sharing," in Joseph D. Sneed and Steven A. Saldhorn (eds.), *Approaches to Accountability in Post-Categorical Programs* (Menlo Park: Stanford Research Institute, 1973).

[19] Douglas Yates, "Neighborhood Government," *Policy Sciences*, 3 (1972), 209–217.

[20] Wallace B. Sayre, "Smaller Does Not Mean Better, Necessarily," *New York Times*, April 8, 1972, p. 29.

[21] Sayre, p. 29.

[22] Daniel Bell and Virginia Held, "The Community Revolution," *The Public Interest* (Summer 1969), 155–188.

[23] Donald Haider, "The Political Economy of Decentralization," *American Behavioral Scientist* 15 (1971), 108–129.

[24] Haider, p. 127.

[25] Peter Marris and Martin Rein, *Dilemmas of Social Reform* (New York: Atherton, 1969); Daniel P. Moynihan, *Maximum Feasible Misunderstanding* (New York: Free Press, 1969).

[26] For the origin of the phrase, see Saul Alinsky, *Reveille for Radicals* (Chicago: University of Chicago Press, 1946).

[27] Tom Wolfe, *Radical Chic and Mau-Mauing The Flak Catchers* (New York: Bantam, 1970), p. 118.

[28] Quoted in Moynihan, opposite title page.

[29] John and Sally B. Van Til, "Citizen Participation in Social Policy," *Social Problems*, 17 (1970), 321.

[30] Moynihan, p. 164.

[31] Robert A. Wilson, "Anomie in the Ghetto: A Study of Neighborhood Type, Race, and Anomie," *American Journal of Sociology*, 77 (July 1971), 66–88.

[32] Lee Sloan, "Good Government and the Politics of Race," *Social Problems*, 17 (Fall 1969), 161–175.

[33] J. Kenneth Benson, "Militant Ideologies and Organizational Contexts: The War on Poverty and the Ideology of 'Black Power,'" *Sociological Quarterly*, 12 (1971), p. 333.

[34] Charles V. Hamilton, "The Nationalists vs. the Integrationist," *New York Times Magazine*, October 1, 1972, p. 36+.

[35] Hamilton, p. 40.

[36] Hamilton, p. 42.

[37] Hamilton, p. 42.

[39] Bayard Rustin, "The Failure of Black Separation," *Newsweek* (November 13), 18–19.

[39] Allan C. Ornstein, *Race and Politics in School/Community Organizations* (Pacific Palisades, Calif.: Goodyear, 1974), p. 187.

[40] Jason Epstein, "The Politics of School Decentralization," *The New York Review of Books*, 10 (June 1968), 31–32.

[41] Daniel Katz and Robert L. Kahn, *The Social Psychology of Organizations* (New York: Wiley, 1966).

[42] Max Weber, *The Theory of Social and Economic Organization*, A. M. Henderson and Talcott Parsons (New York: Oxford University Press, 1947).

[43] Weber, p. 337.

[44] Roy Mansfield, "Bureaucracy and Centralization: An Examination of Organizational Structures," *Administration Science Quarterly*, 18 (1973), 477–488.

[45] David B. Tyack, *The One Best System: A History of American Urban Education* (Cambridge: Harvard University Press, 1974).

[46] Stokely Carmichael and Charles V. Hamilton, *Black Power* (New York: Vintage Books, 1967), p. 166.

[47] See, for example, Marilyn Gittell, "Urban School Politics: Professionalism vs. Reform," *Journal of Social Issues*, 26 (Fall 1970), 69–84; Mario Fantini, "Participation, Decentralization, Community Control, and Quality," *The Record*, 71 (September 1969), 93–107.

[48] For opposing views on this issue see Maurice R. Barube, "Achievement and Community Control," in Patricia Sexton (ed.) *School Policy and Issues in a Changing Society* (Boston: Allyn & Bacon, 1971), 224–33; Harold W. Pfautz, "The Socialization Process" in S. Levin, *Community Control of Schools* (Washington: Brookings, 1970), 37–45.

[49] Fantini, p. 99.

[50] Fantini, p. 107.

[51] David O'Shea, "School District Decentralization: Conflicting Approaches," *Generator*, 4 (1973), 11–19.

[52] Diane Ravitch, *The Great School Wars* (New York: Basic Books, 1974).

[53] Ravitch, p. 32.

[54] Quoted in Ravitch, p. 37.

[55] Ravitch, p. 79.

[56] Ravitch, p. 138.

[57] William R. Grant, "Community Control vs. Integration—the Case of Detroit," *Public Interest*, no. 24 (Summer 1971), p. 68.

58 Grant, p. 73.
59 George LaNoue and Bruce L. R. Smith, *The Politics of School Decentralization* (Lexington, Mass.: Heath, 1973).
60 LaNoue and Smith, p. 103.
61 LaNoue and Smith, p. 106.
62 LaNoue and Smith, p. 112.
63 LaNoue and Smith, p. 73.
64 LaNoue and Smith, p. 81.
65 LaNoue and Smith, p. 83.
66 Fred J. Foley, Jr., "The Failure of Reform: Community Control and the Philadelphia Public Schools," *Urban Education*, X (1976), 389–414.
67 Dale Mann, "Ten Years of Decentralization," *IRCD Bulletin*, 10 (Summer 1975).
68 Herbert Kohl, "Community Control—Failed or Undermined?" *Phi Delta Kappan*, 57 (1976), p. 370.
69 Bert Shanas, "New York School Decentralization, A Mixed Bag," *New York Affairs*, 3 (1976), 69–82.
70 Diane Ravitch and William R. Grant, *School Decentralization in New York City and Detroit's Experience With School Decentralization* (Washington, D.C.: Center for Governmental Studies, 1975).
71 Shanas, p. 73.
72 Bernard Bard, "Is Decentralization Working?" *Phi Delta Kappan* (December 1972), 238–243.
73 Shanas, 73–74.
74 Shanas, p. 78.
75 LaNoue and Smith, ch. 6.
76 "Ocean Hill School Board Told To Answer Charges," *New York Times* (October 16, 1971), p. 24.
77 Martin Schiff, "Community Control of Inner-City Schools and Educational Achievement," *Urban Education*, X (1976), 415–428.
78 LaNoue and Smith, p. 107.
79 Quoted in Bernard Bard, "The State of the Schools," *New York Post* (January 23, 1974), p. 31.
80 Schiff, p. 423.
81 Bert E. Swanson, Edith Cortin, and Eleanor Main, "Parents in Search of Community Influence in the Public Schools," *Education and Urban Society*, 1, no. 4 (August 1969), 383–403.
82 Fantini, p. 107.
83 LaNoue and Smith, p. 101.
84 Melvin Zimet, *Decentralization and School Effectiveness* (New York: Teachers College, 1973).
85 LaNoue and Smith, p. 101.
86 Ravitch and Grant, p. 4.
87 Zimet, p. 108.
88 Diane Ravitch, "Community Control Revisited," *Commentary* (February 1972), 69–74.
89 LaNoue, p. 101.
90 Ravitch and Grant, p. 4.
91 Thomas La Verne, *et al.*, *School Decentralization in New York City* (New York: State Charter Review Commission, 1974), 34–35.

Appendix.
Interpreting Correlations

Suppose we know the IQ scores of a group of pupils and, having given them a test in vocabulary knowledge, we are interested in the connection between their IQ's and their verbal ability on our test. One way of putting it is: can we *predict* how they will do on the test if we know their IQ's? Still another way of expressing it is: how much of the variation in test scores among this group of children can we *explain* by examining the variations among their IQ scores? Table A.1 shows the two scores for each student.

A careful examination of the two sets of scores will show that for each three-point increase in IQ score there is exactly a six-point increase in test score. If we plot each set on a graph, as in Figure A.1 (called a scattergram), the dots form a straight line. Each of the dots in this graph represents two scores; for example, the one with the circle shows the position of the student with an IQ score of 91 and a test score of 52.

This is a perfect positive correlation and is an exceedingly unlikely state

Table A.1 IQ Scores and Test Scores Showing a Perfect Positive Correlation

Student	IQ Score	Test Score
1	85	40
2	88	46
3	91	52
4	94	58
5	97	64
6	100	70
7	103	76
8	106	82
9	109	88
10	112	94

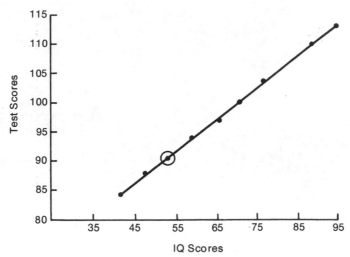

FIGURE A.1   Scattergram of test scores in Table A.1.

of affairs. It would mean that IQ alone is a *sufficient* explanation for how well the students in this group did on the test, without regard to such factors as attention, motivation, previous experience with the words, and a host of other variables, most of which we would expect to have some effect on test performance.

There are a number of ways to show that one variable bears a consistent relationship to another, but most of the studies reported in this book demonstate a relationship through the use of correlation, and report the degree of the relationship in the form of a *correlation coefficient, r*. In the perfect example above, $r = +1.00$; it is positive because there is an *increase* of test score with each increase in IQ. Table A.2 shows test-score data for the same range of IQ scores, indicating a correlation of $r = -1.00$; the scores *decrease* with each increase of IQ score; again, clearly, an improbable situation. If IQ was no help at all in explaining the performance on this particular test, the two sets of scores would bear no relation to one another, and in this case r would equal 0.00.

Table A.2   IQ Scores and Test Scores Showing a Perfect Negative Correlation

Student	IQ Score	Test Score
1	85	94
2	88	88
3	91	82
4	94	76
5	97	70
6	100	64
7	103	58
8	106	52
9	109	46
10	112	40

Thus, the correlation coefficient fluctuates between -1.00 and $+1.00$; the closer it is to zero the less important is the relationship between the variables being studied.

The question of how to interpret its importance as it grows larger can be answered in several ways. If the sample under investigation is small (including only twenty or thirty persons, for example), even a fairly sizable-seeming r (.40, for example) might not be an indication of significant correlation. The statisticians would put it this way: it is possible to obtain a coefficient this large in such a small sample simply by chance.

On the other hand, in large samples, which tend to be characteristic of educational studies, a very small correlation coefficient, even one as low as $r = +.05$, may be statistically significant. In this case, it is not necessary to accept the finding as important just because it exceeds chance; one must make an independent judgment of the magnitude of the relationship it indicates between the variables, and a coefficient of .05 is rather trivial by anyone's definition.

As coefficients go beyond .20, however, it becomes more difficult to judge their importance. Because of the way in which it is calculated, for instance, one cannot consider an r of .40 as twice as great as an r of .20. The simplest and most accurate basis for judging significance is to square the correlation coefficient to obtain a coefficient of determination. With a correlation of .40, r^2 becomes .16 and may be interpreted this way: 16 percent of the variation in the scores of Y can be explained (or predicted) by the variations in the X scores. This leaves a good deal of the variation in Y unaccounted for, but it is still a respectable proportion to have explained; science comes to understand relationships slowly, and to understand almost a fifth of something is a step forward.

Implied in the foregoing is the assumption that in a complex world one is unlikely to find *one* cause for any phenomenon, an assumption that social scientists generally make. One finds occasional very high correlations in nature; Figure A.2, for example, shows the scattergram of temperature readings and the related chirps-per-minute of crickets. In this case $r = +.99$, and one can be fairly certain that nothing else in cricketdom has much to do with a cricket's frequency of chirping. Man, however, is more complicated; and if we are interested in what causes different levels of academic achievement, which is itself a complicated phenomenon, we can expect to find many interrelated factors having some influence.

In order to study the influence of a number of factors at the same time, simple correlation is an inadequate tool, because any one of our X variables may overlap with another. Variations in IQ influence differences in achievement level, and so do variations in social class; but we know that *some* of the variation in IQ itself can be explained by social class position. These two independent variables share some *common* explanatory powers. In the natural sciences, it is often possible to control the influence of a number of independent variables by holding one constant at a time; for example, one can repeat the same experiment, keeping the same temperature each time

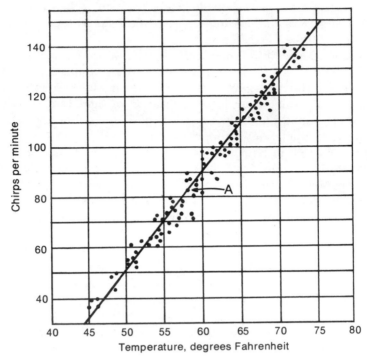

FIGURE A.2   Temperature and cricket chirps per minute of 115 crickets. Frederick E. Croxton, Dudley J. Cowden, and Sidney Klein. *Applied General Statistics* 3d ed. (Englewood Cliffs, N.J.: Prentice-Hall, Inc., 1967), p. 390. Data provided by Mr. Bert E. Holmes.

and varying the humidity or some other relevant factor. This is difficult or impossible to do in social science research, but the statistical tool of partial correlation provides a way of holding one or more of the independent variables constant to permit one to observe what happens to another. An example of partial correlation is given below to demonstrate the process and the way in which it can be read and interpreted.

The example is taken from the Gross and Herriott study of school leadership whose general findings are discussed in Chapter 12. The major independent variable of interest here is the measure of EPL, the aspect of the principal's leadership that involves his interest in and support of the teacher's professional role in the classroom. The higher the principal's EPL score, the greater his involvement with the support of his teachers as professionals. The study gives us first the simple correlations between EPL scores for the principals and a number of other variables (these simple correlations are in this context called "zero order r's"). Each one of the variables is assigned a number that will be used throughout to identify it:

1.   EPL score of the principal

2. teacher morale
3. teacher professional performance
4. pupil academic performance

The zero order correlations are:

$r_{12} = + .50$ (that is, the correlation between the principal's EPL score and his teachers' morale)
$r_{13} = + .36$
$r_{14} = + .06$

We know that family socioeconomic level has a considerable influence on pupil academic performance by itself; and the study found some evidence that the low correlation between EPL and pupil performance indicated above was not true of all socioeconomic levels. Let us assign the subscript 5 to the variable "family income"; r_{54}, the correlation between family income and pupil performance, turns out to be a sizable $+ .61$.

Now we can "partial out," or hold constant, the effect of family income on our zero-order correlations. We will in effect be saying: to what extent do EPL and teacher morale (or professional performance or pupil performance) vary together when we look at groups of schools whose pupils have the *same* average family income? Or, for schools that have the same average family income but different levels of teacher morale: to what extent are the variations in morale accompanied by variations in the principal's EPL score? With family income held constant our zero-order correlations change:

$r_{12.5} = + .55$ (read: the correlation between EPL and teacher morale, independent of the family income of the school population, is .55)
$r_{13.5} = + .41$
$r_{14.5} = + .25$

This procedure has clearly increased the estimate of the EPL's influence on all these factors, considerably so in the case of its effect on pupil performance. The way the principal behaves makes more of a difference for some children than others, a fact that was obscured by our treating children as a total, undifferentiated group.

Gross and Herriott go on to examine another interesting question on which partial correlation can throw some light: does the principal's interest and supportiveness have a *direct* effect on pupil performance or is it merely that his type of leadership helps to create high morale and more professional teaching, which in turn influences pupil performance? With pupil performance as the dependent variable, and with family income of the school population held constant, here is the situation as shown in Figure A.3. Taking EPL as the independent variable of major interest, we can hold constant not

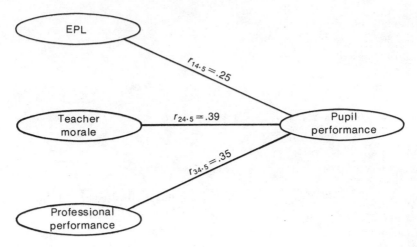

FIGURE A.3   Relation of three school variables to pupil performance holding family income constant. Based on data from Neal Gross and Robert E. Herriott, *Staff Leadership in Public Schools* (New York: John Wiley & Sons, Inc., 1965), p. 55.

only family income but teacher morale. For schools of the same socioeconomic composition and the same average level of professional performance, $r_{14.5}$ turns out to be only .13. If we also remove the effect of teacher morale, $r_{14.532} = .05$. So, the influence of EPL falls almost to nothing. The original relationship between EPL and pupil performance is apparently due to its indirect influence on morale and professional performance.

Index

X